Rio de Janeiro

timeout.com/riodejaneiro

Published by Time Out Guides Ltd, a wholly owned subsidiary of Time Out Group Ltd.
Time Out and the Time Out logo are trademarks of Time Out Group Ltd.

© **Time Out Group Ltd 2007**

10 9 8 7 6 5 4 3 2 1

This edition first published in Great Britain in 2007 by Ebury Publishing
A Random House Group Company
20 Vauxhall Bridge Road, London SW1V 2SA

Random House Australia Pty Limited 20 Alfred Street, Milsons Point, Sydney, New South Wales 2061, Australia
Random House New Zealand Limited 18 Poland Road, Glenfield, Auckland 10, New Zealand
Random House South Africa (Pty) Limited Isle of Houghton, Corner Boundary
Road & Carse O'Gowrie, Houghton 2198, South Africa

Random House UK Limited Reg. No. 954009

For further distribution details, see www.timeout.com

ISBN 10: 1-84670-045-0
ISBN 13: 978184670 0453

A CIP catalogue record for this book is available from the British Library

Printed and bound by Firmengruppe APPL, aprinta druck, Wemding, Germany

The Random House Group Limited makes every effort to ensure that the papers used in our books are made from trees
that have been legally sourced from well-managed and credibly certified forests. Our paper procurement policy can be
found on www.randomhouse.co.uk.

Edited and designed by
Time Out Guides Limited
Universal House
251 Tottenham Court Road
London W1T 7AB
Tel +44 (0)20 7813 3000
Fax +44 (0)20 7813 6001
Email guides@timeout.com
www.timeout.com

Editorial

Editor Andy Footner
Consultant Editor Tom Phillips
Managing Editor Mark Rebindaine
Deputy Editor Matt Chesterton
Marketing Director Andrés Castro
Listings Checker Jennifer McLaughlin
Proofreader/Editorial assistance Anna Norman
Indexer Sally Davies

Managing Director Peter Fiennes
Financial Director Gareth Garner
Editorial Director Ruth Jarvis
Deputy Series Editor Dominic Earle
Editorial Manager Holly Pick

Design

Art Director (Buenos Aires office) Gonzalo Gil
Graphic Designer (Buenos Aires office) Sofia Iturbe
Art Director Scott Moore

Advertising

Sales Director Mark Phillips
International Sales Consultant Ross Canadé
International Advertising Manager Kasimir Berger
International Sales Executive Charlie Sokol
Advertising Sales (Rio) Enio Santiaeno
Advertising Assistant Kate Staddon

Marketing

Group Marketing Director John Luck
Sales & Marketing Director, North America Lisa Levinson
Marketing Manager Yvonne Poon

Production

Production Director Mark Lamond
Production Manager Brendan McKeown
Production Co-ordinator Caroline Bradford
Guides Co-ordinator Susan Whittaker

Time Out Group

Chairman Tony Elliott
Financial Director Richard Waterlow
Group General Manager/Director Nichola Coulthard
TO Magazine Ltd MD Richard Waterlow
TO Communications Ltd MD David Pepper
Time Out International MD Cathy Runciman
Group Art Director John Oakey
Group IT Director Simon Chappell

Contributors

Introduction Andy Footner. **History** Lucy Beney. **Rio Today** Tom Phillips. **Carnival** Tom Phillips. **Football** Alex Bellos. **Where to Stay** Ismay Atkins, Lucy Beney, Simone Bromerschenckel, Matt Chesterton, Andy Footner, Jennifer Mclaughlin (*Naughty and nice* Tom Phillips; *The Fasano factor* Helen Clegg). **Sightseeing: Introduction** Andy Footner. **The Centre** Vik Birkbeck (*Building blocks* Colin McMahon; *Rambling in Rio* Sam Logan). **The Bay** Brian Hagenbuch. **The Hills** Duncan Crossley, Brian Hagenbuch (*Slumming it* Sam Logan). **The Beaches** Helen Clegg (*Find your place in the sun* Colin McMahon; *Flip Flop Don't Stop* Andrew Downie). **The Lake** Helen Clark (*Rambling in Rio* Sam Logan). **Zona Oeste** Lucy Beney. **Zona Norte** Jan Onoszko. **Niterói** Helen Clegg. **Restaurants** Lucy Beney, Helen Clark, Duncan Crossley, Andrew Downie, Brian Hagenbuch, Colin McMahon, Jan Onoszko, Alice Pereira, Ana Schlimovich, Joshua Schneyer (*The light bite* Andrew Downie; *On the menu* Duncan Crossley). **Bars, Cafés & Botecos** Lucy Beney, Helen Clark, Helen Clegg, Duncan Crossley, Andrew Downie, Brian Hagenbuch, Colin McMahon, Joshua Schneyer, (*Cool, cold beer* Andrew Downie). **Shops & Services** Jennifer McLaughlin (*Buying the body beautiful* Helen Clegg). **Festivals & Events** Andy Footner. **Children** Helen Clark. **Film** Brian Hagenbuch. **Galleries** Jennifer McLaughlin. **Gay & Lesbian** Christopher Curtain. **Music** Tom Phillips, Joshua Schneyer. **Nightlife** Helen Clegg. **Performing Arts** Brian Hagenbuch. **Sport & Fitness** Sam Logan. **Trips Out of Town: Parati** Monica Guy. **Angra & Ilha Grande** Brian Hagenbuch. **Búzios** Mark Rebindaine. **Upstate Rio** Lucy Beney. **Directory** Jan Onoszko (*Staying safe* Sam Logan).

Maps Nexo Servicios Gráficos, Buenos Aires, Argentina (www.nexolaser.com.ar).

Photography by Ana Schlimovich (artwork on page 76, 122, 144 by Adao Iturrusgarai, page 200 by Mercedes Jáuregui), except: pages 10, 11, 12, 16, 17, 159 Archivo General de la Nacion; pages 14, 19 Fotojornalismo Agencia Estado; pages 18, 21, 171 Clarín Contenidos; page 23 Richard Keenan; page 49 JW Marriot; pages 33, 38, 51, 75, 80, 123, 243 Mark Rebindaine; page 93, 217, 219 Lucy Beney; pages 114 Belem Com; pages 162, 163 César Charlone; page 176 Fabian Jolivet; page 180 Andy Footner; page 192 Greg Vanderlans; pages 207, 209, 210 Georgina Gil and Andres Castro; pages 212, 213 Casas Brancas.

The Editor would like to thank: All the writers and editorial team, Ismay Atkins, Lucy Wood, Giuseppe Bizzarri, Jenny and Hélcio, Batman Zavareze, Lucy Beney, Miriam Cutz (TurisRio), Patricia Alquéres (RioTur), María Sol Sánchez Coria (SECOM), Sheyla Tauffner (Prefeitura Municipal de Parati), Amanda Salazar (TurisAngra) and Carolina Podestá.

Contents

Introduction

'Her name is Rio and she dances in the sand...' Duran Duran's lyric could have been written for the Marvelous City, as could Barry Manilow's bi-polar 'Copacabana' have been about the world famous beach neighbourhood – but they weren't.

Rio has enough poets of its own and they've created some of the world's most danceable music – which is a good thing, as Rio's one of the world's best places to dance. It's the combination of the thrilling natural beauty and iconic backdrops, the informal atmosphere and smiling people – and the fabulous music. The city's poet laureate (and lyricist of 'The Girl from Ipanema') Vinicius de Moraes wrote: 'Sadness has no end, but happiness does... Happiness is like a feather floating through the air. It glides so easily, but only briefly. To stay aloft it needs a constant wind.'

For Vinicius that 'constant wind' tended to be whisky – as he put it, 'man's best friend, like a bottled dog' – but Rio's pursuit of happiness is as many-stranded as it is infectious and overwhelming. The city is full of life, love and laughter and there's little option for visitors but to join in the fun.

The endless sadness is also a part of the puzzle. Rio is very open about its faults and they're there for all to see, much of the time – there's often a feeling of tension on the streets, the news reports and stories of violence are shocking and scary and many parts of the city are best avoided altogether. But it's these same parts of the city that are throwing up the rough sounds of *funk Carioca*, rapidly becoming known round the world as *baile funk*, just as they gave birth to samba many years before. And as with samba, the lyrics are still about the troubles, the poverty, the endless sadness.

In the minds of many people who've never visited the city, Rio is still stuck in the 1980s of Duran Duran, easy money and tacky fashions – and there's still nowhere else in the world where you'll feel as right in a white suit on the beach (especially during the world's biggest New Year's Eve celebrations) – but take a closer look and there's plenty more going on. Rio's designers are running riots in colour and style, its film industry is as hot as anywhere else in the world, its musicians are off the hook. After many years of bean stews, even its chefs are now cooking up a storm. For a city that's got so little association with hard work, it's an incredibly productive place.

But in the end it always comes back to fun, happiness, hedonism, pleasure – call it what you will, but make sure you get in on it, it's the oxygen of the city. Find it in the non-stop activity of the beach, after a few drinks in a boteco, in sport, whether you're watching or playing, in the commotion of the markets or the solitude of the jungle. Our tip? Find a place where you can laugh, dance and sing all at the same time. The samba clubs are there for that, and so are the football stadiums, the nightclubs, most of the restaurants, the bars, the beaches, the sidewalks and, of course, the New Year's Eve parties and Carnival.

And then, when you find Rio's got under your skin, it's time to dig a little deeper.

ABOUT TIME OUT GUIDES

This is the first edition of *Time Out Rio de Janeiro*, one of an expanding series of Time Out guides produced by the people behind the successful listings magazines in London, New York and Chicago. Our guides are all written and updated by resident experts, who have striven to provide you with all the most up-to-date information you'll need to explore the city or read up on its background, whether you're a local or a first-time visitor.

THE LIE OF THE LAND

Although Rio sprawls for a long way inland, the main areas of the city for visitors are close to the coast. We have divided the city into several areas (the Centre, The Bay, The Hills, The Beaches and so on), and then *bairros* or neighbourhoods within those (Santa Teresa, Copacabana, Botafogo, Gávea and so on). For more details, *see p52*. Every place is listed with its exact address – written in Portuguese, to help you tell a taxi driver or ask a local.

THE LOWDOWN ON THE LISTINGS

Above all, we've tried to make this book as useful as possible. Addresses, telephone numbers, websites, transport information, opening times, admission prices and credit card details are all included in our listings. And, as far as possible, we've given details of facilities, services and events, all checked and correct as

we went to press. However, venues can and frequently do change their arrangements according to seasons, fashions or whims. During holiday periods, in particular, some businesses and attractions have variable hours, and Rio has a lot of holidays.

While every effort has been made to ensure the accuracy of information contained in this guide, the publishers cannot accept responsibility for any errors it may contain.

PRICES AND PAYMENT

The prices we have supplied are correct as we go to press but are subject to change and should be treated as guidelines. All prices are quoted in Brazilian Reais. As a quick reference, one US dollar was worth around R$2 at press time.

We have noted whether venues such as shops, hotels and restaurants accept the following credit cards: American Express (**AmEx**), Diners Club (**DC**), MasterCard (**MC**) and Visa (**V**). A few businesses may take travellers' cheques. If prices vary wildly from those we've quoted, ask whether there's good reason. If not, go elsewhere. We aim to give the best and most up-to-date advice, so we always want to know if you've been badly treated or overcharged.

TELEPHONE NUMBERS

To phone Rio de Janeiro from outside Brazil, dial your country's international code, then 55 (for Brazil) then 21 (for Rio) and finally the local eight-digit number, which we have given in all listings. If you are calling from within Brazil, but outside the city, you will need to add 021 before the eight-digit number. Within the city just dial the eight digits.

ESSENTIAL INFORMATION

For all the practical information you might need for visiting the city – including visa and customs information, emergency phone numbers, information on local weather, details of local transport, language tips and a selection of useful websites – turn to the **Directory** chapter at the back of the guide. It starts on page 222.

MAPS

The map section at the back of this book includes orientation and neighbourhood maps of the central areas of Rio, and street maps of the parts of the city covered in the guide, with a comprehensive street index. The street maps start on page 244, and pinpoint specific locations of hotels (**1**), restaurants (**1**) and bars, cafés and botecos (**1**).

LET US KNOW WHAT YOU THINK

We hope you enjoy the *Time Out Rio de Janeiro Guide*, and we'd like to know what you think of it. We welcome tips for places that you consider we should include in future editions and take note of your criticism of our choices. You can email us at guides@timeout.com.

Advertisers

We would like to stress that no establishment has been included in this guide because it has advertised in any of our publications and no payment of any kind has influenced any review. The opinions given in this book are those of *Time Out* writers and entirely independent.

There is an online version of this guide, along with guides to over 100 international cities, at **www.timeout.com**.

In Context

Features

PEDRO ALVARES CABRAL DESCOBRE O BRAZIL,
ALLI DESEMBARCA, E TOMA POSSE D'AQUELLA REGIÃO.

History

Out of the shadows of slavery, military dictatorship and economic meltdown, the *cidade maravilhosa* emerges.

The enormous popularity of soap operas in Brazil should come as no surprise. The country's history over the last five centuries would put even the most imaginative plot to shame. The story of Brazil has everything – colonists and conquistadores, royalty and republicanism, slavery and splendour, exile and execution, boom and bust, religion and riots, violence and vanity. While the military has rarely missed a cue to step in, and corruption is endemic, Brazilians have shown an enormous capacity to forgive and forget. Political comebacks are the norm rather than the exception and the *jeito* – that uniquely Brazilian way of dealing with seemingly intractable problems – is all important. Yet while the sun shines, the sea is blue and the beer is cold, then life is good for Rio's inhabitants – even if little seems to change in the long run.

EARLY HISTORY
Very little is known about pre-Columbian Brazil. When the first European arrivals landed on the eastern coast of the new world at the very beginning of the 16th century, there were no great cities or ancient civilisations awaiting them.

South America, like North America, had been settled thousands of years earlier, by hunter-gatherer tribes who originally crossed the Bering Strait from East Asia at the end of the last ice age. Whereas the Spanish conquistadores came across the great cities of the Aztecs, the Mayans and the Incas, Brazil was sparsely populated by largely nomadic tribes. Tamoio Indians inhabited the area where Rio now stands.

Although these tribes frequently engaged in warfare and practised ritual cannibalism, initial contacts with Europeans were allegedly friendly. This situation changed, however, once it became clear that the Portuguese were interested only in exploiting both the natives and the land. Once serious colonisation began and these tribes were treated as a perfect reservoir of slave labour, the situation quickly deteriorated. The Portuguese were even forced to abandon the region around Rio during Brazil's early history.

THE ARRIVAL OF THE PORTUGUESE
In April 1500, Pedro Álvares Cabral arrived on the Brazilian coast, near Porto Seguro in Bahia. He claimed the territory, which he named Terra

The slave trade

The first people whom the Portuguese tried to enslave were the native 'Indians'. Since many tribes were nomadic, and there were no great centres of civilisation, some early settlers made their living hunting slaves. Brazil's labour shortage problem remained unsolved, however, and landowners began to look back across the ocean, to Portuguese Africa.

By the end of the 16th century, around 20,000 black African slaves were working on Brazilian sugar plantations. These were the first of around four million Africans who made the journey across the south Atlantic in horrific conditions, until the trade was finally outlawed in the mid 19th century. Overall, around 40 per cent of slaves brought from Africa to the New World ended up in Brazil, and around a half of those came through the port of Rio.

The riches of Minas Gerais were extracted with slave labour. Slaves also built the Estrada Real – a track paved with enormous stone slabs by which this treasure could be carried by mule to the state of Rio and then shipped to Europe. The lives of most slaves were nasty, brutish and short – many succumbed to disease and most worked long hours in harsh conditions.

Some slaves bought their freedom, while others escaped to quilombos, self-governing communities of former slaves in isolated locations, where it was hoped the authorities would not come after them. While the suffering was undoubtedly terrible, there is some evidence to suggest that divisions in Brazilian society were less stark than they were in North America. There is more evidence of interracial marriage, and while some landowners were undoubtedly brutal, many viewed their slaves as part of an extended family.

The coffee boom of the 19th century brought about another wave of slave shipments. Numbers being brought into the country increased year on year. While some landowners conceded that the trade was cruel, many continued to deny that slavery was inhumane and most agreed that it was necessary.

Brazil was the last country in the Americas to outlaw slavery. It was not until 1888 (25 years after Abraham Lincoln's Emancipation Proclamation), while Pedro II was seeking medical treatment in Europe, that his daughter, Princess Isabel (pictured), acting as regent, signed the act outlawing the ownership of slaves.

The legal practice of slavery could be consigned to history with the stroke of a pen. Its legacy of inequality, violence and human rights abuses is a spectre not so easily banished, and one that has haunted Brazil into the modern age.

de Vera Cruz (Land of the True Cross) for the Portuguese crown and celebrated mass, astonishing the Indians with the construction of a large wooden cross. They had never seen metal tools before. In early May, he continued his journey eastwards.

Portuguese king Manuel I was nonetheless intrigued. While he was disappointed that Brazil apparently did not offer the treasures the Spanish conquistadores had found (and looted) elsewhere on the continent, in 1501, another expedition set out that included Amerigo Vespucci. On New Year's Day, 1502, the adventurers arrived in Guanabara Bay. Mistakenly thinking that the bay was the estuary of a great river, Vespucci named the site Rio de Janeiro, or 'River of January'.

CONSOLIDATION AND COLONISATION

In order to secure his new territory, in 1531 King João III dispatched the first settlers to Brazil. The Brazilian coast was divided into capitanias (captaincies) in which wealthy Portuguese emigrants were encouraged to settle and so secure the coastline.

By the mid 16th century, Portugal was only just holding on to its territory in the Americas. The interior of Brazil remained unexplored, as the timber traders were content to stick to the coast, living off the land and taking what they wanted. The Portuguese Crown realised that it must act if Brazil was not to be lost.

In 1549, a Captain-General was appointed to administer the territory, based in the new capital, Salvador, in Bahia. His powers were

The early inhabitants: Tamoio Indians.

limited, however, and town councils had a degree of autonomy. The first few governors were successful in reducing pillage by other Europeans and Indian attacks, and gradually, in the second half of the 16th century, more settlers began to arrive.

The French, however, continued to be a thorn in the flesh of the Portuguese. Many Frenchmen lived freely among the Tamoio Indians, forming relationships with their women and fathering Brazilian children. (The French are also credited with introducing shorts to Rio, as they decided to stop keeping up appearances and dress more suitably for the climate.)

In 1555, the French claimed 'French Antarctica', on the site where Rio now stands. The first three forts built in the city were the work of the French Commander, Nicolas Durand de Villegagnon. While the Portuguese skirmished with the French, whom they treated as pirates, it was only in 1565 that Mem de Sá, then Governor-General of Bahia, garnered sufficient forces to try to wrest the area finally from French – and Tamoio – control.

FOUNDING THE CITY

The Portuguese decided to build first on a hill called the Morro do Castelo, from where it was easy to keep a lookout for attacks from all sides. Unfortunately, there were no sources of fresh water on the Morro do Castelo, and it was not

long before the fledgling city, lacking the defined grid plan so favoured by the Spanish, started to straggle downwards and outwards. Building was not easy. Much land was unsuitable for construction, as the terrain was marshy, with many lagoons. There were also many hills. Over the centuries, many of these *morros* were flattened, with the rock and soil used to reclaim the lagoons – and eventually part of the coastline too.

EL DORADO

Rumours of a fabulously rich and fertile land on the other side of the sea had long been circulating in Europe before any evidence appeared. Once the conquistadores set about subduing Spanish America, large shipments of treasure, pillaged from the native people, appeared in Europe, only firing further the fever to discover 'El Dorado'.

It took a while for the Portuguese to discover their own treasure in the rich soil of Brazil. Alluvial gold was found in Minas Gerais at the end of the 17th century, just as the sugar production passed its zenith. It sparked a gold rush. Prospectors came from Portugal, from the overworked sugar plantations of the northeast and from the coastal settlements further south.

And so began Rio's rise to supremacy, as large quantities of Brazilian gold passed through en route to the Portuguese court. Rio's pre-eminence was finally confirmed in 1763, when the capital of Brazil was moved from Bahia to this up-and-coming younger brother in the country's south east.

THE NEW CAPITAL

Rio had developed significantly over the previous decades. The Paço Imperial, or Governor's Palace, was built in 1743 and Igreja de Nossa Senhora do Carmo do Antigo da Sé, which was Rio's cathedral until 1976, was started in 1749. The Arcos de Lapa were constructed, to carry water to the rapidly expanding city.

Now, more money and people flowed in to the new capital. The first lavish public projects were inaugurated, such as the Passeio Público (Public Walk) in 1783. Situated in Lapa and still open to the public, it offered marble walkways and terraces, decorated with fountains and sculptures and even bars and cafés.

More churches were built. In 1775, work started on Nossa Senhora da Candelária. This church remains one of the city's great landmarks, despite being hemmed in by office blocks, and was also the site of the infamous Massacre of Candelária in 1993, when military police murdered sleeping street children on the church steps.

THREATS TO PORTUGUESE RULE

As the new capital was finding its feet, the first rumblings of discontent with Portuguese rule – and the first calls for independence – could be heard. In 1789, the Inconfidência Mineira was put down. Inspired by the forces propelling the French Revolution, a group of prominent citizens from the gold town of Ouro Preto, led by a dentist nicknamed Tiradentes ('teeth-puller'), had tried to organise a rebellion against the government. They were betrayed before anyone could act. Tiradentes was eventually executed, while other conspirators were exiled to Mozambique.

'The Portuguese royal family were shocked at the lax dress code of the Brazilians.'

The comparatively relaxed attitude of the Portuguese Crown offered it some protection against the kind of revolutionary movements evident elsewhere in Latin America. The

Grand designs: the **Arcos da Lapa.**

Portuguese had never imposed the degree of control over Brazil that the Spaniards exerted across their empire. Ultimately, one event caused the history of Brazil to diverge dramatically from the other South American republics, and set the seal on the prominence of Rio de Janeiro. That event was the arrival of the Portuguese court in Brazil in January 1808.

ROYAL BRAZIL

In late 1807, with Napoleon snapping at the gates of Lisbon, Dom João VI and the entire Portuguese court (numbering many thousands of people) set sail from Lisbon. After a stopover in Salvador, where the people of Bahia were shocked by the dishevelled appearance of their rulers (the queen wore an elaborate turban to disguise the fact that her head had been shaved to rid her of a lice infestation), the royal family arrived to tumultuous welcome in Rio. Dom João was the first reigning monarch to set foot in the New World.

The royal family, however, was a little taken aback by what they found. While they soon appreciated the natural beauty of their new home, they found Rio shabby and dirty. Roads were unpaved, sanitation non-existent and domestic animals roamed the streets. They were shocked at the laxity in dress of the Brazilians – they found men wearing open-necked shirts and women in sleeveless dresses in the summer heat.

The most pressing problem was a shortage of housing. The population of Rio was then about 60,000, and swelled in a very short time to over 70,000. While the king was housed in the hastily converted viceroy's palace, there was no suitable accommodation for most of the new arrivals, many of whom were accustomed to living in luxury.

The city of Rio was still at that time confined to the central area around the port – there was no access through the thick tropical forest and marshy lagoons to today's *bairros* of Copacabana, Ipanema and Leblon. Soon after his arrival, a wealthy merchant offered his estate to the king. The house, which was already among the best in Rio, was subsequently enhanced and became the Quinta da Boa Vista palace. Over the years it was embellished to such an extent that it became known as the 'tropical Versailles'.

It soon became obvious that a full-scale European-style government was going to be run from Brazil, and there was much jostling for position, both by the new arrivals and the long-standing residents of Rio. Finally, Brazil was allowed to trade with any friendly nation, not just the motherland. The number and variety of imports increased enormously. The British in

The fortunes of coffee

The events of Pedro II's reign (*see p15*) took place against the unfolding backdrop of Brazil's fourth great economic cycle, when java provided the biggest financial boom of all.

By the beginning of the 19th century, the sugar trade in Brazil was in decline, with plantations suffering from depleted soil and with increased competition from elsewhere. Many sugar planters had used profits to fuel increasingly luxurious lifestyles, rather than investing in new equipment to enhance profitability. The gold rush in Minas was over and the mineral deposits exhausted, so a mobile workforce was looking for the next way to earn a living.

Coffee bushes had been grown in Rio on a small scale since the early 1700s. The terrain proved to be ideal and, from around 1840, coffee took over almost the entire state. More swamps were drained and much particular established the strong trade links they had long coveted, even if the selection of cargoes was not always appropriate – once a shipment of ice-skates arrived.

British influence during this time is reflected in the establishment of an Anglican church in the city in 1810, the successor of which still thrives in Botafogo. Many plaques on the wall testify to the hardships that new arrivals faced in Rio. Lord Strangford, the architect of the flight across the Atlantic, also founded the Cemitério dos Ingleses (the English cemetery, which is still in use) in Gamboa, on farmland at the edge of the bay ceded by João VI. Until then, non-Catholics had been buried at sea, in slave cemeteries or even along the beaches.

Dom João loved Brazil. He was a cultured man with many interests and the growth of the city reflected this. His interest in all things French (in spite of Napoleon) gave rise to a French Quarter in Rio, centred on the Rua do Ouvidor. He invited a group of French painters and sculptors to come and work in Rio and later founded the Imperial Academy of Fine Arts.

He inaugurated the Bank of Brazil and the country's first printing works; he also founded the Botanical Gardens, a landmark to this day.

Dom João had arrived in Brazil as regent for his mother, the elderly and mad Queen Maria I. She died, however, in Rio in 1816 and Dom João became king in his own right. He then decided that Rio would be the capital not just of Brazil, but of the United Kingdom of Portugal, Brazil and the Algarves. Latin America had its first and only monarchy – and the king had every intention of staying, ruling his empire from the southern hemisphere.

INDEPENDENCE

Unfortunately for Dom João VI, duty in Portugal finally called, and he returned to Lisbon in 1821, to deal with a rebellion which could have swept away the monarchy entirely. He left his son, Pedro, to be regent in his place and governor of Brazil. Bereft of their monarch, and with Lisbon once more trying to exert authority, murmurs of independence were heard once more.

of Rio's Atlantic rainforest was laid waste in the rush to plant coffee bushes.

Coffee cultivation was labour intensive, favouring bigger *fazendas* and prolonging landowners' interest in slave labour. After the abolition of the slave trade, the need for workers on the coffee plantations fired the late 19th century wave of immigration from Europe. People flocked to Rio and, by 1860, it was the biggest city in Latin America.

By 1889, coffee accounted for two thirds of all Brazil's exports (it had become a very fashionable drink in Europe), and around 75 per cent of the world's total supply came from here. Modernisation, mechanisation and immigration helped ease the transition from slave labour and the great plantation houses become ever more opulent – and the coffee barons ever more powerful.

The seeds of the coffee boom's destruction had, however, already been sown. Like the sugar plantations before them, 'slash and burn' of the forests led to soil erosion and depletion, and increased competition came from elsewhere in Central and South America. When the Great Depression hit in the 1930s, the bottom fell out of the coffee market. A 65 per cent slump in global prices was a national disaster.

In September 1822, accosted by yet more messengers bearing instructions from Portugal, Pedro uttered the so-called Cry of Ipiranga – 'Independence or death!' – and had himself crowned Pedro I, Emperor of Brazil. Portugal was too weak to fight back and had no desire to alienate the British, who also had much to gain from an independent Brazil. Portuguese forces, for the most part, withdrew quickly.

'The War of the Triple Alliance became the bloodiest in South American history.'

Dom Pedro's reign was, however, brief. He was far more interested in amusing himself than ruling over a large and disparate country. While independence was welcomed, some of the Emperor's habits were less appealing – to administrative incompetence he added scandal, fathering a number of children by different mistresses. In 1831, he abdicated and returned to Europe, leaving his infant son, Pedro II, as Emperor of Brazil.

Compared with the huge armies and battles which characterised the split of the Spanish empire into 19 separate republics, Brazilian independence was established remarkably peacefully. The glue of an administrative system put in place during the Portuguese exile smoothed the transition, while the establishment of the Empire provided continuity with the past.

PEDRO II

Pedro II was a cultured and enlightened man who travelled widely. An autocratic ruler, he respected the constitution, supported freedom of speech and allowed limited democracy. He found the slave trade distasteful, although felt he had insufficient power to stop it until the very end of his reign. Plantation owners were still the dominant force in the country.

Brazil made huge strides economically under Pedro II. Between 1849 and 1856, foreign trade doubled. The great estates produced ever more sugar, cotton, cattle – and now, coffee (*see left* **The fortunes of coffee**) – and were assisted by the building of roads and railways, the introduction of telegraph, steamship routes to Europe and the founding of banks. Foreign investment poured into the country – most of Britain's investment in Latin America at that time went to Brazil.

There was, however, one blot on Pedro II's reign – the War of the Triple Alliance. Brazil allied with Argentina and Uruguay, to drive back a Paraguayan force which sought to put an end to Brazilian interference in Uruguay and secure access to the Rio de la Plata. This war became the bloodiest in South American history, and while Brazil was on the winning side, she alone suffered over 100,000 casualties. Many of these were slaves, drafted into the army in return for freedom after the war.

All the while, clouds were gathering over the Empire in Brazil. A growing, affluent middle class felt the monarchy was outdated; the church, which had supported the Emperor, was offended by his liberal views; slavery was finally abolished, stoking the wrath of the great landowners; and army officers, fresh from the disastrous war with Paraguay, wanted a greater role in politics. Pedro II was not the kind of man to resist the will of the people, and when asked to abdicate following a military uprising led by Marechal Deodoro da Fonseca, he did so. One of the army officers who delivered the letter requesting his departure was the grandfather of Fernando Henrique Cardoso, who would play a pivotal role in Brazilian politics a century later. Dom Pedro II died in Paris in 1891.

THE BRAZILIAN REPUBLIC

The new government faced a set of enormous challeges, the greatest being to establish some semblance of a democracy in an enormous and diverse country, with a scattered and largely illiterate population. Republicans wanted a centralised constitution, while provincial leaders were strongly in favour of a more federal version.

A republican constitution was established in 1891, but it was another three years before a civilian President took office, in 1894. Although the government was theoretically elected, in fact only about two per cent of the population was eligible to vote. Power remained in the hands of a landowning elite, while the military saw themselves as the defenders of the constitution.

'The 1920s and '30s saw Rio's emergence as a modern, glamorous destination.'

Quickly, the *café com leite* (white coffee) principle became established, with the presidency rotating between candidates from São Paulo, where most of the coffee was grown, and Minas Gerais, renowned for its dairy

The truly iconic **Cristo Redentor**.

production. Presidents made an effort to work constructively with the executive in Rio and the state governors. It was not, however, democratic. As early as 1904, a protest in Rio against compulsory vaccination was bombarded by the military and 300 protestors were exiled to the Amazon.

The early years of the republic were also characterised by huge waves of immigration, growing cities and industrialisation. Between 1890 and 1930, over four million immigrants arrived, around a third of them from Italy, another third from Portugal and the rest fleeing poverty and turmoil elsewhere. While the coffee boom was underway in the south, a rubber boom in the Amazon attracted workers to the jungle in large numbers.

THE GROWTH OF RIO

At the beginning of the 20th century, Rio had a population of around one million people and continued to develop at a fast pace. Mayor Francisco Pereira Passos was responsible for some major improvements, such as the introduction of public health programmes. An engineer by profession, Passos had constructed Rio's first purpose-built tourist attraction – a steam railway up Corcovado, at that time yet to be adorned by the statue Cristo Redentor. In 1912, this would become the first electric railway in Brazil.

While he was in office, a tunnel was built connecting Botafogo with Copacabana, which heralded the start of the development of the city's Zona Sul. Roads were widened, the most impressive being today's Avenida Rio Branco, which was referred to as the Champs Elysées of its time. The construction of many elegant, neoclassical buildings added to the French atmosphere. The Theatro Municipal, founded in 1905, was modelled directly on the Paris opera house.

One of Passos' less wise moves was to attempt slum clearance. With their homes in the centre of the city destroyed, the poor and destitute moved into the hills – which to this day are covered in the slums, or favelas, of the 21st century. The first favela dates from 1897 and grew up behind the English cemetery on the Morro da Providência – victorious republican troops arrived in Rio having put down an insurrection in the north, and camped on the hill while waiting for their just reward. The hill became known as the Morro da Favela, supposedly after the hill near Canudos, where the troops had camped during the campaign. It was the first of an ever-increasing number of poverty-stricken neighbourhoods in Rio.

The next couple of decades, however, saw Rio emerge as a modern, glamorous destination, while the rest of the world saw political and military upheaval. The Copacabana Palace Hotel (*see p42*), still the most desirable lodging in Rio, opened its doors in 1923. The myth of the tropical paradise lived on, as film stars and the famous arrived to claim a Brazilian connection. Films like *Flying Down to Rio* (1933) added to the glamour, but while the cultural life was vibrant and the scenery alluring, all was not well.

Two failed uprisings against the government took place in 1922 and 1924. There was a feeling that somehow Brazil was lagging behind other democracies and the government was unequal to the challenge. To prove this point, a most extraordinary event occurred – the Prestes Column. During the 1920s, for over two years, a group of young army officers marched a total of 25,000 kilometres (13,670 miles) through southern and western Brazil, their only goal being to evade capture and so illustrate the powerlessness of the government. Finally, in 1930, as yet another election was rigged, a revolt by the military put President Getúlio Vargas into office. Not wishing to stir up more civil unrest, the outgoing President, Washington Luís, disappeared into exile.

THE VARGAS YEARS

Vargas took office as the Great Depression hit. Hordes of hungry, homeless and jobless people descended on Brazil's cities looking for work. Most were singularly ill equipped – over half the adult population was still illiterate. While he was authoritarian, many saw Vargas as a benevolent father figure. His skill lay in steering a middle course between the rival doctrines of communism and fascism, as they dominated the world stage. The famous Brazilian compromise, or *jeito*, became a feature of the first 15 years of Vargas's rule, as he sought to co-opt his enemies and broaden his power base.

President Vargas was also the first President to try to harness the power of the growing urban working class. He relied on a combination of nationalism and economic growth. He encouraged the steel industry at Volta Redonda in Rio state, established a labour ministry and permitted the formation of syndicates, or unions, for workers. By 1930, São Paulo had overtaken Rio as the country's industrial heart. The start of World War II provided unrivalled opportunities for the growth of Brazilian industry, to serve markets both at home and abroad.

When war broke out, initially it had been unclear whether or not Brazil would support the Allies. In the event, following a combination of carrot-and-stick on the part of the Americans, Brazil declared war on the Axis powers in 1942.

Populist dictator **Getúlio Vargas**.

Around 25,000 Brazilian troops were committed to the war effort, of which 500 died liberating Italy. German submarines attacked shipping off the Brazilian coast. Military parades and a fever of nationalism briefly united the country.

This ultimately backfired on Vargas. After fighting in Europe to defeat the forces of totalitarianism, the army was not content with a dictator at home. Vargas was deposed by a military coup in October 1945.

THE POST WAR PERIOD

The election which followed saw the start of universal suffrage in Brazil, and President Eurico Gaspar Dutra was elected. He quickly outlawed communism and, as the Cold War dawned, declared Brazil's support for the United States. Continuing urbanisation brought the rich and poor together and favelas started to proliferate in the big cities. Slum residents were no better off in terms of health or education than their predecessors had been half a century earlier.

In 1951, Vargas was returned to power. His government was swiftly dogged by industrial unrest and accusations that he was a communist. He lost any remaining support when one of his bodyguards was implicated in the attempted

Fourth and fifth times lucky: **Luiz Inácio Lula da Silva**.

murder of outspoken journalist Carlos Lacerda. The military finally called for his resignation and, rather than follow so many predecessors into exile, he shot himself in the Catete Palace in Rio.

> **'Brasília was inaugurated in 1960, and brought Rio's days of political intrigue and glory to an end.'**

The departure of Vargas resulted in an unseemly scramble for power. Finally, Juscelino Kubitschek, known familiarly as JK, was installed as President. This marked another first for Brazil – the first Brazilian President without Portuguese origins. JK was keen to promote advancement and change. Many on the left disapproved of his drive for foreign investment and his strengthening of a market economy, and the extravagances of his administration led to the emergence of high inflation.

Appropriately, he is remembered most for the construction of Brasília, the new cutting-edge, purpose-built capital. The work of Oscar Niemeyer and Lúcio Costa, Brasília was inaugurated in 1960 and brought Rio's days of political intrigue and glory to an end.

The peculiar Jânio Quadros – best remembered for trying to ban bikinis – followed Kubitschek as President but resigned after only six months. The military tried to prevent his deputy, João Goulart taking office, relenting only when he agreed to a be President of a more European, parliamentary style of Government, complete with a Prime Minister in the form of Tancredo Neves. Goulart proved to be weak and incompetent. Growth slowed and inflation soared. He made an attempt at land reform, which antagonised the powerful landowners who felt that the democratic experiment had failed. In March 1964, troops from Minas marched on Rio and the military took over again.

MILITARY RULE

Initially it was assumed that military rule was a temporary measure. It would, however, be over 20 years before democracy returned. All over Latin America, democracy came under sustained attack, as the military took over. Unlike other countries, Brazil never had one dictator, as the presidency continued to rotate among the generals. In the early years, resistance grew to military government, manifesting itself in street demonstrations in Brazil's major cities.

The real break with democracy came in December of 1968, when, following Institutional Act 5, Congress was purged of dissidents, many judges and mayors were dismissed and press censorship was enforced. All political parties except the official opposition were banned. Many who opposed these measures fled into exile. The following five years saw the most brutal period – most of the deaths, disappearances and imprisonments happened during this time. During two decades of military rule, over 300 people were killed and more than 1,500 were tortured.

DEMOCRACY RETURNS

A combination of economic downturn and the success of the Diretas-já! campaign (Direct Elections Now!) finally forced the end of the dictatorship. After much political manoeuvring, Congress finally voted for the opposition presidential candidate, a rare statesman who was acceptable to both sides – Tancredo Neves, who had already served under Goulart as Prime Minister. Unfortunately, he died without ever having been sworn in.

His deputy, José Sarney, took over and presided over economic meltdown. Brazil had three new currencies in five years and, by 1988, annual inflation had reached 1,038 per cent. By 1989, over two thirds of the population had no confidence in the government. Things went from bad to worse when later that year, Fernando Collor beat one Luiz Inácio Lula da Silva, who was standing for President for the first time. Lula, a seasoned trade unionist, was viewed as being too radical at a time when communism was imploding around the world. Collor, by contrast, wanted to privatise, reduce bureaucracy and encourage investment. Unfortunately, it seemed that much money was being 'privatised' to individuals and Collor resigned in 1992, just before he was impeached.

By 1993, inflation had reached a staggering 2,500 per cent. Itamar Franco, Collor's successor, was struggling. His Finance Minister, Fernando Henrique Cardoso, finally turned things around, with the implementation of the *plano real* and yet another new currency. Fernando Henrique went on to win the presidential elections in both 1994 and 1998 and is widely credited as being one of Brazil's most successful presidents.

INTO THE 21ST CENTURY

As a new century dawned, Brazil took a significant step that demonstrated the maturity of its democracy. In 2002, Brazil was finally

ready for Lula – and he was ready for Brazil. At his fourth attempt, he was elected President by a large majority of voters. Having abandoned some of his more radical views, Lula has followed many of the economic policies which he so roundly condemned when Fernando Henrique introduced them. As a result, while Brazil's growth has not equalled that of some other developing countries in recent years, investment has remained good and inflation is low.

While few doubt that Lula's heart is in the right place, his government has failed to address the huge burden of Brazilian bureaucracy and 'jobs for the boys'. The poor have benefited significantly from a number of measures, but much remains to be done – not least in Rio.

In many respects, Rio remains the same city that visitors described centuries ago: stunningly beautiful but, on closer inspection, displaying a shockingly ugly face. Nobody arriving at the international airport can fail to see the favelas stretching as far as the eye can see. Various big budget projects are trying to integrate the marginalised into the city's mainstream, but unless the twin issues of corruption and violence are resolved, any success will be limited. New state governor Sergio Cabral is exploring various options, from military deployment to copying the 'zero tolerance' policies that transformed New York. In the meantime, the drug trafficking and murder continue reminding everyone of the fragility of life and of the future prosperity of the city itself.

Tancredo Neves died before taking office.

Rio Today

Forget tomorrow, welcome to the city where the present is paramount.

Ask any Brazilian to describe Rio de Janeiro and the chances are they will reply by quoting a lyric from a track by Gilberto Gil, Brazil's omni-popular pop star turned Minister for Culture. 'Rio de Janeiro continua lindo,' they'll tell you. 'Rio de Janeiro continues to be beautiful.' And despite the city's numerous problems – the violence, the drugs, the social chasm between the haves and the have-nots and the appalling poverty levels – there really is no way of denying it.

Cradled between a patchwork of vast rock formations and lush forests, Rio de Janeiro is without doubt one of the world's most naturally beautiful cities. It's a tropical paradise with around 6.5 million inhabitants, hemmed in by giant strips of sands and towering mountain ranges, and is home to some of the world's most glamorous beaches, like Copacabana, Leblon and Ipanema, made famous by the 1950s bossa nova hit 'The Girl from Ipanema'.

The centrepiece of what locals call the *cidade maravilhosa* (marvellous city) is Rio's Christ the Redeemer statue – a magnificent concrete effigy that towers over the city and can be seen from all corners of the city – but it's just one of many spots from which to marvel.

As well as its physical beauty, Rio must also rank as one of the most exuberant cities in the world, famed for its all-night parties, its unrivalled cultural scene and a level of unashamed debauchery that is marvelled at the world over. Rio, make no mistake about it, is the cultural capital of Brazil.

CARIOCA CULTURE

There is a little bit of everything for visitors to Rio. Music lovers can find some of the countries most exciting young musicians on show virtually every night of the week. Beach bums can spend endless afternoons soaking up sun on the city's seemingly endless sands. Architecture fans, meanwhile, can marvel at the colonial elegance of Rio antigo, gradually being renovated by the town hall. After years of abandon an ever growing number of spectacular mansions and town houses in central Rio are now being restored to their former glory and turned into museums, cultural centres, restaurants and stylish nightclubs.

And how can you speak of Rio without mentioning its footballing past? The city is also a feast for sports lovers, who can tour the Maracanã football stadium and tread where the king of Brazilian football, Pelé, once trod.

Cariocas have a reputation for having a macho society, yet these days the city is even being touted as one of the world's most popular gay destinations. The annual gay pride march, usually held in July on Copacabana beach, is one of the largest and most colourful in the world and there are a growing number of GLS bars, clubs and restaurants, aimed at 'Gays,

Lesbians and Sympathisers'. In 2005, around 500,000 gay tourists from Brazil and overseas made the pilgrimage to Rio's Carnival, according to the tourist board.

Cariocas are proud of describing their city as a cultural melting pot and they are right to do so. Rio is home to immigrants from all corners of Brazil, as well as sizeable Angolan, Japanese, Chinese and German communities. It's a place where one can eat sushi on Monday, dance samba on Wednesday and perhaps take in a ballet on Thursday, and grabbing some sauerkraut during the interval certainly isn't unheard of.

Working-class hero?

On 27 October 1945, a boy called Luiz Inácio da Silva was born in the dusty and impoverished backlands of Pernambuco in Brazil's northeast. Almost exactly 61 years later, on 29 October 2006, the same Luiz was re-elected for his second term as President of the world's fifth largest democracy. Only, by now, people no longer called him Luiz. They referred to him as President Lula.

The rags-to-riches story of Luiz Inácio 'Lula' da Silva is the stuff of fairytales. After fleeing poverty in the arid northeast, he was raised in São Paulo, where he sold peanuts and shined shoes. From there he rose through the union ranks into politics. In the 1980s, he was one of the founders of the Workers Party (PT) and in 2002 he made history after being elected as Brazil's first working-class leader – at the fourth time of asking.

It was almost too much to believe. How, in one of the world's most unequal nations, could a former peasant rise to become the most important man in the country?

Ask most people to explain why Lula is so popular and they're likely to tell you it's because he is the 'mirror image of Brazil'. Lula understands the people. He is the 'boy done good' or, as the president likes to paint himself, the '*Pai dos Pobres*', the 'Father of the Poor'.

Despite repeated corruption scandals during his first term involving members of Lula's government – Y-fronts filled with dollars, high-class call girls and vote buying, to name just a few – his approval rating remains high. In Brazil's poorest areas, government benefit schemes have helped maintain Lula's popularity. The middle and upper classes, meanwhile, who were once fearful of Lula's radical leftism, have been

pleasantly relieved at how moderate the former union leader has turned out to be.

What's more, while during the 1980s Lula was known as a firebrand who threatened to default on Brazil's foreign debt and constantly railed against the International Monetary Fund (IMF), in power he has been far more moderate, improving relations with the US and to a certain extent shunning Venezuela's outspoken leader Hugo Chávez.

Lula is not without his detractors, particularly among what remains of the militant Left, who accuse him of betraying his roots and of not doing enough to speed up land reform or reduce poverty. What is undeniable, though, is that when Brazil's impoverished masses, not least the inhabitants of Rio de Janeiro's shantytowns, look in the mirror, they still see the shoeshine President staring back at them.

Rio vs São Paulo

Once upon a time, there was a Carioca who went to spend his holidays with his family in São Paulo. One day, he went into a hardware shop to buy a potty for his child.

'Don't think we have any of those,' the attendant told him. 'Yes you do,' replied the Carioca, pointing to a large potty on the shelf behind him. 'Look up there.'

'Ah!' said the Paulista shop attendant. 'Here we call those Cariocas.'

The Carioca, infuriated, frowned. 'Well, please give me a Carioca then, so I can fill it with Paulista.'

Cariocas and Paulistas have never exactly seen eye to eye. While their cities are only a few hundred kilometres apart, a gaping chasm separates the personalities of Rio and São Paulo's residents. Snide jokes abound about the Carioca-Paulista rivalry: mostly as puerile as the one above.

Like all great intercity squabbling, it is a culture clash of lifestyles and outlooks. In the blue corner, São Paulo: the organised, money-hungry megalopolis whose European work-ethic has made it Brazil's economic bastion. In the red corner, Rio de Janeiro, the laid-back beach paradise, whose relaxed population and tropical climate have created one of the world's great cultural capitals; the home of samba and carnival.

São Paulo is sold as the city whose devastatingly efficient metro service carries millions of *trabalhadores* to the office each day. Rio, on the other hand, is the city of samba, caipirinhas, cancelled dinner dates and the 'Girl from Ipanema'.

São Paulo is painted as Brazil's gastronomic capital, pausing between slivers of sashimi to deride the bean-stew cuisine of their lowly neighbours. Rio might come up short on the food front, but it wins hands down in terms of culture – or so the Cariocas believe. Paulistas, increasingly, counter that their city is even usurping the culture crown from Rio. Why? Because São Paulo works harder, and thus has more money to pay artists and musicians to perform, of course – sometimes even managing to tempt them to relocate to their city.

There is, it has to be said, more than a hint of truth in the comparisons as any visitor will quickly realise. But that doesn't make the rivalry any less ridiculous. One of the most amusing points of contention is crime. Every time the Brazilian government releases new crime statistics, the Brazilian media reopens the debate. Which city is more dangerous, Brazilians wonder, Rio or São Paulo? The finger pointing begins again, like two men arguing over whose girlfriend is the least ugly.

A TALE OF TWO CITIES

Yet the marvellous city, as residents like to call it, is a city with two faces. It's a divided, schizophrenic city, as any visitor who ventures outside the tourist bubble of the southern beach districts will soon find out.

Rio de Janeiro is undoubtedly one of the world's most stunning cities, but it's simultaneously one of the world's most unequal, divided places, where absolute poverty and extreme wealth pass each other in the street, without exchanging so much as a glance.

The daily reality for most Cariocas is radically different from the rosy vision found in most tourist brochures. A huge majority of residents for example, never even go to the beaches; they are simply too busy trying to scratch together a living in a city where many earn just R$400 (US$200) a month.

Twenty per cent of the population, or around one million people, live in often violent favelas – sprawling, redbrick slums controlled by ruthless, heavily armed drug lords, or increasingly paramilitary vigilantes, who dish out justice through the barrel of an AK-47.

'Cariocas are a resilient lot who constantly strive to look on the bright side.'

Outside the favelas, many people also suffer from a chronic lack of security – or at least the chronic sense of insecurity that pervades almost all aspects of life here. The vast electric fences that encircle many of Rio's more luxurious homes in the glitzy beach neighbourhoods of Leblon and Ipanema are a constant reminder that all is not well in this beachside paradise. Bullet-proof cars are increasingly popular among the rich, while the less well-off invest in black plastic screens to cover their car windows or avoid taking certain routes at certain times.

Rio is undoubtedly also a decadent city. Once touted as the 'tropical Paris' by Eurocentric city planners, it spent much of the second half of the 20th century slowly slipping into decline. Today, in many parts it's a bewildering hodge-podge of ugly high-rise apartment blocks and pollution-stained shanty towns. Since Rio lost its status as the country's capital to Brasilia in 1960, industry has increasingly moved out, while drug traffickers and criminals have moved in. Besides the violence, many other aspects are out of control – the public services, the prison system, law enforcement and pollution – all problems that would tear a lesser city apart.

Yet, despite this, Rio has lost little of its allure or indeed its hopes for a better future. Cariocas are a resilient lot, who for better or worse constantly strive to look on the bright side of life. Fundamental to this ability to ride out the highs and the lows of life is the *jeitinho*, the 'little way'. The little way is basically a form of cunning by which cariocas manage to sidestep all of the irritations and obstacles in life. They skip queues, tell white lies and generally fudge their way through life with hardly a thought for the consequences.

The upside of the *jeitinho* is that Cariocas manage to wriggle themselves out of all manner of fixes without ever losing their trademark smile. The downside is that civil responsibility is not a well-known concept here. Dinner dates are easily forgotten. Promises are made without thought and just as quickly discarded.

It will take more than a *jeitinho* to fix all of Rio's problems, however. In fact, Rio's big hope is that petrol money can help fund a much needed revival. Vast offshore oil

Flying the flag: a poodle shows his colours.

The **Rocinha** favela – giving new meaning to the term 'upwardly mobile'.

reserves – located near the once sleepy fishing village of Macaé, now a bustling city of 160,000 inhabitants – are touted as the first part of a redevelopment programme that will help drag Rio out of social and economic stagnation. In the last decade, Macaé's economy has grown by 600 per cent, bucking a trend of decline that has defined most other parts of the state of Rio. The problems are too great to solve overnight, but this may be a good start.

UNFINISHED BUSINESS

Rio is a city at a crossroads. Either it will gain a new lease of life and propel itself back towards its past glory, or the city will slip further and further into lawlessness and mayhem, with the rich getting richer and richer and retreating further inside their fortress-like apartment blocks and the poor remaining the principal victims.

On a brighter note, there are a number of exciting grassroots cultural movements growing up in the favelas, offering alternatives to some of the country's most deprived young people. The initial signs are mixed. Rio's new governor, Sergio Cabral, has brought hopes that change is at last on the cards, promising to combat crime with an iron fist, to stamp out corruption and jump-start public services. In 2007, Mr Cabral visited Colombia in order to study security policies that have brought about a miraculous drop in crime in cities like Bogotá, Medellín and Cali.

Cabral has hailed such policies, which involved urban redevelopment, massive police reform, weapons amnesties as well as increased repression. Some such plans have already begun to be put in place. The award-winning Brazilian architect Luiz Carlos Toledo, for example, is currently preparing a massive urban redesign of Rocinha, Rio's largest favela, which will include street lighting, hotels and even a cable car designed to improve transport.

Whether such policies are workable in Rio remains to be seen. Few doubt, however, that Cabral has the will to change things. In the first few months of his government (which began in January 2007), he had already signalled the need for a new approach, commanding over a growing assault on Rio's traffickers and a partial restructuring of the security forces. Links between the Federal Government and Rio's state government are also on the up, after two successive administrations that bickered constantly with central government. Rio's new governor has cemented a friendship with left-wing president Luiz Inácio Lula da Silva, which Cariocas hope will see much greater investment in their once great city.

Only time will tell whether such words represent a genuine and workable commitment to a better future or simply more of the empty rhetoric to which Cariocas are so used to. In the meanwhile, in spite of it all, Rio de Janeiro continues to be beautiful.

The **Sambódromo**. See p26.

Carnival

The world's best party. Period.

Reaching a consensus on the roots of Brazilian Carnival is like discussing which is the best samba school in Rio with a Carioca: everyone seems to have a different opinion. But one thing is certain. Long before samba was even a twinkle in Rio's eye, the city was already the scene of riotous street parties.

Like the giant, multicoloured floats that parade through Rio each year, the city's Carnival has undergone many face-lifts since the tradition first sprung up here in the 1500s. The first Carnival celebrations are said to have arrived in Brazil with the Portuguese in the 16th century. Known as the *entrudo*, the festivities were boisterous, irreverent gatherings where locals hit the streets in colourful costumes and with giant dolls.

The first versions of Rio Carnival proper were imported from Paris during the 1830s by middle class Brazilians who held lavish balls at which masked revellers made merry until the early hours of the morning. Over the following years, Carnival survived several attempts at

▶ For dates of Rio's Carnivals up to 2010, *see p154*. Events and parties begin in the week preceding Carnival. For practicalities, visit www.riodejaneiro-turismo.com.br.

repression and evolved into an increasingly debauched musical spectacle, becoming the centre point of the Brazilian year.

SAMBA SCHOOLS

Towards the beginning of the 20th century, a new ingredient was thrown into the cauldron. A musical revolution took place in Rio that would forever change the face of the city's Carnival festivities. It was called samba (*see also p174*). Before long, dozens of informal samba groups – called *blocos* (*see p28* **Bloco rocking beats**), *cordões* or *ranchos* – appeared in Rio. Then, in the late 1920s, the samba schools appeared.

The first official *escola de samba* went by the name of Deixa Falar ('Let them speak') and was created on 12 August 1928, by three giants of samba: Ismael Silva, Bide and Marçal. It was called a 'school' because Deixa Falar's HQ was next to a local primary school in Estácio, a neighbourhood in the north of the centre. The region was full of African culture, brought to Rio by former slaves and their descendants who lived in poor districts around the city centre such as Saude, Morro da Favela (now called Providencia), Morro de Sao Carlos and Gamboa. Immigrants from all over Brazil gathered here, mixing a variety of regional sounds including *maxixes*, *jongos* and *lundus*. The result was samba.

Deixa Falar only lasted until 1931. But it had paved the way for other schools to appear and had guaranteed Estácio's place in samba history. A series of other groups sprung up in its place and, in 1983, merged into the Estácio de Sá (www.gresestaciodesa.com.br) – to this day one of Rio's most respected and innovative schools, which carries the slogan 'The cradle of samba' on its red and white uniform.

The king of all samba schools was also born in 1928, just outside the city centre in the Mangueira shantytown. Nicknamed 'Estação Primeira' (first station) because of its location on the train line outside Central Station, Mangueira (www.mangueira.com.br) was a hilltop shantytown that hosted weekly samba celebrations, drawing visitors from far and wide.

The Mangueira has produced some of Brazil's best-loved *sambistas,* including Cartola, Nelson Cavaquinho, Carlos Cachaça and Padeirinho. Female samba divas have also flocked to perform with the Estação Primeira, among them Alcione and Beth Carvalho.

'It wasn't always sequins and hedonism. Samba used to be looked down on like many today dismiss funk.'

Rio's first official Carnival parade, in 1932, was won by the Mangueira school, triggering an avalanche of nostalgic sambas in the coming years, paying tribute to their 'darling Mangueira'. 'I've had the happiness to live here, and the other schools even cry, envious of your position,' Cartola sang in Sala de Recepção. 'My Mangueira is an entrance hall. Here we embrace our enemies as if they were brothers.'

The School quickly became the Manchester United of Brazilian Carnival. Today, its pink and green colours are worn in virtually every corner of the country. Mangueira was a poor and, as the century went on, increasingly violent shantytown, yet it has never lost its label as the home of samba. A large part of this success is down to Jamelão, Mangueira's most famous *puxador* (Carnival singer), whose thundering, deep voice has graced the school's parades for decades. Until suffering health problems in 2006, Jamelão was an ever-present at Mangueira rehearsals and parades, belting out the school's annual anthem or *samba enredo*.

CITY OF SAMBA

These days, samba is very much part of the mainstream. In 2005, the town hall opened the **Cidade do Samba** (*see p63*), a permanent mega-monument located in the port area where Deixa Falar sprung up 80 years before.

As well as housing so-called 'Samba Factories' – warehouses where the city's top 13 schools prepare their floats – the City of Samba boasts a museum and live shows. Some have criticised the development as a slightly watered down, tourist version of Carnival, yet the renovation of the Port area, of which the City of Samba is part, can only be a good thing, bringing life back to a long-forgotten part of town.

But it wasn't always sequins and hedonism. Until the 1950s, samba was still considered the music of crooks, drunks, prostitutes and, worst of all from the perspective of the high society, Afro-Brazilian slave descendants. Samba was looked down on in the same way that many today dismiss funk, the latest sound to emerge from Rio's favelas.

In journalist Sergio Cabral's excellent study of Rio's Carnival he recalls a newspaper editorial from the early 1940s that underlines the prejudice around what is today a national passion. 'There must, in future, be more rigorous censorship of the productions, in order to avoid the possibility of encouraging low-level themes,' the paper wrote. 'There are lots of interesting things to touch on, just as there are intelligent ways to free our people of the African ideas that are imposed on them by the 'maestros' and 'poets' from the favelas.'

But Rio's samba schools refused to be silenced, and in the post-war period continued to grow in number. By the 1960s, samba had ceased to be the sound of the poor – hoards of Rio's middle and upper classes were also heading to the samba schools, inspired by the crossover between favela *sambistas* and radio crooners like Dick Farney and Elizeth Cardoso. Twenty years later, Rio's samba schools would receive a permanent tribute in the centre of Rio.

One of those responsible for transforming the Carnival parade into an event for the masses was Joãosinho Trinta, a larger than life Carnival designer from Maranhão, whose designs have won him eight Carnival titles since 1965 for schools including the Salgueiro, Beija-Flor and Viradouro. Trinta – a theatre set designer by trade – injected a much-needed dose of drama into the samba parades and frequently compared Rio's Carnival to the opera. 'This is my life,' he said of the samba parades in a recent interview. 'This is what I am. I don't work. I carry out a mission.'

THE SAMBODROMO

If Trinta was key to the transformation of Carnival, Leonel Brizola also did his part. Brizola, who governed Rio from 1982 to 1986, was the man behind the controversial Sambódromo da Marquês de Sapucaí, better known simply as the **Sambódromo** (*see p60*).

Bloco rocking beats

Their names say it all. 'What shit is this?', 'Suck but don't dribble' and even 'Christ's armpit'. These are the Carnival *blocos* – probably the world's most brazenly debauched form of street party.

Most gringos have the impression that the samba schools are the heart of Rio de Janeiro's Carnival, but they're wrong. *Blocos* are what it's really all about.

Mobile street parties that come to life weeks before Carnival proper, the *blocos* come in all shapes and sizes and can be found in most neighbourhoods. There are kids' blocos for the younger generations, animal *blocos* to take your poodles to and alcohol-soaked 'piranha' *blocos*, where muscle-bound Brazilian men run riot dressed up in drag. Botafogo is even home to its own *bloco* run by the local psychiatric hospital, with its predictably irreverent name 'Going, Going, Gone Mad'.

Blocos usually take place at the same time and place each year, but are subject to some changes. Check the Friday arts guide in *O Globo* newspaper a few weeks before carnival for a completely up to date run-down, or search for 'Blocos de Carnaval' on the Portuguese version of www.wikipedia.org.

Here is a small selection of some of the *blocos* to watch out for:

Suvaco do Cristo

Named Christ's Armpit for its location in Jardim Botânico, which sits directly underneath the outstretched right arm of the Christ the Redeemer statue.
Where The party starts at Bar Jóia on the corner of Rua Jardim Botânico and Rua Faro.
When The last Sunday before Carnival usually at 1pm, although organisers sometimes change the time to keep away the riff-raff.

Monobloco

Organised around a huge drum troupe founded in 2000 by the musician Pedro Luis and his band A Parede. Made up of over 100 drummers and a huge mobile sound system, the party attracts thousands of devotees with its mix of regional and ear-splitting rhythms, and is one of Rio's most famous *blocos*.
Where Copacabana beach, Posto 6.
When 9am, an early start on the Sunday immediately following Carnival.

Bloco das Carmelitas

The queen of Santa Teresa's *blocos*. According to urban legend the *bloco* received its name after a nun fled the nearby Carmelitas convent to join in the festivities. The *bloco* draws huge crowds and proceeds through Santa Teresa twice during Carnival.
Where Bar do Serginho, Rua Dias de Barros with Ladeira de Santa Teresa.
When Two outings, at 6pm on the first Friday of Carnival and then at 5pm on the Tuesday of Carnival.

Bloco Clube do Samba

A bloco for samba purists, organised by Ângela Nogueira, the wife of the late João Nogueira, one of Rio's most beloved *sambistas*.
Where On Avenida Atlântica, at the corner with Rua Santa Clara in Copacabana.
When At 2pm, on the Tuesday of Carnival.

Banda de Ipanema

Founded during the 1964 military dictatorship the Banda de Ipanema is one of Rio's most harmonious, irreverent *blocos*, drawing a happy mix of transvestites, OAPs, students businessmen and the rich and poor alike.
Where Catch it at its starting point in Praça General Osório in Ipanema or as it progresses down the beach towards Leblon.
When Twice: 3pm on the Saturday of Carnival and again at 3pm on the Tuesday of Carnival.

Imprensa que eu Gamo

A *bloco* run by Rio-based journalists, whose annual theme tune sends up politicians and, occasionally, humiliates foreign journalists who write nasty things about Brazil.
Where At the Mercadinho São José on the corner of Rua Das Laranjeiras with Rua Gago Coutinho, in Laranjeiras.
When An early party, from 4pm onwards, on the Saturday two weeks before Carnival starts.

Keen to be remembered for giving Rio a makeover, Brizola commissioned Brazil's superstar architect Oscar Niemeyer to remodel parts of the city, creating a series of futuristic-looking state schools as well as the definitive tribute to Carnival – a 650-metre- (2,100-foot-) long concrete catwalk for the samba groups to parade down each year.

From the off, Niemeyer's project was mired in controversy. Some said it would be impossible to create a half-decent, safe stadium in the 110 days allotted for its construction. Others said it would change irreparably the style and atmosphere of the samba school processions. One thing was certain: the Sambódromo marked the beginning of another new era in Carnival.

THE ERA OF MEGABUCKS

Rio's samba schools never lost their links to Rio's shantytowns. Many of the schools are located in or near the favelas, or in the impoverished suburbs, while the majority of the dancers and those involved in preparing the floats are residents of these communities.

'In 2006, three top samba schools banned foreigners for fears the gringos were ruining their performances.'

Yet the spectacle has certainly moved on from the days of Cartola's Mangueira. Cartola spent much of his life living in a wooden shack, selling sambas and washing car windscreens to scrape by. These days, samba schools receive six-figure sponsorship deals from all imaginable sources: mining companies, tourist boards and even, in 2007, the Venezuelan president Hugo Chávez, who bank-rolled a giant effigy of the revolutionary Simón Bolívar.

Carnival's increasing commercialisation has led several key samba figures to shun the annual procession, arguing that Carnival has sold its soul. The increasing presence of foreigners in the parades has also caused controversy. In 2006, three of the city's top samba schools announced they would ban foreigners from participating in their Carnival parades because of fears that the gringos were ruining their performances.

Yet the money continues to pour in. In 2007, Rio's samba association – LIESA – raked in no less than R$38 million (US$20 million) through ticket sales alone. Exact figures are hard to come by but it's rumoured in the Brazilian press that the whole spectacle costs at least R$100 million (US$50 million) to put on each year.

Unsurprisingly, perhaps, Rio's Carnival has not been immune to the corruption that permeates so many levels of Brazilian life. In 2007, a Parliamentary Inquiry, the CPI do Samba, was opened after allegations that that year's Carnival procession had been fixed by local mafia bosses.

At the beginning of 2007, the President of Rio's Samba Association, Ailton Guimarães, was arrested as part of a massive sting operation intended to crack down on illegal gambling rackets in Rio. Among others arrested was Anísio Abraão David, the honorary president of the Beija-Flor samba school, champions of that year's Carnival.

THE PARADE

Despite all this, Rio's *desfile*, or parade, remains one of the world's great visual events, an electrifying, throbbing and relentless spectacle that's a must-see for all visitors to Rio. Since the 1930s, the format of Carnival parades has suffered several mutations. These days, the competition is arranged in leagues or *grupos*, rather like a football league. The top flight of the Carnival parade is the *Grupo Especial* or Special Group, followed by groups A, B, C, D and E. The Special group performs each year on the Sunday and Monday of Carnival and the results are announced on Ash Wednesday. The top teams are given 80 minutes to parade, during which they repeatedly sing that year's samba theme or *enredo*.

The *enredo*, pioneered in the 1930s by groups like Mangueira, is a specially composed theme tune that usually picks up on some aspect of Brazilian history, culture or current affairs and attempts to capture the zeitgeist. Recent themes have included a tribute to Chico Buarque, a samba about the legacy of slavery, and tracks singing the praises of the Amazon rainforest or a particular piece of its fruit.

Each school's procession is based around the *enredo* and it's virtually impossible to spend Carnival in Rio without memorising at least one of the catchy tunes. If you're in Rio in the lead up to Carnival you can swot up on the lyrics of your chosen school by buying a copy of the annual *Grupo Especial* compilation CD, available in most record shops.

Many samba *enredos* have been written since the beginning of last century, paying tribute to Rio de Janeiro and Carnival. Perhaps the most fitting remains Mangueira's 1954 theme, 'Rio de Janeiro, Today and Yesterday': 'Rio de Janeiro... your sumptuous panorama [is] incomparable, sublime, vibrant,' it croons. 'You are the model city. You are the heart of Brazil.'

Gushing, over the top and full of itself – it's the spirit of Carnival in a nutshell.

Football

Never say 'it's only a game'.

In Rio de Janeiro, everyone is touched by football. Even those rare citizens who profess not to give two hoots for the game will – when pressed – admit to having a preference for one of the city's four main clubs. It's inconceivable that you could live in Rio and be unable to list Flamengo, Fluminense, Vasco and Botafogo, to not know their team colours or to be incapable of humming along to at least one of their songs. Aligning yourself (and, almost as crucially, your next of kin) with one of the big four is not so much about liking football – it's about functioning as a Carioca.

In order to best fit in to Rio society and conversations, there comes a time (usually not long after arrival) when you have to decide which club to support. It pays to make the decision carefully, since the Rio clubs are strongly divided along social and cultural lines. Botafogo, for instance, is the club of intellectuals, poets and the superstitious – and the club of Garrincha, the best footballer Rio (some would say Brazil) ever produced.

Discovering what the clubs stand for is as good a way as any of learning about Rio's history, and also about the emergence of Brazilian football, which by the 1950s was the best in the world. Even though Rio de Janeiro has not been the national capital for almost 50 years, and even though the São Paulo clubs have been consistently better for the last decade, the city is still the administrative and spiritual heart of Brazilian football. Rio retains its essence as the city that best represents the nation; and football is one of the fundamental aspects of that national identity.

Football arrived in Brazil (from England) in 1894, down the coast in Santos. It was only a few years later that the game made it to Rio. In 1902, Oscar Cox, an Anglo-Brazilian, and his friends founded Rio's first club, Fluminense. Slavery had only just been abolished and the club was an exclusively white affair, a institution that upheld the social divisions of the day. When, slowly, black and mixed-race players started to emerge, they were made to feel uncomfortable. Most famously, the mulatto Carlos Alberto covered his face in rice-powder to disguise his skin-colour. When fans saw the make-up dissolve in the sweat and sun, they began to chant 'pó de arroz' ('rice powder') at him. The phrase was then adopted as Fluminense's nickname – possibly the least politically correct club nickname in football. Yet, rather than feel embarrassed about such racist beginnings, the fans turn it into a big

Keep it up

You may not get to see a football match when you are in Rio, but – barring non-stop tropical rainstorms – you will definitely see some footvolley. The game is a form of volleyball using only one's feet, head and chest, and is played all along the beaches of Copacabana and Ipanema.

It's a dazzling sight, all about close-body control skills, athleticism and flamboyance. There is a sense that footvolley, which was invented in the 1960s, has distilled the spirit of Brazilian football.

As there is no possibility of volleyball-style smashes, footvolley rallies can last for an unexpectedly long time. The game has a relaxed beauty to it and when two top doubles

are playing – usually, games are played in a two-a-side format – huge crowds can gather.

The game is played on beach volleyball courts, and emerged when footballers confined themselves to the courts when beaches became too busy to play 11-a-side football. Many women play footvolley, and competitions often involve mixed doubles.

Footvolley has a reputation for attracting rebellious souls, like footballers Edmundo and Romário. One of the sport's pioneers was Almir, a pugnacious maverick who confessed to taking drugs when playing for (São Paulo state club) Santos and was shot dead after getting involved in a brawl in Copacabana. A footvolley match was arranged as a tribute.

The clubs

Flamengo

Mascot The *urubu* – a black Brazilian vulture.
Stadium Gavea, although almost all matches are played at the Maracanã.
Origin of name It's a neighbourhood of Rio.
Historic figures Junior (857 appearances for the club), Leônidas da Silva, Zizinho and Zico.
Fascinating fact Flamenguistas believe that with upwards of 25 million fans in Brazil alone, they are the best-supported club in the world.

Fluminense

Mascot Man in bib and tucker.
Stadium Laranjeiras, although most matches played at the Maracanã.
Origin of name It is an adjective used to describe people from the city of Rio, which means river.
Historic figures Renato Gaúcho (currently Fluminense manager), Rivelino, Telê Santana.
Fascinating fact After an argument in 1911, nine players moved to Flamengo to start a new club there. The club's first idol was Harry Welfare, a Liverpudlian centre-forward who originally came to Rio to teach maths and geography at the Anglo-American school.

Botafogo

Mascot Manequinho, a statue of a boy urinating outside the club.
Stadium No stadium, play most games at the Maracanã.
Origin of name It's a district of Rio.
Historic figures Garrincha, Didi, Gerson, Jairzinho.
Fascinating fact In the 1940s, Biriba, a stray dog, became the club's lucky charm and was paid the same bonuses as the players.

Vasco

Mascot Fat, moustacheod caricature of a Portuguese.
Stadium São Januário.
Origin of name Named after the Portuguese navigator Vasco da Gama, the first person to go directly from Europe to India.
Historic figures Bellini, Romário, Vavá.
Fascinating fact The terracing at the stadium cannot go all the way round the pitch because the club chapel is in the way.

joke – Fluminense fans still throw talcum powder all over themselves before big games.

Fluminense maintains a reputation as the team of aristocrats. Fans assimilate these values to such an extent that a poor favela dweller who supports Fluminense will see himself as more refined than his equally poor Flamengo-supporting neighbour, purely on the basis of club allegiance.

It was on Fluminense's ground, in 1914, that the Brazilian national team played its first ever match, winning 2-0 against Exeter City. Five years later the club built terracing around the pitch, the result being the Estádio das Laranjeiras, the first stadium in the country.

(The stadium still stands and has a capacity of about 8,000. It's an impressive relic, located next to what is now the governor's palace.)

While the elite were passing their afternoons at Fluminense, the rest of the city was also taking to football. So much so that by the 1910s the city reputedly had more pitches than anywhere else in South America. It's thought that one of the reasons that the Brazilians became so good was that they learnt to play outside the official institutions: play was a lot more creative and flamboyant. Also, poverty meant that most of the have-nots learnt to play using coconuts, bundles of socks or anything else of a vaguely spherical nature.

The suburban leagues started to throw up excellent non-white players, but they were often forbidden from playing against the top clubs. The club that broke the white domination of the game was Vasco da Gama (normally referred to simply as 'Vasco'), the club of the Portuguese immigrant community. Unable to choose poor black players in the amateur era because they did not have other jobs, Portuguese businessmen gave them jobs in their shops so they could make the team. Eventually, all barriers against black players collapsed in the early 1930s – and with racially mixed teams, Brazilian football finally came into its own.

Vasco's other great contribution to Rio football was the construction, in 1929, of São Januário. The stadium was the biggest in the city, with a capacity of about 30,000, and is still in use. It retains many of its original features, such as intricate ironwork and Portuguese tiling with nautical scenes, and is probably the most charming stadium in Brazil.

The 1930s was the decade in which Brazilian football established itself as world class – particularly with the performance of the national team at the 1938 World Cup in France, where Leônidas da Silva was voted best player. He played for Flamengo and was in his time the greatest sports star that Brazil had produced.

Leônidas' fame helped establish Flamengo as the most popular club in Brazil. Even though it started off in the 19th century as a regatta club for the rich, as football came to dominate, it achieved the opposite reputation. The 'Rubro-Negro', the Ruby-and-Black, is the team of the masses. So much so that the word Flamenguista is often used as a euphemism for a favela dweller. In truth, Flamengo's fanbase is drawn from both ends of Rio's social and economic spectrum. It occupies a role like Manchester United in England or Juventus in Italy – they are the team that the most people love, and that everyone else loves to hate.

The national self confidence created by Brazil's performance in 1938 (the team won third place) resulted in the country hosting the first post-war World Cup in 1950. Rio was the capital city and the venue for the construction of the largest stadium in the world, the Maracanã. In a city with such awesome natural features – Corcovado, the Sugar Loaf, Copacabana beach – the gigantic Maracanã is still worthy of its place in the landscape. When it was inaugurated it had an official capacity of 183,000. The attendance figures for Brazil's final game of the 1950 World Cup, where they lost 2–1 to Uruguay, were an estimated 200,000, still considered the largest crowd of all time. (Note: this was *not* the final game, but the decisive match of the tournament.)

The Maracanã was built by the Brazilians as a metaphor for the team's greatness and ambition. After the catastrophic defeat against Uruguay, however, which lost them the title with 12 minutes to go, it became a parallel symbol of failure. Even so, the Maracanã became Brazilian football's grandest stage for the golden years of the 1950s and 1960s, an era in which the national team dominated world football.

Even though Pelé never played for a Rio team, many other Brazilian legends did, and in those decades domestic football in Brazil was arguably the best in the world. The Maracanã would fill on a weekly basis to see the skills of players like Garrincha, Nilton Santos, Didi, Zagalo, Amarildo, Jairzinho and Gerson – all crucial members of the World Cup victories in 1958, 1962 and 1970. Each of these legends wore the colours of Botafogo, the smallest of the big four, which helps to explain why its fans are the most superstitious – they need all the help they can get. Garrincha was the symbol of Rio football – he was the game's most talented dribbler, possibly because he was born with legs bent in parallel curves. He was was also a famous womaniser and married Elza Soares, the top samba singer of the time, who still performs regularly in Rio. Garrincha could not adapt to life after he retired and, in 1983, died an alcoholic. A bust of him is positioned by one of the Maracanã gates. Botofogo fans touch it as they walk in to the stadium.

'Streamers, drums and firecrackers are de rigueur for all matches.'

Brazil established a new way of playing football – coined by Pelé as the 'beautiful game' – but their contribution goes beyond the pitch. Brazilians pioneered a more passionate, exuberant and colourful way of supporting their clubs and the national side. This all began in Rio and possibly can be dated to Mário Filho, a journalist who in 1934 organised a competition between Flamengo and Fluminense fans for a derby game. He encouraged them to put on the best show, and they brought along streamers, drums and firecrackers. The game was hyped as the 'Fla-Flu', which is the name now given to all matches between the teams and is the most famous fixture in Brazil. Now streamers, drums and firecrackers are de rigueur for all matches.

A decade later, Flamengo fan Jayme de Carvalho formed the Charanga, a brass band that was the first outfit to play music on the terraces. Now, every Brazilian match that you go to will have drummers and a trumpeter or

The **Maracanã**.

two. Jayme also played up to the carnivalesque aspect of fan behaviour – he dressed up in team colours and brought banners and flags to the stadium. In those days there was no merchandising or replica shirts so he and his wife would spend ages sewing them all together. Thanks to men like Mário Filho and Jayme de Carvalho, going to watch football became as much about taking part in a spectacle as watching one.

At around the same time, Lamartine Babo, one of the great samba composers, wrote theme tunes for each of Rio's main clubs. These delightful songs are still sung by fans and are as well known as the national anthem.

The last great era for Rio football was the 1970s and 1980s, when Flamengo were all-conquering, with their greatest idol, Zico. Since then the clubs have gone into decline. There are many reasons for this, the most important being that most of the best Brazilians now play in Europe. Attendence figures for the national league are pitiful. Average crowds for the 2006 national league were 15,000 for Flamengo, 11,000 for Fluminense and 9,000 for Botafogo – and since these clubs tend to use the Maracanã as their home ground, it means that the matches are almost entirely devoid of atmosphere. (Brazil is too big, and people too poor, for there ever to be more than a handful of away fans for matches between teams from different cities.)

The national league was only introduced in 1971 – after their third World Cup victory – and has never stirred the passions in the way that the state league, where the rivalries are a century-old, still does. The best matches to go to are the state league finals, usually held in March, when the Maracanã will fill to capacity with an exuberant, colourful crowd. A Fla-Flu final on a clear-skied Sunday is still one of the most exhilarating experiences in sport.

Yet it's not all nostalgia for the glory days. Despite the poor attendences of most games, Rio is still a city that lives and breathes *futebol*. *O Globo* has a front page football story every day, almost every shop or bar has the insignia of one of the big four clubs, football tune ringtones are as common as birdsong and the most common form of male apparel is a football top. Fans have a tendency to don the club shirt on the day after a victory, but not on the day after a defeat. This fashion is so pronounced that you can usually work out who has won a match just by looking out the window and watching passers-by.

And there is football going on 24 hours a day. Workers who clock off after midnight – like waiters and hotel porters – play until sunrise on the public pitches by the Aterro de Flamengo. Throughout the day, football is played wherever there is space – even the most vertical of favelas on the hillsides has a *quadra* for kickabouts. Rio is a city shaped by its football culture and the sport's bootmarks are still strongly felt.

• *Alex Bellos is the author of* Futebol: The Brazilian Way of Life, *published by Bloomsbury, New York and London.*

Where to Stay

Where to Stay 36

Features

Where to Stay

Rio's hotel industry is finally widening its net.

Rio's hotels are mostly for holiday makers and have traditionally been as close to the beach as real estate values will allow. A change is starting to come, though, with a proliferation of hostels and affordable accommodation opening up near the shores of the Guanabara bay in Botafogo and a few choice places to stay in the quieter streets of Santa Teresa.

The first steps in exploring other areas are being taken by smaller, more personal lodgings, which herald another change in Rio's hotel landscape. In the last couple of years a handful of what could be classed as boutique hotels and design bed and breakfasts has sprung up. There are sure to be more in their wake, in other interesting places off the beaten tourist trail.

Most of Rio's hotels and hostels, though, are in the Zona Sul in Copacabana and Ipanema, where nothing is far from the beach. There's not so much between a lot of them in quality

either. The ones listed here represent a cross section of the city's hotels as well as the unusual or outstanding.

Another option is to rent a flat for your stay and there are a few agencies specialising in this. These include www.rioflatrental.com, www.rioapartments.com, www.rioapartment services.com and www.redeprotel.com (look under *Hoteis*, in Portuguese). These can get booked up a long time ahead, especially in high season. About the only time Rio doesn't reward spontaneity is when you're trying to sort out accommodation.

Our listings are divided into the following categories solely by price for a double room: **Luxury** (over R$500, around US$250); **Expensive** (R$300-$500, US$150-250); **Moderate** (R$150-300, US$75-$150); and **Budget** (under R$150, US$75). Prices go crazy during Carnival and over the New Year, when even the worst hotels can book up completely (and often insist on a minimum stay). These two enormous celebrations approximately mark the beginning and end of the high season, in which you should expect to pay more than in other months, though all year round it's worth asking the hotels directly, or via their websites, for cheaper rates or promotions.

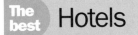

Hotels

The best

For designer rooms

Extravagant French touches at **Fasano** (*see p39*) or **La Suite** (*see p48*); best of Brazilian at **Marina All Suites** (*see p43*) or **Hotel Portinari** (*see p45*).

For blending in

See the city from the local point of view with **Cama e Café** (*see p40*); make yourself at home at **La Maison** (*see p48*) or get linked in to Rio's creative community through the **Relais Solar** (*see p40*).

For lounging by the pool

Enjoy the secluded garden of **Mama Ruisa** (*see p40*) or rub shoulders with history at the **Copacabana Palace** (*see p42*).

For spectacular views

Get high in the **Sofitel Rio Palace** (*see p43*) or look down over the Sugar Loaf mountain from the favela at the **Maze Inn** (*see p38*).

For extremely sporty types

Join the surfing crowd near the beach at **Hotel Priaia Linda** (*see p50*) or climb the walls at **Tupiniquim Hostel** (*see p40*).

The Centre

Expensive

Guanabara Palace

Avenida Presidente Vargas 392, Centro (2195 6000/ www.windsorhoteis.com.br). Metro Uruguaiana/128, 132, 2018 bus. **Rates** R$350-$400 double. **Rooms** 485. **Credit** AmEx, DC, MC, V. **Map** p245 I1 ❶
This shimmering glass monster of a hotel is one of the dominant structures in Rio's Centro, its upper floors tall enough to gaze over the tall buildings of the centre to Corcovado and the hills. In the other direction you get good views of Guanabara Bay, ensuring the hotel's roof terrace is a popular spot at both dawn and dusk. The hotel has almost 500 standard rooms and suites, all well maintained and appointed with chunky hardwood furnishings and

> ❶ Green numbers given in this chapter correspond to the location of each hotel on the street maps. *See pp244-253.*

good storage space. Air-conditioned vans provide complimentary transport to Copacabana beach.
Bar. Business services. Concierge. Disabled-adapted rooms. Gym. Internet (high-speed). No-smoking rooms. Parking. Pool (outdoor). Restaurant. Room service. TV.

The Bay

Luxury

Hotel Glória
Rua do Russel 632, Glória (2555 7272/www. hotelgloriario.com.br). Metro Glória/158, 409, 464 bus. **Rates** R$505-$725. **Rooms** 610. **Credit** AmEx, DC, MC, V. **Map** p245 J5 ❷

Opened in 1922 to chime with the centenary of Brazilian independence, the Glória's glory days came and went between the wars, meaning that you're unlikely to see many celebrities or dignatories here these days – though they do provide a helipad on the roof for anyone who fancies a shot at the high life. The hotel still puts on a great front with its gleaming white façade, but the maintenance of the 600-plus rooms is haphazard, as is the service, and these days the majority of the hotel's guests are on a corporate or academic junket. In the pros column, the communal facilities – fitness centre and spa, decent sized pool, fair breakfast buffet – are better than the rooms (mostly cream and chintz, with the occasional Louis Quinze imitation in the suites), the views of Sugar Loaf and Guanabara Bay are special, and those with a fetish for faded glamour (that old chestnut), will love this place. Hardly worth the rack rates (though they do fall sharply for additional nights), but do check the website for special offers.
Bar. Business centre. Concierge. Disabled-adapted rooms. Gym. Internet (high-speed). No-smoking rooms. Parking. Pool (outdoor). Restaurant. Room service. Spa. TV.

Moderate

Provence Golden Park
Rua do Russel 374, Glória (2555 2700/www.hotel goldenparkrio.com.br). Metro Glória/158, 409, 464 bus. **Rates** R$150-$170 double. **Rooms** 68. **Credit** AmEx, MC, V. **Map** p245 J5 ❸

Just a few blocks down from the Hotel Glória (*see above*), the Golden Park is a moderately priced option, particularly suited to business travellers needing quick access to Centro or the Santos Dumont Airport nearby, but good for anyone who's not focussed only on the beach. Rooms are fairly standard but include a comfy leather sofa. The Parque do Flamengo, across the busy street, is ideal for a morning jog or walk along the beach, although sadly it's not really suitable for swimming.
Business centre. Disabled-adapted room. Internet (high-speed R$30/day). Parking (free) Pool (outdoor). Restaurant. Room service. TV.

Creative colours at **Relais Solar**. *See p40.*

Budget

Alpha Hostel

Praia de Botafogo 462, Casa 3, Botafogo (2286 7799/www.alphahostel.com). Metro Botafogo/121, 434, 571 bus. **Rates** R$80-$100 double; $35 dorm bed. **Rooms** 11. **Credit** MC, V. **Map** p247 H10 ④
On a safe and atmospheric street just a shell's throw from Botafago beach and one block from a metro station, Alpha is well run and good fun. Five dorms and six private rooms (the latter book up fast in high season) are there to bunk down in and the friendly staff will help you get the best out of your time in the city. They'll also make you breakfast, which is included in the rates. Internet access is not and incurs a R$5 surcharge.
Bar. Internet (high-speed). TV room.

Maze Inn

Rua Tavares Bastos 414, Casa 66, Catete (2558 5547/http://jazzrio.info). Metro Catete/84, 434, 498 bus. **Rates** R$70 double. **Rooms** 11. **No credit cards. Map** p245 H6 ⑤
It may be in the Favela Tavares Bastos but it's an, ahem, a-maze-inn place to stay, and not just for its staggering views over the bay and the Sugar Loaf mountain. Your host is pretty extraordinary too. Bob Nadkarni has been settling into Rio for some years now, with a community centre underneath his home in the favela. With his tall tales and the help of his jazz nights (*see p181*) he's become quite a local personality – and now his B&B is becoming well known too. It has seven rooms, four self-service flats, more under construction and plenty of grand plans to spare, including one to bring the internet to the favela. But this isn't about top facilities and comfort, it's about imagination and, yes, the view.
TV room.

El Misti Hostel

Praia de Botafogo 462, Casa 9 (2226 0991/www. elmistihostel.com). Metro Botafogo/121, 434, 571 bus. **Rates** R$80-$120 double; R$25-$50 dorm bed. **Rooms** 14. **Credit** MC, V. **Map** p247 H10 ⑥
Owned and run by friendly Argentinians, El Misti has all the elements of a good hostel: an excellent breakfast, knowledgeable and helpful staff, easy access to the centre and the beaches and an extensive and tasteful music collection. The first hostel on a small alleyway where there are now three (including the Alpha Hostel; *see above*), there's a comfortable seating area where friends are easily made and lost. The staff speak enough English to point you to where to get tickets to clubs, parties, samba schools and just about anywhere else you might want to go. An in-house chef also makes good dinners for R$10 to $15 and Friday night's Argentinian-style *asado* (barbecue) brings out the best in everyone. One warning: it's best avoided during Carnival and the New Year when it fills to an uncomfortable capacity.
Bar. Internet (high-speed). TV room.

The art of good bed and breakfast: **Cama e Café**. *See p40.*

The Fasano factor

Designed by French master Philippe Starck, this new addition to the Ipanema beachfront raises the bar for stylish accommodation in Rio. The luxury hotel market has thus far been dominated by the Victorian Copacabana Palace and perhaps the nearby Caesar Park and a couple of other big chain names. The Fasano hopes to attract a fresher, more discerning and, let's face it, trendier clientele.

The Fasano Hotel and Restaurant is the brainchild of the Fasano family, who are of Italian origin and have been stalwarts in the Brazilian gastronomic industry since the early 1900s. They began their business in São Paulo, where they are clearly top of the pile with their Parigi and Gero restaurants and a new Fasano hotel; but now they also have a branch of the Gero in Rio and the Forneria Rio, both within walking distance of the hotel.

The property, a new building, looks relatively unassuming from the outside, dominated by a dark wood façade, and with each room having individual balconies – in itself an unusual feature in Ipanema. A nice touch is that the balconies are separated by mirrored screens, which give an added level of privacy. Inside, the Philippe Starck touches come to the fore, such as the curved light fittings, the leather chairs and the use of luxury materials such as marble and granite for surfaces. It's all surrounded by dark wood, again quite unusual in a beachfront hotel.

The downstairs area is dominated by an Italian seafood restaurant and club-bar, which promises to have cutting-edge DJs and live musicians. These areas are open to the public so if you can't afford to stay there you can at least don your finest gear for a fresh fruit caipirinha at the bar.

The rooms themselves have Starck's much imitated but rarely surpassed signature as well as the usual luxury accoutrements. There are 82 rooms in total, including seven suites and three deluxe suites. From these, it's possible to lie in your king-size bed and see the whole length of Ipanema beach. Only a few of the regular rooms have a sea view, and because of the dark wood some can be a little gloomy. The hotel promises signed pieces from the 1950s and '60s and this is evident in the leather chairs and the Dali esque mirrors.

The hotel's crowning glory, both literally and figuratively, is the rooftop pool and bar. The vista here is drop-dead stunning, looking along the whole of Ipanema beach and round to the Cristo statue behind you. Just in case you start forgetting there's another world out there, you can also see the local favela.

Fasano Hotel & Restaurant

Avenida Viera Souto 80, Ipanema (3896 4000/www.fasano.com.br). **Rates** R$833 double; R$2,037 suite. **Rooms** 82. **Credit** unconfirmed; phone ahead. **Map** p249 G17.

Tupiniquim Hostel

Rua São Manuel 19, Botafogo (2244 1286/ www.tupiniquimhostel.com.br). Metro Botafogo/ 107, 434, 512 bus. **Rates** *R$80-$100 double; R$25-$35 dorm bed.* **Rooms** *6.* **No credit cards.** **Map** p247 H11 **❼**

Just off a narrow, tranquil alleyway in the heart of Botafogo, this converted Portuguese colonial-style house has plenty of space (four dorms and two private rooms) and bags of charm. The hexalingual (no, really) Brazilian owner is a professional climber and will happily put guests through their paces on the property's climbing wall. Among the other amenities are a multilingual library, games room, bikes and surfboards for rent and old fashioned gramophone to listen to that scratchy samba album you just picked up at the flea market.
Bar. Internet (high-speed). Parking. TV room.

The Hills

Luxury

Mama Ruisa

Rua Santa Cristina 132, Santa Teresa (2242 1281/ www.mamaruisa.com). Both tram lines/206, 214 bus. **Rates** *R$600-$900 double.* **Rooms** *7.* **Credit** *AmEx, MC, V.* **Map** p245 H5 **❽**

A former private home on the side of the hill, the Mama Ruisa has been restored by Jean-Michel Ruis, a young French recent arrival to Rio who's very much involved in the running of the hotel and in checking that his guests have everything they desire. The rooms are themed after flamboyant stars (Maria Callas, Collette, Picasso and Josephine Baker) with views over the Sugar Loaf and Guanabara bay. The shared living room is a large, airy space, again with great views, perfectly suited for getting to know your fellow guests, as is the small pool in the garden, surrounded by sun loungers and covered alcoves for taking breakfast or a caipirinha. With ambitious and developing plans for the future, this boutique hotel sometimes shows it's still a work in progress, but it does succeed in providing a beautiful oasis of calm perched above the bustle of the city.
Internet (high-speed). No-smoking rooms. Pool (outdoor). TV.

Expensive

Relais Solar

Ladeira do Meireles 32, Santa Teresa (2221 2117/ www.relaissolar.com). Both tram lines/206, 214 bus. **Rates** *R$335-$565.* **Rooms** *5.* **Credit** *AmEx, MC, V.* **Map** p245 H5 **❾**

A jewel crowning Santa Teresa, the Relais Solar, a tastefully restored colonial villa, is not just in a happening part of town, its priorities are in all the right places too. Known locally as the Solar de Santa, the hotel has an editing suite, some excellent local art on display and a small but immaculate bistro and bar catering for special events. Breakfasts give you

the best possible start to your day – a wealth of colour and vitamins served on the sunny veranda with the verdant garden stretching out in front. The hotel only has five rooms, including a secluded garden suite — and can accommodate up to 13 people if the whole property is booked (less when rooms are booked separately as some share bathrooms). As well as this, the staff run a creative tourism agency and have the contacts to link guests with the right people in Rio, from gastronomy to extreme sports, but especially for artists, clowns (it's run by a circus impresario), film crews and others in creative industries. Highly recommended. *Photo p37.*
Concierge. Internet (wireless and high-speed). No-smoking rooms. Pool (outdoor). Room service. TV room.

Moderate

Cama e Café

Rua Pascoal Carlos Magno 5, Santa Teresa (2224 5689/www.camaecafe.com.br). Tram Largo das Neves/214 bus. **Rates** *vary.* **Map** p245 H5 **❿**

This bed and breakfast organisation gives hope that Santa Teresa just might be able to avoid the curse of being picked out as the next big tourist destination. Well versed in theories of sustainable tourism, Cama e Café works with Santa Teresa residents to provide a personalised experience, matching up guests with hosts in some of the most beautiful homes in the neighbourhood. Get in touch before you arrive and they'll ask you to fill in a questionaire about you and your trip – and then try to work out who of their growing roster of over 50 trained hosts you'd benefit most from staying with. Rates vary according to your budget and the kind of place you're looking for, but the welcome is always warm and friendly and in many cases the beds are in spectacularly grand old houses and the breakfasts served in gardens overflowing with life. *Photo p38.*

Budget

Casa Mango Mango

Rua Joaquim Murtinho 587, Santa Teresa (2508 6440/www.casamangomango.com). Both tram lines/ 206, 214 bus. **Rates** *R$120-$190 double; R$35 dorm bed.* **Rooms** *11.* **Credit** *MC, V.* **Map** p245 H4 **⓫**

Just next to the Convent in Santa Teresa stands a sprawling old mansion, now run by its friendly Irish owner Julie as the ultra-relaxed Casa Mango Mango. What it lacks in spotlessness it more than makes up for in charm, and provides an affordable base for those aiming to spend a while getting to know the city a little better.
Bar. Internet (high-speed). Pool (outdoor).

Rio Hostel

Rua Joaquim Murtinho 361, Santa Teresa (2224 6903/www.riohostel.com). Both tram lines/206, 214 bus. **Rates** *R$100-$120 double; R$37 dorm bed.* **Rooms** *6.* **Credit** *MC, V.* **Map** p245 I4 **⓬**

Copacabana Palace. *See p42.*

Sofitel Rio Palace.

This sweet and laid-back crashpad is in the heart of charming, cobblestoned Santa Teresa, an area where, according to Rio Hostel's website, you'll encounter artists and monkeys. And who doesn't love monkeys? There are three dorms and three doubles to choose from, a bar for caipirinhaphiles and a small outdoor pool to cool off in.
Bar. Internet (broadband with surcharge). No-smoking rooms. Pool (outdoor). TV room.

The Beaches

Luxury

Caesar Park Rio de Janeiro

Avenida Vieira Souto 460, Ipanema (2525 2525/ www.caesar-park.com). Bus 175, 503, 2018. **Rates** R$500-$1000 double. **Rooms** 228. **Credit** AmEx, DC, MC, V. **Map** p249 E17 ⑬

The exterior doesn't exactly shout 'luxury' but the Caesar's lobby, with its restrained masculine tones, suited doormen and buffed floors will hint at the five-star prices in store. One of Rio's most expensive hotels, the 23-floor Caesar manages to command dizzying room rates for its unbeatable beachfront location – slap in the middle of Ipanema, and a few easy strides from the sand – and its huge 21st floor Imperial Suite, which puts up many of Rio's highest profile visitors. The pampering continues on the hotel's strip of beach, where loungers, shades, beach towels and 24-hour surveillance are all part of the deal. Spoilt globetrotters will find all the facilities they expect from a five-star: efficient, multilingual staff; a (small) rooftop pool; a business centre; a well-equipped gym with spectacular ocean views; and a lavish breakfast buffet. But don't expect design fireworks in the rooms: they are spacious but the conventional and slightly faded decor falls squarely in the 'corporate luxury' category. *Photo p46.*

Bar. Business centre. Concierge. Gym. Internet (high-speed). No-smoking rooms. Parking. Pool (outdoor). Restaurants (2). Room service. Spa. TV.

Copacabana Palace Hotel

Avenida Atlântica 1702, Copacabana (2548 7070/ www.copacabanapalace.com.br). Metro Cardeal Arcoverde/126, 503, 2016 bus. **Rates** R$830-$1,400 double. **Rooms** 222. **Credit** AmEx, DC, MC, V. **Map** p250 I14 ⑭

It's grand, it rules the beach and if there's a hotel in South America more famous than the Copacabana – well, we haven't heard of it. The Copacabana Palace almost single-handedly stands in defence of the reputation of the magnificent Copacabana beach from the varied assaults of tourism, decay and Barry Manilow – and does so effortlessly. The whole operation just whispers 'luxury', from the breakfast by its beautiful pool to the turning down of the beds at night. Behind the beautifully maintained stucco façade (when illuminated at night the structure looks like a giant, candle-lit wedding cake), lie 222 rooms and a million anecdotes, some of which are true. Ava Gardner trashed her room here after breaking up with Sinatra. Orson Welles defenestrated a sofa (it ended up in the pool) after a tiff with Dolores del Rio. Lana Turner, Carmen Miranda, Marlene Dietrich, er, Ricky Martin – the visitors' book reads like a roll call of 20th-century celebrity. Anyone who's ever been anyone, plus the contenders, the wannabes and the nobodies, has either stayed in or partied at the Copacabana since its opening in 1923. While all rooms are regularly refurbished, many still have their original mahogany fittings as well as sumptuous, swishable drapes over large windows and – what you find only in classic hotels – ceilings that are higher than is strictly necessary. There are fitness and business centres, two very good if predictably pricey restaurants (the Cipriani and the Pergula), a beauty salon,

a rooftop tennis court and without question the best hotel pool in the city (unless there's a jilted auteur staying in one of the overlooking suites). Meander across the road to the beach for more discreet pampering where hotel staff are on hand to dust the sand off your sunlounger and keep an eye on your things while you go for a dip in the ocean. If you'd like to get a taste of the experience but don't have the budget to stay, make a reservation for their very good Sunday brunch by the pool. *Photo p41.*
Bar. Business centre. Concierge. Gym. Internet (dataport, high-speed). No-smoking rooms. Parking. Pool (1 outdoor). Restaurants (2) Room service. Spa. TV.

Marina All Suites

Avenida Delfim Moreira 696, Leblon (2172 1100/ www.marinaallsuites.com.br) Bus 128, 524, 2018. **Rates** R$695-$1,960 double. **Rooms** 38. **Credit** AmEx, MC, V. **Map** p248 B17 ⑮
The hotel of choice for chic Brazilians, the all suite Marina has 30 basic suites and eight design suites, the latter created by top architects and designers and arguably the most exclusive rooms in the whole city. Supermodel Giselle Bünchen, for example, prefers the Diamante, set in tones of yellow, orange and red like the Leblon sunset. The whole hotel is awash in elegant touches like the staff uniforms by designer Lenny Niemeyer. The in-house Bar d'Hotel (*see p107*) is a funky bar-restaurant that attracts beautiful locals and tourists alike and the view from the small pool rooftop pool – on the Health Floor with massage rooms, a fitness centre and a steam room – is nothing short of awesome. All this and an enviable position on the Leblon seafront, just across the road from the beach.
Bar. Business Centre. Concierge. disabled-adapted floors. Internet (high-speed wireless or cable, R$30/day). Parking (R$16/day). Pool (outdoor). Restaurant. Room service. Spa. TV.

JW Marriott

Avenida Atlântica 2600, Copacabana (2545 6500/ www.marriott.com). Metro Siquiera Campos/136, 434, 2016 bus. **Rates** R$1,050-$1,500 double. **Rooms** 245. **Credit** AmEx, DC, MC, V. **Map** p249 H15 ⑯
The five-star JW Marriott is just a few steps from the white beaches of Copacabana. It was patently built for corporative tourism and with middle-aged Americans in mind: hearty breakfasts, tip-top service, spotless rooms, plenty of front door security and lifts that announce their destination with an American slur. Nevertheless, there are enough reasons for any nationality to enjoy this 245 room behemoth, the most obvious being the swimming pool, gym and sun-drenched terrace that – perched on the top of the hotel – afford breathtaking views across Corcovado, the bay and out beyond the Sugar Loaf mountain. It's an impressive hotel, with the large lobby area sitting under a towering multi-coloured, stainless glass front and the recommendable Taiyou Sushi Restaurant and bar area. *Photo p49.*
Bar. Business centre. Concierge. Gym. Internet (high-speed). No-smoking rooms. Parking. Pool (outdoor). Restaurants (3). Room service. Spa. TV.

Sofitel Rio Palace

Avenida Atlântica 4240, Copacabana (2525 1232/ www.accorhotels.com.br). Bus 126, 426, 2018. **Rates** R$500-$600 double. **Rooms** 388. **Credit** AmEx, MC, V. **Map** p249 H17 ⑰
The mighty Sofitel reigns from her strategic perch at the western tip of Copacabana, within short walking distance of Ipanema. Hang poolside all day long in sun or shade, with the luxury of having two strategically built pools to choose from. The sixth, seventh and eighth floor have recently been totally renovated. The hotel is joined to the next door Shopping Cassino Atlântico (*see p132*), which is chock full of antique shops and art galleries and the hotel's Le Pré Catalan restaurant serves the very finest in French cuisine (*see p110*).
Bars (2). Business centre. Concierge. Disabled-adapted rooms. Internet (R$20/day wireless, high-speed). No-smoking floors. Parking (free). Pools (2 Outdoor). Restaurants (2). Room Service. Spa. TV/DVD.

Expensive

Best Western Sol Ipanema

Avenida Vieira Souto 320, Ipanema (2525 2020/ www.solipanema.com.br). Bus 127, 474, 512. **Rates** R$370-$460 double. **Rooms** 90. **Credit** AmEx, MC, V. **Map** p249 F17 ⑱
A privileged beachfront spot across from the beautiful people at Posto 9 make the Sol Ipanema a top choice among in-the-know beach bunnies. The lobby has been recently renovated and the rooms are well appointed and clean. The rooftop pool is quite small, but the spectacular view makes up for it.
Bar. Concierge. disabled-adapted rooms. Gym. No-smoking floors. Internet (wireless, high-speed R$30/day). Pool (outdoor). Restaurant. Spa. TV.

Naughty and nice

The love motel is a Brazilian institution, just like football or samba. Young or old, single or married, almost everybody is familiar with these mind-blowingly kitsch liaison points, which range from the absurdly luxurious to the downright sordid and carry a variety of sidesplitting names like 'Sinless' and 'Love Land'. Northern Rio even boasts its very own 'Motel Baghdad'.

Top range motels beat most hotels hands down in terms of service and luxury. Most motels operate a system of 12-hour periods. Oversleep and you'll probably get charged twice the price when you leave, but you can just check in and stay as long as you like – as long as you are paying. So if you can handle that awkward moment, bumping into sweaty-palmed couples at reception, why not check into a motel for your stay in Rio?

There's no shortage of motels in Rio de Janeiro. In the southern zone one of the best known is the **Hotel Panda**, located in Botafogo directly under the disapproving gaze of the Christ the Redeemer statue. The presidential room here boasts a swimming pool complete with fake waterfall, a sauna and a mini dancefloor equipped with strobe lights. Most rooms have separate dining rooms, vast bathrooms and, of course, very, very large beds.

Another favourite among residents of the south zone is the **Elegance Hotel**, not far from the Catete Palace. The building's brash red façade hides a luxurious set of rooms, where you can dance the night away in your own private nightclub, take your pick from an excellent menu of Brazilian delicacies and even order sex toys from room service (they arrive on a silver platter, in the hands of the motel's ever discreet waiters).

If you're looking for something more raunchy, head to the **Villa Reggia Hotel** in the Saude neighbourhood in central Rio. The Villa Reggia boasts thematic rooms, whose superbly tacky decor promises to transport you to Versailles, Japan or the rather less exotic São Paulo. For the really adventurous, the motel even boasts a 'Sado' themed room, complete with chains, handcuffs and some intimidating gothic paintwork.

If you've been out in Lapa and fancy slipping away to somewhere more comfortable, there's the **Hotel Villa Rica** on the corner of Joaquim Silva, with cramped but clean rooms, or the Viña Del Mar, a huge motel with rooms that resemble concrete goldfish bowls.

Vip's motel, on Avendia Niemeyer, is one of the few motels in Rio to boast a sea view. Located on the coastal road between Leblon and São Conrado, Vip's is one of Rio's more expensive motels but the spectacular views from its penthouse suites are well worth the extra price tag. One of its recent additions is a special room, known as the Nuth, where (perhaps stemming from a misunderstanding of the term auto-eroticism) you can actually park your car inside the room.

For photos of the Nuth complete with car and most of the other rooms in Brazil's motels, plus everything you need to know on the art of motel going (including special offers and discounts) see the comprehensive and frequently updated site www.guiade moteis.com.br (in Portuguese).

All of the following motels accept most major credit cards.
Elegance Hotel Rua Correia Dutra 19, Catete (3235 9000/www.elegancehotel.com.br).
Hotel Panda Rua São Clemente 298, Botafogo (2537 3134/www.panda hotel.com.br).
Hotel Villa Rica Rua Conde de Lages 2, Lapa (2232 2983/www.hotelvillarica.com.br).
Villa Reggia Rua Sacadura Cabral 136, Saude (2223 4104/www.villareggia.com.br).
Vina del Mar Rua Joaquim Silva 57, Lapa (2509 1857/www.vinadelmar.com.br).
Vip's Motel Avenida Niemeyer 418, Leblon (3322 1662/www.vipsmotel.com.br).

Excelsior Copacabana

Avenida Atlântica 1800, Copacabana (2195 5800/www.windsorhoteis.com). Metro Cardeal Arcoverde/126, 503, 2016 bus. **Rates** R$380-$585 double. **Rooms** 233. **Credit** AmEx, DC, MC, V. **Map** p250 I14 ⑲

If fortune is more important to you than fame, you might well want to stay here, right next door to the world renowned Copacabana Palace but three times as cheap. The Excelsior looks great for a three-star, with Brazilian redwood panelling in the corridors and bathrooms with marble and granite fittings and laminate flooring. The buffet breakfast is a star turn, offering pancakes, smoked salmon, over ten types of smoothie and fruits you never knew existed. There are 233 clean and comfy rooms and suites, some with views of the ocean, others with views of the hotel's garbage skips – enquire in advance. Staff members are vivacious, mostly English-speaking, and eager to please. Particularly welcome is the hotel's *barraca* (beach shack) on Copacabana beach where staff dole out complimentary towels and parasols and prepare the sun loungers. If you're after sun without sand, head for the roof. The pool is only a couple of backstrokes long but it has a bar and terrific views across the bay. There's nothing like catching the eye of Christ the Redeemer while you're downing your fourth caipirinha...
Bar. Business centre. Concierge. Gym. Internet (high-speed). No-smoking rooms. Parking. Pool (outdoor). Restaurant. Room service. Spa. TV.

Ipanema Plaza

Rua Farme de Amoedo 34, Ipanema (3687 2000/ www.ipanemaplazahotel.com). Bus 127, 474, 512. **Rates** R$350-$405 double. **Rooms** 140. **Credit** AmEx, MC, DC, V. **Map** p249 F17 ⑳

Part of the Golden Tulip chain of international hotels, this is a popular choice for gay travellers due to its prime position on the main strip of Farme de Amoedo. But its location could also be a drawback: light sleepers may be bothered by the noise from the street below on weekend nights during peak season, as the party carries through till dawn. The Ipanema Floor, inaugurated in 2006, is its swankiest offering: hip Italian furnishings, a 29 inch TV with DVD and all the finest touches like bathrobes, a free daily newspaper, unlimited internet access and a champagne welcome. Modern facilities include a gym, sauna, steam bath and full-sized rooftop pool.
Bar. Business centre. Gym. Internet. No-smoking floors. Internet (high-speed R$35/day). Parking (R$20/day). Pool (outdoor). Restaurant. Room service. TV.

Mercure Apartamento Arpoador

Rua Francisco Otaviano 61, Arpoador (3222 9603/ www.accorhotels.com.br). Bus 126, 426, 2018. **Rates** R$328-$459 double. **Rooms** 56. **Credit** AmEx, MC, V. **Map** p249 H17 ㉑

Formerly known as the Parthenon, all of the Mercure's apartments are good-sized with a separate living and bedroom, stocked with modern furnishings

and an 'American kitchen' – as they like to call the open concept kitchenette. Due to its popularity with business travellers, the apart-hotel rates are surprising low on the weekends, which might be a handy bonus for vacationers.
Business Centre. Concierge. Gym. No-smoking floors. Internet (high-speed, free). Parking (R$8/day). Pool (indoor). Restaurant. Room Service. TV/DVD.

Moderate

Arpoador Inn

Rua Francisco Otaviano 177, Arpoador (2523 0060/www.arpoadorinn.com.br). Bus 126, 426, 2018. **Rates** R$180-$370 double. **Rooms** 50. **Credit** AmEx, MC, V. **Map** p249 G17 ㉒

The only hotel from Leme to Leblon that can claim to be right on the beach – you step out the door and onto the sands of Praia do Arpoador. Whether you choose an ocean-view room or the cheaper street facing option, rooms have all the standard trappings with modern bathrooms. Highlights include breakfast served overlooking the beach, and watching the surfers in the sunset from nearby Arpoador rock.
Concierge. Internet (shared terminal R$10/hr). Restaurant. Room service. TV.

Grande Hotel Canadá

Avenida Nossa Senhora de Copacabana 687, Copacabana (2557 1864/www.hotelcanada.com.br). Metro Siqueira Campos/119, 154, 434 bus. **Rates** R$158-$175 double. **Rooms** 68. **Credit** AmEx, MC, DC, V. **Map** p249 H14 ㉓

A decent option for travellers on a budget who demand a little more comfort than you find in a hostel, the Grande Hotel Canadá is on the busy, main commercial street in Copa, handy for quick access to shops and services and just a couple of minutes walk from the beach. You won't find much in the way of luxuries, but the service is welcoming and facilities are clean and in good condition.
Bar. Internet (high-speed R$10/hr). Restaurant. Room service. TV.

Hotel Portinari

Rua Francisco Sá 17, Copacabana (3222 8800/ www.hotelportinari.com.br). Bus 404, 464, 521. **Rates** R$250-$350 double. **Rooms** 66. **Credit** AmEx, MC, V. **Map** p249 H16 ㉔

Nine different Brazilian designers have lent their name to the Portinari's design hotel concept. The ninth floor is by ecologically-minded Gilmar Peres and uses only wood from reforestation and completely avoids artificial dies in the textiles, while the bold and colourful 11th and 12th floors, credited to Stella Orleans e Bragança, each have one ultra-modern disabled-adapted room. Although the hotel lacks a pool, guests can soak in a Jacuzzi in the top-floor fitness centre.
Bar. Business Centre. Concierge. disabled-adapted rooms. Gym. Internet (high-speed R$18/hr). No-smoking floors. Parking (R$30/day). Restaurant. Room Service. Spa. TV/DVD.

Hotel Santa Clara

Rua Décio Vilares 316, Copacabana (2256 2650/ www.hotelsantaclara.com.br). Metro Siqueira Campos/434, 463, 521 bus. **Rates** R$150-$170 double. **Rooms** 25. **Credit** MC, V. **Map** p249 H13 ㉕
Copacabana's Bairro Peixoto is an unlikely thing, a quaint little neighbourhood with a small-town feel that backs onto, and is a part of, one of the most densely occupied neighbourhoods in the continent. Still just a few blocks from the beach and the nightclubs and the commercial centre, the Santa Clara is a cute little hotel whose services are basic and decorations homely with simple wooden furniture. The best rooms at the front have a small balcony overlooking the street where you can ask to have your breakfast served.
Concierge. disabled-adapted rooms. Room service. TV.

Ipanema Inn

Rua Maria Quitéria 27, Ipanema (2523 6092/ www.ipanemainn.com.br). Bus 127, 474, 512. **Rates** R$170-$250 double. **Rooms** 56. **Credit** AmEx, DC, MC, V. **Map** p249 E17 ㉖
On one of the hippest streets in the 'hood and just a couple of blocks from the lively Praça General Osório, the Ipanema Inn is an excellent small hotel with above-standard facilities to complement its sweet location, which even allows some sea views. It's particularly good value for small groups or large families, as the top floor has two suites which can sleep up to six people each. Just off the lobby you'll find Brasil e Cia (*see p146*) a pleasant little shop that sells Brazilian handicrafts.
Internet (high-speed shared Terminal R$10/hr). No-smoking rooms. Restaurant. TV.

Relaxing on the roof at the **Caesar Park**. *See p42.*

Martinique Copa

Rua Sá Ferreira 30, Copacabana (2195 5200/
www.windsorhoteis.com.br). Bus 125, 415, 503.
Rates R$200-$220 double. **Rooms** 117. **Credit**
AmEx, DC, MC, V. **Map** p249 H16 **27**
Another solid mid-range option from the Windsor
group – behind the Martinique's eight-storey glass
façade lie 117 rooms (divided into 'standard' and
'superior'), friendly and efficient staff and a fair
range of amenities for a hotel in this grade, including a rooftop pool with bar, sizeable bathrooms with
marble tubs and power showers and Wi-Fi access in
the public areas. It's nothing spectacular, but if the
weather's nice you won't care.
Bar. Business centre. Concierge. Disabled-adapted
rooms. Gym. Internet (high-speed, wireless).
No-smoking floors. Parking. Pool (outdoor).
Restaurant. Room service. TV.

Ritz Plaza Hotel

Avenida Ataulfo de Paiva 1280, Leblon (2540
4940/www.ritzhotel.com.br). Bus 132, 433, 521.
Rates R$270-$390 double. **Rooms** 56. **Credit**
AmEx, MC, V. **Map** p248 A17 **28**
On Leblon's main commercial street, the Ritz Plaza
offers impeccably clean and well-lit rooms with mod
ern furniture. Elegant touches abound, from the artwork in the rooms to the stained glass panels
throughout the hotel. Rio's ritziest shopping and
restaurants, including Shopping Leblon and the Rua
Dias Ferreira, are just a stone's throw away.
Business centre. Concierge. Disabled-adapted rooms.
Gym. Internet (high-speed wireless R$15/day). No-
smoking floors. Parking (R$25/day). Pool (indoor).
Restaurant. Room Service. Spa. TV.

Budget

Edifício Jucati

Rua Tenente Marones de Gusmão 85, Copacabana
(2547 5422/www.edificiojucati.com.br). Metro
Siquiera Campos/434, 463, 521 bus. **Rate** $100
double; R$30 dorm bed. **Rooms** 57. **No credit**
cards. Map p249 H13 **29**
This no-frills apartment hotel in a no-frills art deco
building offers excellent value for money. Each of
the 57 apartments has bedroom, bathroom and
kitchen spaces and can sleep up to six – if everyone
gets along ok. Air-conditioning units and ceiling
fans come as standard. Rooms can be rented by the
night, week or month, with good discounts for long
stays. You have to find your own breakfast. If you're
Michael Johnson you'll be able to make Copacabana
beach in 43.18 seconds from here.
Internet (high-speed). No-smoking floors. TV room.

Hotel São Marco Ipanema

Rua Visconde de Pirajá 524, Ipanema (2540 5032/
www.sanmarcohotel.net). Bus 127, 474, 512. **Rates**
R$136-$169 double. **Rooms** 56. **Credit** AmEx, MC,
V. **Map** p248 D17 **30**
One of the best options for budget travellers who
would rather be near the beach, but don't make a

fuss over being pampered. The rooms at the family
owned San Marco have recently been renovated but
remain small and the view is nothing to write home
about – but you are in the heart of Ipanema with the
city's finest offerings at your fingertips.
Bar. Internet (shared terminal R$18/hr). Restaurant.
Room service. TV.

Ipanema Beach House

Rua Barão da Torre 185, Ipanema (3202 2693/
www.ipanemahouse.com). Bus 154, 474, 523.
Rates R$140 double; R$45 dorm bed. **Rooms** 13.
No credit cards. Map p249 E16 **31**
As you'd expect in upscale Ipanema, the rates at this
excellent hostel are a tad higher than you'll find elsewhere; but with facilities galore and Ipanema beach
just a couple of blocks away, you won't feel ripped
off. As well as the ten dorms and three doubles, the
IBH has a swimming pool (the real McCoy rather
than just a tub on a patio), bar, barbecue area, sports
equipment for rent, round-the-clock internet access
and one of the best breakfast spreads in town. If
you're going in summer it's worth knowing that two
of the dorms have air-conditioning.
Bar. Disabled-adapted rooms. Internet (high-speed).
No-smoking rooms. Parking. Pool (outdoor). TV room.

Lemon Spirit

Rua Cupertino Durão 56, Leblon (2294 1853/
www.lemonspirit.com). Bus 177, 434, 464, 572.
Rates R$120 double; R$40 dorm bed. **Rooms** 6.
No credit cards. Map p248 C17 **32**
In the heart of Leblon, and enjoying the neighbourhood's relative exclusivity and calmness, this small
hostel is housed in a lovely restored heritage building just one block from the beach and a short and
pleasant walk along the beachfront to Ipanema. All
of the rooms are kept cool with air conditioning,
while the welcome is warm.
Bar. Internet (high-speed). No-smoking rooms.
TV room.

Lighthouse Hostel

Rua Barão da Torre 175, Casa 20, Ipanema
(2522 1353/www.thelighthouse.com.br). Bus 175,
432, 464. **Rates** R$100-$120 double; R$40-$45 dorm
bed. **Rooms** 2. **No credit cards. Map** p249 F17 **33**
Owned and run by a New Zealander and a Brazilian,
this relatively restrained (by Rio's standards) lodging is a simple and spotless home from home, with
a lovely outdoor area and barbecue. Three blocks
from Ipanema beach.
Internet (high-speed). No-smoking rooms. TV Room.

Mellow Yellow

Rua General Barbosa Lima 51, Copacabana
(2547 1993/www.mellowyellow.com.br). Metro
Cardeal Arcoverde/119, 464, 2019 bus. **Rates**
R$100-$110 double; R$33-$42 dorm bed. **Rooms**
13. **Credit** MC, V. **Map** p250 I13 **34**
Hedonists will reckon they've died and gone to
heaven when they check in here. The friendly staff
welcome guests with a complimentary caipirinha,
which sets the tone for what follows. Facilities

include a spa, a chill-out lounge (with hammocks, sofas and bean bags), a games room, a herb garden and a bar with regular live music and great tunes 24/7. The cable television service means that football fans can keep track of games back home and the restaurant has theme nights running the gamut of international culinary standards from Thai curries to Mexican burritos. There are 11 lively dorms and a couple of quieter private rooms. If that's not enough, there's even a beach called Copacabana just one block away.

Bar. Internet (broadband). No-smoking rooms. Spa. TV room.

Stone of a Beach

Rua Barata Ribeiro 111, Copacabana (3209 0348/ www.stoneofabeach.com.br). Metro Cardeal Arcoverde/119, 464, 2019 bus. **Rates** R$100-$110 double; R$30-$39 dorm bed. **Rooms** 11. **Credit** MC, V. **Map** p250 I13 ③⑤

Whoever thought up the name should be dangled from the top of the Christ statue by their ankles until they recant, but Soab is nonetheless a top-notch hostel, with seven dorms and four private rooms in a big old mansion on one of Copacabana's main streets. It's a party-oriented place with facilities galore, including a roof terrace with barbecue, a games and TV room and the Clandestino bar (open from 6pm Wednesday to Saturday to both guests and the public), which has live music, imported beers and giveaway happy hour deals. Like everywhere else, rates go sky-high for Carnival week.

Bar. Internet (high-speed). No-smoking rooms. Pool (outdoor). TV room.

The Lake

Luxury

La Maison

Rua Sérgio Porte 58, Gávea (3205 3585/www.la maisonario.com). Bus 176. **Rates** R$500-$650 double. **Rooms** 5. **No credit cards. Map** p253 F2 ③⑥

Up on the hill in leafy Gávea, around the corner from Gilberto Gil's studio and under the gaze of the Rocinha favela, is Jacques' house. More of an extravagant bed and breakfast than a hotel, Jacques is the consummate host and bursting with suggestions for tour options, restaurant and bar recommendations and with passion for Rio and this hotel, designed and decorated by his brother Francois-Xavier Dussol (who also designed La Suite; *see below*). Breakfasts – and other meals if you order in time – are served around a central dining table in the open-sided living room, with a view over the small swimming pool to the Corcovado. With all the rooms different (named Shanghai, Tiffany, Copacabana and others), all the details individual and no safe deposit boxes (or even need to lock your room), it's a far cry from the anonymous corporate hotels lining the beaches. *Internet (high-speed, wireless). Parking. Pool (outdoor). Restaurant.*

Zona Oeste

Luxury

Sheraton Barra

Avenida Lúcio Costa 3150, Barra da Tijuca (3139 8000/www.sheraton.com/barra). Bus 179, 523, 2113. **Rates** R$545-$625. **Rooms** 292. **Credit** AmEx, DC, MC, V. **Map** p253 A4 ③⑦

Luxury hotels are fairly new to Barra, and the Sheraton was the first, completed in 2003. All rooms have balconies (some have more than one) and at least a partial view of the ocean. The closer to the front of the building you are, the more of the beach you see. Most rooms are comfortable and spacious, if unremarkable, with good bathrooms. The Terral Restaurant offers a high quality but fairly limited menu, and the red-lit bar is a relaxing place for a caipirinha. The pool – at the back of the hotel – is beautifully landscaped. There is a play area for children, a gym and a spa service. The Palmeiras Bar offers relaxed poolside dining. The hotel can arrange a full range of city tours, along with various other sightseeing and sporting options. There is a beach service, providing towels, chairs and umbrellas – even a massage. In the lobby, there is a hairdressing salon and a small branch of jeweller H Stern. *Bars (2). Business centre. Concierge. Disabled-adapted rooms. Gym. Internet (dataport, high-speed). No-smoking rooms. Parking. Pool (outdoor). Restaurant. Room service. Spa. TV.*

La Suite

Rua Jackson Figueiredo 501, Joatinga (2484 1962/ no website). Bus 179, 524, 557. **Rates** R$800-$900 double. **Rooms** 7. **No credit cards. Map** p253 C4 ③⑧

La Suite is a little way out of town, accessible more or less only by taxi (although they do also have a rooftop helipad), but that's not the reason why you'll be reluctant to stray too far from this elegant lodging. Its seven rooms, named after their different colours (and all with marble bathrooms in matching hues) have all been boldly decorated by Francois-Xavier, your host, who also designed the whole building from the ground up and continues to develop it, as he has already done, with considerable success, with La Maison (*see above*). The pile of fashion magazines featuring the hotel, from Brazil and the world, is only a hint at the extent to which the location and decoration grab the imagination. It doesn't stop there, though, as your host and his partner, Rodrigo, are always on hand to help with suggestions and to create a convivial atmosphere among the guests. In this, they're helped in no small measure by a fantastic chef whose fine cuisine helps the hidden dining room balance the extravagant living room as the building's heart. A small plunge pool shares the incredible views from the deck and a larger pool is planned closer to sea level. If you want to feel spoilt, this is the place. *Photo p50.* *Internet (high-speed, wireless). Parking. Pool (outdoor).*

JW Marriott. *See p43.*

Life is sweet at **La Suite**. *See p48.*

Windsor Barra Hotel

Avenida Sernambetiba 2630, Barra da Tijuca (2195 5000/www.windsorhoteis.com). Bus 179, 523, 2113. **Rates** R$472-$711 double. **Rooms** 338. **Credit** AmEx, DC, MC, V. **Map** p253 A4 ➌➒
Completed only in 2005, the Windsor Barra offers the latest in luxury hospitality. The rooms are very comfortable and tasteful. Many have wooden floors, all have lovely paintings by Brazilian artists and some have unusual touches – such as a window (with a blind!) between the bathroom and the bedroom, which gives a great feeling of light and space. The bathrooms are generous and the bathtubs even more so. For a special treat, try a luxury corner room, with a 180 degree view. Unfortunately, the hotel doesn't do balconies. There is currently only one restaurant, although there are plans to open another. The pool is rather exposed, being on the top of the building without much shade. There is a gym and a sauna. The showers for de-sanding by the special beach entrance are a nice touch – no need to traipse through the lobby in your bikini. The hotel can arrange the full range of Rio sightseeing tours.

Bar. Business centre. Concierge. Disabled-adapted rooms. Gym. Internet (high-speed). No-smoking rooms. Parking. Pools (2 outdoor). Restaurant. Room service. Spa. TV.

Moderate

Hotel Praia Linda

Avenida Pepê 1430, Barra da Tijuca (2494 2186/ www.hotelpraialinda.com.br). Bus 179, 523, 2113. **Rates** R$210-250 double. **Rooms** 60. **Credit** AmEx, MC, DC, V. **Map** p253 A4 ➍➍
The Praia Linda is popular with surfers – as it's just across from the beach known as Praia do Pepê (after an extreme sportsman who became something of a national hero) – and with hang-gliders, as it's close to the Pedra da Gávea. Despite being in the concrete jungle of Barra da Tijuca, its beachside location helps it to retain a neighbourhood feel. The 21 deluxe ocean-view apartments are well-worth the price, and the 'super luxos' have recently been redecorated in bright tones.
Internet (shared terminal R$10/hr). Parking (free). Restaurant. Room service. TV.

Sightseeing

Introduction

Your holiday starts here.

Rio's sights fall into a few distinct categories, headed by the standout natural landmarks – **Corcovado**, the **Sugar Loaf** and the **Dois Irmâos** mountains at the end of Leblon; the beaches; the bay, and the forest. Then there are the man-made additions – the **Maracanã** stadium, the modernist architecture, the grand old palaces and theatres and the narrow cobbled streets of the **Centro** and of **Santa Teresa**. Just as important are the Carioca people, whether they're parading at Carnival or laughing and singing in a Lapa nightclub, sunning themselves on the beach or displaying otherworldly *futevolei* skills, dancing round red tape or just dancing. Cariocas often get accused of being too full of themselves, but with a constant stream of tourists for over 80 years from all around the world admiring their city and their *joie de vivre*, it's easy to see why.

NEIGHBOURHOOD GUIDE

Rio is divided into four different parts: **Centro, Zona Sul, Zona Norte** and **Zona Oeste**. These are divided into *bairros* (neighbourhoods), of which Ipanema and Copacabana are already world famous. As most of the attractions and best restaurants, bars and hotels are in the Zona Sul and the Centro, we've divided these two into five sections, with a chapter each for the Zona Norte and Zona Oeste and an extra chapter for Niterói – a separate city the other side of the Guanabara Bay.

The **Centre**, including the downtown district, the port area and Lapa, is the historical heart of the city and where the work happens. Monday to Friday it's a hive of activity but on the weekends it's deserted, apart from the revitalised neighbourhood of Lapa, which comes alive at night.

Putting the 'awe' into 'orientation': **Gávea**, **Jardim Botânico**, **Leblon** and the ocean.

The **Bay** covers the *bairros* of Catete, Glória, Flamengo, Botafogo and Urca. Despite their football teams and the Sugar Loaf mountain, the area is often overlooked between of the more obvious claims for attention of its neighbours; but it's an ideal base in the middle of town and has some of the best cultural life in the city.

The **Hills** are a must for every visitor for the statue of Cristo Redentor and the view from Corcovado, but the district also covers Santa Teresa, a tiny hilltop *bairro* with a great spirit that so far seems to be coping well with its rapid introduction to the mass tourist trail. Also in this section are Laranjeiras and Cosme Velho, much passed through on the way to the Corcovado but little explored.

Although Rio has miles on miles of them, The **Beaches** chapter concentrates on just the famous ones, Copacabana, Ipanema and Leblon. Cut off from the city until major tunnels were built in the 1920s, these are now the ultimate urban beaches, and the narrow strips of flat land behind them are chock full of people and life.

The **Lake** groups the upmarket residential areas away from the coast in the Zona Sul – Gávea, Jardim Botânico and the other small *bairros* and parks around the Lagoa.

Zona Oeste stretches for miles and miles along the ocean coast, through the wealthy districts of São Conrado and Joatinga, the huge concrete and sand expanses of Barra de Tijuca and Recreo dos Bandeirantes, with their shopping malls and beaches, to the sleepy village life of Vargem Grande and beyond.

Zona Norte is the catch-all district encompassing the urban sprawl to the north and west of the centre. The part closest to the centre holds the Maracanã, the Zoo and the grand gardens and buildings of the Quinta da Boa Vista, but most of the rest is not recommended for solo exploration.

Niterói is another city, facing Rio on the other side of the Guanabara Bay, and blessed with fantastic beaches of its own, marvellous views and some of world-class architect Oscar Niemeyer's best buildings.

TOUR GUIDES

There are plenty of guides in Rio. Most taxi drivers will happily spend the afternoon showing you around for a modest fee; all hotels and hostels also have a huge stack of guide brochures and options.

Solar de Santa Creative Tourism, the offshoot of the hotel (*see p40*) offers creative and personalised tours for fashion, art, gastronomy, film-making and more. Travel agencies like **Blumar Turismo** (Avenida Borges de Medeiros 633, Unit 405-408, 2142

9300, www.blumar.com.br) and **Hallmark Tourismo** (Avenida Almirante Barroso 63, Sala 2809, Centro, 2524 9931, www.hallmarktur.com.br) can show you around the city, organise car rentals, hotel reservations and plane tickets around the country. Tailor-made luxury vacations are offered by **Dehouche** (2512 3895, www.dehouche.com), which also offers an Ipanema penthouse to their clients. For a short, intense buzz, **Helisight** (2511 2141, www.helisight.com.br) has a variety of helicopter tours, or for a more mellow trip **Marcos Rosauro** (mobile 7845 6033, www.traineira.com.br) offers boat trips. For a list of jungle tour operators, *see p90* **The urban jungle**; and for options for favela tours, *see p73* **Slumming it**.

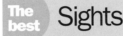

The best Sights

Absolute must-dos

Appreciate the natural beauty from the top of **Pão de Açúcar** (*see p64*) and the **Cristo Redentor statue at Corcovado** (*see p74*) and experience the exhilaration of the beaches of **Zona Sul** (*see pp75-80*).

Churches

Marvel at the architectural daring (or folly) of the **Catedral Metropolitana** (*see p63*), the sparkling gold of the **Igreja do Mosteiro de São Bento** (*see p63*) and the views from around the quaint **Igreja de Nossa Senhora da Glória de Outeiro** (*see p69*).

Flora and fauna

Get up close to some of the world's most exotic animals at the **Jardim Zoologico** (*see p96*), discover amazing and unlikely plantlife at the **Jardim Botanico** (*see p83*) or get both at once in the **Floresta da Tijuca** (*see p90* **The urban jungle**).

Grand designs

The **Maracanã** football stadium (*see p94*), Niemeyer's **Museu de Arte Contemporânea** (*see p98*) and the landscape wonders of the **Sítio Roberto Burle Marx** (*see p93*).

Urban oases

Relax in the gardens of the **Palácio do Catete** (*see p68*) or the **Centro Cultural Parque das Ruinas** (*see p72*), do some holiday reading at the **Real Gabinete Português de Leitura** (*see p60*), or head for the hills in the **Parque da Cidade** (*see p86*).

The Centre

Buildings of Empire and State – and Rio's take on the rush hour.

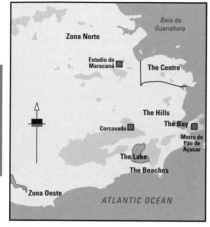

The Centre is a clash of styles, with old buildings imported from Europe pitted against modernism, and people trying to work their way through endless red tape in a city known mostly for play. Most of Rio de Janeiro's historic buildings can be found within the area that includes **Praça XV**, **Cinelândia**, **Lapa**, **Praça da Carioca**, **Praça Tiradentes**, **Praça da República**, **Gamboa** and **Saúde**. The city was effectively shaken from its slumbers by the arrival of the entire Portuguese court, led by the regent João VI and his queen, Carlota Joaquina, in 1808. Fleeing from the irresistible advance of Napoleon across Europe, they sailed to Rio with the protection and encouragement of the British government, which was casting its beady eye on the fabulous wealth of the young colony. At the time of their arrival, the city's entire population was a mere 50,000.

Although Don João is credited with planting the **Jardim Botânico** (*see p83*) and inspiring the future creation of the **Museu Nacional de Belas Artes** (*see p167*) and the **Biblioteca Nacional** (*see p56*), the royal family survived the tropical heat, the hostility of the local elite and the clamours of the abandoned Portuguese for just 14 years. In 1822, they went home, leaving their son to take up the Brazilian throne as Don Pedro I. Before the century was out, in 1889, the royal family made a grand exit with the last ball of the empire at the **Ilha Fiscal** (*see p62*).

Cinelândia

Despite the superior historical claims of Praça XV, the heart of central Rio is Cinelândia, the result of the grandiose project of modernisation of the republican capital. The square is dominated by the imposing **Theatro Municipal** (*see p193*), built in 1909 as a copy of the Opera of Paris, part of an architectural complex which includes the **Câmara Municipal**, seat of the city council, the Biblioteca Nacional, the Museu de Belas Artes, the **Centro Cultural da Justiça Federal** (*see p55*) and the **Clube Naval**.

This rectangular square has been the stage for many political dramas – the traditional route for protest marches is to begin at **Ingreja da Candelária** church, march down Rio Branco Avenue and terminate with a rally in Cinelândia – followed by discussions long into the night over a *chope* of beer at the **Amarelinho** terrace café (*see p119*). From students opposing the military dictatorship being pursued across the square by the cavalry in the 1960s and massive demonstrations for direct elections in the early 1980s to regular strikes and protests today, all have passed through Cinelândia. The square is also the stage for frenetic street parties, Carnival, world cup victories and various cultural events on temporary stages erected in front of the Câmara Municipal.

The best way to get to Cinelândia is by metro. From the Praça Floriano exit you emerge close to the Theatro Municipal. It's a fair old sight – red-carpeted marble staircases, painted panels, columns, alcoves and balustrades with details in bronze, quartz and onyx. There are guided tours on the hour on weekdays (tickets at Rua Manoel de Carvalho, at the back of the theatre; previous arrangement should be make for English-speaking guides) but an even better way to appreciate its gilt and glamour is to join the throngs for the popular priced classical concerts at 11am on Sunday mornings.

Crossing Rio Branco to the other side of the square is the **Biblioteca Nacional**, which also dates from the early years of the Republic (1910) and combines a neoclassical design with elements of art nouveau. The entrance hall is dominated by an imposing marble staircase and illuminated by an intricate skylight; what follows is the largest public library in Latin America and the eighth biggest in the world, containing 13 million volumes, most of them available for public consultation. It is hard to believe that until the arrival of Don João VI, books were banned from the colony. Among the works in the Biblioteca Nacional are a section of manuscripts, one of rare and ancient books, a selection of musical scores accompanied by a sound archive, and the 1462 Mogúncia Bible.

Further along Rio Branco, the **Museu de Belas Artes** belongs to the same period and architectural style and was constructed between 1908 and 1923. Apart from the collection of 16th- to 18th-century Flemish art and a small number of earlier works bequeathed by Don João VI, it has a unique collection of 19th- and 20th-century Brazilian art, including some fine modernist works. The most important of these are by Lasar Segall, Anita Malfatti, Tarsila do Amaral, Di Cavalcanti, Guignard and Portinari.

Turning back past the Biblioteca Nacional is the **Centro Cultural da Justiça Federal**, an old courthouse turned cultural centre that contains exhibition halls, a cinema, a small café and an interesting gift shop. In similar style to its larger neighbours it has interesting wrought-iron stair-rails, stained-glass windows and beautiful patterned tiles on the floor. Behind it, on Avenida Presidente Wilson,

is the present home of the Academia Brasileira de Letras, a neoclassical copy of the Petit Trianon in France's Versailles.

Crossing Rio Branco back to Cinelândia, the **Odeon Cinema** (*see p161* **Cachaça and popcorn**) is at the corner of the square. The elegant 600-seat cinema with its grand circle and stage also houses a café and restaurant and a sophisticated second hand bookshop. One of only two surviving cinemas of those which gave the square its name in the 1930s, the Odeon was completely refurbished in 1999. It has an impressive year-round programme that includes various film festivals, a monthly marathon all-night film session interspersed with *discothèque*, and seasonal 'Miscelanea' events that spill out into the square.

At the sea end of the square is the **Monroe Fountain** (1861), which was bought by Don Pedro II in 1878 and transferred to Cinelândia in 1979. At the side is a massive iron statue of Mahatma Ghandhi striding purposefully forward in his dhoti and sandals. To the right are the gardens of **Passeio Público** (*see p56*), designed by Mestre Valentim in 1783 and a shady meeting place for Cariocas ever since. The gardens were restored in 1864 and again in 2004 and every Sunday morning host a small street market specialising in old coins and stamp collections.

Old-world charm and great cakes at the **Confeitaria Colombo**. *See p59.*

Sightseeing

The imposing façade of the **Igreja de Nossa Senhora Candelária**. *See p60.*

On the corner, the massive **Cine Palácio** is the other survivor of Cinelândia's golden age, with its art deco façade and stained-glass windows. Parallel with Rio Branco, the tiny cobbled street of Álvaro Alvim contains the basement **Teatro Rival**, a cosy venue for some of Rio's best and most popular singers, and a number of informal bars that spill out onto the street on Friday nights.

Biblioteca Nacional
Avenida Rio Branco 219 (2220 9484/www.bn.br). Metro Cinelândia/409, 434, 571 bus. **Open** (by guided tour only) 11am & 3pm Mon-Fri. **Admission** R$2. **No credit cards. Map** p245 H3.

Centro Cultural da Justiça Federal
Avenida Rio Branco 241 (3212 2550/www.ccjf. trf2.gov.br). Metro Cinelândia/409, 434, 571 bus. **Open** noon-7pm Tue-Sun. **Admission** free tickets available for cinema sessions. **Map** p245 H3.

Passeio Público
Metro Cinelândia/409, 434, 571 bus. **Open** 9am-5pm daily. **Admission** free. **Map** p245 I4.

Largo da Carioca

Behind and left of Theatro Municipal is Largo da Carioca, dominated by the 17th/18th-century church and monastery of **Santo Antônio** and

the church of **São Francisco da Penitência**. Access is just beside the exit of Carioca metro station, by means of a lift at the end of a dank tunnel. During the annual festival of Santo Antônio on 19 June, the main gates are opened and crowds of people swarm up the hill to line up for bread blessed in the name of the saint and therefore, it is popularly supposed, embued with special powers.

Built between 1657 and 1772, and restored in 2002, the church of São Francisco da Penitência is a particularly fine example of Baroque architecture. The details of the church's interior, carved from cedar wood, are entirely coated with over 400 kilograms (880 pounds) of gold. Portuguese sculptors created the lifelike figures of saints and the altarpiece that represents São Francisco's vision of a winged Christ. Their work was a major inspiration for Brazil's famous Baroque sculptor Aleijadinho. The ceiling, painted by Portuguese master Caetano Costa Coelho, is the first Brazilian example of architectural perspective in painting. The Franciscan order was formerly famous for its Ash Wednesday processions calling the faithful to the penitence of Lent, but, appalled by the licentiousness and irreverence of a population still bleary eyed from Carnival, it finally gave up the processions at the end of the 19th century.

Building blocks

It took Brazilian architecture two and a half centuries to get from the colonial Imperial Palace (*pictured*) in central Rio de Janeiro to the modernist Museum of Contemporary Art (*see p97*) in Niterói. Hop on a ferry across Guanabara Bay and you can do it in around 30 minutes.

In both time and temperament, the two buildings represent the opposing poles of Rio architecture, and between them lies a whole world of different styles. Across the city, contrasting materials, uses and functions butt up against, loom over and peek out from underneath one another. Change, and the remarkable power and beauty of nature, have been the only constants in Rio's architectural development. Those and the inevitable rows over the pros and cons of modernist architecture – a movement which to many is synonymous with the work of Oscar Niemeyer, the country's most famous architect. Niemeyer is a Brazilian icon who has defined for the world the modernist style that reshaped Brazilian cities from the mid 20th century onwards.

Brasília, the capital, is the modernist mecca, for good and ill. But Rio has its share of standout structures. Start with the building where Brazilian modernism itself began, Gustavo Capanema Palace (Rua da Imprensa 16, Centro). Still known to many Cariocas as the Ministry of Education and Public Health (its initial function) the building was designed with the help of Le Corbusier, the Swiss-French architect who was the leading voice of European modernism, and conforms closely to his style and strictures. It also bears the pencil marks of Niemeyer, then just a trainee. Several other Brazilians who would become the country's modernist visionaries also worked on the project, including Lúcio Costa, Jorge Machado Moreira and the landscape architect Roberto Burle Marx. Capanema Palace might look common today, but when completed in 1945 – with the whole structure resting on pilings 12 metres (40 feet) high, and with an open plaza underneath – the building was considered revolutionary. It embraced Le Corbusier's five principles of design and was the world's first high-rise with a glass façade. It shaped the way in which Niemeyer, Costa and other modernists would build the new Brazil over the next decades.

Rio's other notable modernist structures are the Metropolitan Cathedral, the Museum of Modern Art (*see p67*) and the Monument to the Dead of World War II (*see p68*).

Modernism was aimed not merely at revamping architecture. It also rejected the architecture that had come before, particularly the eclecticism of the 19th century. For Rio, that came as more bad news. The early 20th century had already seen authorities demolish some of the city's colonial past In search of a new urban style. That continued in the middle decades and into the 1970s, with different goals and different targets.

The result is that little is left of Rio's colonial heritage. But what remains is compelling. The main colonial square downtown, Praça XV (*see p60*), the Imperial Palace and the 250-year-old buildings and residences that line the narrow cobblestone streets of the area all radiate charm. And the post-colonial era of eclecticism left a dramatic mark on the city. The Municipal Theatre, the National Museum of Fine Arts and the National Library endure as fine examples from that period.

The challenge now is a contemporary movement that will be able to stand up to the critics, and to the wrecking balls, over the coming decades.

The monastery church of Santo Antônio is from the same period. There is a good view from the square in front of the monastery, which seems to float above the city.

Along Rua Uruguaiana, a pedestrian street beginning at Rua da Carioca, is the **Igreja Nossa Senhora do Rosário e São Benedito dos Homens Pretos** (1737). As slaves were not allowed to frequent the churches of the elite, they built their own, thus providing a burial place for the dead who up until this time had been unceremoniously thrown into ditches. Every Thursday at noon there is the highly popular Missa de Cura e Libertação (Healing and Liberation Mass) during which the church is packed with people for nearly three hours. To the side of the church is the Museu do Negro, which contains some vicious instruments of torture brought to the church by ex-slaves who had won (or bought) their liberty. There are also images of Escrava Anastácia, a beautiful slave with an iron gag, now the object of a special cult.

In the parallel street of Gonçalves Dias, the **Confeitaria Colombo** (see p120; photo p55) maintains its turn-of-the-century elegance. A tea room and restaurant, its saloons are walled with Belgian crystal mirrors creating an opulent atmosphere. It has always been a favourite meeting place for politicians and artists and has hosted receptions for illustrious visitors, including Queen Elizabeth II in 1968. Enjoy an afternoon tea with Portuguese pastries or a buffet lunch on the first floor gallery looking down on the saloon below. The gift shop specialises in commemorative items.

Igreja e Convento de Santo Antônio

Largo da Carioca (2262 0129/2262 1201). Metro Carioca/119, 128, 177 bus. **Open** 8am-6pm daily. **Admission** free. **Map** p245 I3.

Igreja Nossa Senhora do Rosário e São Benedito dos Homens Pretos

Rua Uruguaiana 77 (2224 2900). Metro Carioca or Uruguaiana/119, 128, 177 bus. **Open** 7am-5pm Mon-Fri. **Map** p245 I2.

Igreja de São Francisco da Penitência

Largo da Carioca (2262 0197). Metro Carioca/ 119, 128, 177 bus. **Open** 9am-noon, 1-4pm Tue-Fri. **Admission** R$2 (includes Museum of Sacred Art). **Map** p245 I3.

Tiradentes & Praça da República

From Confeitaria Colombo you can cross back over Uruguaiana to the **Largo de São Francisco**. The **Instituto de Filosofia e Ciências Sociais** (IFICS), on the square, was originally a military academy inaugurated by Don João VI in 1810. There's a small photographic archive inside telling the story of the labour movement (Memória da Luta Operária). On the other side of the square is the church of **São Francisco de Paula**, built in 1759. It contains work by Mestre Valentim.

Turning down Rua de Camões is the magnificent **Real Gabinete Português de Leitura** (1887), a royal reading room dating from the last gasp of the monarchy, with checkered marble flooring and tiers of leather bound books stretching up to the stained-glass dome that illuminates the interior. The columns are garlanded with wooden flowers and resemble maypoles. It's a grand place for a quiet read, and fortunately the whole area is full of second-hand bookstores, many of which stock English-language books.

Further down Rua de Camões, the **Centro Cultural Hélio de Oiticica** (see p167) is a small gallery in memoriam of one of Brazil's most eclectic modern artists, famous, among other things, for dressing up kids from Mangueira favela in magic capes called Parangolés. On the corner in front of the cultural centre, two *pé sujo* (dirty feet) bars maintain an array of vintage fruit machines and a constant jukebox duel – on one side of the street, local sensual funk; Queen and vintage rock on the other.

Just down the street, Praça Tiradentes is dominated by Dom Pedro I on his horse surrounded by friendly indians. This square was once the centre of Rio's theatreland. The surviving theatres, **Teatro Carlos Gomes** (early 19th-century art deco) and **Teatro João Caetano** (for both, see p193) are two of Rio's most important, whose programmes sometimes include dance or music events. Rua da Constituição links Tiradentes to Praça da República. Half way down, the new **Museu do Rádio** (see p60) is a photographic record of the history of radio with its glamorous stars of the 1950s and '60s.

Praça da República is a large square with wonderful old trees, extraordinary little animals called cutias and a pond full of ducks. On one side of the square is the **Igreja de São Jorge**. On Saint George's day, 23 April, the life-sized image of Jorge on his white horse processes round all the streets of the centre of the city, accompanied by crowds of devotees mostly dressed in red – São Jorge is immensely popular in Rio. In the church giftshop you can find banners and images of the horseman saint. On the other side of the square is the largest emergency hospital in Latin America, Hospital Souza Aguiar, and the **Arquivo Nacional**, an imposing neoclassical building in which Don

Sightseeing

João VI originally installed the Museu Real in 1818. The National Archive took it over in 1907.

Crossing Avenida Presidente Vargas on the other side of the square is **Central do Brasil**, the train station inspired by the British but built by Dom Pedro II and later imortalised in Walter Salles' film of the same name. Suburban trains have long been the principal means of transport for millions of workers coming from the suburbs to the centre and Zona Sul, the metro being a recent alternative for many routes. From here, on 2 December, National Samba Day (*see p155*) trains full of samba players and enthusiasts leave Central from 4pm onwards for the 40-minute trip to the suburb of Oswaldo Cruz where a massive samba festival goes on all night. During Carnival the samba schools wait for their turn to perform in the **Sambódromo** lined up on the side of the avenue. During the weekends preceding Carnival, the biggest Escolas de Samba (samba groups) have dress rehearsals in the Sambodromo. This is when all the local people involved in making Carnival have a real chance to enjoy their group's performance, since entrance is free for all. The Sambódrome itself is not very exciting when empty – a bit like looking at a race track without the horses – but was designed by Niemeyer, one of the few architects in the world capable of giving a personal touch to armoured concrete. Nearby, in the middle of Avenida Presidente Vargas, is a bust of slave and freedom fighter Zumbi dos Palmares. It's a massive bronze head on a pyramidal shaped plinth, a copy of the wonderful 19th-century yoruba sculptures from Benin and Nigeria.

Igreja de São Francisco de Paula

Largo São Francisco de Paula (2509 0070). Metro Carioca or Uruguaiana/119, 128, 177 bus. **Open** 11am-12.30pm Mon-Fri. **Admission** free. **Map** p245 I2.

Museu do Rádio Roberto Marinho

Rua da Constituição 78 (2232 6172). Metro Uruguaiana or Central/107, 125, 415 bus. **Open** noon-5pm Mon-Fri. **Admission** free. **Map** p245 H2.

Real Gabinete Português de Leitura

Rua Luís de Camões 30 (2221 3138/www.real gabinete.com.br). Metro Carioca or Uruguaiana/ 119, 128, 177 bus. **Open** 9am-6pm Mon-Fri. **Admission** free. **Map** p245 H2.

Praça XV

On one side of Praça XV is the **Palácio Tiradentes**, another early 20th-century neoclassical pile that is now the legislative parliament of Rio de Janeiro State. Inside there is a well-organised photographic exhibition of the political history of the republic that can also be accessed in English on two computer terminals. Before the Guanabara Bay was earthed in, eliminating Glória beach and creating **Aterro do Flamengo Park** (*see p67*), Praça XV was on the seafront, so as soon as Don João VI and his court stepped out of the boat he could transform the 1743 **Paço Imperial** into his new palace. Nowadays, it houses exhibitions and a cinema.

Some of Rio's most beautiful architecture is to be found in and around the square. **Arco dos Telles**, a fine 18th-century arch, survived a fire that destroyed much of this part of the city in 1790. It leads to Travessa do Comércio, a little street of antique buildings converted into bars and restaurants (Carmen Miranda lived at no.13). Further on, the Rua do Mercado is being revitalised by a co-operative of artists led by Grupo do Anônimo, a theatre group that organises samba sessions on Friday nights.

Paço Imperial

Praça XV de Novembro 48 (2533 4491/www.paco imperial.com.br). Metro Carioca or Uruguaiana/ 123, 128, 132, 172 bus. **Open** noon-6pm Tue-Sun. **Admission** free. **Map** p245 J2.

Palácio Tiradentes

Rua 1º de Março (2588 1251). Metro Carioca or Uruguaiana/123, 128, 132, 172 bus. **Open** 10am-5pm Mon-Fri. **Admission** free. **Map** p245 J2.

Candelária

Around the corner from Praça XV, the **Centro Cultural Banco do Brasil (CCBB)** is a thriving multimedia cultural centre. The Banco do Brasil was founded by Dom João VI, who later cleaned out the vaults when he returned to Lisbon. It's a fine building with a lofty luminous dome in the central hall whose circular balconies lead off into a series of galleries. The CCBB runs a succession of exhibitions, as well as theatres, cinemas, a bookshop and two restaurants. In the same block, the **Casa França-Brasil** is another charming building with a large exhibition hall and cinema. Just down the street **Centro Cultural dos Correios** completes the trio. CCBB faces into the beginning of Avenida Presidente Vargas, dominated by the magnificent **Igreja de Nossa Senhora Candelária** (*photo p56*), built in 1775 and restored in 1898. It was built on the site of the city's first church (1630). The interior was painted by some of Brazil's best 19th-century artists – Zeferino da Costa, Oscar Pereira da Silva and Barnadelli. Even though there are modern skyscrapers on all sides, its twin domes dominate the long avenue. In front of the cathedral a simple wooden cross marks the spot of the infamous massacre of a group of sleeping street kids that made world news in 1994.

Rambling in Rio Centro

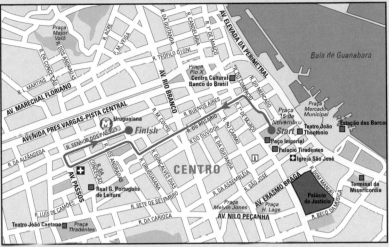

A short walk from the waterfront to the market zone gives a feel for old Rio and a taste of how the city's planners (and their sometimes laissez-faire methods) have blended the ancient with the new. This walk begins with some history, passes through some of the city's best street shopping and ends at a convenient metro stop.

An important note before you start: during the week this route is bustling, but safe. On Sundays and public holidays, much of the centre tends to be deserted and tourists become a target for thieves.

Begin at Praça XV, one of the oldest areas of Rio de Janeiro, where Dom João II was dethroned and Brazil was declared a republic in November 1889. Here is the Paço Imperial, former home of the Portuguese royalty, just a short walk from the ferry terminal from where boats leave for Niterói.

With the water on your right, cross the street at the **Arcos dos Telles**. The opening to this ancient passageway is marked by concrete arches between two buildings. It's hard to miss. This alleyway is a perfectly preserved street from Rio's colonial days. The arches that pass overhead have been restored, as have the two-storey colonial buildings that now house over 15 small bars and restaurants. On Thursdays and Fridays especially, this area fills with locals unwinding after work.

Cross over Rua do Ouvidor, one of the oldest streets in Rio, and after the next block turn left on to Rua do Rosário. The following street to your right, Rua Visconde de Itaboraí, leads to **Cais do Oriente**, a wonderful restaurant with an indoor garden (*see p101*). Just beyond that is the **Banco do Brasil Cultural Center**, a space transformed from Brazil's national bank headquarters to a well- preserved and active cultural space.

Walking down Rua do Rosário, you'll cross Rua Primeiro de Março. Keep going over this and the next big thoroughfare, Avenida Rio Branco, until you reach Rua Gonçalves Dias, where on the left is the outstretched awning of **Confeitaria Colombo** (*see p59*), one of the oldest and most celebrated coffee and dessert shops in the city.

Rua Rosário ends on Rua Uruguaiana at the entrance to the **Igreja de Nossa Senhora do Rosário e São Benedito**. This ancient church was built in 1669 on top of a hill, but moved to its present-day location in 1772.

One block to the right, the rough and ready **Camélodromo Market** starts on Rua Buenos Aires. For more shopping, continue down Rua Buenos Aires to Avendia Passos, take a right, then right again on to Rua Senhor dos Passos for the **Saara** (*see p134* **Market daze**).

The walk ends at the end of Rua Senhor dos Passos. Take a left on Rua Uruguaiana for the Uruguaiana metro stop.

A labour of love and a constantly changing work of art: **Escadaria Selarón**.

On the other side of the avenue, in the tiny Rua Dom Gerardo, a steep drive leads up into the leafy courtyard of the **Mosteiro São Bento**. The best times to visit are for the crowded Sunday 10am mass or at evensong when the magnificent gold interior of the recently restored 17th- and 18th-century church is accompanied by the Gregorian chant of the monks. The painted panels are from the 17th century and the flues of the ancient organ (1773) are linked to the modern ones (1945). Nearby, at the **Espaço Cultural da Marinha**, a cultural centre maintained by the navy, visitors can inspect a World War II anti-torpedo boat and climb into a sinister black submarine – not for the claustrophobic. Dom João VI's galleon is also on display, along with a series of maps and navigational instruments and curious collections of objects salvaged from shipwrecks.

Here you can buy a ticket for a schooner trip round Guanabara Bay or to visit the charming **Ilha Fiscal**, a strange green palace built by Dom Pedro II. Amazingly, this neo-gothic folly was constructed as a customs office, replete with English stained glass and a wonderful parquet floor in the upper saloon, inlaid with the wood

of 16 different species of tree. It came into its own in 1889 when the money raised by the populace to assuage the ravages of a drought in the north-east was blown on the last fling of the empire, O Último Baile do Império. There was no resistance when Marechal Deodoro de Fonseca proclaimed the republic three days later. The political regime changed but scandals regarding the investment of public money continue to this day. Ilha Fiscal was the only public building to maintain images of the monarchy in the charming stained glass portraits of Dom Pedro and Princesa Isabel. From the sea there is a wonderful view of the whole bay, with traffic flowing over the hoop of the Niterói bridge (one of the longest in the world), as well as boats, barges, liners and tankers in the water, and planes swooping down into the local city airport of Santos Dumont.

Back on dry land, follow the avenue round past Praça XV to the **Museu Histórico Nacional**. Besides porcelain busts of all the royals, an authentic imperial carriage and a complete 19th-century apothecary, it has a new exhibition with cultural artefacts and historical records of different indigenous groups.

Centro Cultural Banco do Brasil

Rua 1° de Março 66 (3808 2020/www.bb.com.br/
cultura). Metro Carioca or Uruguaiana/123,
128, 132, 172 bus. **Open** 10am-9pm Tue-Sun.
Admission free to exhibitions; tickets available
for cinema sessions and theatres. **Map** p245 I1.

Espaço Cultural da Marinha

Avenida Alfredo Agache (2104 6992/2104 9165/
www.sdm.mar.mil.br). Metro Carioca or Uruguaiana/
123, 128, 132, 172 bus. **Open** noon-5pm Tue-Sun.
Admission free; tickets available here for trips
round Guanabara Bay and Ilha
Fiscal. **Map** p245 I1.

Igreja do Mosteiro de São Bento

Rua Dom Gerardo 68 (2206 8100/www.osb.org.br).
Metro Carioca or Uruguaiana/123, 128, 132, 172
bus. **Open** *Church* 7am-noon, 2-6pm Mon-Sat. *Mass*
10am Sun; shortened version 7.15am Fri, Sat.
Admission free. **Map** p245 I1.

Igreja de Nossa Senhora da Candelária

Praça Pio X (2233 2324). Metro Carioca or
Uruguaiana/123, 128, 132, 172 bus. **Open**
7.30am-4pm Mon-Fri; 8am-noon Sat; 9am-1pm
Sun. **Admission** free. **Map** p245 I1.

Museu Histórico Nacional

Praça Marechal Âncora (2550 9224/www.
museuhistoriconacional.com.br). Metro Carioca.
Open 10am-5.30pm Tue-Fri; 2-6pm Sat, Sun.
Admission R$6; R$3 students; free under-5s
& over-60s; free Sun. **Map** p245 K2.

Gamboa

Long abandoned by the municipal authorities,
the port district in the north of the Centro
is currently making something of a social
and cultural comeback, led by the enormous
Cidade do Samba – the Samba City.
Providing huge warehouse-like workshops
for the numerous samba schools to prepare
their floats and costumes, it's also intended
to work as a kind of out-of-season Carnival,
with short demonstrations throughout the day,
huge weekly shows and a series of 'cultural
activities' planned for the future.

Whether or not the remainder of this
district will benefit from the drive remains
to be seen, but the **Trapiche Gamboa**
(*see p177*) a gigantic old brick warehouse
converted into a joyful and inexpressibly
cool samba club, demonstrates that the area
is ripe for rejuvenation.

Cidade do Samba

Rua Rivadávia Corrêa 60 (2213 2503/2213 2546).
Bus 127, 128, 170. **Open** 10am-5pm Tue-Sat.
Shows from 8pm Thur. **Admission** R$10; R$5
reductions. *Shows* R$150; R$75 reductions.
Credit MC, V. **Map** p245 I1.

Lapa

Lapa has been ground zero for Rio's Bohemia
for over two centuries. The preferred haunt for
artists and politicians in the 19th century, replete
with brothels and taverns, it inevitably fell into
a temporary decline, only to return in style over
the last 20 years. The great landmark is the
viaduct – **Arcos da Lapa** – now graced by
Rio's last remaining tramline, which leaves
from the city centre and winds up the hill of
Santa Teresa (*see p70*). From the square under
the arches you can see the strange 96-metre (315-
foot) cone of the **Catedral Metropolitana**.
An ugly upturned bucket from the outside, a
quick look inside is necessary to appreciate
what architect Edgar Oliveira da Fonseca was
thinking. In the basement is the throne of Dom
Pedro II, and an assortment of other artefacts
are displayed in the **Museu Arquidiocesano
de Arte Sacra** (Sacred Art Museum).

Under the arches, **Fundição Progresso**
and **Circo Voador** (for both, *see p180*) are
both venues for eclectic musical events ranging
from samba to rock, funk, hip hop and trance.
They also promote seasonal daytime events,
workshops and festivals. Fundição Progresso
also maintains permanent rehearsal spaces
for theatre/circus groups like **Intrépida
Trupe** (*see p192* **Super trupers**) and Grupo
Anônimo, both of which have helped elevate
circus to a modern art form. The street behind,
Rua do Lavradio, is full of antique shops that
double as bars and music venues at night. On
the first Saturday of every month the street
hosts a Portobello Road-style market, mixing
antique bric-a-brac with clothes, handicrafts
and a happy crowd imbibing beer in the sun.

At the Santa Teresa end of Arcos da Lapa are
the first signs of an amazing one-man art project,
the **Escadaria Selarón**, a constantly changing
mosaic of coloured tiles and wall paintings on
a flight of steps. Over the years, Chilean artist
Selarón has single-handedly transformed the 215
steps from Joaquim Silva street leading up to the
Ladeira de Santa Teresa into a riot of colour with
painted tiles sourced from all over the world.

Arcos da Lapa

Metro Cinelândia/410, 433, 464, 571 bus.
Map p245 I4.

Catedral Metropolitana

Avenida República do Chile 245 (2240 2669/
www.catedral.com.br). Metro Carioca/107, 157
bus. **Open** 6am-7pm daily. **Admission** free.
Map p245 I3.

Escadaria Selarón

Rua Joaquim Silva 81-85. Metro Glória/
434, 571, 572 bus. **Map** p245 I4.

Sightseeing

The Bay

A mountain you may have heard of and some of Rio's lesser-known pleasures.

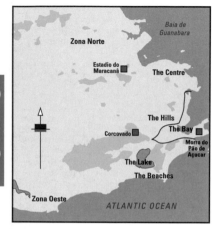

The low-lying neighbourhoods that separate downtown from Copacabana and Ipanema tend to get outshone by their more illustrious neighbours. The iconic **Sugar Loaf** is assured of its place on the Rio must-see list but the rest of genteel **Urca** and the adjacent districts of **Glória**, **Flamengo**, **Catete** and **Botafogo** are easier to discount when set against the history of the centre and the glamour of the ocean beaches. Take the time to get to know them, however, and you'll discover another side of Rio; less glamorous, perhaps, but easier to live in, especially if you're planning on staying for more than just a week.

These neighbourhoods of residential streets and shopping centres are now becoming home to a new generation of clubs and bars popular with the student and alternative crowds. The hotels and hostels are also promoting themselves as a base within easy distance of both the beaches and the nightlife of Lapa.

Stretching along the scenic (but sadly polluted) arc of Guanabara Bay, there's a mix of parks, stately colonial architecture, 1950s *botecos* and cutting-edge cuisine. Without Ipanema's white sands and clean waters to chill things out, the area fairly bustles with extra-curricular activities. People fish, skate, jog, bike and fly model aeroplanes and play football, basketball, volleyball and endless other variations on the theme. The sheltered bay also draws water sports enthusiasts.

Urca

Most people equate Urca with **Pão de Açúcar** (the Sugar Loaf; *photo p69*) and although the granite monolith and its quixotic cable car are an undeniably singular and breathtaking experience, there are other things to see in the neighbourhood as well.

But to get it out of the way, the cable car leaves from the parking area at **Praia Vermelha** and runs from 8.15am to 10pm. A two-stage affair, the cable car first stops at Sugar Loaf's lower counterpart, the 218 metre (715 feet) Morro da Urca. A large, flat top has allowed developers to put in gift shops, an outdoor café, a restaurant, clean – yes, clean – public toilets and an amphitheatre that shows a film tracking the short history of the cable car. Concerts like the **Oi Noites Cariocas** series (*see p183*) held during the summer are wildly popular because of the stunning setting. A new structure currently under construction promises even better hilltop services for shows and parties.

From there, a second cable car climbs again to an altitude of 396 metres (1,219 feet) and the Sugar Loaf peak, where nearly all of Rio is exposed below in all its rollicking chaos. Off the front of the smallish viewing platform is Niterói and beyond that the open ocean. The all-encompassing view is a great way to wrap your mind around the layout of the city. If your turned off by crowds, it's best to go at off-peak hours.

The small beach just past the parking lot for the cable car is **Praia Vermelha**, named for its reddish sand. While large groups of tourists amble the short boardwalk, the beach itself is usually not crowded. Generally the water is clean and clear in the morning, but an unfortunate pattern of currents fills it with garbage nearly every afternoon.

Leading off the Sugar Loaf end of the beach is a nice, paved trail, **Pista Cláudio Coutinho**, which winds along the base of the Morro da Urca. With the waves breaking on rocks below, frigate birds and vultures floating in the drafts along the steep walls above and monkeys cavorting among tropical vegetation right next to you, the trail is a must-see for nature lovers. An established trail leaving from Cláudio Coutinho climbs to the platform at Morro da Urca. It takes about 20 minutes and is a gentle walk. A tip for the parsimonious: after 7pm the cable car back down is free.

There are climbing routes on both Morro da Urca and Sugar Loaf. You'll need full gear and knowledge of the routes or a good climbing guide to make the ascent – look for climbing expeditions at travel agencies or among the hostels in Botafogo (*see pp38-40*).

On the downtown side of the hill is the heart of the residential section of Urca. Built entirely on landfill and relatively isolated from the rest of the city, it's the safest and quietest area in Rio. It feels like a rich fishing village and was once home to Carmen Miranda. It still is home for Roberto Carlos, the 'king of Brazilian pop'; an evening stroll along Urca's boardwalk with the sun setting behind the Christ statue and fishermen casting into the pink waters of the bay, and it's not hard to see why he likes it.

For a trip out into the bay and the ocean beyond, converted fishing boats leave for fishing, diving or just fun days out from the tiny harbour behind the Domingos Fernandes Pinto bridge on Avenida Portugal. For more information about group bookings and special trips, call Marcos Rosauro (7845 6033, www. traineira.com.br).

The word structure in front of the small **Praia da Urca** was once a casino and hotel built in the 1930s. Rumours of restoration circulate constantly, but nothing has been done to date. At the end of the residential area, the land continues out into a spit with a military base, **Fortaleza São João**. Civilians need to make special arrangements to enter.

Bondinho Pão de Açúcar

Avenida Pasteur 520 (2461 2700/www.bondinho. com.br). Bus 511, 512. **Open** *Ticket office* 8am-8pm daily. **Admission** R$35; R$17.50 6-12s; free under 6s. **Map** p250 K11

Botafogo

With theatres, museums, cinemas, bars, a historic cemetery, a classic soccer club, three malls and numerous shops and restaurants, Botafogo isn't lacking much. It even has its own beach. Well, kind of. The waters of **Enseada de Botafogo** (an inlet that is part of Guanabara Bay) are far too polluted for swimming, relegating the crescent of sand to something of a large, energy-sapping sports field (it's hard to run on the sand). Despite the tainted water, the bay, with its bobbing boats and dramatic backdrop, is always a pleasant sight.

A must-see in Botafogo is the **Cemitério São João Batista** (Cemetery of St John the Baptist). Mirroring the city surrounding it, the lower flat part of the cemetery is filled with

The beach at **Enseada de Botafogo**.

Praia Vermelha. *See p64.*

opulent tombs honouring Rio's upper-class, but as the large cemetery creeps up the hill, the budget drops. Eventually, the towering marble tombs are replaced first by cabinets of cramped *gavetas* (concrete drawers) filled with Rio's poor and then by unmarked crosses dotting fields of dirt. Fittingly, the cemetery gives way to a slum at its top end. Views of the Santa Marta favela, Sugar Loaf and the Christ statue heighten the cemetery's dramatic effect. Particular graves to look out for are those of Brazil's musical elite: Antonio Carlos Jobim, Vinicius de Moraes, Baden Powell and Clara Nunes. Also buried here are Carmen Miranda, aviator Alberto Santos-Dumont and Roberto Marinho, founder of Globo and one of most influential figures of 20th century Brazil. The cemetery gates are on Rua General Polidoro – entrance is free and it's open during daylight hours.

The **Museu do Índio** (*see below*) houses Rio's most comprehensive collection of artefacts and information relating to the indigenous populations. Funded by Funai (National Indian Foundation), the museum has a good permanent collection and hosts up-to-date exhibits, seminars and documentaries exploring current issues.

Further towards the water, bookworms, historians, mansion connoisseurs and those in search of a green garden in Botafogo will want to stop by **Museu Casa de Rui Barbosa** (*see below*). Nicely restored in 2003, the neoclassical mansion was once the home of journalist and statesman Rui Barbosa (1849-1923). Now, besides showing his personal belongings and a historic collection of texts from Brazilian literature, the museum holds regular seminars, concerts and cinema screenings.

From there to Avenida Praia do Botafogo and extending south toward Copacabana is the neighbourhood's main commercial centre. **Praia Botafogo Shopping** is a quiet, multilevel affair where you can buy daring swimwear without being scrutinized by impossibly glamorous shop employees. There is also a cinema in the complex (*see p163*). The most fashionable mall in Botafogo is **Rio Sul** (*see p132*), located between the two tunnels that lead Copacabana along the Avenida Lauro Sodré, a Rio landmark selling the hippest local and international brands. Next-door to Rio Sul is the huge **Canecão** performance venue (*see p180*).

At the south end of Botafogo's beach is something resembling a huge concrete submarine in dry dock. It is, in fact, Club Botafogo's football stadium, though they have not played here for years. Across the street is **Club Guanabara**, a complex with two swimming pools, work-out facilities, a restaurant and a boating club.

The recent proliferation of hostels in Botafogo has made the neighbourhood a new centre for young, budget-minded travellers looking to avoid inflated prices closer to the desirable beaches. The influx has given Botafogo a shot in the arm and the enterprising owners of the Casa Matriz group, among others, are building on the trend with places like **Casa Matriz** (*see p185*), **Maldita Drinkeria** (*see p121*) and other on-again, off-again party spaces in the neighbourhood's old colonial homes.

Museu Casa de Rui Barbosa

Rua São Clemente 134 (3289 4600/www.casarui barbosa.gov.br). Metro Botafogo/176, 457, 592 bus. **Open** 10am-5pm Tue-Fri; 2-6pm Sat-Sun. **Admission** R$1. **Map** p247 H10.

Museu do Índio

Rua das Palmeiras 55 (2286 8899/www.museu doindio.org.br). Metro Botafogo/176, 457, 583, 592 bus. **Open** 9am-5.30pm Tue-Fri; 1-5pm Sat, Sun. **Admission** R$4. **Map** p246 G11.

Flamengo

Before the **Copacabana Palace** (*see p42*) and the consequent blasting of the tunnel that opened access to the ocean beaches, Flamengo held the torch as the swanky, beachside neighbourhood set apart from the chaotic downtown. Copa long ago usurped Flamengo's place in the sun, but it manages to retain some hints of its former glory while developing as part of metropolitan Rio.

The neighbourhood is dominated by **Parque do Flamengo** – also known as the **Aterro** (landfill) – a massive park packed with palms, flowering trees and sports courts and cut through by a bike and running track that span the park's four-kilometre length. As its popular name suggests, this area was formerly submerged under the bay before ambitious urban planners decimated much of the historic centre by levelling two hills – one where the Metropolitan Cathedral now stands and the other in today's Lapa. The rubble was shunted into the water, creating what is now the airport and the park.

Completed in 1965, this beautiful park was designed by the modernist landscape architect Roberto Burle Marx, who imagined so many of Rio's public spaces. The park now has over 300 species of trees and large expanses of grass. At the north end of the park, close to downtown, the **Museu de Arte Moderna** (*see p68*) has stood since 1948, though it needed to be restored and restocked after a tragic fire in 1978. The museum houses a decent permanent collection and attracts quality national and international exhibits. A recent add-on to the side of the

Sightseeing

museum holds the music venue **Vivo Rio** (*see p181*). Just south of the museum – in the middle of one of those strangely hushed modernist spaces reminiscent of the capital Brasília – stands the **Monument to the Dead of World War II**, a towering sculpture built in honour of the Brazilians who died fighting in Italy.

The circular **Marina da Glória** (*see below*), on the spit of land that separates the bay from Flamengo Beach, has a small yacht club with a number of beautiful old boats moored, their rigging tinkling in the breeze, and restaurants and bars for visitors. It also plays host to trade shows, Fashion Rio, the TIM music festival and a huge musical New Year's Eve party that draws thousands.

The beach at Flamengo might once have been a long, attractive stretch of white sand, but the pollution of the bay has since spilt over onto the shore. Despite the daily water toxicity reports in *O Globo*, which usually qualify Flamengo as 'swimmable', unseasoned visitors would do well to head to the ocean beaches instead. Swimming aside, it's a great place for a jog or a gentle stroll and the evening views can be breathtaking. Planes arc in and out of the airport, the bay is dotted with sails keeled under an ocean breeze and a pink puff of cloud plays around the top of the Sugar Loaf – though it is best to clear out before dark. At the south end of the park is the Porcão restaurant (*see p102*), and for a touch of high glamour and camp there's the flamboyant **Museu Carmen Miranda** (*see p171*).

The park is bordered by two large fast-moving avenues, Avenida Aterro and Avenida Praia do Flamengo, that mainline downtown to Botafogo and Copacabana. Most of Flamengo's residential area is packed with mid- to high-income apartment buildings, but there are a couple gems of interest tucked among them. The **Espaço Cultural Oi Futuro** (*see p167*) is a lively proving ground for contemporary performing and visual arts. At Avenida Praia do Flamengo 158 is the **Castelinho do Flamengo** ('Flamengo's little castle'). A ruddy pink architectural oddity pocked with balconies spiked by towers, its used as a cultural centre dedicated to the visual arts, but the real visual wonder is the building itself.

Marina da Glória

Avenida Infante Dom Henrique s/n (2205 6716/ www.marinadagloria.com.br). Map p245 K5.

Museu de Arte Moderna

Avenida Infante Dom Henrique 85, G (2240 4944/ www.mamrio.org.br). Metro Cinelândia/176, 422, 474, 484 bus. Open noon-6pm Tue-Fri; noon-7pm Sat, Sun. Guided tours 3pm, 4pm, 5pm Sat, Sun. Admission R$5. Map p245 J4.

Catete

The bustling Rua do Catete is Catete's main drag, and lined by brightly painted but crumbling colonial homes built by wealthy 19th-century denizens looking to escape from downtown. The north end that runs into Lapa is quite rough and not to be traversed at night. Similarly, the hills on the west side of Rua do Catete give way quickly to favelas and should be avoided. Climbing east, however, are winding cobblestone streets hiding gems for the adventurous.

The neighbourhood's most striking attraction is the **Palácio do Catete**. Originally built in the 1860s as an opulent home for coffee magnate Barão de Nova Friburgo, the palace became the seat of the republic shortly before the turn of the century and functioned as such until Brasília was completed in 1960. Under overwhelming pressure from the right wing and military, President Getúlio Vargas famously took his own life here in 1954 in a bedroom on the third floor. Now in the palace grounds is the **Museu da República** (*see below*), a café, a cinema and various spaces for the visual and performing arts. The palace gardens, extending all the way from Rua do Catete to Praia de Flamengo, are a refuge of peaceful greenery, duck ponds and babbling fountains. The park, café and cinema hold longer hours than the museum.

Next door to the Palácio do Catete is the **Museu de Folclore Edison Carneiro**. It has an excellent collection of colourful ceramics, traditional costumes and other motley elements sprung from the fertile mash of Catholicism, African rituals and native beliefs.

At the south end of Rua do Catete is the plaza known as **Largo do Machado**. A transportation hub, the busy square is another creation by landscaper Burle Marx. While often chaotic, the elongated plaza with its towering trees and market stands make it a nice place to sit and take in a bit of Carioca life. Leading east from the square is **Laranjeiras** (*see p72*) and the road to the **Corcovado** (*see p74*).

Museu de Folclore Edison Carneiro

Rua do Catete 181 (2205 0090/www.museudo folclore.com.br). Bus 409, 464, 472, 498, 572. Open 11am-6pm Tue-Fri; 3-6pm Sat, Sun. Admission free. Map p245 I6.

Palácio do Catete & Museu da República

Rua do Catete 153 (3235-2650/www.museudare publica.org.br). Bus 409, 464, 472, 498, 572. Open noon-5pm Tue, Thur, Fri; 2-5pm Wed; 2-6pm Sat, Sun. Admission R$6; free Wed & Sun. Map p245 I6.

The views only get better: looking back from the **Bondinho Pão de Açúcar**. *See p65.*

Glória

The waters of Guanabara Bay once reached as far as Glória, but the glory days ended when urban planners exploded a good part of the downtown districts to use for filling the bay. The waterline moved back away from the hill and it diverted the district into a slow and seemingly inexorable decline.

Because it was removed from the spotlight, however, most of Glória's old, dramatic structures escaped the wrecking ball of progress, and the hill – like a tiny, closer-to-everything Santa Teresa – has become something of a time capsule, capped with huge old homes and ringed by historic structures. A stroll through the twisting, cobbled streets and steep staircases leads to rewarding 360-degree views of the peak, but do it during the day: the relative wealth and proximity to downtown make it a target for thieves when night falls.

The most important building in the neighbourhood is the **Igreja de Nossa Senhora da Glória de Outeiro** (*see below*). Completed in 1739, the church is arguably Rio's most interesting surviving colonial structure. It was a favourite among the Portuguese royal family, and Emperor Dom Pedro II was baptised at the church. The simultaneously imposing and intricate wooden altar is generally attributed to the venerated sculptor Valentim da Fonseca e Silva. The church is going through extensive rennovations but is still open for services and also has a library and a small museum to visit, complete with a display of religious figurines.

At the base of the hill is the blinding white façade of **Hotel Glória** (*see p37*). A belle époque landmark finished in 1922, the 1924 opening of Copacabana Palace made its supremacy in luxury short-lived. Renovations have come and gone without managing to dispel the feeling of decline, but it's grand entrance still sells it well to the conference crowd. Next door to the hotel at Rua do Russel 632 is the **Teatro Glória**. Once the hotel's bar, the theatre was taken over by the city government and, after a recent restoration, has a regular schedule of good quality plays and musicals.

Igreja de Nossa Senhora da Glória de Outeiro

Praça Nossa Senhora da Glória 135 (2557 4600/ www.outeirodagloria.org.br). Metro Glória/571 bus. **Open** 8am-5pm Tue-Fri; 8am-noon Sat, Sun. **Admission** free. **Map** p245 J5.

The Hills

Closer to God.

Most of the best views in Rio have been left for the favela dwellers, but the resurgence of the Santa Teresa district has given others the chance to get a look-in.

While the package tourists dash from the beach to the Corcovado, there's now much more opportunity to discover the breezy, cobblestone streets in between, and to witness the rapidly rising confidence of the artists and communities that inhabit them.

Santa Teresa

Located on a hill overlooking the city centre, Guanabara Bay and the Zona Norte, Santa Teresa is at once a window onto Rio and a neighbourhood apart. Not only does it boast the only surviving tram network in the city but it also plays host to Rio's most vibrant artistic community. Ageing mansions and cobbled streets combine with the clatter and rattle of the 19th-century trams to lend Santa Teresa the air of a bygone age.

Santa Teresa became part of the city's history in 1629 when a small chapel dedicated to Nossa Senhora do Desterro was built on the hillside above Lapa. The word 'desterro' (exile) hints at how difficult it was to reach the chapel. In 1750, a Carmelite convent was founded here dedicated to Santa Teresa D'Avila, founder of the Order of the Shoeless Carmelitas. The district went on to adopt her name.

Access to Santa Teresa remained difficult until the mid to late 19th century, making it an ideal hideaway for runaway slaves who formed *quilombos* (slave refuges) there. Bounty hunters were frequently dispatched to Santa Teresa and the surrounding hills. But it wasn't only slaves who recognised the attraction of Santa Teresa. From the mid 19th century the Carioca elite was drawn to the region by its cooler, more salubrious climate, and its consequent lack of the yellow fever-carrying mosquitoes that plagued the lower lying parts of the city.

The district grew significantly in the late 19th and early 20th centuries with mass migration from Europe. Santa Teresa was especially popular among the wealthier immigrants who built sumptuous homes here, some of which can still be visited by the public.

In the late 1960s a series of devastating landslides triggered a wave of panic in the neighbourhood that caused many of the wealthier families to move away. Numerous fine buildings fell into a state of neglect and house prices plummeted. The 1970s heralded the beginning of the neighbourhood's slow revival, with, as ever, artists and Bohemians leading the way.

The revival continues to this day and can be seen in the numerous restaurants, crowded bars and well cared for cultural centres and museums. Santa Teresa's street carnival is now one of the best in the whole city, attracting thousands of revellers to its narrow, cobbled streets, and live music can be heard throughout the year in Santa. During the excellent annual **Portas Abertas** (*see p155*) initiative, Santa Teresa's artists open their ateliers to the public for a long weekend.

One of the great attractions of Santa Teresa is getting there by tram, known as the **Bonde** (Rua Lélio Gama behind the huge Petrobras building, every 30 minutes, 7am-8.30pm, R$0.30). Excellent guided tours of Santa Teresa depart from here every Saturday at 10am costing around R$4. Arrive 20 minutes or so beforehand to ensure you get a seat, though generally a tradition holds that those who ride the running board don't have to pay. Before reaching Santa Teresa the tram crosses the narrow Arcos da Lapa, as it has since 1896 – an unforgettable experience and now a tourist attraction in its own right. Be cautious, though, when using the tram. Thefts on board are not uncommon. Dress down and don't flash money or expensive cameras around. Similar care should be taken when walking around the other parts of Santa Teresa.

There are two tram lines, both of which make a stop at **Largo dos Guimarães**, the Bohemian heart of Santa Teresa where many of the best bars, cafés, restaurants and handicraft shops can be found. From Largo dos Guimarães, one line (Paula Mattos) takes a north-western route terminating at **Largo das Neves**, a very pleasant, shaded square surrounded by small bars that swarm with locals on Friday and Saturday nights. The other line (Dois Irmãos) continues uphill from Largo dos Guimarães, affording some breathtaking views across the city to the faraway mountains near Teresópolis.

Most people get off the tram at Largo dos Guimarães. Much of Santa Teresa can easily be discovered on foot and, as there is little traffic, walking is a pleasure. A short walk down Rua Carlos Brant is the one-room **Museu do Bonde** (*see p72*). The old workshop that houses the trams is also worth a look; it was here that Eurydice meets her fate in the 1959 Oscar-winning classic *Orfeu Negro*.

From the Tram museum it's an easy stroll down Rua Pascoal Carlos Magno to the **Centro Cultural Laurinda Santos Lobo** (*see p72*). The centre takes its name from the Brazilian heiress who lived in a grand mansion nearby now known as the **Parque das Ruinas** (*see p72*). The pink and white mansion that now houses the Cultural Centre was built in 1907. A majestic marble stairway leads to the upper porch, which is supported by white columns with beautifully carved capitals and decorated with coloured glazed tiles with Italianate floral motifs. The gardens are well maintained and contain numerous medicinal plants and stone benches shaded by a huge mango tree – an ideal spot to sit and contemplate the subtle elegance of the building. Both modern and classical concerts are held regularly in the auditorium and on the upper porch near to the gardens.

A few minutes' walk down Rua Monte Alegre is the **Museu Casa de Benjamin Constant** (*see p72*), dedicated to one of the founding fathers of the Brazilian Republic. Built around 1860, the house now exhibits a collection of documents, photographs, sculptures, furniture and personal items, while the gardens afford a panoramic view over the city.

A short tram ride away, near **Largo do Curvelo**, is the Parque das Ruinas. The house was built in the middle of the 19th century as

All aboard the **Bonde** – Santa Teresa's main mode of transport.

the home of Joaquim Murtinho, a wealthy tea plantation owner and minister of the economy. On his death in 1911, Murtinho left the mansion to his niece Laurinda Santos Lobo, who encouraged distinguished Brazilians and visiting foreign celebrities to visit – when Rio was attracting them in droves. After her death in 1946 it fell into neglect, was burgled and eventually became a ruin. However, in the mid 1990s the house was partially restored and nowadays the park hosts open-air concerts at the weekends. The ruins themselves and the adjoining terrace offer stunning views of the Sugar Loaf Mountain, Guanabara Bay and the city centre.

The ruins are connected by a footbridge to the neighbouring **Museu da Chácara do Céu** (*see p167*).

Centro Cultural Laurinda Santos Lobo
Rua Monte Alegre 306 (2224 3331/2242 9741). Tram Paula Mattos/65, 214 bus. **Open** 10am-8pm Tue-Sun. **Admission** free. **Map** p244 G5.

Centro Cultural Parque das Ruinas
Rua Murtinho Nobre 169 (2252 1039). Either tramline/206, 214 bus. **Open** 8am-8pm Tue-Sun. **Admission** free. **Map** p245 H4.

Museu do Bonde
Rua Carlos Brant 14 (2242 2354). Either tramline/206, 214 bus. **Open** 9am-4pm daily. **Admission** free. **Map** p245 H5.

Museu Casa de Benjamin Constant
Rua Monte Alegre 25 (2509 1248). Tram Paula Mattos/214 bus. **Open** 1-5pm Wed-Sun. **Admission** R$0.75; free Sat. **Map** p244 G5.

Laranjeiras

Most visitors only pass through Laranjeiras to get to **Corcovado** and the Christ statue, but the neighbourhood is one of Rio's hidden gems. Mostly residential, Laranjeiras (literally 'orange trees') is dotted with shops and restaurants and even a couple of clubs, designed to accommodate the area's solidly middle-class residents.

Heading up Rua das Laranjeiras from Largo do Machado, to the right is the massive, over-the-top **Palácio das Laranjeiras** (*see p74*). Hidden on a hill among greenery, the palace is tough to spot but worth the effort. A private house designed by Armando Carlos da Silva Telles in 1909, the city government took over the building in 1946, using it as luxurious quarters for illustrious visitors. When Brasilia was built, it became the president's Rio outpost. Tours of the building are highly recommended but must be set up beforehand by phone.

The adjacent **Parque Guinle** was conceived as hunting grounds for the Palácio, but is now a beautifully landscaped city park bisected by a small brook. Entrance to the park is free and it's open during daylight hours.

Continuing up Rua das Laranjeiras toward Corcovado, look for the street Rua da Alice, a narrow street replete with Bohemian charm. Stacked with shops and restaurants, it winds up the hill, with spectacular views. **Casa Rosa** (*see p123*) is a great excuse to explore the nether regions of Laranjeiras.

The heart of Laranjeiras' residential neighbourhood starts where Rua General Glicério turns off Rua das Laranjeiras. It's

Slumming it

Travelling from the international airport to the centre of Rio, visitors can't help but notice the expanse of corrugated tin and brick houses full of mystery and intrigue. For many years these slums, or favelas as they're called in Brazil, were strictly off limits to the curious traveller, but as security became the norm in a few of Rio's favelas, enterprising locals began inviting foreigners to enter and explore the colourful life therein. Soon after, favela tours were born.

Many local tour companies offer a very passive type of favela tour that often combine a pass through Rocinha, Rio's largest favela, with a number of stops along the way back to Leblon on Avenida Niemeyer, where there are a number of photo opportunities. Tour operators have outfitted jeeps with benches that can hold up to a dozen tourists in the back. Don't expect scenes from *Cidade de Deus*, though; the tours are a generally safe view of favela life, even if they are a little anti-climactic – most of the favelas in the south zone are comparatively safe and far more integrated into city life than the shantytowns on the northern and western outskirts.

Other favela tours get more interactive. Funk dance parties are perhaps the best and most enjoyable way to see the good life in the favela. Local operators will pick you up from your hotel around midnight and deliver you home just before sunrise.

Samba schools can also offer a tour of sorts inside the favela. Some of these schools, such as the famous **Mangueira**, are based in a favela. Members of the school act as ad hoc tour guides to walk tourists through the favela to the school building where *sambistas* practice singing, playing, and dancing. Escorts will normally meet you near the entrance to the favela after dark and, once the samba school rehearsal is over, will deliver you to a taxi at the base of the favela around midnight. They also have a samba museum for daytime visits.

Finally, for an overnight stay in a favela in or around the Zona Sul, there are an increasing number of options with small guest houses marketing their beds to foreign visitors only, moving away from the less lucrative market of hosting other Brazilians in town to visit relatives or friends. These guest houses, called *pousadas*, are generally clean, run by very friendly locals, and offer some of the best views you'll find in Rio.

Baile funk tour
Mobile 9643 0366/www.bealocal.com.

Favela tour
Marcelo Armstrong (3322 2727/ www.favelatour.com.br).

Indiana Jungle tours
2484 2279/www.indianajungle.com.br.

Mangueira
Rua Visconde de Niterói 1072, Mangueira (3872 6786/www.mangueira.com.br).

Pousada Favelinha
Rua Antonio Joaquim Batista, Casa 13 Morro Pereira da Silva, Laranjeiras (no phone/www.favelinha.com).

Cristo Redentor has the whole wide city in his arms.

a quiet, decidedly domestic and landlocked area that meanders up the hill and feels worlds apart from the beach life of Zona Sul. Saturday morning's huge market at the bottom of General Glicério, selling food, flowers, arts and crafts, is spectacular.

Palácio das Laranjeiras

Rua Paulo César de Andrade 407 (2299 5233). Bus 406A, 422, 498, 583. **Open** *call ahead for guided tours.* **Map** 247 H7.

Cosme Velho & Corcovado

The statue of **Cristo Redentor** (Christ the Redeemer) (*see below*) atop the 710-metre- (2,300-foot-) high granite dome of Corcovado (Hunchback) mountain attracts over 300,000 visitors every year. No amount of hyperbole can do justice to the views over Rio that the mountaintop affords. The statue itself is hardly less impressive, measuring 30 metres (98 feet) in height and weighing 1,145 tonnes, its arms wide open as if to embrace the city and its 11 million inhabitants. Plans for a statue of Christ the Redeemer were first discussed in 1921; the monument was initially conceived as a way of commemorating the first 100 years of Brazilian independence. In 1923, a project put forward by the Brazilian engineer Heitor da Silva Costa was chosen and a national fundraising campaign was launched to pay for the construction of the statue. It took five years to build and was opened to the public on 12 October 1931.

Keep a close eye on the weather and choose a fine day to go up. It's not much fun looking down on a blanket of cloud in the knowledge that you should be appreciating one of the most spectacular views in the world.

The **Corcovado Cog Railway** (*see below*) that departs from Cosme Velho is the most popular way of reaching the peak and its statue.

Predating the statue, the four-kilometre railway was opened on 9 October 1884, by Emperor Dom Pedro II. The journey takes about 20 minutes with the train climbing steeply through lush tropical forest. Sit on the right-hand side when ascending for the best views. From the terminus you can either walk the 200 steps to the top, hop on the escalator or ride the elevator.

A short walk up Rua Cosme Velho from the Corcovado railway station, **Largo do Boticário** (no.822) is a beautiful shaded square surrounded by colourful houses that date back to the early 19th century. The cobbled square is named after former resident Joaquim Luiz da Silva Souto, who lived here from 1831 and ran a *boticário* (apothecary) patronised by the royal family.

For a wilderness experience, take the Corcovado railway only as far as the **Paineiras** station. It's an ideal place for biking, walking and jogging among monkeys and exotic birds in their natural habitat. The best time to visit is on Saturdays and Sundays when Paineiras is closed to traffic.

If approaching Paineiras by car or taxi it's worth stopping at the **Mirante Dona Marta**. This view point stands 340 metres (1,115 feet) above sea level and offers magnificent views. The Mirante Dona Marta can be accessed from Estrada do Mirante Dona Marta; the turning is clearly signposted and can be found on the left-hand side of the road about a quarter of the way up Estrada das Paineiras.

Cristo Redentor & the Corcovado Cog Railway

Rua Cosme Velho 513, Cosme Velho (2558 1329/ www.corcovado.com.br). Bus 180, 184, 583, 584, then train from Cosme Velho to Corcovado. **Open** *8.30am-6.30pm daily (trains leave every 30 mins, last train at 6pm).* **Tickets** *R$33; R$18 6-12s; free under-6s.* **Map** 246 F9.

The Beaches

If life's a beach, this is where to live it.

Think of Rio and you immediately think of the beach. On a fine day – and there are plenty of them – old and young, rich and poor descend to the beach in their droves. It's a great place to see the 'melting pot' that is Brazil as locals spend days on end playing *futevôlei*, *frescobol*, running, skating, surfing, flexing their pecs and generally parading and bronzing their bodies, finely honed or not, on the city's golden sands. Nowhere is this truer than on the truly marvellous beaches of the Zona Sul.

Zona Sul's sands stretch from the **Morro do Leme**, just round the corner from the Pão de Açucar, to the **Dois Irmãos** (Two Brothers) mountain at the end of **Leblon**, via Copacabana, Arpoador and Ipanema. They are marked by Postos, lifeguard look out points numbered one (in Leme) to 12 (in Leblon), all with their own demarcation and significance.

Ipanema.

Find your place in the sun

Brazilians like to think of the beach as a great equaliser. The worker who cleans offices can lay claim to the same strip of sand as the executive whose office he cleans.

But as Rio de Janeiro residents will tell you, some beaches are more equal than others.

Rio's beaches have their own personalities. Or, to put it less generously, they have their own pecking orders.

Differentiated by street names or, more commonly, by the numbers of their lifeguard posts, the various beaches have their own customs, cultures and rules. And though these rules are unwritten, they are often followed more closely than the official beach regulations posted by city authorities.

A common question Cariocas will ask one another is, 'Which beach do you go to?' It's not just making conversation. It's shorthand, a quick way for Rio residents to learn something about the other person.

The beaches of Copacabana, particularly near lifeguard Postos 3 and 4, attract a diverse local crowd but also a fair share of sunburned foreign tourists and sex workers hoping to do business with them. Posto 7 in Ipanema is the surfer scene and the beach for many residents of Rio's favelas. Gays and lesbians gravitate to the area around Posto 8, with its trademark rainbow flag. Posto 11 in

Leblon has become the beach for families and couples, while the sporting crowd shows off their football, volleyball and *frescobol* skills at Posto 10.

And then there is Posto 9. Here is where you'll find the beautiful people, the hipsters and the ageing remnants of the intellectual left. Posto 9 is home to those who consider themselves the crème de la crème – and we're not talking about sunscreen here.

You won't be kicked off the sand if you show up where you don't fit in. Brazilians are class-conscious, but not boorish. But you might not be made to feel welcome either, and this rule applies to fellow Brazilians as well as to foreigners.

There are some tips to blending in: Skimpy swimsuits are not just acceptable but even encouraged, for both sexes. But women who try to go topless are scorned, another example of the sometimes complicated Brazilian take on sexuality. Skip the beach towel; Cariocas do not use them. Leave the book at home; the story of the day is unfolding before your eyes. Be liberal in applying the sunblock but judicious in ingesting the caipirinhas. Fear the waves, but trust the vendors.

Finally, find a beach where you feel comfortable and chances are you will be welcomed. That's what Cariocas do.

Leme

Sitting at the bottom of the Morro do Leme is Leme beach – one of the only areas where lush rainforest still backs on to the sands. In 1990, the hill was declared an environmental protection area and is now a refuge to 90 bird species and four native endangered flora species. The Morro now belongs to the military and for R$4 it's possible to wander up through the army buildings of the **Forte Do Leme**. It's open on weekends and holidays between 9am and 6pm. The **Forte do Vigia** sits at the top, from where there's an excellent panorama of the entrance to Guanabara bay, Sugar Loaf mountain, Niterói, Cristo Redentor and the offshore island of Cotunduba. It also gives a fantastic view along the arch of the four kilometres of Leme and Copacabana beach.

The huge Avenida Princesa Isabel, which runs off the beachfront road, Avenida Atlântica, marks the end of Leme beach and the start of one of the most famous stretches of sand in the world, Copacabana beach. Riotur has a tourist information centre at Avenida Princesa Isabel 183 (2541 7522). Go here for good information and maps of the area.

Copacabana

For many people Copacabana is still the fantasy destination in Rio, but the reality is rather different. Much of the old-fashioned glamour of Copacabana has now disappeared, supplanted by endless cheap chain stores, a glut of traffic, a thriving red-light district, a constant background of petty crime and a general feeling of decay. On the other hand, there are still stacks of good-value restaurants, some great little bars and buzzing nightlife, a world famous hotel and, of course, the amazing three-kilometre stretch of beach.

Copacabana was a tiny fishing village cut off from the rest of Rio until the opening of the Tunel Velho in 1892, which links it with Botafogo and completely changed the layout of the city. On 6 July of that year it was made an official barrio or district. Now Copacabana has a barely credible 400,000 inhabitants and is one of the most densely populated neighbourhoods in the world.

The district came into its own in the 1930s and '40s when it became a playground for Hollywood's rich and famous. These glamorous sojourns were popularised in the 1933 film *Flying Down to Rio* in which Fred Astaire and Ginger Rogers skipped the light fantastic to such tunes as 'The Carioca'. This old world glamour is still in evidence in Rio in the form of the magnificent **Copacabana Palace Hotel** (*see p42*), about a third of the

Copacabana: the world's busiest beach?

way down the beach from Leme. The gleaming white French neoclassical façade of this building is an unmistakable sight on the Avenida Atlântica. Inspired by hotels in the French Riviera, Copacabana Palace opened its doors in 1923 and has been welcoming everyone from royalty to footballers (often classed as the same thing in Rio) ever since. To get the feel of it without staying there, splash out on a Sunday brunch in the Pergula restaurant.

Almost opposite the hotel is the gay section of Copacabana beach, marked by the rainbow flags. Demarcation on the beach is a common theme in Zona Sul (see p76 **Find your place in the sun**). Another great symbol of Copacabana is its wavy pavement – an early 1930s design by the prolific Roberto Burle Marx, based on Portuguese mosaics.

At the far end of Copacabana beach are the 12-metre- (39-foot-) thick walls of the **Forte de Copacabana** and the **Army History Museum** inside. Built on the **Ponta de Copacabanca**, the site of the old Nossa Senhora de Copacabana chapel, the building is more or less how it looked when it was built in 1914. The fort also serves as a good spot to sit and watch the activity in Guanabara Bay, away from the crowds of Copacabana. The area is known as **Posto 6**, though there's no actual lifeguard point here. There are, however, the last remnants of

Copacabana's fishing village. Local fisherman leave here on their boats at dawn and sell their catch here when they return at around 8am.

It's not possible to walk around the coast to reach the neighbouring district of **Arpoador**. Instead, a short walk past the busy surf shops on Rua Francisco Otaviano, and a left turn through the **Parque Garota de Ipanema** brings you to **Posto 7** and **Praia do Arpoador** (Arpoador beach).

Arpoador

Arpoador rock is one of the best places to watch the sun set over Ipanema. Walking up it gives a picture-postcard shot of Ipanema and Leblon beach. To the left of the rock is the small, hidden-away **Praia do Diabo** (Devil's Beach). Named for its vicious waves, it's a favourite with the local surfers but also makes a pleasant place to sit and is normally a lot fresher and less crowded than neighbouring Arpoador. As well as the surfers, there's always a crowd of muscle men toning their already incredibly toned bodies on the old-school beach gym overlooking the beach.

Arpoador beach is a favourite with families and many come down from the local favela **Cantagalo**, which you can see clinging to the mountainside opposite. It can get a bit hectic but it's a good place to watch local kids jumping

Ipanema.

off the rocks into the calmer sea or fishermen whiling away the hours waiting for a catch. Arpoador actually means 'fisherman with a harpoon' and the area gets its name thanks to the abundance of fish in the area. It's much better for swimming on this side but does also get crowded with local surfers. To join in, rent a surfboard on the beach from Jean at Surf Favela. He's an interesting fellow who runs a surf club that brings together a mixture of local kids regardless of background or wealth – a rare thing in Rio.

Walking down the paved area from Arpoador leads to Avenida Vieira Souto and the start of Ipanema beach. Note again the pavement, built soon after the one in Copacabana.

Ipanema

Beautiful people cruise up and down Ipanema every day, and at the weekend it's absolutely packed. The seafront is backed by tree-lined streets with small cafés, shops and restaurants.

Nowhere is demarcation on the beach more evident than on Ipanema. The rainbow flags mark the start of the gay area that continues up the whole of Rua Farme de Amoedo opposite. Continuing along the beach you get to **Posto 9**, formerly a hippy hangout but now dominated by the hip and happening set. The current height of fashion is the area by the tallest palm tree, but it's always subject to change. You'll be hard-pushed to squeeze yourself in here at the weekend as Cariocas mingle to check each other out and catch up with what's going on.

Posto 9 is a hive of activity. Young lads in *sungas* line the waters edge to play *futevôlei*; people skate, run or cycle along the seafront; and it's possible to hire bikes from Special Bike (Rua Teixero de Melo 53, 2513 3951, www.special bikebotafogo.com.br, R$15 per hour) or many other places. If you're not feeling that active, all along the beach from Leme to Leblon are kiosks where you can sit and sip a drink. *Agua de coco* (coconut water) drunk straight from a green coconut is highly recommended: Carioca's swear by it as a hangover cure.

For a day at the beach, head to one of the many *barracas* (tents), where you can rent a chair for about R$4 a day. They also sell drinks and some food, but Ipanema beach, and especially Posto 9, is packed with food sellers offering everything from pineapple and brownies to the Brazilian staple *açai*, each salesperson with his or her own unique selling chant. The Uruguay kiosk serves a mean sausage sandwich.

'Ipanema' is an Indian word for dangerous water. The currents here can be very strong so take extra care when a red flag is flying. Even seasoned Cariocas have sometimes been swept out to sea. Lifeguards are in constant

Flip-flop don't stop

If proof were needed of just how present Havaianas are in Brazilian life, it comes in the name. For Brazilians rarely speak of *chinelos* (flip-flops). They speak of Havaianas. Like Sellotape and Hoover, the brand name has become synonymous with the object.

In a city where a T-shirt with sleeves is considered formal wear, everyone owns a pair of these rubber sandals. Stylish, durable and simple, they are an indispensable part of the Carioca wardrobe.

That is partly because they are so cheap (the basic models sell for less than US$4), partly because they look good with just about anything and partly because they are perfect for Rio's hot climate. Next time you're at the beach see how many pairs you can spot before you lose count.

The sandals were first made in 1962 and are based on Japanese Zori shoes. The difference was that Havaianas were made from 100 per cent rubber. Those early models comprised a basic white sole with coloured straps but that changed in the early 1990s when a cash crisis forced the company into making a monochrome model.

The success of the so-called Havaiana Top prompted them to explore new directions and the factory in Alagoas now produces 39 different styles, including high-heeled sandals for the ladies, tiny ones for infants and special lines designed by some of Brazil's most irreverent cartoonists. Periodically, the company produces exclusive offers such as the diamond-encrusted versions for jewellers H Stern that cost more than US$30,000.

Forty-five years later, 3.7 billion pairs have been sold, a number that is increasing by 160 million pairs per year. What was made for Brazilian beaches are now sold to 83 countries, some of which are landlocked.

Sightseeing

Leblon.

watch at the Postos for a reason. The strong currents generally mean that the water around the beaches in Zona Sul is cleaner than the rest of Rio, although it does have off-days, particularly after heavy rain. Local papers publish a useful daily report on water quality and surf conditions.

An important daily ritual around Posto 9 is the marking of sunset. A few minutes beforehand, locals stop and begin to watch, cold beer or caipirinha in hand, and cheer as the sun goes down over the famous **Dois Irmãos** mountain at the end of Leblon.

A good day to be in Ipanema is Sunday when Avenida Vieria Souto is closed off to traffic and, on a sunny day, the beach fills to bursting point with Cariocas and tourists. Sundays also see the **Feira Hippie** (*see p133*) come to **Praça General Osório**, a block back from the beach up Rua Teixeira de Melo, selling local handicrafts.

A walk up **Rua Vinicius de Moraes** takes you to the restaurant now named **Garota de Ipanema** (*see p127*), which will forever be connected with the song that introduced Bossa Nova to the world.

Just past Posto 10, the canal and gardens of **Jardim de Alah** mark the junction between Ipanema and Leblon. The seafront road changes its name here from Avenida Vieira Souto to Avenida Delfim Moreira.

Leblon

Away from the crowds of Posto 9, Leblon beach is much more tranquil and generally dominated by young families who live in the area's affluent neighbourhood. There's even **Baixo Bebê**, a special section for babies and toddlers (*see p156*). It's also good place to get a massage from one of the local masseurs that set up their stalls under many of its shady trees.

Away from the beach, Leblon is a pleasant and an easy place to wander round with a host of exclusive boutiques and the fancy new fashion centre, **Shopping Leblon** (*see p132*). The area has a great and steadily expanding range of restaurants and bars. They're mostly a little more expensive than those in other areas, but fashionable with it.

At the end of the beach at Leblon is another surf hangout where the waves crash against the rocks under **Avenida Niemeyer** and the Morro Dois Irmãos. If the surf's good – and it often is – the **Mirante do Leblon** is a perfect lookout from which to see the daredevil skills of the boardriders below. Leave the beach and take a stroll up Avenida Niemeyer to get there, then grab a drink and a snack from a kiosk and take it all in.

Incidentally, the houses you can see crawling up the Dois Irmãos are part of the favela Vidigal.

The Lake

In Rio, even the pedalos are cool.

With such famous beaches, it's maybe a surprise that Rio should make so much of its lake; but in the neighbourhoods that surround it are some of the city's most upscale streets and some of its best restaurants, bars and cultural spaces. Altogether more mellow than the beach districts, the area still vibrates with life, from the runners round the lake to the forests running up the hills to the favelas at the top.

Lagoa Rodrigo de Freitas

More than just a lake, the Lagoa is an expansive leisure area surrounded by mountains, apartment blocks and some of Rio's most exclusive sport and social clubs. Well utilised by local residents and visitors for running around, boating in and gazing at, the lake is a valuable addition to the variety of Rio.

Before the arrival of the Portuguese, Tupinambá Indians named the lake Sacopenapan, after the heron-like birds that wade in its waters. When the Portuguese arrived they used the surrounding land to grow sugar cane and at one time there were three sugar mills nearby. Other factories followed, manufacturing textiles, gunpowder and food. In the 1920s, a large landfill and drainage project was undertaken to smarten the area up and the swampy margins of the lake were transformed into prime building land. Desirable residences began to spring up and with them three favelas.

In the favela removal programmes of the 1960s and 1970s these slums were cleared and the residents were rehoused. Cidade de Deus, the favela-cum-housing estate made famous by the film of the same name, was originally populated by former residents of these slums. Now the lake is bordered by some of Rio's most sought after neighbourhoods and the Sacopenapan herons still remain – joined now by anglers standing knee-deep in the water or drifting around in small skiffs.

A handful of famous sports clubs have facilities for training their rowing and sailing crews here and the teams can be seen putting in their early morning training during the week and competing at weekends. Several of Rio's private leisure clubs are situated close by and the two islands of the Lagoa are home to the most exclusive of these, **Clube Piraquê** and **Clube Caiçaras**. The lake was the site for the canoeing, waterskiing and rowing competitions in the Pan American games, with a grandstand viewing area built especially for the event.

For those who like to keep their feet on dry land the 7.5-kilometre (4.5-mile) track that circles the lake is heavily used by joggers, cyclists and skaters as well as by many who come for a stroll or to visit the bustling restaurants and recreation facilities of the area.

At the beginning of each December, an elaborate ceremony accompanies the lighting of a spectacular illuminated Christmas tree, the largest floating decoration in the world. Until the end of December, visitors who wish to see the tree close up can take boat trips operating from the pontoon next to the Arab restaurant (see p116) nightly.

The two most popular areas of the lake are around **Parque Cantagalo** (see p82) on the Ipanema side and **Parque Patins** (see p83) on the Gávea shore. As well as a play area and sports facilities, there are a number of kiosks at Parque Cantagalo with food and live music. The swan boats that bob about the lake can be hired from the small pier here. One of the most agreeable places in Rio, Parque Patins bustles with joggers, skaters, cyclists, walkers and diners – its biggest draw is the cluster of kiosks. Here they have grown into open-air restaurants with a range of gastronomic offerings and live music to suit just about every taste. In the evenings the area gets even more lively. First, the families arrive: parents eat, drink and chat,

A gentle end to the day: sunset reflected in the **Lagoa Rodrigo de Freitas**. *See p81.*

oblivious to their children who hurtle about on bicycles, running over unwary pedestrians. As the families leave and the night wears on, tables become harder to find and the hum of conversation rises in competition with the MPB, jazz, samba and choro from the talented musicians who play here. Parque Patins is also home to a busy heliport, offering a variety of sightseeing helicopter tours. Prices range from R\$150 per person for a six to seven-minute flight to R\$875 for a comprehensive hour-long tour. For details, contact Helisight (2511 2141, www.helisight.com.br).

Less busy, but worth a visit for the view alone, is **Parque Catacumba** (*see p83*), which also holds the amazing collection of the **Fundação Eva Klabin** (*see below*). Parque Catacumba takes its name from the catacombs of its original inhabitants, who were fleeing slaves, and was a hillside favela until it was cleared during the government rehousing programmes of the 1970s. Today the park is a sculpture garden, exhibiting works by many respected artists including Franz Weissmann, Bruno Gioni and Mario Agostinelli. The trail to the top of Pico da Sacopã takes about 25 minutes and the view from the top is stunning. Display boards along the trail have information about the flora, fauna and history of the park, with English translations. The path is a one-way loop that starts at the top left-hand side of the sculpture garden.

The Fundação Eva Klabin holds an amazing private collection of more than 1,000 pieces, including paintings, furniture, ceramics, silver and oriental rugs. It includes many items from ancient Egypt and Rome, pre-Columbian treasures from Peru, objects from the Chinese dynasties as well as important European pieces and examples from Brazil. Entrance for guided tours only.

Fundação Eva Klabin

Avenida Epitácio Pessoa 2480, Lagoa (3202 8550/ www.evaklabin.org.br). Metro Cantagalo/461, 415, 473 bus. **Open** by guided tour only 2.30pm & 4pm Wed-Sun. **Admission** R\$10; free Fri. **Map** p249 F15.

Parque Cantagalo

Avenida Epitácio Pessoa, Lagoa. Metro Cantagalo/ 415, 461, 473 bus. **Map** p249 F16.

Parque Catacumba & Morro dos Cabritos

Avenida Epitácio Pessoa, Lagoa. Metro Cantagalo/ 415, 473 bus. **Open** 8am-5pm daily. **Map** p249 F15.

Parque Patins

Avenida Borges Medeiros. Bus 157, 461. **Map** p248 C14.

Jardim Botânico

A leafy well-to-do residential neighbourhood, Jardim Botânico (which refers to both the district and the botanical garden) has become increasingly popular with artists defecting from Santa Teresa. Wandering its streets the visitor can stumble across hidden shops, studios and some of the most sophisticated bars and restaurants in the city. Each August many of the artists open their studio doors to the public for two weekends. (Visit www.circuito dasartes.com.br for details.)

A morning or afternoon visit to the botanical garden is well worth the cab ride from any part of town and can easily be combined with lunch at **Couve Flor** (*see p114*); shopping for handicrafts at the fair-trade shop **O Sol** (*see p147*); and, on weekends, a trip to one of the races held at the **Jockey Club** (*see p204*).

In a city that's already blessed with more that its fair share of green and pleasant spaces, **Jardim Botânico** (*see p86*) takes its place as the jewel in the crown. Indeed, it was originally a royal plant nursery that was laid out according to the whims of Prince Dom João VI. Wanting to expand the collection quickly, he offered payment to anyone who brought along seeds from exotic plants or spices to the nursery. Today the gardens are home to an extensive range of flora with over 8,000 species of plants and over 5,500 trees from Brazil and around the globe.

The gardens have now matured into a lush haven of tranquility. Wide shady avenues are lined by skyscraping imperial palms, some now over 150 years old. The scale of these trees is staggering and it's common to see visitors dwarfed by their immensity, staring up in awe. Monkeys and many native birds, including hummingbirds, toucans and parakeets, inhabit the park and visitors will have a good chance of spotting them while wandering around.

Many paths in the garden gravitate towards the Lago Frei Leandro. The area around this small lake makes a good resting place and offers a stunning view of the towering imperial palms overshadowed by Corcovado mountain itself. Equally impressive at ground level are the gigantic floating leaves of the Amazonian water lily Victoria Regia – they can reach a diameter of

Lagoa Rodrigo de Freitas. *See p81.*

Rambling in Rio Ipanema & Lagoa

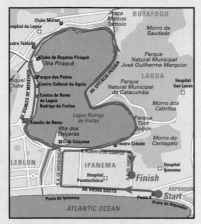

Around the Lagoa and Ipanema beach are some of Rio's most beautiful neighbourhoods and along this trail you'll find spots on the beach for future sunbathing, a whole load of exercise opportunities, a cluster of restaurants and some top shops. Pick up the trail from anywhere along this circular walk, or to really fit in, jog or rent a bike. The track around the Lagoa is just over five kilometres, and it's in great condition – ideal for walking, running or riding on.

The walk starts as Arpoador turns to Ipanema, at **Posto 8** life-guard post (just a couple of blocks from two bike rental shops, *see pxxx*). Follow the pavement along Avenida Veira Souto, past two volleyball nets (open to the public during the day) and the area of the beach around the end of Farme de Amoedo street, well known as a popular GLS (gay, lesbian and *simpatizantes*) spot, to the eternally hip **Posto 9**.

The crowd thickens as you reach Posto 9, with a young and hip crowd of beautiful people whose patch extends as far as the row of coconut trees in front of the Caesar Park hotel. The *coqueirão*, the tallest of these trees, is a popular meeting spot for locals, especially college kids and young families. The kiosk just before the row of trees is one of the few kiosks on the beach that remains open all night.

Continue along the beach to **Posto 10**, crossing the street here to follow Rua Anibal de Mendoça up to the Lagoa. Once you

cross Rua Epitácio Pessoa, take a right onto the jogging track or bicycle path.

This is the area of stretch and workout stands, and further down the path, as it curves to the left around the Lagoa, are small, fenced-in public football courts. At around 4pm, young locals who live in the area often organise a game. If there's room, they'll be happy to bring you on the pitch, but if you've got two left feet, consider instead a less competitive diversion – the kiosks in **Parque Cantagalo** rent duck and swan-shaped paddle boats.

Farther down, the path bends sharply to the left and then to the right around the **Ponta do Pires**, about one third of the way around the Lagoa. Soon after the point is the boathouse of the Flamengo rowing team. Serious rowers can stop by here between 10am and noon on weekdays to find out about taking a scull out or joining a crew.

Passing the boathouse, the trees clear to give a lovely view across the Lagoa. Looking almost directly across, you'll see the tall palm trees of the **Jardim Botânico**. Scanning to the left of the trees, you'll notice the **Jockey Club** and the Rocinha favela creeping over the ridge towards the neighbourhood of Gávea below. The view remains open as you pass the far end of the Lagoa. Looking across the water to the left you'll see the neighbourhood of Ipanema – an ideal photo spot.

Next is the exclusive private **Piraquê Naval Club** and just beyond there are more football courts. Larger and floodlit, games here generally start later and are more organised, but if you're lucky, there might be room for just one more.

Arab Quiosque (*see p116*) is part of a small cluster of popular restaurants and night clubs that sit on the edge of the Lagoa, next to a heliport. Continuing around along the south of the lake there's a small skate park on your right opposite the private **Clube Caiçaras**. It's a public park, but some of the city's best free-style skaters hang out here on the weekends.

Complete the loop of the lake and cross Epitácio Pessoa at the Shell station onto Rua Alberto de Campos. Follow this road and turn right onto Farme de Almoedo, which leads to **Beach Sucos**, a juice bar on the corner of Visconde de Piraja, for an energy-boosting mango juice without sugar. One block to the left is the bike rental store.

2.5 metres (8 feet) and support a weight of up to 40 kilograms (88 pounds).

Elsewhere in the gardens, make for the orchid house where you'll find a collection of over 600 species from all over Central and South America. A 600-metre (1,950-foot) 'Mata Atlântica' trail wanders through a stretch of Atlantic forest vegetation typical of that which covered the region before the arrival of the Portuguese and their axes.

Other delights include a Japanese garden, an area displaying edible plants, a zone with plants from the Amazon, a rose garden, a sensorial garden and the carnivorous plant house. A different kind of attraction is the recently opened **Espaço Cultural Tom Jobim** (2239 4562). Dedicated to the memory of one of the garden's most famous admirers,

it holds frequent open concerts with respected performers. Look out for the **Museu do Meio Ambiente** (Museum of the Environment) scheduled to open its doors in 2008.

Further down Rua Jardim Botânico, the lush gardens of **Parque Lage** were laid out in 1849 by the English landscape architect John Tyndale. The combination of Victorian design along with the verdant tropical vegetation lends the place a jungle feel. The mansion was built in the 1920s and was later owned by Henrique Lage, a wealthy ship owner. It's now an art school, exhibition space and home to **Café du Lage** (*see p128*), a small establishment that's become famous for its weekend brunches.

A steep path to the Cristo Redentor on Corcovado starts in Parque Lage and takes

The **Jardim Botânico**, overlooked by the Corcovado mountain. *See p83.*

about two hours to ascend. Assaults have occurred on the trail, though, so it's better to go with a guide or in a group and to leave valuables at home.

Jardim Botânico

Rua Jardim Botânico 920, Jardim Botânico (3874 1808/www.jbrj.gov.br). Bus 172, 511, 521. **Open** 8am-5pm daily. *Guided tours* free on weekdays by prior arrangement. **Closed** Christmas Day & New Year's Day; special hours during Carnival. **Admission** R$4. **Map** p248 B14.

Parque Lage

Rua Jardim Botânico 414. Bus 503A, 592. **Open** 8am-6pm daily. **Admission** free. **Map** p248 D13.

Gávea

Gávea is a bustling residential and commercial neighbourhood. The main thoroughfare, Rua Marquês de São Vicente, leads past upscale shopping centres, residences, schools, the **Pontifícia Universidade Católica (PUC)**, the **Solar de Grandjean de Montigny** (*see below*), the **Fundação Planetário** (*see below*), the **Instituto Moreira Salles** (*see p167*) and the **Museu** and **Parque da Cidade** (*see below*), on to the not-so-luxurious favelas of Rocinha and Parque da Cidade.

At the start of Rua Marquês da São Vicente is the **Praça Santos Dumont**, a small park with shady trees, fountains and a playground. It's flanked on one side by the Jockey Club and on the other by the popular streetside restaurants **Braseiro** (*see p128*) and **Hipódromo** (*see p130*). On weekend nights things get very lively as the square becomes a meeting place for a young party crowd. It's also host to a Friday produce market and a flea market on Sundays that runs from 9am to 5pm.

Inside the Hipódromo once or twice a month, and every weekend in the run up to Christmas, there are clothes and accessories and a whole lot more at the **Babilônia Feira Hype** (*see below*). It's an eclectic mix of alfresco shopping, eating, live music, bouncy castles and horse racing. The choice is excellent – some of Rio's trendiest designers started their clothing lines in these tented stands and bargains abound. Check the website or call ahead for the date of the next event.

Further down the Rua Marquês de São Vicente is the former residence of French architect Grandjean de Montigny, who moved to Brazil in 1816 and was subsequently responsible for the design of many of Rio's impressive public buildings. He designed the **Solar de Grandjean de Montigny** (*see below*) in Brazilian neoclassical style, with Tuscan columns and breezy verandas.

Surrounded now by the tall trees and modern buildings of the PUC university campus, the space is used for temporary art exhibitions. The Solar contains a small library of art, architecture and history materials that's open to the public.

Close by is the **Fundação Planetário** with two state-of-the-art domes, that are open to the public on weekends and holidays, and which offers free telescope viewing sessions of the southern sky at 6.30pm and 8.30pm each Tuesday, Wednesday and Thursday. In the same building is the **Museu do Universo** (Museum of the Universe), an excellent, imaginative museum with a wealth of interactive displays. Curiously enough (or perhaps appropriately, considering the various connotations of the word 'star') the Planetarium is also home to the very fashionable restaurant and dance club, 00 (*see p170 and p189*).

Rambling up hill from Gávea into the mountains of the Tijuca forest is the beautiful, peaceful **Parque da Cidade** (*see below*) with its abundance of trails and picnic spots. It's also home to the **Museu Histórico da Cidade**, which houses a collection of important paintings, porcelain and other pieces related to the history of the city. Next to the museum is a small chapel (the museum curator has the key) whose walls are painted with a bizarre and controversial mural by the artist Carlos Bastos. The mural depicts scenes from the life of Saint John and uses famous Brazilian personalities as the characters (not all of whom are in the same league of holiness as the apostle). The painting was never finished: the Catholic Church objected to some of the personalities used and these were subsequently painted over.

Babilônia Feira Hype

Tribuna C do Jockey Club Brasileiro, Gávea (2267 0066/www.babiloniahype.com.br). Bus 172, 511, 571. **Open** 2-10pm, dates vary. **Admission** R$4. **Map** p248 B15.

Fundação Planetário & Museu do Universo

Rua Vice-Governador Rubens Berardo 100, Gávea (2274 0096/www.rio.rj.gov.br/planetario). Bus 157, 432, 571. **Open** *Museum* 10am-5pm Tue-Fri. **Admission** R$6. **Map** p258 A16.

Parque da Cidade & Museu Histórico da Cidade

Estrada de Santa Marinha 505, Gávea (2512 2353/ www.rio.rj.gov.br/culturas). Bus 592, 593. **Open** *Museum* 11am-4pm Tue-Fri; 11am-3pm Sat, Sun. *Park* 8am-5pm daily. **Admission** free. **Map** p253 F2.

Solar de Grandjean de Montigny

Rua Marquês de São Vicente 225, Gávea (3527 1435). Bus 158, 523, 592. **Open** 10am-5.30pm Mon-Fri. **Admission** free. **Map** p253 F1.

Zona Oeste

The best of the west – wild and otherwise.

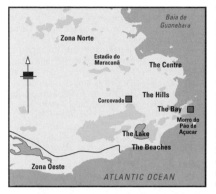

Watching the sun slip behind the landmark mountains at the end of Leblon beach is a Rio must-do, but surprisingly few visitors to Rio venture west to see what lies beyond the picture postcard backdrop. In short, there's a lot more to the city than meets the eye.

For most people, the main draw is **Barra da Tijuca**, known locally as Barra (and pronounced BA-ha). Zona Sul diehards will tell you that Barra isn't even worthy of the name Rio. That is not what the statistics say, since increasing numbers of Rio's residents choose to make Barra home. The place is a strange mix of Brazil's *nouveaux riches* (very rich, in many cases) and ordinary middle-class families, sick of the cramped apartments and the crime elsewhere in the city.

Sunset boulevards: **Barra da Tijuca** stretches into the distance.

The population of Barra grew by 44 per cent between the censuses of 1990 and 2000, with the rate of growth speeding up towards the end of the decade. Today, that development continues apace, with new homes and office blocks being built not only in Barra, but in the neighbouring *bairros* of **Recreio** and **Vargem Grande**.

These areas might lack character – but they do have space and open views. The plan for the Metro to come this far is still a pipe dream, so currently the best way to get to Barra and beyond is by bus. Services from the Zona Sul and Centro are frequent – any service marked Barra da Tijuca will do. A taxi from the Zona Sul to Barra Shopping will cost around R$30.

São Conrado

Technically, São Conrado is part of the Zona Sul, but it lies the far side of the great divide. There's a choice of two routes into São Conrado from the Zona Sul, one considerably more scenic than the other but both prone to serious delays during rush hour. The main road, the Auto Estrada Lagoa-Barra, leaves the Zona Sul in Leblon, and passes through the 1.5-kilometre **Túnel Zuzu Angel**, emerging in São Conrado directly below the **Rocinha** favela.

The second route, infinitely preferable if you're expecting a delay, is along Avenida Niemeyer, from the western end of Leblon beach. This road snakes around the foot of the Dois Irmãos mountains and the Vidigal favela, taking you along the coast and past some of the 'love motels' closest to the Zona Sul and the Sheraton Rio hotel.

The divisions between Rio's haves and have-nots are well documented, but the contrasts are seldom seen as starkly as they are in São Conrado. Home to the **Gávea Golf Club** (*see p198*), one of Rio's most exclusive establishments, and the **Fashion Mall** (*see p132*), one of the city's glitziest shopping malls, São Conrado is dominated by Rocinha, possibly Latin America's largest favela.

While Rocinha is officially home to 56,000 people, in reality the population is probably three times that size. Although Rocinha is now so well established that it's counted as a *bairro* in its own right, it continues to grow as yet more people arrive from the north-east and from Brazil's interior, in search of a better life. The community now has its own branches of fast-food restaurants and banks and some shopping chains have established outlets there.

The little church, **Igreja de São Conrado**, which gave the *bairro* its name, still stands above the main road on the right-hand side as you head towards Barra. It dates from the beginning of the 20th century, and its

construction was funded by Conrado Jacob Niemeyer, who owned the surrounding land at that time and who gave his last name to the main avenue. Another Niemeyer, the architect Oscar, also left his mark on the area with the Casa das Canoas (*see below*) of 1951, now seen as one of the most important examples of Brazilian modernism. It houses a permanent exhibition of his furniture designs.

Whether passing through on the way to Barra, or stopping in São Conrado, look up for the arresting sight of hang-gliders and paragliders catching the thermals around the stark face of **Pedra da Gávea**. Novices are welcome to give it a go, with tandem flights launching from the ramp on **Pedra Bonita** (*see p198*). Depending on the weather, between ten and 30 minutes later, pilot and passenger should land on the grass above **Praia do Pepino**, at the far end of São Conrado. The beach in itself may look inviting, but the water is almost always polluted.

Casa das Canoas
Estrada das Canoas 2310, São Conrado (3322 3591/ www.niemeyer.org.br). Bus 710. **Open** 1-5pm Tue-Sun. **Admission** R$8; R$4 concessions; free under-10s & over-65s. **Map** 253 D2.

Joatinga

At the western end of São Conrado, the road disappears into a tunnel once again, reappearing on the *elevado*, a double-decker highway on stilts over the ocean, which hugs the base of Pedra da Gávea. An alternative is to take the **Estrada do Joá**, which winds up through the trees over the lower slopes of the mountain. The views back over São Conrado and the sea are spectacular. Hidden away from sight is the **Praia da Joatinga** (Joatinga beach), largely empty on weekdays. The beach is reached by car from the Estrada do Joá, but access down to the sand can be difficult for the elderly, the infirm and for small children. At the tip of the peninsula, reached by a footbridge, stands the private **Costa Brava Club**, overlooked by **La Suite** hotel (*see p48*) and the Rio residence of a certain Edson Arantes do Nascimento (more commonly known as Pelé).

Barra da Tijuca

Often referred to as the Miami of the south, Barra da Tijuca is both loved and hated by Cariocas in equal measure – including by those who live there. Emerging from the road from São Conrado a large poster bears the entreaty, 'Smile, you're in Barra'. After a quick glimpse of the sea, a multi-lane highway stretches ahead towards a shimmering forest of tower blocks, shopping malls and advertising hoardings. Car

Wet and wild: **Joatinga beach**.

ownership is taken for granted here. There is nowhere to walk in Barra, except of course along the beach, which is the biggest – and in the eyes of many people, the best – in Rio.

There are two main thoroughfares through Barra – Avenida das Américas, which runs in an almost straight line through the centre of Barra and into Recreio, and Avenida Lúcio Costa, still popularly known as Avenida Sernambetiba (although the name has officially been changed), which runs along the beach, parallel to Avenida das Américas.

A third great thoroughfare, Avenida Ayrton Senna, takes traffic inland from Barra, eventually joining the Linha Amarela – a quick cut through the mountains to the centre of town and the international airport.

Close to the junction of Avenida Ayrton Senna and Avenida das Américas is the relative calm of **Bosque da Barra** (*see p91*), a well-maintained environmental refuge, full of bird-life and home to many small animals. There are trails, a cycle track and a flower-filled lake, where herons can often be seen. The beach is

The urban jungle

As if the spectacular coastline was not enough, Rio is also home to the world's largest urban forest, the **Floresta da Tijuca**. The Floresta is, however, only one section of the **Parque Nacional da Tijuca** (2492 2252), open to the public daily from 8am to 5pm and free to enter.

The biggest and best known part of the park, which covers a total area of 39.5 square kilometres (15 square miles), is the **Serra Carioca**; anyone visiting Corcovado and Cristo Redentor passes through this sector. Even with the large volume of tourist traffic, the tranquility and lushness of the surroundings are a welcome contrast to the hustle and bustle below. The **Vista Chinesa**, from which there is a great view of the city, and the **Mesa do Imperador** are two other landmarks in this area.

But for real peace and quiet, the Floresta da Tijuca sector is the place to go. Two imposing pillars mark the entrance from the Alto da

Barra's redeeming feature – 18 kilometres (11 miles) of prime white sand stretching as far the eye can see and fading into the distance where the mountains meet the sea. Even in high summer, there's always room for another deckchair. The crowds thin out the further west you go. **Praia do Pepê**, at the beginning of the beach, is one of the most fashionable sections, widely popular with the young and pretty. Pepê, who the beach is named after, was a radical-sports champion and national hero who died in a hang-gliding accident.

The beach is a magnet for water sports enthusiasts, principally surfers, windsurfers and kite surfers. A lot of surf schools have set up shop along the beach and many offer a trial lesson (*see p201*). For surfers of all kinds, often the biggest battle is getting out through the waves in the first place. While the water is usually clean, the beach can be very treacherous because of strong currents and a powerful

undertow. Observe warning notices and flags, but above all, watch what the locals are doing. If nobody is in the water, it's probably for a good reason. The **Surf Bus** (*see p91*) is useful for choosing the right place to take the plunge, as it takes the scenic route from Largo do Machado in the Zona Sul, passing along Rio's beaches as far as **Prainha**. The bus has special stowage space for boards, and is equipped with a sound system, DVDs and a minibar service.

The first section of the beach is backed by extensive condominium and hotel development. Both of Barra's five-star hotels are located here, facing on to the beach. Beyond the turn-off for Avenida Ayrton Senna, the beach is wilder, until it reaches Recreio. During the summer months, the beach road is one-way only at weekends, with traffic travelling in the Recreio direction.

The far end of Barra beach is part of the Reserva de Marapendi, an ecological reserve,

Boa Vista, which runs between Tijuca and Barra da Tijuca. The road then wends its way around a one-way system past lovely waterfalls, huge trees and overwhelming greenery. In places, the environment is almost prehistoric, with only water, wood and giant ferns. There are views across the forest canopy to the sea beyond that are totally unimpeded by any sign of urban development.

Over 1,600 plant species grow in the park, most of which is categorised as late secondary forest, replanted after the clearances of a century ago and now in an advanced state of regeneration. Rainforest rejuvenation is taken seriously – there is a nursery containing 60,000 native plant seedlings. The park is also home to many bird species and small mammals, including coati, gambá, anteater and hedgehog.

A variety of trails are marked throughout the forest, catering for all ages and conditions, although some require guides. A highlight is the trek (categorised as medium level of difficulty) up the one-kilometre **Pico da Tijuca**. The views from the top are breathtaking; it is the highest summit in Rio. There are two restaurants in this sector, both of which ooze character – **Os Esquilos** and **A Floresta** – plus several picnic areas.

The third sector of the park includes Pedra da Gávea and Pedra Bonita. Pedra da Gávea offers one of the most challenging hikes in Rio, while Pedra Bonita, a fairly gentle trek, is better known for its hang-gliding opportunities.

There is a trail guide (in Portuguese and English) called *Trilhas do Parque Nacional da Tijuca* (R$60), published by Instituto Terra Brasil and a map (R$3), both available from the souvenir shop just inside Alto da Boa Vista park entrance.

Many tour operators run trips to the park, all with English-speaking guides. Here are a few recommendations:

Indiana Jungle Tours

(2484 2279/www.indianajungle.com.br).
An ecotourism operator. In addition to jeep tours through the Floresta da Tijuca, Indiana Jungle tours can also arrange horse treks in Vargem Grande and hang-glider/parachute flights from Pedra Bonita.

Rio Adventures

(2522 5024/www.rioadventures.com)
This adventurous outfit offers several 4x4 tours of the Tijuca Forest. Guides speak English, French and Spanish and tours can be arranged with as little as 6 hours' notice.

Trilhas do Rio

(2424 5455/www.trilhasdorio.com.br).
Trilhas do Rio is an adventure and ecotourism operator, offering environmental tourism plus various sporting and adventure activities in beautiful locations throughout the city.

and as such has not been developed. The reserve is home to *jacarés* (alligators), monkeys, *capivaras* (water hogs), *gambás* (a kind of skunk) and more. Although the road continues along this stretch, there's nowhere to park and no refreshment kiosks. Access to the beach is permitted, though, so it's a good spot for getting away from it all.

Much of Barra beach is backed by the **Lagoa de Marapendi**, a brackish waterway enclosed by a tangle of mangrove swamps on which cormorants perch in large numbers. Many housing complexes on the far side of the lagoon offer a small boat service across to the beach. The lagoon offers opportunities for windsurfing, a good option for beginners who might appreciate a more sheltered environment than the open ocean.

An excellent-quality cycle track runs along the length of Barra beach and then on into Recreio. The superb views on offer to those cycling in both directions make it well worth the pedalling – hook-nosed Pedra da Gávea at one end and the Morro do Pontal at the other, with the sparkling South Atlantic right beside you all the way.

Bosque da Barra

Avenida das Américas, kilometre 7, Barra da Tijuca. (3151 3428). Bus 179, 703, 2018.
Open 6am-5pm Tue-Sun.

Surf Bus

(2539 7555/8702 2837). **Tickets** R$2.
The bus leaves Largo do Machado for Prainha at 7am, 10am, 1pm and 4pm each day. It returns from Prainha at 8.30am, 11.30am, 2.30pm and 5.30pm. At weekends, the bus only goes as far as Macumba. After 10am, there are additional stops at Rio's main hotels.

Itanhangá

Tucked away at the foot of Pedra da Gávea, most travellers are only likely to pass through

Itanhangá on the way to the **Floresta da Tijuca** (*see p90* **The urban jungle**). The leafy Estrada da Barra da Tijuca is lined with residential complexes, hidden away in the trees. Much of the left-hand side of the road as you leave Barra is taken up by the **Itanhangá Golf Club**, another of Rio's more exclusive establishments, but the real reason for coming here is the **Empório Tropical**, a true emporium of Brazilian *artesanato*, located inside the **Chácara Tropical**, a large garden centre that also has a delightful small restaurant and a coffee shop.

Empório Tropical

Rua Dom Rosalvo da Costa Rêgo 420 (2493 0394/www.chacaratropical.com.br). Bus 748, 750. **Open** 8am-5.30pm daily. **Credit** varies.

Recreio dos Bandeirantes

Things are a bit rougher and readier in Recreio – or Recreio dos Bandeirantes as it's properly known – than in Barra, although perhaps not for much longer. The construction boom reached this part of town some time ago, and the rate of development speeds up each year. That said, much of Recreio is still relatively low-rise and many residential backstreets are still unpaved, giving the place a laid-back, small-town atmosphere.

Praia dos Bandeirantes is essentially a continuation of Barra beach, but the water is more sheltered here and usually safe for swimming. At the far end, the **Morro do Pontal** divides it from the **Praia do Pontal** (also known as Macumba beach), popular with surfers and families alike. At low tide, there's a causeway linking the Morro to the beach.

Inland from the beach, the **Parque Ecológico Chico Mendes**, named after an ecologist murdered for his work, offers another sanctuary for wildlife, including *jacarés* (alligators) and *jabutis* (red-footed tortoises). The 40-hectare (99-acre) park offers guided tours, a wildlife observation tower and a children's play area.

The sightseeing highlight in Recreio, however, is the **Museu Casa do Pontal** (*see below*). This folk art museum has over 5,000 works of art in its permanent collection, dating from 1950 to the present. Many are imaginatively worked ceramic figures depicting all aspects of life – there's even an erotic section. There are also wood carvings, sculptures, mechanised tableaux and rooms dealing with folk celebrations and religious rites. Explanatory texts are in English and French as well as Portuguese. The museum is set in a large garden, specifically designed to complement the galleries.

Museu Casa do Pontal

Estrada do Pontal 3295, Recreio dos Bandeirantes (2490 3278/www.popular.art.br/museucasado pontal). Bus 703, 749. **Open** 9.30am-5pm Tue-Sun. **Closed** Mon. **Admission** R$10; R$5 concessions.

Parque Ecológico Chico Mendes

Avenida Jarbas de Carvalho 679, Recreio dos Bandeirantes (2437 6400). Bus 703, 749. **Open** 8am-5pm daily. **Admission** free.

Prainha & Grumari

Beyond Recreio, even the last vestiges of the city are left behind. The road rises around the curve of the hillside, high above the sea, then descends again to Prainha. The beach here is a favourite spot for *surfistas* from all over Brazil. It's a small cove, enclosed and picturesque, surrounded by a thickly forested hillside. Kiosks on the beach serve drinks and sandwiches and there are a couple of beach restaurants. Prainha is not recommended for surfing beginners though – experts dominate the scene here. This is the final stop for the Surf Bus (*see p91*).

After Prainha, the Avenida Estado da Guanabara continues on to Grumari. A magnificent, peaceful place with four kilometres of unspoilt golden sand, it's one of the few wilderness beaches left within the city limits. The beach is backed by a hillside clad in Atlantic rainforest, mingling with banana palms and large cacti. Buses are banned from the beach and car numbers are strictly limited, as the area is an environmental protection zone. Sometimes, waves form natural pools in the sand. **Abricó** beach, hidden away behind thick undergrowth and some big rocks at the Prainha end of Grumari, is Rio's only nudist beach. Kiosks and vans offer refreshments, but otherwise the infrastructure is much less well developed here. During the week, the beach is often deserted except for a handful of fishermen and the omnipresent surfers.

At the end of Grumari, the road climbs the hillside again – offering more gorgeous views – before descending to Guaratiba. Ahead, the salt marshes stretch into the distance. Tucked away on the Estrada da Barra da Guaratiba, as the road heads back towards Barra, is a landscape architect's dream, the **Sítio Roberto Burle Marx**. Formerly a banana plantation, this large estate was bought by landscape architect and designer Roberto Burle Marx in 1949 to house his enormous collection of plants that he'd brought back to Rio from the four corners of the globe. Marx restored the original house and the small 17th-century chapel. He died there in 1994, but had already donated the estate to the nation

The 'Miami of the South': **Barra da Tijuca.** *See p88.*

in 1985. Today visitors can walk around the house, see the large garden nursery, marvel at more than 3,500 species of plant, admire Marx's tasteful collection of *objets* and visit his studio, part of which is an old coffee warehouse, brought brick by brick from the dockside of Rio's old port.

Sítio Roberto Burle Marx
Estrada Roberto Burle Marx 2019, Barra de Guaratiba (2410 1412) Bus 854. **Open** (by guided tours only) 9.30am & 1.30pm Tue-Sun (reserve in advance 8am-4pm Mon-Fri). **Admission** R$5.

Vargem Grande

Vargem Grande is small-town Brazil at its best – and most accessible. There are horses in the main street and banana palms on the street corners. Come for a visit and see how easy it is to forget that the town sits on the fringes of a huge metropolis.

Just 20 kilometres (12.5 miles) from Barra Shopping, Vargem Grande nestles at the foot of the *serra* (mountain range). When the pace of Rio gets too much, people come here to get away from it all. The area is gradually becoming better known, though, mainly because of its Centro Gastronômico. A cluster of top-quality restaurants to suit all budgets

are scattered throughout the town (for **Quinta** and **Skunna**, *see p116 and p118 respectively*). In September every year, the town hosts an art and gastronomy festival that draws big crowds.

Vargem Grande is ideal as a base for trekking into the mountains, either on foot or on horseback. There are many stables in the area, offering lessons in both classical riding and *hipismo rural* (country-style riding). Horse treks, or *cavalgadas*, are popular here. There are trails to follow that lead through sumptuous, scented groves of avocado and banana trees, to waterfalls and into the jungle beyond. Ease incipient saddle soreness by stopping to have a beer and a *pastel* at a bar accessible only by horse or on foot, complete with a tethering post outside.

If something more lively appeals, Vargem Grande also offers Rio's two water parks – **Rio Water Planet** (*see p158*) and Wet 'n Wild, both of which offer a range of aquatic attractions for adults and children alike.

Haras Horse Shoe
Estrada do Sacurrao 498, Vargem Grande (2428 1023/www.horseshoe.com.br). Bus 703, 707. **Open** 9am-5pm Tue-Sun.
To really get along in Vargem Grande, Haras offers horse treks and lessons in both classical and country riding. Teacher Anna speaks English.

Zona Norte

A stupendous stadium and a whole city beyond.

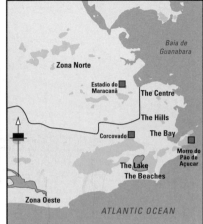

West of the Centre and north of Corcovado and the Floresta da Tijuca, Rio sprawls for miles along Guanabara Bay and between the mountains. This indeterminate area is known as the Zona Norte, a part of the city that many visitors only see when passing through on the way to and from the international airport. It feels a world away from the golden beaches and glamorous hotels of the Zona Sul. The people in the Zona Norte tend to be poorer, the buildings smaller and there are more favelas. Crime is also more prevalent here than in the better-policed Zona Sul. That said, the vast majority of people living in the Zona Norte are good natured, law-abiding citizens and there are several places that really do demand a visit. The key is to blend in (wear plain clothes, leave valuables and jewellery behind, keep cameras and maps hidden), walk purposefully and don't wander too far off the beaten track.

Maracanã

If there's one place that tourists will make a pilgrimage to in the north of the city, it's the iconic **Maracanã** football stadium in Tijuca. Built in 1950, the Estádio Jornalista Mario Filho, as it's officially called, is still the biggest in the world and holds the record for the highest attendance at a football match: 199,854 people watched Uruguay beat Brazil in the decisive

match of the 1950 World Cup here. These days, with new safety regulations, the maximum capacity is a still stupendous 96,000.

A tour of the stadium takes in the changing rooms and warm-up areas and English-speaking staff are available along the way to answer questions. The turf is immaculate and the stadium is a perfectly shaped amphitheatre, where so many dramas of the world's greatest footballing nation have been played out.

Brazil's top players, like Zico, Pelé and Ronaldo, have made their mark not only on the stadium's history, but also on its *Calçada da Fama* (Pavement of Fame), just by the entrance.

Here are also details of forthcoming matches, by far the best way to experience the Maracanã. Rio's top four clubs – Flamengo, Fluminense, Botafogo and Vasco – play here, and because Brazil has both national and state leagues, there's football played all year round (for ticket information, see p204). By Gate 18 there's also the **Museu do Futebol** devoted to Brazil's football history including, of course, plenty of World Cup highlights.

Maracanã Football Stadium
Rua Professor Eurico Rabelo, Maracanã (2299 2442). Metro Maracanã/249, 435, 455, 464 bus. **Open** 9am-5pm daily; 8-11am match days. **Admission** R$20. **No credit cards. Map** p252 A3.

São Cristóvão

One stop down the metro line from Maracanã is **São Cristóvão**, known as the *bairro imperial* (imperial district) and easily Zona Norte's most interesting neighbourhood.

When the Portuguese royal family arrived in Rio in 1808, Dom Joao VI chose to make São Cristóvão their home. Previously, the area had been mainly covered in mangrove swamps but during the 19th century the neighbourhood grew to become the wealthiest and most desirable area of the city.

São Cristóvão's fall from grace, though, was just as quick. Since the beginning of the 20th century the area has become heavily industrialised, the beach turned into a port and viaducts carrying noisy roads now tower over the once quiet residential streets. The upper class families have long gone, but reminders of the past still remain, most notably in the faded regal glory of the neoclassical **Palácio de São**

Maracanã
Football Stadium.

Cristóvão – formerly dubbed the 'Tropical Versailles' – set on the highest ridge of the **Quinta da Boa Vista**. For the 80 years that Rio was the seat of the Portuguese Empire (and after independence, the Brazilian Empire), this was where the royal families lived.

The **Museu Nacional** (*see below*) is housed in the Palácio and is said to be the best natural history museum in South America. One of the most interesting collections is the ceramics and artefacts of Tupinambá and Guaraní Indians, the two main pre-Columbian cultures to be found in Brazil. Check out the *tapa sexos*, ceramic micro-bikinis worn by women and used in fertility rituals.

Behind the Museu Nacional is the **Jardim Zoológico** (*see below*) known also as Riozoo. It's a refreshingly modern and pro-active zoo in a delightful setting. The **Museu da Fauna** next door is dedicated to ecological issues.

A five-minute walk to the east of the Quinta is the **Museu do Primeiro Reinado** (*see below*), a French-inspired neoclassical house given by Dom Pedro I to his lover, the Marquesa de Santos, in 1827. The ground floor has been well preserved and includes furniture from the royal families, but ask to look upstairs too to see the lush frescoes that cover almost every part of the walls and ceilings.

A five-minute walk north of the Quinta leads to the area's modern heritage, the **Campo de São Cristóvão**. This 1950s redbrick building, towering as high as the viaduct that passes overhead, is the Centro de Tradições Nordestinas Luiz Gonzaga, better known as the **Feira de São Cristóvão** (*see below*). Within its walls are over 600 different market stalls, bars and restaurants offering the tastes and traditions of the north-east of Brazil. The best time to come is on a Friday or Saturday evening when the market is open round the clock and the stages at either side of Avenida do Nordeste are crowded with people listening to the live music and dancing forró.

On the Campo's north-eastern side is the neogothic **Educandário Gonçalves de Araújo**, one of Rio de Janeiro's last remaining boarding schools. The domes visible on the hill behind it are home to the telescopes of the **Observatório Nacional** (Rua General Bruce 586, São Cristóvão, 3878 9100, www.on. com.br). It moved to this purpose-built location in 1922 and star-gazers can call to arrange to view the southern skies.

Feira de São Cristóvão
Campo de São Cristóvão (2580 0501/www.feira desaocristovao.com.br). Bus 261, 310, 312. **Open** 10am-4pm Tue-Thur; 10am Fri to 10pm Sun non-stop. **Admission** R$1. **No credit cards.** **Map** p252 C1.

Jardim Zoológico
Quinta da Boa Vista (3878 4200/www.rio.rj.gov.br/ riozoo). Metro São Cristóvão/232, 461, 462, 474, bus. **Open** 9am-4.30pm Tue-Sun. **Admission** R$5. **No credit cards.** **Map** p252 A2.

Museu Nacional
Quinta da Boa Vista, São Cristóvão (2568 8262/ 2254 4320/www.acd.ufrj.br/museu). Metro São Cristóvão/232, 460, 462, 474 bus. **Open** 10am-4pm Tue-Sun. **Admission** R$6. **No credit cards.** **Map** p252 A2.

Museu do Primeiro Reinado
Avenida Pedro II 293, São Cristóvão (2299 2148/ www.sec.rj.gov.br/webmuseu/mpr.htm). Bus 261, 310, 346, 472, 474, 624. **Open** 11am-5pm Tue-Fri. **Admission** free. **Map** p252 C2.

Beyond São Cristóvão

Elsewhere in the Zona Norte, other places worth visiting are some distance away and, because they're located in areas that are potentially dangerous for tourists, it's strongly advisable to take a taxi to visit them. The **Fundação Oswaldo Cruz** (*see below*) in Manguinhos is centred around the breathtaking Pavilhão Mourisco, a neo-Moorish palace built in the early 20th century. Inspired by the Alhambra Palace in Spain, the Pavilhão's walls and floors are lavishly decorated with mosaics and tiles imported from Europe.

In Engenho de Dentro there's a small and fascinating museum, the **Museu de Imagens do Inconsciente** (*see below*). Started during the 1950s by art therapy pioneer Nise da Silveira, it showcases the art of schizophrenics who have no formal art training, but whose work has been acclaimed by critics.

The district of Penha is home to the **Igreja de Nossa Senhora da Penha**, an impressive 17th-century church that can be seen for miles around because of its location on top of a 160-metre- (525-foot-) high rock. The church is a place of pilgrimage for thousands of worshippers, especially during the church's annual festival in October. Many climb the 382 steps hewn from the rock on which it stands on their bare knees – for the less devout, or the plain lazy, there's a small funicular tram.

Fundação Oswaldo Cruz
Avenida Brasil 4365, Manguinhos (2598 4242/ www.fiocruz.br). Bus 393, 395, 397. **Open** by appointment only Mon-Fri; 10am-4pm Sat. **Admission** free.

Museu de Imagens do Inconsciente
Rua Ramiro Magalhães 521, Engenho de Dentro (3111 7465/www.museuimagensdoinconsciente. org.br). Bus 249, 260, 691. **Open** 9am-4pm Mon-Fri. **Admission** free.

Niterói

Modern architecture, classic views and characterful beaches.

Sightseeing

Rather than being just an offshoot of Rio, Niterói is actually a thriving city in its own right, facing Rio across the Guanabara Bay. It's principally famed for its Niemeyer-designed museum, but with more than half a million inhabitants it also has a decent nightlife and live music scene, largely powered by its big student population. It's an attractive option too for commuters and those seeking a less frenetic stay in the city, with direct and easy access to the centre of Rio but with a quieter, more residential feel. Its beaches too have a lot to recommend them, with great views back to Rio from the bay and some absolutely stunning and often empty stretches of sand along its ocean coastline.

Niterói is divided into two principal areas, the bay district, where most of the buildings are, and the ocean beaches, which are fairly easily accessible by bus from the centre. From Rio, both the ferry (from Praça XV, every 15 minutes, 24-hour service, R$2) and the bus across the 13-kilometre (eight-mile) bridge arrive among the numerous shops and banks of the centre.

Arriving at the main Niterói ferry terminal, turn right for buses along the bay and to the ocean beaches. There's a useful tourist information office, just outside the terminal, open from 9am to 6pm every day, with up-to-date information on the progress of the **Caminho Niemeyer** (*see p98*) and current attractions.

The bay

The **Museu de Arte Contemporânea** (MAC; *see p98*) is Niterói's biggest attraction, and for good reason. It rises up out of a reflecting pool on a cylindrical base only nine metres (29 feet) in diameter, juts out slightly over a rocky promontory and appears to hover over the bay. Often there's not that much to see inside as far as exhibitions go, but most visitors come to see the building rather than the art, and few leave disappointed.

The building was designed by Brazilian architect Oscar Niemeyer, who was responsible for much of the architecture in Brasilia and is now considered one of the most important names in modern architecture. Construction was completed in 1996.

From the MAC building you can look down over **Praia da Boa Viagem** on one side and the arch of **Praia das Flexas** and **Praia de Icaraí**. As pleasant as these beaches look, their waters are not great for swimming. It's worth holding out for the ocean beaches further out.

Continuing round the bay is **Praia de São Francisco**, which is lined with restaurants and bars. From São Francisco, a taxi up to the **Parque da Cidade** on the Morro da Viração gives a fantastic view of pretty much all of Niterói, the bay and Rio. It's a great place to watch the sunset over Sugar Loaf.

The next beach along, **Praia de Charitas**, has the Charitas ferry terminal, another Niemeyer-designed building, which also links to Rio's Praça XV. Continuing round the bay past the relaxed fishing villages of Jurujuba beach is the **Fortaleza de Santa Cruz**. The fortress was the first to be built on Guanabara Bay and is still the largest. Visits to its colonial chapel, built in 1612, its lighthouse and impressive battlements are by guided tour only (in Portuguese, although they do their best to provide information in English). The tourist information office in the Fortress has a leaflet on other forts in Niterói.

A good destination for a wander through the centre of Niterói is the **Museu da Imprensa** (Brazilian Press Museum; *see p98*), which displays front cover headlines of many key events in Brazilian history, and has exhibits illuminating the history of print, including a replica of Gutenberg's first printing press.

There are also several notable churches in Niterói, including the pretty colonial **Igreja São Francisco Xavier** (Avenida Quintino Bocaiúva, 2711 1670) on the way to Jurujuba. On the last Sunday of each month the **Ilha Da Boa Viagem** is open to visitors, with the little 17th-century church of **Nossa Senhora da Boa Viagem** at the top, which affords yet more great bay views.

There's still more Niemeyer to come too (like many great architects, he seems to work harder as he gets older), with the huge **Caminho Niemeyer** project only just started as he reached his 100th birthday. The modernist white curved building near the ferry terminal is the **Teatro Popular** (www.culturaniteroi. com.br), the only other currently completed part of a huge ten-piece suite of Niemeyer buildings.

Fortaleza de Santa Cruz

Estrada Eurico Gaspar Dutra, Jurujuba (2711 0462). Bus 33. **Open** *9am-5pm Mon, Sat; noon-5pm Tue-Fri.* **Admission** *R$4.* **No credit cards.**

Museu de Arte Contemporânea

Mirante Boa Viagem (2620 2481/www.macniteroi. com.br). Bus 47B. **Open** *11am-7pm Tue-Sun.* **Admission** *R$4.* **Credit** Call to check. **Map** p251 I14.

Museu da Imprensa

Rua Marquês de Olinda 29 (2620 1122). Bus 47b. **Open** *10am-5pm Mon-Fri.* **Admission** *free.* **Map** p251 J12.

To get away from the crowded sands of Rio, head to the ocean beaches. The *praias* of **Piratininga**, **Camboinhas**, **Itaipu** and **Itacoatiara** consist of endless stretches of empty sand backed by lush vegetation and a scattering of residential houses. Many wealthy Cariocas come to this area (with the size of the houses as evidence of this) to set up home away from the madness of the city.

Piratininga and Camboinhas, reached by the no.39 bus from the ferry terminal, cover around five kilometres between them. Alongside Piratininga is the isolated **Praia da Barra**, with calm, sheltered waters.

At the end of Camboinhas beach and across the Lagoa are the calm waters of Itaipu, an excellent beach for swimming. Take the no.38 bus to the end of Francisco da Cruz, from the ferry terminal or from Praia de São Francisco at the junction of Avenida President Franklin Roosevelt. The beach is surrounded by a lovely little fishing village where you can dine on the local catch at many of its fish restaurants.

The farthest beach, but worth the trip, is **Praia de Itacoatiara**. It's backed by spectacular mountains covered in vegetation. Itacoatiara has a great vibe and is a favourite with surfers although there is a calm spot near the rocks for swimming.

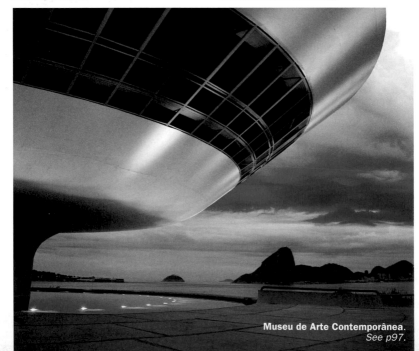

Museu de Arte Contemporânea.
See p97.

Sightseeing

Eat, Drink, Shop

Features

Restaurants

Good food and plenty of it.

Rio's restaurants offer something for all tastes and budgets, and eating out with friends – or sharing a table with new acquaintances – is a frequent activity for Cariocas and a common start to a late night on the town.

Rio's *por kilo* (pay by plate weight) eateries feature a cornucopian selection of salads, mains and desserts. A growing number of *botequins* (taverns or gastropubs) serve up traditional *petiscos* (tapas) and main dishes with modern flair. Meat is king at the city's ubiquitous *churrascarias*, where waiters circle with skewers of filet mignon *a volonte* and just about anything else that can go on the grill. Exotic and spicy north-eastern and northern Brazilian dishes can be found on many menus. The city's sandwich stands and juice bars are a spot to rub shoulders with fitness-minded Cariocas or late-night hedonists. Brazilian rice and black beans are staples of many traditional meals, but the city's worldly options include nouvelle French and Italian cuisine with tropical flourishes, as well as Portuguese, Lebanese, Italian, Japanese and vegetarian options.

The Zona Sul of Rio is home to most of the city's most eclectic restaurants with both chic and simple options. Lunch is the main meal in Rio, while late (but not always light) dinners are common (around 10pm). Fresh juice and very cold, light beer (*chope*) are favourites to accompany restaurant fare, and go well with Brazil's often spicy and salty cuisine. Respectable wine lists are available at top restaurants and Brazilian wines are starting to come into their own. Many restaurants serve the national dish, black bean and pork *feijoada*, on Saturday, typically accompanied with a high-octane caipirinha. Brazilian portions tend to be large, and main dishes at most restaurants will serve two. Waiters sometimes bring a *couvert* of bread or breadsticks, butter, quail eggs and pickled vegetables. This is billed unless you refuse it.

Tipping (ten per cent) is included as an itemised charge on sit-down restaurant bills, and additional tipping is optional, but not common. Overcharging tourists is not unusual, so check your bill. A word to the wary: credit-card cloning is a concern in Rio, especially at touristy spots with high turnover. Like the locals, ask the waiter to bring over the credit-card swiper (*pode trazer a maquina?*) and swipe your card tableside.

Get them while they're hot: spicy peppers on sale at a Botafogo street market.

The Centre

Traditional Brazilian

Nova Capela
*Avenida Mem de Sá 96, Lapa (2232 1907). Bus
410, 434, 572.* **Open** from 11am-last customer daily.
Main courses R$16-$48. **Credit** AmEx, DC, MC, V.
Map p245 H3 ❶
Roasted baby goat, wild boar and a late kitchen that
keeps Lapa alive even after the music dies down are
just part of what distinguishes this Rio institution
– and more than make up for the grumpy service and
the plain decor. The boar and the goat are late-night
favourites and some regulars swear by the trout with
broccoli rice. The *bolinho de bacalhau* (fried balls of
potato and cod) are better than average but the salads are best given a wide berth. Nova Capela survived Lapa's roughest time, when even the savviest
Cariocas avoided these streets at night, but now that
the 300-year-old neighbourhood is enjoying a boom,
it's full of the same kind of Bohemians, intellectuals
and hustlers who used to give Lapa its character. Not
to mention hipsters and young people with money.

Modern Brazilian

Cais do Oriente
*Rua Visconde de Itaboraí 8, Centro (2233 2531/
www.caisdooriente.com.br). Bus 404, 2018.*
Open noon-midnight Tue-Sat; noon-4pm Mon,
Sun. **Main courses** R$40-$50. **Credit** AmEx, DC,
MC, V. **Map** p245 J1 ❷
Located in a picturesque backstreet, the heavy,
plush armchairs at the entrance are invitation
enough to come in and make yourself at home.
Inside, East meets West, as the stripped stone walls
of this 19th-century building are softened with
Oriental rugs, huge vases and wicker furniture.
The Cais cleverly manages to be both cosy and
freshly tropical – there's plenty of colour and candlelit tables, but out the back you'll find a marvellous covered terrace. The food reflects this fusion,
with Thai chicken sitting alongside Brazilian beef
dishes. On most weekends there are live performances by local musicians.

German

Bar Brasil
*Avenida Mem de Sá 90, Lapa (2509 5943).
Bus 410, 434, 572.* **Open** 11.30am-11pm Mon-
Wed; 11.30am-midnight Thur, Fri; 11.30am-6pm
Sat. **Main courses** R$20-$26. **Credit** MC, V.
Map p245 H3 ❸

❶ Purple numbers given in this chapter
correspond to the location of restaurants
on the street maps. *See pp244-253.*

The best | Restaurants

For gourmet food
Eat gourmet nosh for less at **Da Silva**
(*see p112*) and **66 Bistrô** (*see p115*).
Splash out at **Le Pré Catelán** (*see p110*),
Margutta (*see p113*), **Olympe** (*see p115*)
and **Roberta Sudbrack** (*see p115*).

For fashionable nibbles
Get in with the in-crowd at **Aprazível** (*see
p104*), **Bar d'Hotel** (*see p107*), **Clube
Chocolate** (*see p118*) and **Miam Miam**
(*see p102*).

For traditional food
Savour local flavours at **Adega da Velha**
(*see p102*), **Quinta** (*see p116*),
Restaurante Quinta da Boa Vista (*see
p118*) and **Siri Mole e Cia** (*see p107*).

For a meaty treat
Visit the city's best *churrascarias*, such
as **Barra Brasa** (*see p107*) and **Palace
Churrascaria** (*see p107*).

For food by the kilo
Match quantity to appetite at a *por kilo*
joint; **Ataulfo** (*see p107*), **Celeiro** (*see
p110*), **Couve Flor** (*see p114*) and
Fellini (*see p109*) are among the best.

For live music
Find forró at **Severyna** (*see p103*) or MPB
and jazz at **Quiosque Arab** (*see p116*).

The refrigerator tells you all you need to know about
Bar Brasil: Traditional, Dependable and, well, cool.
More than a metre wide and nearly two metres tall,
the hulking wooden icebox by the bar does not quite
date back to 1907, when the place was founded. But
along with the scuffed wood floor and the bronze tap
for the draft beer, it looks like it could. The menu is
German and Brazilian, good with beer and heavy on
meats – any doubts and the waiters can help with a
suggestion that's more like an order. The smoked
pork dishes and sausage platters are signatures. Bar
Brasil also has quick dishes for R$10-$15, and the
steak and fries are popular at lunchtime. But the
smoked chicken tops all. Try for a table by the big
windows, but even on a suffocatingly hot day Bar
Brasil is breezy and comfortable, helped by large
fans suspended from the six-metre (17-foot) ceilings.
And you can relax and imagine, without too much
strain, how Lapa must have been in the 1930s, '40s
and '50s, when the resurgent neighbourhood was
home to musicians and poets, artists and writers,
and their clubs and cabarets.

The Bay

Traditional Brazilian

Café Lamas
Rua Marquês de Abrantes 18, Flamengo (2556 0799/www.cafelamas.com.br). Bus 178, 571, 573. **Open** 9.30am-3am Mon-Thur, Sun; 9.30am-4am Sat. **Main courses** R$19-$99. **Credit** AmEx, DC, MC, V. **Map** p247 I7 ❹

Lamas has been around for more than 130 years, and there are many reasons why, starting with the cold draft beer that sharp-eyed waiters keep bringing. They waste no time in taking your order and getting you fed, but don't let their white coats and black bow ties fool you: this isn't a formal place. For a century, in its original location, Lamas was known as a gathering spot for journalists, politicians and intellectuals. The move in 1976 to its current location is betrayed by the unattractive tiles and panelling of the era, but the charm and lively discussions of the old Lamas live on. The menu is extensive, but you won't find much invention. Try the *bolinhos de bacalhau* (fritters of minced fish and potato) or the steak dishes, big enough for two and served with a variety of sauces and sides. The fried onions are a Lamas tradition – don't pass them up. Its late kitchen makes it perfect for a bite and a beer on the way home from a concert or movie.

Bar do Arnaldo. *See p104.*

Porção
Avenida Infante Dom Henrique, Parque do Flamengo, Flamengo (3389 8989/www.porcao.com.br). Bus 127, 128, 404. **Open** 11.30am-midnight Mon-Thur, Sun; 11.30am-1am Fri, Sat. **Set menu** R$66. **Credit** AmEx, DC, MC, V. **Map** p247 J8 ❺

The unique location, great view and extravagant layout of numerous square metres of food make Porção a singular experience. It's one of the few buildings and the only business in Parque do Flamengo, sitting right on the beach. A friendly army of red-uniformed waiters circulate with an almost overwhelming variety of meat on a stick (don't be afraid to ask, it may be beef or ostrich) and a self-service buffet area has just about anything else you may want. The Flamengo outpost is the most famous of a chain that includes branches around Rio as well as in Miami and New York. **Other locations**: throughout the city.

Praia Vermelha Bar e Restaurante
Círculo Militar de Praia Vermelha, Praça General Tibúrcio, Urca (2275 7292). Bus 511, 512. **Open** noon-midnight daily. **Main courses** R$10-$25. **No credit cards. Map** p250 K11 ❻

This is a sublime place to round off any visit to Pão de Açúcar (Sugar Loaf mountain). Situated at the end of the tiny Praia Vermelha beach, the restaurant is housed in a military club. Seating is arranged on three patios, all of which have views across the bay to Sugar Loaf. The food served is simple fare such as pizzas, steaks and sandwiches. After 6pm, the rhythm of the lapping waves is accompanied by live music – and a R$6 cover charge is added to the bill.

Modern Brazilian

Miam Miam
Rua General Góis Monteiro 34, Botafogo (2244 0125/www.miammiam.com.br). Bus 126, 457, 584. **Open** 7.30pm-12.30am Tue-Fri; 8pm-1.30am Sat. **Main courses** R$25-$50. **Credit** AmEx, MC, V. **Map** p247 I11 ❼

In an old restored home close to the Rio Sul Mall in Botafogo, Miam Miam is a stylish affair serving good food. The menu shows French influences that have been given a Brazilian twist, served after creative cocktails. The decor is decidedly New York, or at least 'new' something, with low-slung sofas covered in zebra-print, 1950s chrome and nogahyde chairs and strange designer knick-knacks. The end result is reasonably harmonious, probably because staff are nice and the dishes, like fish with palm hearts and cashew butter, very satisfying. It also caters on occasion for the cutting-edge Moo electronic nights, which helps to keep the attention of the hip crowd. *Photo p106.*

North-eastern Brazilian

Adega da Velha
Rua Paulo Barreto 25, Botafogo (2286 2176). Bus 176, 583, 592. **Open** 11.30am-1am daily. **Main courses** R$7-$40. **Credit** DC, MC, V. **Map** p247 H11 ❽

The light bite

What links a sunny, carefree day lying on the beach with Carioca friends with a frustrating few hours spent bumper to bumper in a rainy traffic jam alongside a seething favela? The answer, as anyone in Rio would agree, is **Biscoitos Globo**. In both places, relief comes in a bag of biscuits.

Street vendors sell the bag of half-biscuit, half crisps anywhere there is a captive audience, and that audience has grown considerably over the years as Biscoitos Globo has established itself as the snack of choice for Cariocas. Up to 10,000 bags are sold each day in the summer, and its success among Cariocas of all ages, incomes and colours has made it a Carioca icon. The distinctive yellow logo appears on everything from T-shirts to lampshades to beachwear. Today, Biscoitos Globo are as ubiquitous as bikinis and beer on Rio's beaches. They have even featured in an exhibition at the city's Museum of Contemporary Art, something Andy Warhol would surely have approved of.

First made in São Paulo in 1953, Biscoitos Globo arrived in Rio the following year when the brothers who produced them at a São Paulo bakery called Globo decided to return to their home town with their new product. The biscuits quickly took off, their unsophisticated packaging and light and airy form particularly appropriate for a Carioca society that was and remains just that. Before long they were a staple and the brothers were obliged to open a factory in Rio to meet demand. Sometimes known as *biscoitos de vento*, or wind biscuits – because that's what's in their crunchy hollow shell – the snack comes in two basic versions of sweet and salty. Cariocas swear by their ability to fill a hole between meals and with just 135 calories per pack, it's guilt-free gluttony.

Despite Adega da Velha's vast menu of well-prepared meals from north-eastern Brazil, most people come for just one thing: the award-winning *feijão* (bean stew). Voted on more than one occasion to be the best in Rio (the city most associated with the dish), the *feijão completo* comes with a pile of cheese and dried meat for a mere R$7, making it one of the better deals in the city. But don't be afraid to branch out either as the place has a reputation for turning out some of Rio's best plates à la Bahia. Some also claim that the *bolinhos do bacalhau* (fried cod balls) are also the best in town, but it's a subject best not to broach with Cariocas. Short servers use their low centre of gravity and quick feet to get you a beer when the other is almost finished – sometimes whether you want another one or not.

French

Carême

Rua Visconde de Caravelas 113, Botafogo (2537 2274). Bus 463, 511. **Open** 8pm-midnight Tue-Sat. **Main courses** R$30-$60. **Credit** AmEx, V. **Map** p246 F12 **➒**

Gallic food, just like its heritage and culture, holds certain Cariocas in a hypnotic trance. It's the French connection, and TV chef Flavia Quaresma seems to be in to a good thing by dedicating her restaurant to it. The decor is typically French with starched table cloths, tiled floors and tall mirrors. Off the menu come rich classics like filet mignon in wine sauce, lamb chops wrapped in pastry and, when the season is right, Flavia will cook up an exemplary *magret de canard*. The desserts are regularly touted as the best in Rio. An expensive restaurant, but if you go by all the plaudits and romancing couples filling this place, it hardly seems to matter.

Italian

Fiammetta

Rio Plaza Shopping 220, Rua General Severiano 97, Botafogo (2295 9096/www.fiammetta.com.br). Bus 404, 512, 592. **Open** noon last customer daily. **Main courses** R$22-$30; R$17-$29 lunch buffet. **Credit** MC. **Map** p247 I11 **➓**

Fans of Italian food flock to Fiammetta. Although located in a shopping centre the space is made warm and inviting, with a bowed wooden ceiling and a towering pizza oven at the centre. For lunch there's a hearty buffet that feeds office workers; in the early

Eat, Drink, Shop

evening the restaurant caters to families, and later on the queue outside grows as couples and groups of friends arrive. The pizza deserves its reputation as being some of the best in Rio – alongside the traditional toppings are some original creations such as the Fiamma with sausage, aubergine and fennel.

Peruvian

Intihuasi
Rua Barão do Flamengo 35D, Flamengo (2225 7653/ www.intihuasi.art.br). Bus 434, 573, 574. **Open** noon-3.30pm, 7-11.30pm Tue-Sat; noon-3.30pm Sun. **Main courses** R$25-$36. **Credit** DC, MC, V. **Map** p247 I7 ⑪
It's strangely hard to find good food from the rest of Latin America in Brazil, but Intihuasi is a notable exception. This welcoming little place owned by a Peruvian-Brazilian duo serves up the best of Peruvian home-style cooking, including *ceviche*, stuffed chiles, *majarisco* (seafood casserole), meat and vegetarian options. They can also magic up one of Rio's best pisco sour cocktails.

The Hills

Traditional Brazilian

Bar do Mineiro
Rua Paschoal Carlos Magno 99, Santa Teresa (2221 9227). Both tram lines/206, 214 bus. **Open** 11am-2am Tue-Sat; 11am-1am Sun. **Main courses** R$22-$40. **Credit** AmEx, DC, MC, V. **Map** p245 H5 ⑫
One of Santa Teresa's most popular meeting points, the Bar do Mineiro serves up tasty traditional dishes from Minas Gerais as well as offering a good selection of quality cachaças and ice-cold beers. Saturday's *feijoada* is famous and should not be missed, nor should the deep-fried bean pasties. It's not always easy to get a table but the pavement outside is a lively place to sip a caipirinha while you wait. The decoration of the bar reflects the artistic sensibility of its owner, Diógenes Paixão, the eponymous Mineiro, a Brazilian art collector of some renown. One of the walls is covered with an array of old black and white photographs of great MPB stars like Gal Costa and Caetano Veloso, while above the bar there's an interesting collection of vividly coloured paintings playfully depicting small town Brazilian life; enormous copper pots adorn the other walls. What's more, the bar is now part of local culture and a great compilation CD was released in 2004 as a tribute to its reputation.

Sobrenatural
Rua Almirante Alexandrino 432, Santa Teresa (2224 1003). Both tram lines/206, 214 bus. **Open** noon-midnight daily. **Main courses** R$20-$60. **Credit** AmEx, DC, MC, V. **Map** p245 H5 ⑬
Popular with Cariocas and tourists alike, this mid-priced seafood restaurant has a rustic feel, with

exposed brickwork and a hardwood ceiling. Colourful abstract paintings with Brazilian motifs decorate the walls. The delicious *moquecas* (shrimp or fish stew cooked in coconut milk and palm oil) are especially popular. Lunchtime specials are good value and shouldn't set you back more than R$7.

Modern Brazilian

Aprazível
Rua Aprazível 62, Santa Teresa (2508 9174/ www.aprazivel.com.br). Tram Dois Irmãos line/ 206 bus. **Open** noon-midnight Thur-Sat; 1-6pm Sun. **Main courses** R$41-$78. **Credit** AmEx, DC, MC, V. **Map** p245 H5 ⑭
This is the place to go for something special, and its summer season High Noon parties on Sunday afternoons have been attracting an in-the-know crowd from Zona Sul. Hidden away high on a hill on a quiet cobbled street, surrounded by lush tropical vegetation and with fabulous views over the city centre and Guanabara Bay, Aprazível offers a truly delightful experience. You can choose to dine in a charming garden setting or an indoor space reminiscent of a country home. The menu is based on family recipes with a touch of the exotic. Grilled breast of duck in plum and white wine sauce served with wild rice and apple purée is just one of the many delicacies to choose from. Live *chorinho* can be heard every Thursday from 9pm to midnight. Not for those on a tight budget.

Espirito Santa
Rua Almirante Alexandrino 264, Santa Teresa (2508 7095/www.espiritosanta.com.br). Both tram lines/206, 214 bus. **Open** 11.30am-6pm Mon-Wed; 11.30am-midnight Thur-Sat; 11.30am-7pm Sun. **Main courses** R$30-$60. **Credit** AmEx, DC, MC, V. **Map** p245 H5 ⑮
In a little house just off the tramlines, the Espirito Santa serves up innovative Brazilian cuisine with Amazonian touches and decent vegetarian options in the heart of Santa Teresa. Chef Natacha Fink has drawn up a menu from across the country to be served on the little patio gazing over Santa Teresa, where live music is also performed each weekend and for special events. On a menu dominated by fish and seafood, there's also a *moqueca de banana*, a vegetarian version of the ubiquitous fish stew.

Northeastern Brazilian

Bar do Arnaldo
Rua Almirante Alexandrino 316B, Santa Teresa (2252 7246). Both tram lines/206, 214 bus. **Open** noon-9pm Mon; noon-11pm Tue-Sun. **Main courses** R$19-$39. **Credit** MC, V. **Map** p245 H5 ⑯
An honourable Santa Teresa institution, this small, cosy restaurant tastefully decorated with Brazilian handicrafts has been serving first-rate, reasonably priced north-eastern Brazilian fare for almost 40 years. *Carne do sol* (sun-dried beef) is

Aprazível.

Eat, Drink, Shop

the menu's must-order item, but also consider the delicious *feijão de corda* (brown beans and herbs) and, for those whose cholesterol levels can take it, the *manteiga de garrafa* (melted butter in a bottle), which should be slathered over the sun-dried beef. Be warned: north-eastern cuisine is not for the fainthearted! *Photo p102.*

Severyna
Rua Ipiranga 54, Laranjeiras (2556 9398/ www.severyna.com.br). Bus 126, 173, 435, 485. **Open** 11.30pm-2am daily. **Main courses** R$24-$40 (plus R$10 music cover charge). **Credit** AmEx, DC, MC, V. **Map** p247 H8 ⑰

The food is spicy at Severyna, but its the music that brings the heat. Even on a sleepy Monday night, the place jumps with the sounds of forró, and a policy of different music on different nights keeps punters on their toes – whatever the sounds, expect people to be dancing. The food is north-eastern, nicely executed but nothing fancy. Ask for one of Severyna's *tábuas*, appetiser sampling plates perfect for groups or a couple wanting to graze. Wash it all down with beer for less than R$3 a bottle, or one of the many juices made fresh from fruits of the north-east. Severyna has a roadhouse feel, with its high ceilings and exposed brick walls, but some of the dancers dress as sharply as they move, so the silk shirt can work here too. It's popular with Cariocas and Brazilian tourists, but enough foreigners show up for the restaurant to have English menus. And dancing lessons too.

Portuguese

Tasca do Edgar
Rua Mario Portela 16, Laranjeiras (2558 5582). Bus 406, 422, 498. **Open** 8am-last customer Tue-Sun. **Main courses** R$30-$60. **Credit** AmEx, DC, MC, V. **Map** p246 G8 ⑱

Tasca do Edgar, and its eponymous host Edgar Costa, are Rio institutions that help to uphold the city's never-ending love affair with *chope* (cold beer) and finger-foods. Located on a happening corner in Laranjeiras, this indoor/outdoor boteco offers Portuguese dishes including codfish, seafood rice, and steaks, but many choose to stick with *petiscos* (finger-foods), including delectable pasties, codballs, and perhaps the city's best *casquinha de siri* (crab au gratin). If it's full, there are several other bars and restaurants nearby, like the similar Bar do Serafim across the street.

The Beaches

Traditional Brazilian

Alvaro's
Avenida Ataulfo de Paiva 500, Leblon (2294 2148). Bus 157, 433, 511, 569. **Open** noon-1am daily. **Main courses** R$25-$80. **Credit** AmEx, MC, V. **Map** p248 C17 ⑲

Retro decor yet a forward-looking menu at **Miam Miam**. *See p102.*

Down-to-earth and traditional, this is a restaurant for Leblon regulars to come and have a gossip and put the world to rights in. Its homely feel and plain decor make it seem like a village local and it has a hearty menu to match. Alvaro's is popular with families, especially during the day, but it's also busy late at night because of its bar and its *pastéis* – these small, fried pasties filled with shrimp, *catupiry* cheese or palm hearts are renowned for being among the best in Rio. They taste even better accompanied by a *chope* (draught beer) after a good night out.

Bar do Beto
Rua Farme de Amoedo 51, Ipanema (2523 1443). Bus 125, 175, 456, 2017. **Open** 11.30am-1am daily. **Main courses** R$30; R$10 snacks. **Credit** AmEx, DC, MC, V. **Map** p249 F17 ⑳

For a low-key retreat a couple of blocks from the beach, there's nowhere better than Bar do Beto. In a pretty tree-lined street, this small, relaxed eatery with its ceiling fans and casement windows thrown open to the pavement affords a great view of the world going by. Old-time waiters in starched white cotton jackets offer a prompt and ever-courteous service. Choose from seafood, beef and chicken dishes, or just stick with a bottle of wine and a selection of snacks. The *frango à francesa* (French-style chicken) and the *lula doré* (deep-fried squid) are exceptional – but be warned, most portions are easily sufficient for two.

Barra Brasa

Avenida Afrânio de Melo Franco 131, Leblon
(2111 5700/www.barrabrasaleblon.com.br). Bus
404, 591. **Open** 11.30am-midnight daily. **Main**
courses R$46-$52. **Credit** AmEx, DC, MC, V.
Map p248 C16 ❹

Secrets to enjoying all that is offered by this modern *churrascaria* are to pace yourself and to take small portions. The buffet has a huge array of fresh dishes including salads, sushi and Lebanese appetisers. But the real draw is the meat – the choice is extraordinary. Anyone who feels in the mood for a TV dinner can request a personal headset and listen to the audio of the flatscreens placed subtly in the dining room. BB has ensured that sports fans don't have to miss a minute of the soccer action for any reason – televisions have been strategically placed in the men's room (but not in the women's). Kids have their entertainment too – in the form of a monitored playground.
Other locations: Avenida Ayrton Senna 2541, Barra (2199 9191).

Brasileirinho

Rua Jangadeiros 10A, Ipanema (2513 5184).
Bus 123, 456, 522. **Open** noon-midnight daily.
Main courses R$18-$34. **Credit** AmEx, DC, MC, V.
Map p249 G17 ❷

Brasileirinho is a typical, workhorse Brazilian restaurant for around 40 diners, offering plentiful, wholesome and tasty dishes, especially from the inland state of Minas Gerais. This is the place for *feijão*, with pork fillet, *couve* (kale) and garlic rice. The buffet offers a great opportunity to give everything a try. The atmosphere brings a wholesome touch of Brazil's great, pulsing *sertanejo* (rural) heart to the big city – all checked tablecloths, wood-burning ovens and soapstone pots. The caipirinhas are among the best around and there's a huge range of own-made produce on sale, so you can come away with a jar of *doce de leite* (caramel spread) or some cachaça from the hinterland.

Palace Churrascaria

Rua Rodolfo Dantas 16, Copacabana (2541 5898/
www.churascariapalace.com.br). Metro Cardeal
Arcoverde/136, 154, 533 bus. **Open** noon-1am daily. **Set menu** R$45. **Credit** AmEx, DC, MC, V.
Map p250 I14 ❸

All the festive excess and expertly prepared meats of a classic Brazilian *churrascaria rodizio*, but at a smaller price than some of Rio's other leading BBQ joints. The Palace serves up skewer after skewer of every imaginable cut of meat, and also offers fish and shrimp. It boasts an impressive salad bar and a lounge piano player to liven things up. Located conveniently in Copacabana's hotel district.

Plataforma

Rua Adalberto Ferreira 32, Leblon (2274 4022).
Bus 178, 465, 570, 571. **Open** noon-late daily.
Main courses R$25-$106. **Credit** AmEx, DC, MC, V. **Map** p248 B16 ❹

A favourite hangout of Bossa Nova idol Tom Jobim, everything in Plataforma is big: the venue, the wine list and especially the *picanha* steaks. The restaurant is famed for its cuts of barbecued meat, but the menu is extensive and has plenty of fish and pasta dishes too. Tourists come here in their droves to see the nightly show upstairs that includes traditional music and dancing from all parts of Brazil. There's also live music every night in the Bar do Tom behind the restaurant.

Siri Mole e Cia

Rua Francisco Otaviano 50, Copacabana (2267 0894/
www.sirimole.com.br). Bus 123, 474, 570, 593.
Open noon-midnight daily. **Main courses** R$45-
$110. **Credit** AmEx, DC, MC, V. **Map** p249 H17 ❺

This is a multiple award-winning restaurant and rightly so. It's the place to come to taste the best Brazilian cuisine in the city. The focus is on cuisine from Bahia and the speciality is the seafood, which is of the highest quality. The *moquecas* (seafood stews) are mouthwatering and generous in size. The exotic African ingredients aren't as overwhelming as can be found in other versions of this dish and the subtlety seems to be the secret, bringing all the flavours to life. For those with a sweet tooth, the *cocada preta* (dark coconut ice) is to die for.

Modern Brazilian

Ataulfo

Avenida Ataulfo de Paiva 630, Leblon (2540 0606).
Bus 157, 433, 511, 569. **Open** 9am-11.30pm daily.
Main courses R$24-$50; R$40/kilo. **Credit** AmEx, MC, V. **Map** p248 B17 ❻

Restaurant, café, patisserie, sushi bar – Ataulfo is many things under one roof. The atmosphere is laid back and customers are soothed by the sound of the huge water feature on the back wall. Even more impressive are the two side walls of soil with dozens of tropical plants growing out of them. The restaurant is busiest at lunchtime and during the afternoon when food is paid for by weight. It's also a good place to grab a coffee and one of their delicious pastries, or indulge in one of the many ice-creams.

Bar d'Hotel

Marina All Suites, Avenida Delfim Moreira 696,
Leblon (2540 4990/www.marinaallsuites.com.br). Bus
175. **Open** *Café* 7am-10pm daily. *Restaurant* 6pm-1am Mon-Wed, Sun; 6pm-2am Thur-Sat. **Main courses** R$25-$48. **Credit** MC, V. **Map** p248 B17 ❼

Serving 'nouvelle tropical' cuisine with Italian touches, this always-in fashion locale boasts a full-on view of one of Rio de Janeiro's most vaunted stretches of surf. Yes, it's a hotel restaurant, but the superb mixed drinks, flattering soft light, sharp decor and inventive food at reasonable prices mean it attracts more locals than guests. A good spot for rubbing elbows with Rio's body-beautiful jet set. The Caipisake (a twist on the caipirinha, with saké) is a house speciality.

Bazzar

*Rua Barão de Torre 538, Ipanema (3202 2884/
www.bazzar.com.br). Bus 154, 573, 2017.*
Open noon-5pm, 7pm-midnight daily. **Main
courses** R$30-$50; R$30 grills. **Credit** DC, MC, V.
Map p248 D16 ❷

Stripped wood, bare brick and very square – the
tables, the chairs and even some of the plates
– Bazzar offers a clean-cut modern ambience, softened with candlelight and a little gentle jazz. The
imaginative and mouthwatering menu is Italian-
influenced Brazilian with an exotic twist (with
touches of Thailand and Japan) and whatever you
choose, it'll be fabulous. Try duck breast with
banana-da-terra (a type of banana). Portions are just
the right size. Browse a fine selection of international cookery books on your way to the loo.
Other locations: Avenida Rio Branco 46,
Centro (2253 1248).

Cafeína

*Rua Farme do Amoedo 43, Ipanema (2521 2194/
www.cafeina.biz). Bus 154, 433, 474, 572.* **Open**
8am-11.30pm daily. **Main courses** R$12-$25.
Credit AmEx, DC, MC, V. **Map** p249 F17 ❷

Similar in style to a European bakery and café, this
is one of the best places in the Zona Sul to get breakfast or a leisurely light lunch. The selection of
breads and pastries is tremendous and the portions

generous (the 'Natural' breakfast can easily stretch
to two people). Service is friendly and efficient and
the terrace is the perfect place to people watch as
Cariocas make their way to and from Ipanema
beach, which is just a stone's throw away.
Other locations: Constante Ramos 44, Copacabana
(2547 8561); Barata Ribeiro 507 (2547 4390); Ataulfo
de Paiva 1321, Leblon (2259 6288); Rio Design 119,
Leblon (2259 4224).

Carlota

*Rua Dias Ferreira 64B&C, Leblon (2540 6821/
www.carlota.com.br). Bus 157, 172, 433.* **Open**
7.30pm-midnight Tue-Fri; 1-5pm, 7.30pm-12.30am
Sat; 1.30-10.30pm Sun. **Main courses** R$38-$75.
Credit AmEx, DC, MC, V. **Map** p248 A17 ❸

A small and cosy environment, Carlota is another
successful São Paulo restaurant to be imported to
Rio. The cuisine is contemporary and owner and
head chef Carla Pernambuco also makes sure it's
not over-complicated or fussy. She uses the influences of her grandmother, her travels around
Europe and experience from years living in New
York to create an eclectic and colourful menu. All
the main courses are created with a view to challenging and delighting the taste buds (like the filet
mignon with port sauce and fig risotto). From the
desserts, the guava soufflé with *catupiry* cheese
sauce is well worth experiencing.

Bright colours and low lights at **Zaza Bistrô Tropical**.

Fellini

Rua General Urquiza 104, Leblon (2540 6486/ www.fellini.com.br). Bus 172, 438, 522, 2018. **Open** 11.30am-midnight daily. **Main courses** R$34-$41 per kilo. **Credit** AmEx, MC, V. **Map** p248 B17 ㉛

Fellini stands out among kilo restaurants for the quality of its food and the range of its menu – one day duck, the next lamb, the next lobster. Every day there's a whole area of creative salads and a separate counter with sushi and sashimi. A wide range of delicious deserts add to the appeal. Regular lunchtime queues attest to its popularity and it regularly gets the nod for the best kilo restaurant in the city from the *Veja Rio* eating and drinking guide. Recently refurbished.

Garcia & Rodrigues

Avenida Ataulfo de Paiva 1251, Leblon (3206 4100, reservations 3206 4109/www.garciae rodrigues.com.br). Bus 132, 433, 573. **Open** 8am-midnight Mon-Thur; 8am-2am Sat, Sun. **Main courses** R$18-$70. **Credit** AmEx, DC, MC, V. **Map** p248 A17 ㉜

Whether you're after a bottle of wine and a baguette, or a full-blown gastronomic experience, there's always an excuse for visiting Garcia & Rodrigues. Deli, brasserie, pâtisserie and vintner to boot, this luscious place simply groans with good things – and all of the highest quality. Chateaubriand with béarnaise sauce or ravioli of duck perfumed with orange – the established and the innovative sit side-by-side in inviting and lively surroundings.

Zaza Bistrô Tropical

Rua Joana Angélica 40, Ipanema (2247 9101/ www.zazabistro.com.br). Bus 512, 574, 2018. **Open** 7.30pm-12.30am Mon Thur, Sun; 7.30pm-1.30am Fri, Sat. **Main courses** R$35-$50. **Credit** AmEx, DC, MC. **Map** p249 E17 ㉝

To walk into Zaza is to walk into an exotic, enchanted emporium – an assault on the senses in every way. The corner house itself could come straight from a fairy-tale illustration. Stay out on the terrace and watch the world go by, enjoy the intimate surroundings of the downstairs bistro – or go the whole hog, kick off your shoes and eat reclined among the plush, deep-red cushions upstairs. Satisfied customers can then fall fast asleep, or just take advantage of the low-lighting to get to know each other better. 'Bistrô tropical' is a good description of the menu – Brazilian favourites, such as *picanha* (a cut of sirloin), but served with curry and couscous, local fish and imaginative salads. The service is attentive and friendly and English is widely spoken, reflecting the place's popularity with *estrangeiros*.

Zuka

Rua Dias Ferreira 233b, Leblon (3205 7154/ www.zuka.com.br). Bus 172, 522, 574, 593. **Open** 7pm-1am Mon; noon-4pm, 7pm-1am Tue-Fri; 1pm-1am Sat, Sun. **Main courses** R$27-$42. **Credit** AmEx, MC, V. **Map** p248 A17 ㉞

The decor is modern and minimalist but any austerity is softened by a potted tree that links the dining room to the magnificent trees that line Rua Dias Ferreira, just outside Zuka's large front windows. Chef Ludmilla Soeiro's best dishes of beef and seafood arrive invitingly arranged on large plates of all shapes that are wonderful to behold, if tricky to swap. The *ceviche* appetizer is firm and fleshy, with just a hint of citrus and, in keeping with the average Brazilian palate, an absent of heat. The greens are served with a dressing of curry and coconut that captures Soeiro's inventive mixing of flavours. Soeiro is only 30, but her creative forays have already won wide acclaim. Sometimes her creativitie impulses go too far though: a penne risotto in a veal sauce is somehow both too salty and too sweet. But the *namorado*, a fish whose name means 'boyfriend' in Portuguese, gets raves for its pairing with a broth of foie gras and the seared tuna is excellent. The best tables are at the front, between those trees, or in the middle, where you can watch Soeiro and her team work the grill in the sunken kitchen.

Far Eastern

Koni Express

Avenida Ataulfo de Paiva 1174E, Leblon (3502 3664). Bus 434, 484. **Open** 11am-3am Mon-Wed; 11am-5am Fri, Sat; 11am-midnight Sun. **Main courses** R$5.50-$8.50. **Credit** V. **Map** p248 A17 ㉟

This is the first Japanese fast food outlet in Rio and has quickly won the hearts and the stomachs of Cariocas who visit the place for quick, cheap and healthy food, enjoyed close to some of the best beaches in the city. Over 20 menu options include tuna, salmon and Philadelphia rolls, plus delicious shrimp tempuras with passion fruit mousse. The delicious sweets are inventive too – caramelised banana, strawberries with Nutella, and the 'Romeo and Juliet' with mascarpone.

Sushi Leblon

Rua Dias Ferreira 256, Leblon (2512 7830/ www.sushileblon.com). Bus 157, 433, 503, 512. **Open** noon-4pm, 7pm-1.30am Mon-Fri; noon-1.30am Sat; 1pm-midnight Sun. **Sushi** R$5-$20. **Credit** AmEx, MC, V. **Map** p248 B17 ㊳

The food served in Sushi Leblon is excellent but that's not the only reason to come here. None of the other four Japanese restaurants within a stone's throw have the glamour of this long-standing Leblon institution. Sushi Leblon is one of the favourite venues of the Carioca elite and there's often a queue outside – as well as traffic jams as the rich and image-conscious leave their SUVs parked outside the door. Once inside, enjoy the creative concoctions and the intimate atmosphere; the tables are arranged close together and you can eavesdrop on the latest gossip from both executives and Globo (Latin American's biggest television network) stars alike.

Eat, Drink, Shop

French

L'Etoile

37th floor, Hotel Iberostar, Avenida Atlântica 1020, Leme (3873 8880/www.iberostar.com.br). Bus 136, 154, 523. **Open** 7.30pm-midnight daily. **Main courses** R$50-$70. **Credit** AmEx, DC, MC, V. **Map** p250 J13 ⊕

This first-rate restaurant located on the top floor of the Hotel Iberostar has recently been refurbished after the property was purchased by a Spanish group. As Le Saint Honoré, the restaurant used to enjoy a widely envied reputation for its exclusively French menu, but now that it sits on top of the Iberostar, Spanish cuisine has been added. The atmosphere is modern and warm, with an extraordinary view over Copacabana beach. Service is excellent and the menu is a deft mix contemporary and classic recipes. The chef is a big fan of Brazilian ingredients and has learned how to adapt the classic French dishes to the country's tropical flavours. The grouper with choron sauce is a constant on the menu – and for good reason. An evening here is expensive, but memorable.

Galeria 1618

Rua Gustavo Sampaio 840, Leme (2295 1618). Bus 472, 504, 505. **Open** noon-1am Mon, Tue, Thur; 9am-1am Sat; 9am-midnight Sun. **Main courses** R$15-$35. **Credit** AmEx, MC, V. **Map** p250 J13 ⊕

A mixture of art gallery, bookstore and café with charming interior decoration, Galeria 1618 is also a French bistro that serves up an excellent brunch on weekends. Regular customers keep returning for the own-made bread, the croque monsieur and the fabulous couscous. Art exhibitions change every couple of months and the bookstore is stocked exclusively with art and design books. There are jazz performances on Wednesday, Saturday and Sunday evenings.

🕯 Le Pré Catelán

Hotel Sofitel, Avenida Atlântica 4240, Copacabana (2525 1232). Bus 121, 175, 484, 2016. **Open** 7.30-11.30pm Mon-Sat. **Main courses** R$52-$65. **Credit** AmEx, DC, MC, V. **Map** p249 H17 ⊕

Rio's hotel restaurants have never enjoyed a high reputation, but the head chef here, Roland Villard, has put the Sofitel's (*see p136*) flagship restaurant near the top of Rio's food chain. He's there every night, gliding from table to table, checking that everything has arrived as ordered and elucidating the finer details of a menu that changes every couple of weeks. The tasting menu costs R$125 and comprises a selection of starters, several main courses and a big plate of puddings, each dish seemingly better than the one before. The three dining rooms (one red, one black and one with a covered terrace) are tricked out in contemporary French style, the decor as tasteful as the food is tasty. And as if that's not enough, the view over the twinkling curve of Copacabana beach will make sure your eyes are kept as busy as your jaw.

Health food

Ateliê Culinário

Rua Dias Ferreira 45, Leblon (2239 2825/ www.atelieculinario.com.br). Bus 172, 438, 574. **Open** noon-8pm Mon-Thur; noon-1am Fri; 9am-1am Sat; 9am-11pm Sun. **Sandwiches/salads** R$16.50-$18. **Credit** V. **Map** p248 A17 ⊕

Opened ten years ago as a take-away counter for a small vegetarian catering company, the Ateliê Culinário is a good find if you can find it, squeezed in between a pizza restaurant and a supermarket. With only four tables on its tiny patio and room for a maximum of about 20 customers at any time, what it lacks in size, it makes up for in class – the menu is sparse but its customers, many of them ladies who lunch and all of them fiercely loyal, revel in the health-food specialities. Desserts are also light and delicious. The chance to observe street life on Dias Ferreira, the most chic street in Leblon, merely adds to the appeal.

Celeiro

Rua Dias Ferreira 199, Leblon (2274 7843/ www.celeiroculinario.com.br). Bus 132, 172, 433, 512. **Open** 10am-5pm Mon-Fri; 10am-6.30pm Sat. **Main courses** R$66/kilo. **Credit** DC, MC, V. **Map** p248 A17 ⊕

Repeatedly awarded honours for tossing the best salads in the city, this very popular sidewalk café serves a comprehensive range of fresh salads, wholesome quiches and soups at its buffet. In the tiny interior there's just about enough space for the buffet, so most of the seating is crammed together on the shady pavement outside. If your timetable is flexible, try to avoid the lunchtime rush as the queue for the buffet can get very long and there's usually a wait for a table.

Delírio Tropical

Rua Garcia D'Ávila 48, Ipanema (3201 2977/ www.delirio.com.br). Bus 433, 571, 572. **Open** 9am-10pm Mon-Sat; 9am-9pm Sun. **Main courses** R$11-$20. **Credit** AmEx, DC, MC, V. **Map** p249 E17 ⊕

For a swift, cheap yet healthy lunch, this is an ideal place to go. It's a counter service restaurant but the choice of salads is enormous and the food is always both fresh and beautifully presented. The menus change every day and can get pretty adventurous with flavours and combinations. In fact, the only problem is the place's popularity – at peak times the queue can stretch out of the door and it can be hard to find a place to sit, a situation that isn't helped by the fact that it's one of the first restaurants in Rio to offer free Wi-Fi. **Other locations**: throughout the city.

Gula Gula

Rua Henrique Dumont 57, Ipanema (2259 3084/ www.gulagula.com.br). Bus 154, 457, 503, 2018. **Open** noon-midnight Mon-Thur; noon-1am Fri, Sat. **Main courses** R$17-$34. **Credit** AmEx, DC, MC, V. **Map** p248 D17 ⊕

Le Pré Catalán.

One of the first restaurants in Rio to focus on producing healthy food, Gula Gula has maintained its place atop the ever increasing list of places dedicated to well-appointed and informal eating. The highlight is its salads, and customers can pick from the range behind the glass counters and then mix and match with options such as chicken salad with pesto, sun-dried meat or Caesar salad. Main courses include a tasty roast-beef salad and grilled salmon with a choice of sauces.
Other locations: throughout the city

Italian

D'Amici

Rua Antônio Vieira 18, Leme (2541 4477). Bus 472, 591, 592, 2011. **Open** noon-1am daily. **Main courses** R$30-$120. **Credit** AmEx, DC, MC, V. **Map** p250 J13 ⓺

When all you want to do is eat well – and we mean really well – this is the kind of restaurant you want to find yourself in. It's a clandestine, in-the-know kind of place, hidden on a side street, its interior invisible from the outside. The clientele mainly comprises celebrities and politicians who want to dine without being seen or photographed. The roast lamb with potatoes is as perfect as the people-watching.

Gero

Rua Anibal de Mendonça 157, Ipanema (2239 8158/ www.fasano.com.br). Bus 154, 583, 591. **Open** noon-4pm, 7pm-1am daily. **Main courses** R$50-$70. **Credit** AmEx, DC, MC, V. **Map** p248 D16 ⓻

A sharp intake of envious breath usually accompanies any mention of Gero – a popular draw with Rio's in-crowd and the first step in the Fasano empire's expansion from São Paolo into Rio (*See p39* **The Fasano factor**). Behind its bunker-like façade, designed by architect Aurélio Martinez Flores (who also designed the prize-winning original São Paulo branch), the menu offers a mouthwatering array of pricey Italian inspired dishes in an atmosphere heavy with an almost industrial chic – lots of bare brick and stripped wood, skylights and tall thin windows. There are, of course, a couple of heavies on the door to keep out the riff-raff.

Middle Eastern

Amir

Rua Ronald de Carvalho 55, Copacabana (2275 5596/www.amirrestaurante.com.br). Bus 154, 433, 523. **Open** noon-midnight daily. **Set menu** R$30. **Credit** AmEx, DC, MC, V. **Map** p250 I13 ⓽

Recently refurbished from the top of its spacious upstairs area to the end of its outdoor patio, Amir could just be the best Middle Eastern restaurant in Rio. It puts on belly dancing shows on a Thursday night but the authentic Arabic food is the main attraction, and especially the mouthwatering banquets. Everything here is worth trying and the

well-priced banquets are the way to do it. The lamb is exceptional and the desserts are out of this world. **Other locations**: Rio Design Barra, Avenida das Américas 7777, Barra da Tijuca (2431 1664).

Polish

A Polonesa

Rua Hilário de Gouveia 116, Copacabana (2547 7378). Metro Siqueira Campos/154, 433, 523 bus. **Open** 6pm-midnight Tue-Fri; noon-midnight Sat, Sun. **Main courses** R$24-$40. **Credit** DC, MC, V. **Map** p250 H14 ⓮

Copacabana isn't the first place you'd expect to find respectable goulash, borscht, dumplings, stuffed cabbage, chilled vodka shots or a chocolate soufflé, but A Polonesa offers up all of these eastern European staples in an unpretentious, grotto-like dining room that, incongruously, attracts Rio's celebrity-set. The service, as you might expect, can be gruff, but that's all part of the charm. Anyway, the portions are hearty enough that you won't need the waiter to come back to the table too often.

Portuguese

Antiquarius

Rua Aristides Espínola 19, Leblon (2294 1049/ www.antiquarius.com.br). Bus 157, 172, 433. **Open** noon-2am Mon-Sat; noon-midnight Sun. **Main courses** R$35-$126. **Credit** AmEx, DC, MC, V. **Map** p248 B17 ⓴

Whereas North America relies on a token of Bill Clinton's presence to know whether a restaurant is great or not, Rio looks to Mick Jagger. Yet even before his visit, Antiquarius could already boast a steady parade of A-list celebrities and international monarchs and politicians. Despite this, it's an intimate restaurant where anyone would feel at home, regardless of status. The menu is mostly traditional Portuguese soul food that tastes like it's been divinely made. There are plenty of salted cod and seafood dishes as well as the classic *arroz de pato* (duck risotto). Ask the maitre d' for tips on what to choose but make sure to leave room for one of the heavenly deserts, accompanied by a cup of percolated coffee and a nip of *amarguinha*, an almond-based liquor.

Da Silva

Rua Barão da Torre 340, Ipanema (2521 1289). Bus 123, 132, 433, 512. **Open** 11.30am-5pm Mon; 11.30am-11.30pm Tue-Sun. **Main courses** R$25-$40. **Credit** AmEx, DC, MC. **Map** p249 E16 ⓵

Da Silva is proof that the cuisine of Portugal is still both alive and well in Rio de Janeiro. The restaurant is a gourmet buffet at lunchtime, when you pay by weight, and serves ample à la carte dishes for dinner. The owners also operate Antiquarius (*see above*), one of Rio's most celebrated gourmet restaurants. The general consensus is that Da Silva offers Antiquarius-quality food at lower prices and

Pizzeria Capricciosa.
See p115.

the recommended dishes are the same – the duck risotto and the many varieties of salt-cod. Desserts include voluptuous Portuguese puddings.

Seafood

Margutta

Rua Henrique Dumont 62, Ipanema (2259 3718/ www.margutta.com.br). Bus 132, 432, 464, 570. **Open** 6pm-1am Mon-Fri; noon-1am Sat; noon-midnight Sun. **Main courses** R$32-$69. **Credit** AmEx, DC, MC. **Map** p248 D17 ⑩

Recommended by star chef and restauranteur Roberta Sudbrack, Margutta is the kind of place that Cariocas can turn to as a weapon with which to defend their city's culinary reputation against derisory comments from Paulistas. Chef Paolo Neroni opened the restaurant with his wife in 1994 and has been impressing customers ever since with pastas and meat dishes, but especially his imaginative plates of seafood, sourced from his native Italy and around the world.

Other locations: Avenida Graça Aranha 1/2, Centro (2563 4091).

Marius Degustare Crustáceos

Avenida Atlântica 290B, Leme (0800 707 9001/ www.marius.com.br). Bus 472, 504, 505. **Open** noon-midnight daily. **Set menu** R$112. **Credit** AmEx, DC, MC, V. **Map** p250 K13 ⑪

The decor is over-the-top maritime-kitsch, with the floor covered in Styrofoam balls to resemble sea foam – so it would be easy to dismiss this place as a tourist trap. But that would be a mistake. There's so much chilled or expertly grilled seafood on offer here that you end up turning away platters of whole lobster, jumbo prawns, crab, oysters and flaky sea bass.

MIO

Rua Farme de Amoedo 52, Ipanema (2523 2886/ 2521 2648/www.mioristorante.com.br). Bus 132, 432, 464, 570. **Open** noon-?pm daily. **Main courses** R$30-R$90. **Credit** AmEx, DC, MC, V. **Map** p249 F17 ⑫

A showboating, attention-grabbing restaurant that's as good to look at as it is to eat in. The first thing you'll see is the huge fish tank, full of scaly delicacies that might well be casting nervous glances at the 'catch of the day' section of the chalkboard. Then there's the bar, surrounded by a table groaning with cheeses of all kinds and a big leg of ham. Next to that is a marble basin full of fresh seafood that, along with the pastas, is the house speciality.

Osteria dell'Angolo

Rua Paul Redfern 40, Ipanema (2259 3148/ www.osteriadellangolo.com.br). Bus 132, 433, 512. **Open** noon-4pm, 6.30pm-midnight daily. **Main courses** R$25-$45. **Credit** AmEx, MC. **Map** p248 D17 ⑬

This comfortable Italian-owned seafood restaurant doesn't bow to fads or kitchen alchemy, but its fresh fish and tasty antipasti have made it a Rio mainstay. Mains include oven-baked whole red snapper or grouper brushed with white wine, olive oil and fresh rosemary and the well-mannered waiters give you a look at your fish before deboning it into perfect fillets.

Shirley

Rua Gustavo Sampaio 610, Leme (2542 1797). Bus 472, 505. **Open** noon-1am daily. **Main courses** R$30-$50. **No credit cards. Map** p250 J13 **54**
A small and straightforward Leme institution, one block back from the beach, Shirley is known for dishing up big portions of tasty Spanish-style seafood in a cosy atmosphere.

The Lake

Modern Brazilian

Caroline Café

Rua JJ Seabra 10, Jardim Botânico (2540 0705/ www.carolinecafe.com.br). Bus 158, 410, 571, 572. **Open** noon-last customer daily. **Main courses** R$18-$89. **Credit** AmEx, V. **Map** p248 C13 **55**

A hip and happening American style bar-restaurant with a terrace that pulls in a young and well-heeled party crowd. The atmosphere is always lively, particularly at weekends when it's a popular place for groups to gather for a drink and a bite to eat before hitting the clubs. The menu offers a mixture of Brazilian, American and Mexican dishes as well as a separate sushi bar. There's also an impressive array of cocktails – some old regulars and some inspiringly novel concoctions. The restaurant is well known for its themed events when staff lay on special menus and deck the place out accordingly.

Couve Flor

Rua Pacheco Leão 724, Jardim Botânico (2239 2191/ www.couveflor.com.br). Bus 125, 511. **Open** noon-4pm, 7-11pm Mon-Fri; noon-11pm Sat; noon-9pm Sun. **Main courses** R$33-$38/kilo. **Credit** AmEx, DC, MC, V. **Map** p248 A13 **56**
There's nearly always a queue of hungry people waiting outside this popular and casual kilo restaurant, a short stroll from the Pacheco Leão gate of the Botanic Garden. There's a salad bar, wide selection of hot dishes, sushi and a *churrascaria*, which serves beef and chicken. If you're famished or on a tight schedule, ask to be seated upstairs and the wait will be shorter.

Food fit for kings: **Roberta Sudbrack** keeps it fresh.

Guimas

Rua José Roberto Macedo Soares 5, Gávea (2259 7996). Bus 157, 158, 435, 571. **Open** noon-1am daily. **Main courses** R$30-$50. **Credit** AmEx, DC, MC, V. **Map** p248 A15 ⑤
Beloved of artists and thinkers, Guimas is a lively, quirky place, serving the very best modern Brazilian cuisine. While you wait for your order, make your own artistic contribution on the tablecloth – it may end up on the wall, alongside the efforts of the great and the good who have passed through the restaurant's doors before you.
Other locations: Rua Paul Redfern 33, Ipanema (2529 8300).

Roberta Sudbrack

Avenida Lineu de Paula Machado 916, Jardim Botânico (3874 0139/www.robertasudbrack.com.br). Bus 158, 438. **Open** 7.30pm-midnight Tue, Wed; noon-3pm, 7.30pm-midnight Thur; noon-3pm, 7.30pm-late Fri; 7.30pm-late Sat. **Credit** MC. **Map** p248 C13 ⑤
Roberta Sudbrack deserves all the praise and fame she gets: she's brave, charming and a brilliant chef. In her kitchen, there's no room for gimmickry or surplus ingredients, it's all about keeping it fresh and simple. Her secret recipe for hamburgers? Fresh mincemeat, salt and pepper. Of course there are more elaborate dishes to come out of the kitchen, but whether it be a burger or *côte d'agneau*, the emphasis is on technique and the selection of produce. The menu changes every day but only offers one choice per course. It's a totalitarian attitude, but you know from the confidence behind the smile that few leave unsatisfied. For proof, look no further than the pictures on the walls: King Juan Carlos, Prince Charles, Tony Blair, Fidel Castro and President Cardozo (Sudbrack was his personal chef for six years) are just a few to have used her embroidered napkins.

French

66 Bistrô

Avenida Alexandre Ferreira 66, Jardim Botânico (2266 0838/www.66bistro.com.br). Bus 504, 505, 570. **Open** noon-4pm, 7pm-12.30am Tue-Fri; noon-6pm, 7pm-12.30am Sat; noon-6pm Sun. **Main courses** R$40-$56. **Set menus** R$28 lunch; R$72 dinner. **Credit** MC, V. **Map** p249 E13 ⑤
For once the use of the word 'bistro' isn't just an affectation. The menu at 66 – steak tartare, moules marinière, magret, and so on – will be familiar to anyone who has spent more than six hours travelling through France. (Though the carpaccio of fresh shiitake mushrooms with shaved Parmesan probably isn't on the prix fixe at Rouen's Chez Philippe.) This mix of authenticity and audacity isn't surprising when you learn that the man behind the stove is Claude Troisgros, scion of one of France's most famous gastronomic dynasties, who, among other things, have a strong claim to be the inventors of nouvelle cuisine (don't hold it against them, it was just a phase) and who collect Michelin stars for fun. Troisgras is one of Brazil's top chefs but keeps

things fairly simple here, recreating old favourites using fresh local ingredients and offering good set menu and buffet deals for lunch and supper. To sample his more elaborate, and more expensive, creations, book a table at Olympe (*see below*).

Olympe

Rua Custódio Serrão 62, Jardim Botânico (2539 4542/www.claudetroisgros.com.br). Bus 172, 438, 463, 512. **Open** noon-4pm Fri; 7pm-12.30am Mon-Thur, Sat. **Main courses** R$62-$85; R$160 tasting menu. **Credit** MC, DC, V. **Map** p249 E13 ⑤
A smart but informal space with 48 covers, crisp white tablecloths, crimson banquettes and vivid modern paintings, Olympe is superstar chef Claude Troisgros's flagship restaurant in Rio, a magnet for visiting celebrities and the local in-crowd but unpretentious and welcoming with it. If you're willing to spend upwards of R$70 on a main course, staff will be happy to see you. And you'll be happy to see the menu, divided into 'Specialities' and 'Creative', the former a medley of French haute cuisine standards – carpaccio drizzled with white truffle oil, sautéed foie gras, tenderloin au poivre – the latter comprising more idiosyncratic, fusion-type dishes such as tuna tartare with tapioca caviar and wasabe vinaigrette, and veal *picanha* with artichokes and shiitake mushrooms (Troisgros likes his shiitakes). Aptly for a restaurant named for the home of the gods, there's a bottle of nectar on the wine list – a Chateau D'Yquem 1994 that will set you back close to R$5,000.

Italian

Pizzeria Capricciosa

Rua Maria Angélica 37, Jardim Botânico (2527 2656/www.capricciosa.com.br). Bus 463, 569. **Open** 6pm-1am Mon-Fri; 6pm-2am Sat, Sun. **Pizzas** R$25-$39. **Credit** AmEx, DC, MC. **Map** p249 E17 ⑤
High ceilings, hardwood floors, glass-enclosed wine-cellars, exposed brick and other eye candy (often including the clientele) are perks of this pizzeria. The menu makes a big to-do about the provenance of its pizza toppings – creamy buffalo mozzarella, fresh basil and rockets and such specialities as wild mushrooms or authentic San Danilo ham – and Cariocas swear by these plate-sized, light-crust pizzas. While they might not hold their own in Napoli, they can arguably give some (deservedly) vaunted São Paulo pizzerias a run for their money. *Photo p113.*
Other locations: throughout the city.

Quadrifoglio

Rua J J Seabra 19, Jardim Botânico (2294 1433). Bus 158, 410, 571, 572. **Open** 12.30-3.30pm, 7.30pm-midnight daily. **Main courses** R$37-$78. **Credit** AmEx, DC, MC, V. **Map** p248 C13 ⑤
This quiet, romantic restaurant has a cool creamy-white interior decorated with orchids. It offers a menu of traditional Italian food, livened up with some Brazilian flair. Pasta dishes, risottos and exotic meats are followed by some interesting desserts such as roast figs with lavender ice-cream.

Eat, Drink, Shop

Middle Eastern

Quiosque Arab

Espaço Victor Assis Brasil (antigo Parque dos Patins), Quiosques 7&9, Avenida Borges de Medeiros (2540 0747). Bus 157, 434, 504, 505. **Open** 9.30am-last customer daily. **Main courses** R$26-$64. **Credit** MC, DC, V. **Map** p248 C14 ❻❸

The kiosks in the Parque dos Patins get busy with music and good food each evening and offer a chilled spot to sit outside by the lake and watch the lights twinkle from the other side. The Arab kiosk has a varied but regular music programme of jazz, *choro*, and samba and serves up excellent middle-eastern dishes. Its neighbours offer Brazilian *picanha* (steaks that you can cook yourself at your table), German or Italian food. Turn up and have a look at the menus and a listen to the live music before you make your choice, or for a cheaper option, or if you're not too hungry, you can just go, soak up the atmosphere, and buy a snack from the street vendors. **Other locations**: Avenida Atlântica 1936, Copacabana (2235 6698).

Far Eastern

Mr Lam

Rua Maria Angélica 21, Lagoa (2286 6661/ www.mrlam.com.br). Bus 463, 569. **Open** 7pm-12.30am Tue-Thur; 7pm-1.30am Fri, Sat; noon-6pm Sun. **Main courses** R$29-$148. **Credit** AmEx, DC, MC, V. **Map** p249 E13 ❻❹

Apart from an efficient mass transit system and a large central park, one thing every major city needs is at least one decent Chinese restaurant named 'Mr' something. Mr Lam, though, the chef here, was poached from Mr Chow's in Manhattan by local businessman Eike Batista and has become something of a sensation in Rio. The set menus are great for sharing and get you a procession of mixed appetisers such as minced crab wrapped in lettuce, spring rolls, and chicken satay. Follow up with crispy duck (very authentic) or the usual stir-fried meat or fish options with delicious sauces. The cocktails are good, if pricey (averaging around R$20) but the few wines offered by the glass best avoided in favour of beer or soft drinks.

Nakombi

Rua Maria Angélica 183, Jardim Botânico (2246 1518/www.nakombi.com.br). Bus 409, 410, 438, 996. **Open** 7pm-1am Mon-Thur; noon-4pm, 7pm-1.30am Fri; 12.30pm-1.30am Sat; 12.30pm-midnight Sun. **Main courses** R$45-$110. **Credit** AmEx, MC. **Map** p249 E13. ❻❺

There's a seemingly infinite number of places to eat sushi in Rio these days, but this split-level Japanese joint, with its miniature Buddhas smiling up at diners from the stripped-wood floor, and its wonderfully incongruous centrepiece, a mini-van of all things, promises – and delivers – something different. Owner Paolo Barossi had the idea

of putting a sushi bar in one of the aforementioned vehicles – emblematic of the Paulista Japanese community – ten years ago, and now there are three such restaurants in Sao Paolo and this new branch in Rio. Sushiman Ohata 'drives' the van, deftly slicing and dicing over 30 sushi options that impress both eyes and palate. Options include *kobinados*, *tenakis*, *duplas* and special rolls. The upper level, with its private booths, is much in demand thanks to its free Wi-Fi and order-by-intercom system (15 per cent is added to the bill for the latter service).

Organic

Orgânico

Praça Santos Dumont 31, Gávea (2187 0100/ www.enirvana.com.br). Bus 178, 432, 512. **Open** 6am-10pm Mon-Fri; 9am-6pm Sat. **Main courses** R$15-R$20. **Credit** DC, MC, V. **Map** p248 B15 ❻❻

It's early starts in the Nirvana yoga centre for their balanced snacks of healthy and organic food prepared by chef Márcio Valério. The decor is very zen to accompany fresh fruit shakes or daily specials like grilled heart of palm in passion fruit sauce.

Zona Oeste

Traditional Brazilian

Quinta

Rua Luciano Gallet 150, Vargem Grande (2428 1396/ www.quinta.net). Bus 703, 707. **Open** by reservation only Mon-Fri; 1-7pm Sat, Sun. **Main courses** R$40-$60. **Credit** AmEx, MC, V.

This is a good place in which to blow your budget completely. Set in an exquisite colonial-style house (which, predictably, isn't anywhere like as old as it looks), amid a delightful tropical garden, the dining experience at Quinta is one to be savoured. Choose a table on the terrace, overlooking the pond, and *sagui* (cheeky little monkeys) will come and sit on the railings beside you. The menu is imaginative and wide-ranging and all of the the dishes top quality – try the wild boar and seafood crêpes.

Modern Brazilian

In House

Rio Design Barra 345, Avenida das Américas 7777, Barra da Tijuca (2438 7638). Bus 854, 882, 1133. **Open** noon-11pm Mon-Thur, Sun; noon-1am Fri, Sat. **Main courses** R$15-$30. **Credit** AmEx, DC, MC, V.

This is a stylish, clean-cut and friendly place, just as good for a snack lunch with friends as for a dinner for two. Light and bright in the day, the atmosphere in the evening is relaxed and welcoming. There's a comfortable area for drinks before you eat, all squidgy sofas and deep armchairs – and the caipirinhas are encouragingly generous. Foodwise, it's Italy meets Brazil, with a range of pastas and local dishes with a contemporary twist. Try the *escalope dionisio* or for real local flavour, the *brasileirinho* (a juicy steak with the usual Brazilian accompaniments – plus a fried egg). In the unlikely event you've left room for more, try the pecan pie.

French

Clube Chocolate

2nd floor, São Conrado Fashion Mall, São Conrado (3322 1223/www.clubechocolate.com). Bus 175, 524, 750. **Open** noon-11pm Mon-Wed; noon-midnight Thur, Fri; noon-12.30am Sat; noon-10pm Sun. **Main courses** R$28-$68. **Credit** AmEx, DC, MC, V. **Map** p253 E3 ⑰
A fashionable boutique (*see p136*) and a fashionable restaurant rolled into one, this is Latin America's original concept store and the place to rub shoulders with Rio's jet-set crowd of actors, artists and businessmen. The menu is full of French classics so exquisitely created and presented by Parisian chef

Pascal Jolly that it's hard to find their equal elsewhere in the city. Each weekend there's a special menu focusing on the cuisine of a particular region in France, from Normandy to Provence and all the bits in between. But no one's here for the food alone – this is a restaurant to visit for the sheer experience.

Italian

Ettore

Avenida Armando Lombardi 800D/E, Barra (2493 1548/www.ettore.com.br). Bus 387, 523. **Open** noon-midnight Mon-Thur; noon-2am Sat, Sun. **Main courses** R$30-$50. **Credit** DC, MC, V. **Map** p253 A3 ⑱
The bread basket alone makes a trip to Ettore worthwhile – loaves coated with sea salt and rosemary, filled with cheese and ham. Don't fill up too much, though, because the menu is full of fine Italian favourites and new twists on the theme. The atmosphere is cosy and relaxed: trattoria meets Carioca.

Relax and make yourself at home in the comfortable living space of **In House**.

On the menu

acarajé delicious fried-bean cake, fried and stuffed with vatapá (*see below*).
bobó de camarão manioc cooked with fresh shrimp, peppers, tomatoes and coconut milk.
canja chicken broth with vegetables. A good bet for sensitive stomachs.
carne de sol heavily salted, cured beef served with beans, rice, squash and kale.
casquinha de siri stuffed crab with tomato, garlic, onion, green pepper and white wine.
cozido can describe any type of stew. Usually contains a good range of vegetables.
farofa a common side dish made from manioc.
feijoada a classic Carioca dish – black beans and various cuts of pork and beef, served with kale, rice, farfofa and sliced oranges.
moqueca Bahian seafood stew cooked in palm oil and coconut milk. Recommended.
prato feito an inexpensive dish served at lunch usually comprising rice, beans, salad and a choice of fish, chicken or beef.
tutu á Mineira a bean purée from Minas Gerais with manioc flour, onion, garlic, parsley, bacon, sausage and hard-boiled egg.
vatapá Bahian shrimp dish with a thick sauce of coconut milk, tomatoes and palm oil.

Cardápio Menu

café da manhã breakfast; **almoço** lunch; **lanche** snack; **jantar** dinner; **sopa/caldo** soup; **prato principal** main course; **sobremesa** dessert; **sorvete** ice-cream; **garçom** waiter; **conta/nota** bill; **taxa de seviço** service charge; **pão** bread; **queijo** cheese; **leite** milk; **ovos** eggs; **manteiga** butter; **azeite** olive oil; **dendê** palm oil; **alho** garlic; **sal** salt; **pimenta** pepper; **açúcar** sugar; **molho** sauce; **farinha** dried manioc flour; **arroz** rice; **feijão** beans; **mandioca** cassava/manioc; **milho** corn; **palmito** palm heart; **assado** roasted; **churrasco** barbecue; **cozido** boiled; **frito** fried; **grelhado** grilled; **picante** spicy/hot.

Carnes e aves Meat & poultry

bife steak; **carneiro** lamb; **costela** ribs; **costeleta** chop; **fígado** liver; **frango** chicken; **lingüiça** sausage; **pato** duck; **peru** turkey; **peito** breast; **picadinho** stew; **porco** pork.

Peixe/Frutos do mar Fish/seafood

atum tuna; **camarão** shrimp; **caranguejo** crab; **lagosta** lobster; **lula** squid; **mariscos** shellfish; **ostra** oyster; **polvo** octopus; **siri** small crab.

Seafood

4 Estaçóes
Ilha da Coroa 20, Barra da Tijuca (2493 4444/ www.restaurante4estacoes.com.br). Bus 175, 179, 523, 524, 2016. **Open** 6pm-midnight Wed-Fri; noon-1am Sat; noon-8pm Sun. **Main courses** R$30-$50. **Credit** AmEx, DC, MC, V. **Map** p253 B4 ⑨
You can only get to the restaurant by crossing the Marapendi lake by boat, a romantic adventure that sets the tone for an equally seductive candlelit supper. The service is impeccable, as are the dishes prepared by head chef Alex Freire. His speciality is fresh fish and seafood, and the *casquinha de siri* (crab au gratin) is irrefutable proof of his skills.

Skunna
Estrada dos Bandeirantes 23363, Vargem Grande (2428 1213/www.skunna.com.br). Bus 703, 707. **Open** 7pm-midnight Thur; noon-1am Fri-Sun. **Main courses** R$30-$40. **Credit** AmEx, DC, MC.
Skunna is *the* place for seafood in Vargem Grande's Centro Gastronômico and is worth the trek out west in itself. Simple and unpretentious, its appearance belies the wonders which emerge from the kitchen. Prawns in orange sauce with saffron rice, seafood risotto and a magnificent *moqueca* (a typically Brazilian seafood stew) – it's very hard to choose, particularly as most main courses are big enough for two. For those who are not so fish inclined, there is a good choice of steak and chicken dishes. A little gentle live music makes for a very mellow evening out of town.

Zona Norte

Traditional Brazilian

Restaurante Quinta da Boa Vista
Parque Quinta da Boa Vista, São Cristovão (2589 4279/www.restaurantequintaboavista.com.br). Metro São Cristóvão/461, 462, 463 bus. **Open** 11am-6pm daily. **Main courses** R$20-$57. **Credit** AmEx, V. **Map** p252 B2 ⑩
Although off the beaten tourist track, this restaurant deserves a place on it, for its cuisine as well as its history and beautiful park setting. It is housed in the former chapel of the São Cristovão palace and has been tastefully extended. Large picture windows in the dining area bring the green of the park right inside and the atmosphere is serene and relaxed or there's outdoor seating too. The food is fresh and delicious and the main course portions are generous enough to share between two. It opens at lunchtime only but as it is a two minute stroll from the entrances of both the zoo and the National Museum it is the perfect resting place between the two.

Bars, Cafés & Botecos

Beating the heat.

Rio knows a lot about quenching thirst and can be one of the most fun places to take a drink in the world. Separating out the bars and botecos from the restaurants and live music venues has been a near impossible task – you'll be able to fill your belly at almost all of these places, and don't be surprised if a band strikes up too. Equally, many of the restaurants listed won't take offence if you turn up for a drink only, though Cariocas generally don't drink without eating, and some of the city's best bars have such good live music that we've listed them in our Music chapter (*see pp174-183*).

WHERE TO DRINK

Traditional botecos (*see p122* **Cool, cold beer**) are everywhere there are buildings; kioscos and street vendors cover everywhere else – all competing to serve the coldest beers. For a smarter drink, choose between the historical grand cafés of the centre or the new wave of Paulista-style design bars of Ipanema and Leblon. Or hit both – you're on holiday.

But Rio's not really about being smart. Up on the hill overlooking the centre, the bay and the

Sugar Loaf mountain, Santa Teresa is best discovered through its cafés and botecos. Likewise, Laranjeiras and Botafogo, areas that generally get driven straight through by visitors, reward a visit to their innovative bars with a glimpse of a lively alternative scene.

Recommended too is an evening in the laid-back bars of Baixo Gávea or Jardim Botânico. Like the rest of the city, few of the places are going to impress on decor – but stick around to soak up the atmosphere and you probably won't want to leave.

WHAT TO DRINK

If Rio ever had a rule book of drinking etiquette, someone tore it up a long time ago. Order what you like, when you like and nobody's going to question your taste or sobriety.

That said, apart from wine, which is expensive and generally poor compared with other countries, there's not much chance to go wrong. Soft drinks are coffee (espresso) and fruit juices (a multitude); alcoholic drinks are beer and caipirinhas, or some version on the theme (substitute other fruits for lime for taste, and vodka for cachaça to reduce the hangover). Beer – found in the 'Soft Drinks' section of most menus – is almost invariably lager, served in a quick succession of small glasses so it never gets a chance to get warm.

A note: though Cariocas drink a lot and have little respect for decorum, they rarely get drunk and disorderly. Don't spoil the party.

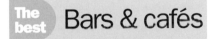

Bars & cafés
The best

For a late-night drink
Prop up the bar at **Pizza Guanabara** (*see p128*) or **Cervantes** (*see p126*).

For postcard-perfect views
Admire the bay from **Bar Urca** (*see p120*).

For flirting
Braseiro da Gávea (*see p128*) or anywhere else there's people around.

For afternoon tea
Have your cake and eat it too at **Confeitaria Colombo** (*see p120*) or **Cafe du Lage** (*see p128*).

For cold açaí
Get fresh and juicy at **Natural e Sabor Juice Bar** (*see p128*) or **BB Lanches** (*see p126*).

For rounding off the weekend
The lively way in **Casa Rosa** (*see p123*) or quietly in the gentle **Goiabeira** (*see p123*).

The Centre

Amarelinho
Praça Floriano 55, Cinelândia (2240 8434/www. amarelinhodacinelandia.com.br). Metro Cinelândia/ 119, 125 bus. **Open** 11am-last customer daily. **Credit** AmEx, DC, MC, V. **Map** p245 I3 ❶
On the historic Praça Floriano, the downtown Amarelinho is the flagship in a chain of several, and a Carioca classic. Its prime location and good reputation have made it a historic meeting point for students, intellectuals and business people over the last 80 years. A perfect pit stop on a downtown

> ❶ Pink numbers given in this chapter correspond to the location of each café, bar and boteco on the street maps. *See pp244-253.*

Eat, Drink, Shop

Social Sunday evenings at **Casa Rosa**. *See p123.*

walking tour, rest your feet while having a beer and slice of pizza and watch the cogs of Rio's business community turn.

Other locations: throughout the city.

Bar Luiz

Rua da Carioca 39, Centro (2262 6900/www.barluiz. com.br). Metro Carioca/107, 154, 158 bus. **Open** 11am-11.30pm Mon-Sat. **Credit** AmEx, DC, MC, V. **Map** p245 I2 ➋

Serving cold meat, cold beer and a highly regarded potato salad, Bar Luiz has been a Rio reference point and a firm favourite for a long lunch since 1887. In between, it's changed location (in 1927) and name (in 1942, from Bar Adolf) but the menu and decor have remained true to the original spirit.

Cachaça Esporte Clube

Rua do Riachuelo 49, Lapa (2242 4580/www. cachacaesporteclube.com.br). Bus 433, 464, 572. **Open** 5pm-last customer Tue-Sat. **Credit** AmEx, MC, V. **Map** p245 I4 ➌

Occupying a classic corner in Lapa, the main attraction at Cachaça Esporte Clube is – guess what? – cachaça. There are over 100 different kinds on offer. To watch the world go by and avoid the crush inside, aim for a table close to the big windows.

Confeitaria Colombo

Rua Gonçalves Dias 32, Centro (2232 2300/ www.confeitariacolombo.com.br). Bus 119, 121, 123. **Open** 8am-8pm Mon-Fri; 9.30am-5pm Sat. **Credit** AmEx, DC, MC, V. **Map** p245 I2 ➍

A Rio institution since 1894, this is *the* place to come to soak up the atmosphere of a bygone age. With a high, stained-glass ceiling, galleried upper floor and magnificent Belgian mirrors throughout, it's easy to see why the *confeitaria* has always been a favourite haunt of the city's artists and intellectuals. A pianist tinkling the ivories of the grand piano adds to the attraction if the mouthwatering array of pastries is an insufficient draw. Try the brulée tart with fresh fruits. A large selection of sandwiches and savoury snacks is also available. Upstairs, the Cristóvão restaurant does a good buffet lunch and an à la carte menu of hearty Brazilian dishes, suffused with a distinct flavour of Spain and Portugal. Also well worth visiting is the Confeitaria Colombo in the Forte de Copacabana.

Other locations: Forte de Copacabana, Praça Eugênio Franco 1, Copacabana (3201 4049).

The Bay

Bar Urca

Rua Cândido Gaffrée 205, Urca (2295 8744/ www.barurca.com.br). Bus 511, 512. **Open** 11am-11pm Mon-Sat; 11am-6pm Sun. **Credit** AmEx, MC, V. **Map** p250 J14 (inset map) ➎

Rio is full of charming settings, but very few are more charming than Bar Urca's. At the tip of one of Rio's quietest neighbourhoods, Bar Urca is a two-storey corner affair that looks out over a picturesque little marina of bobbing boats. Or it would, if there weren't a line of people across the street blocking the view by leaning on the concrete balastrade and drinking beer. And that's the best part about Bar Urca – waiters cross the street to serve extremely cold beer and good bar food like *empadas* (small tarts) and *pastéis* (small fried pies; the *camarão* (shrimp) is highly recommended) – to patrons lingering on the waterfront sidewalk. Views of Niterói and downtown, and a host of colourful regulars make it an ideal spot for an afternoon beer.

Belmonte

Praia do Flamengo 300, Flamengo (2552 3349/ www.botecobelmonte.com.br). Metro Flamengo/ 409, 472, 572 bus. **Open** 7am-last customer daily. **No credit cards.** **Map** p247 J8 ⑥

Late on weeknights when the rest of Flamengo is dark and quiet, perennially boisterous Belmonte is busting at the seams, the crowd overflowing out into the street. If you can get inside, the classic decor will take you back half a century. Long popular with journalists and other professionals who live in the area's numerous high-rise apartment buildings, the concept at Belmonte is simple: go with friends, talk loudly, laugh and drink cold beer. *Photo p124.*

Cobal de Humaitá

Rua Voluntários da Pátria 446, Humaitá (various phones/www.portalducobal.com.br). Bus 173, 410, 522. **Open** 6pm last customer daily. **Credit** varies. **Map** p246 F11 ⑦

In the shadow of the Christ statue, Cobal de Humaitá occupies nearly an entire city block and is a popular gathering place – on a warm evening hundreds line the outdoor tables quaffing cold ones, listening to live music if someone's playing, and eating. With barely a frill in sight, it's a straightforward and none-too-attractive market, but completely functional. The most popular night spots on the Rua Voluntários da Patria side are Espirito do Chopp (2266 5599) serving *estupidamente* cold beer and Manekineko (2537 1510), serving sushi. Also serving outdoor tables are Pizza Park (2537 2603) and Galeto Mania (2537 0616). Lengthy expanses of tables crammed together means service can be slow. Samba and choro is often played live on weekends.

Drinkeria Maldita

Rua Voluntários da Pátria 10, Botafogo (2527 2456/http://matrizonline.oi.com.br/drinkeriamaldita). Metro Botafogo/464, 583, 584 bus. **Open** 6pm-4am Tue-Fri; 6pm-5am Sat, Sun. **Credit** AmEx, MC, V. **Map** p247 H10 ⑧

The latest venture from the owners of Casa da Matriz, Drinkeria Maldita has quickly become a favourite in Botafogo. With Miller Genuine Draft, home-made burgers, industrial-strength air-conditioning and pop decor, it doesn't feel much like Brazil. The kitchen can get a bit bogged down with the heavy volume of orders, but the food is good when it comes. Sidewalk tables extend down the block for those who prefer to be outside, but be fore-warned that the adjacent avenue is noisy and stays that way well into the night.

Mofo

Rua Barão do Flamengo 35, Loja C, Botafogo (2179 8264). Bus 434, 573, 574. **Open** 11.30am-last customer daily. **Credit** MC, V. **Map** p247 I7 ⑨

Thankfully, the oddly named Mofo – Portuguese for mould – has nothing to do with the freshness of the food or the hygiene of the bar. Instead, it's an oblique reference to the owner's dad and his nostalgia of bygone days, which are evoked by black and white photos and art deco antiques. Busy and sociable, Mofo is a 'locals' bar where students and artists from the neighbourhood drop in for chit-chat. The all-important caipirinha range is great, with the delicious watermelon version the pick of the bunch.

O Plebeu

Rua Capitão Salomão 50, Botafogo (2286 0699/ www.oplebeu.com.br). Bus 154, 434, 463, 521. **Open** 8am-4am Mon-Sat; 8am-9pm Sun. **Credit** AmEx, DC, MC, V. **Map** p246 F11 ⑩

Good luck getting a table at this honest Botafogo bar, but don't be shy if it looks hopeless – just wedge yourself in for a look around, then climb upstairs for a peek there too. Tables and patrons spill out of everywhere at O Plebeu, onto the second-floor balcony – the best spot in the house – to the sidewalk, where groups multiply and absorb one another until it's hard to tell who came with whom; and even through the windows, where neighbours gather on soccer nights to peer in and follow the national sport. The beer is served bracingly cold, kept that way with coolers and refilled adeptly by waiters in perpetual motion.

Downtown drinks at **Amarelinho**. *See p119.*

Cool, cold beer

Rio's bars, traditionally rough and ready establishments known as botecos, or sometimes *botequins*, are as good a place to fall in love with the city as its beaches or mountains. While keeping up a steady supply of ice-cold beer, they manage to embody the legendary Carioca informality.

The majority are still the basic, hole-in-the-wall places known as *pé-sujos*, which literally translates as 'dirty feet' – the name coming from the fact that the men (and they are almost always men) who stand at the metal and glass counters are shod either in mucky work boots or sandy flip-flops. More upmarket botecos are nicer, cleaner and more spacious, with tables, cold beer, basic snacks and meals and friendly service from male waiters. (Carioca waiters have traditionally been old men in bow ties.)

In recent years, however, a new kind of establishment has sprung up. Dubbed, not unsurprisingly, *pé-limpos* (clean feet), the new bars blend the casual charm of the traditional Carioca boteco with a more upmarket Paulista-style bar-restaurant. Built with the female customer in mind, their success revolves around their ability to preserve Rio's laid-back informality with a higher standard of service, a wider range of tastier and healthier food and a more spacious and classy environment.

Today, six different chains have capitalised on the desire for *pé-limpos*, all adding branches at a steady rate. The leader is **Manoel e Joaquim** (*see p127*) with 11 bars. The famous **Garota de Ipanema** bar has added nine more outlets in other neighbourhoods and named them accordingly (*see p127*). Other chains include **Botequim Informal** (*see p126*) **Devassa** (*see p126*), **Belmonte** (*p121*) and **Espelunca Chic** (*p126*).

Pé-limpo service, as in many bars, comes through waiters, who generally look after a certain sector – so keep in his good books or you'll go thirsty. No one goes to the bar and the bill is paid at the end of the night. (Under a recent, but relatively untested, law, customers can now request a chart to note down what they consume as a way of avoiding the sadly common practice of bill-padding.)

Food is available and Cariocas never go out just to drink. In many *pé-limpos*, waiters deliver trays of snacks unsolicited, so be careful what you order and ask about the price – they aren't giving it away for free.

Most of the *pé-sujos*, however, are so small that the only places to sit are on bar stools over the counter and if you don't serve yourself, no one else will. Patrons often stand in the street, balancing their drinks on stools. The really tiny places are known as *bunda fora* ('arse outside') because there isn't enough space to get whole bodies in. The food on offer is basic and greasy and if you order anything other than beer, cachaça or caipirinha the barman will look at you like you're from another planet.

A good introduction to the *pé-sujo* experience is to go for lunch. Most serve a plate of beef or chicken with rice and beans for a very affordable price, a Carioca experience not to be missed – if you have the stomach for it.

The Hills

Bar do Gomez

Rua Áurea 26, Santa Teresa (2232 0822). Tram Paula Mattos/214 bus. **Open** 11am-11pm Mon-Sat; noon-11pm Sun. **Credit** MC, V. **Map** p244 G5 **①**
The inimitable Bar do Gomez was founded in 1919 as a grocer's store by Spanish immigrants from Galicia. To this day it retains its idiosyncratic charm and functions both as a bar and a grocer's: household cleaning products, tinned foods and jars of olives and jams fill the shelves above the bar. Its affable Spanish owner, Gomez, has run this Santa Teresa icon for many years. The deep-fried codfish balls and mini shrimp pies are highly recommended. There are over 60 types of cachaça to choose from and good draught beer is served throughout the day. A truly unique bar. Warmly recommended.

Eat, Drink, Shop

Bar do Marcô

*Rua Almirante Alexandrino 412, Santa Teresa
(2531 8787). Either tram line/206, 214 bus.*
Open noon-midnight Tue-Sun. **No credit cards.**
Map p245 H5 ⑫
This bar-cum-restaurant has a cosy feel to it with
two sofas at the back of the bar and a balcony with
a fine view of the Niterói bridge and the mountains
in the distance. A good *feijoada* can be had on
Saturdays and Sundays. The bar also offers a good
range of live music. From Friday to Sunday, for a
small cover charge, you can hear chorinho, bossa
nova, samba, MPB or jazz.

Casa Rosa

*Rua Alice 550, Laranjeiras (2557 2562/www.casa
rosa.com.br). Bus 298, 422, 583, 584.* **Open** from
10pm Fri, Sat; from 5pm Sun. **No credit cards.**
Map p246 F8 ⑬
Once a huge brothel, the 'pink house' is now one of
Rio's more diverse clubs. In the sprawling house on
the hill overlooking Laranjeiras, Casa Rosa is dominated by a spacious open-air patio and rambles on
from there. A smallish stage hosts samba and forró
on Sundays and a wide range of quality bands on
other nights. Two bars keep the booze flowing and
the stairs at the back of the house lead to an air-
conditioned room where DJs play electronica.
There's also table football and pool tables. Sunday
samba nights get going at around 6pm, on Fridays
and Saturdays at around midnight. *Photo p120.*

Clan Café

*Rua Cosme Velho 564, Cosme Velho (2558 2322).
Bus 422, 498.* **Open** 11am-3pm Mon-Fri; 11am-
last customer Sat. **Credit** AmEx, MC, V.
Map p246 F9 ⑭
A trip up the hill in the evening yields the Clan
Café, a bar/music venue with a taste of the old Rio.
Musicians play samba, forró, jazz, MPB and other
native and non-native styles of music. A big open
air patio roofed with ivy makes it ideal for warm
Carioca evenings. If want to hear the music, it pays
to arrive early (or reserve) and get a table close to
the stage. Music normally starts at around 9.30pm.

Goiabeira

*Largo das Neves 13, Santa Teresa (2232 5751).
Tram Paula Mattos/214 bus.* **Open** from 6pm Tue-
Sun. **No credit cards. Map** p244 G4 ⑮
A small traditional bar nestled under the shade of a
large *goiaba* (guava) tree on a corner of a charming
little square at the end of the tram line, Goiabeira
does an assortment of tasty snacks, reasonable pizzas and good cachaças. A great place to go to get
away from the madding crowds of Largo dos
Guimarães. The bar closes when the last customer
has drained their last drink and not a moment before.

Hideaway

*Rua das Laranjeiras 308, Laranjeiras (2285 0921)
Bus 498, 583, 584.* **Open** 6pm-2am Tue-Thur, Sun;
6pm-5am Fri, Sat. **Credit** AmEx, DC, MC, V.
Map p246 G8 ⑯

Open house at **Bar do Gomez.**

Belmonte. *See p121.*

Although Rio isn't known for its pizza, Hideaway could hold its own in Naples. In an old building mercifully set off the noisy Rua das Laranjeiras, there are over 20 available toppings that are layered generously on well-made crispy crusts. Pool tables, board games, good music (mostly jazz, occasionally house music) and extremely cold beer make it an excellent place to kill a few hours with friends.

Jasmin Manga

Largo do Guimarães 143, Santa Teresa (2242 2605). Either tram line/206, 214 bus. **Open** 10am-11pm daily. **Credit** MC. **Map** p245 H5 ⓱
An attractively designed cyber café serving a good variety of sandwiches, salads and pizzas, Jasmin Manga is conveniently located near to the tram stop in Largo dos Guimarães and boasts an indoor space as well as a very pleasant patio surrounded by tropical plants. The breakfasts are good value and a wide range of alcoholic drinks is served. There's live music every Thursday from 8pm to 11pm.

Largo das Letras

Rua Almirante Alexandrino 501, Santa Teresa (2221 8992/www.largodasletras.com.br). Either tram line/206, 214 bus. **Open** 2-10pm Tue-Sat; 2-8pm Sun. **Credit** AmEx, DC, MC, V. **Map** p245 H5 ⓲
Hidden away in a slightly dilapidated early 20th-century mansion just above Largo dos Guimarães is Santa Teresa's only bookstore-cum-café. Decent

coffee along with savoury snacks and Portuguese sweets can be sampled on the patio just in front of the bookstore, which has a good range of books on both Rio and Brazil. It's an ideal spot to watch the world go by in Largo dos Guimarães below.

Mike's Haus

Rua Almirante Alexandrino 1458A, Santa Teresa (2509 5248/www.mikeshaus.com.br). Tram Dois Irmãos/206 bus. **Open** noon-midnight Tue-Thur, Sun; noon-2am Fri, Sat. **Credit** DC, MC. **Map** p244 G6 ⓳
A small, eclectically decorated German restaurant-cum-pub, Mike's Haus serves up authentic German cuisine and offers a good range of imported beers from the motherland. Owned and run by a German (the eponymous Mike) and his Brazilian wife, this moderately priced establishment is popular with both Cariocas and expats. The homemade apple strudel should not be missed. Nor, while you're in the area, should you miss the *acarajé* (a spicy shrimp filled black-eyed pea patty cooked in bubblingly hot palm oil) sold by Mike's neighbour, Nega Teresa, from her decorated roadside stall (Rua Almirante Alexandrino 1458, 2232 1310, 5-10pm Thur-Sun).

Simplesmente

Rua Pascoal Carlos Magno 115, Santa Teresa (2221 0337). Either tram line/206, 214 bus. **Open** 6pm-3.30am Mon-Thur; 6pm-4.30am Fri, Sat. **No credit cards. Map** p245 H5 ⓴

Popular with the local Bohemian crowd, this unpretentious bar has a friendly and funky 1960s feel to it. It's a good bet for late-night drinks and light snacks. The delicious black bean soup is a favourite here. Live *samba de raiz* (roots samba) can be heard every Wednesday from around 9pm (there's a R$2 cover charge). Many people leave their tables to dance, enhancing the joint's informal, let-it-all-hang-out atmosphere.

The Beaches

Academia da Cachaça

Rua Conde Bernadotte 26G, Leblon (2529 2680/ www.academiadacachaca.com.br). Bus 464, 522, 572. **Open** noon-2am Tue-Sat; noon-1am Sun. **Credit** DC, MC, V. **Map** p248 B16 ㉑
The Academia de Cachaça is an unremarkable bar on the edge of an equally unremarkable shopping centre, but something more than its name has struck a chord with the drinking classes. Its wide range of cachaça (it boasts almost 100 different brands), a decent menu of north-eastern delicacies like sun-dried meat and *escondidinho* (a sumptuous mix of mashed cassava and cheese with fillings like shrimp and trout), and its lively atmosphere makes it a huge hit with middle-class Cariocas of all ages. It is almost always busy, with queues outside at weekends – and this just a year after it doubled in size due to demand.

Allegro Bistrô Musical

Modern Sound, Rua Barata Ribeiro 502D, Copacabana (2548 5005/www.modernsound. com.br). Metro Siqueira Campos/154, 433, 523 bus. **Open** 9am-9pm Mon-Fri; 9-8pm Sun. **Credit** AmEx, DC, MC, V. **Map** p250 H14 ㉒
Located in the kind of air-conditioned record megastore, restaurant, café, bar and daytime live jazz venue that you don't really expect to find in the often sweltering, chaotic quarter of Copacabana. Apart from offering perhaps the best selection of music CDs in Rio, Modern Sound features free live Brazilian jazz most afternoons in its Allegro Bistrô, along with a full bar, finger-foods, salads, sandwiches and main dishes. Performance hours vary so check the website for details.

Bar Bracarense

José Linhares 85, Leblon (2294 3549/www. bracarense.com.br). Bus 132, 157, 433, 512. **Open** 7am-midnight Mon-Fri; 8am-midnight Sat; 9am-10pm Sun. **No credit cards. Map** p248 B16 ㉓
The Bracarense enjoys an almost fabled status among Brazil's drinkers for its beer and snacks. The draught is creamy and freezing and is consistently rated among the best in Rio, and the bar snacks, particularly the fried balls of shrimp and catupiry cheese, are right up there. Other than that, though, there isn't much to shout about. The Bracarense has a real outdoor energy but it's basically a glorified

pavement, with tables strewn along the edge of the street. A recent refurbishment has spruced the place up and given it a cleaner, less studenty feel (gone are the plastic tables and chairs, replaced by smart wooden ones) and the once disgusting toilets are now more presentable. Popular with bathers coming straight from the beach a few blocks away, especially at weekends.

BB Lanches
Rua Aristides Espinola 64A, Leblon (2294 1397). Bus 132, 157, 433, 512. **Open** 9am-3am daily. **No credit cards. Map** p248 A17 ㉔
BB Lanches is not the only juice bar in Leblon but it was the first and is the most famous. Service is fast and friendly and there's always someone standing at the right-angled counter on the corner of Ataulfo de Paiva, and normally a few sitting on the wooden benches on the pavement sipping on an *açaí* juice. There are 28 different kind of fruit juices on offer and almost 100 different sandwiches, snacks and hearty meat pastries.

Botequim Informal
Rua Conde de Bernadete 26, Leblon (2540-5504/ www.botequiminformal.com.br). Bus 132, 157, 433. **Open** 6pm-1am Mon-Fri; noon-1am Sat, Sun. **Credit** AmEx, DC, MC, V. **Map** p248 B16 ㉕
A typical *pé-limpo* (*see p122* **Cool, cold beers**), Informal creates an easy environment to appreciate as good a *chope* at Brahma as you'll find in Rio. In a bid for this all-important title, Informal has imported technology from São Paulo. The key? A two tap system, one pouring liquid, the other adding a creamy head. The new tactic is serving them well enough, they've now got five branches dotted around the city, and one in Niterói.
Other locations: throughout the city.

Cervantes
Rua Barata Ribeiro 7B, Copacabana (2275 6147). Bus 154, 433, 523. **Open** noon-4am Tue-Thur; noon-6am Fri, Sat. **Credit** DC, MC, V. **Map** p250 I13 ㉖
Trust in the pineapple. Cervantes has been serving what many Cariocas consider the best sandwiches in Rio since 1959, so if the man behind the counter offers you a slice of pineapple with your sandwich, go for it. Two things can be difficult about Cervantes. One is getting in and out without any unpleasantness, especially in the wee hours when the streets can be dodgy but when, ironically, Cervantes sees a rush of punters. This is a part of Copacabana, after all, that's also home to prostitutes, pimps and the drug trade, but a little awareness should get you through fine. The other tricky part is deciding which sandwich to order from the comprehensive range. Cervantes also has one of the better ranges of draught beers in Copacabana.
Other locations: Park Palace, Avenida das Américas 5777/112, Barra da Tijuca (2438 1458); Via Parque Shopping 2068, Avenida Ayrton Senna 3000, Barra da Tijuca (2421 1068).

Cobal do Leblon
Rua Gilberto Cordoso (various phones/www. portaldacobal.com.br). Bus 464, 522, 572. **Open** 6pm-last customer. **Credit** varies. **Map** p248 C16 ㉗
Tucked away in the backstreets between Leblon and Gávea is Cobal Leblon, a market by day and collection of eateries by night, with a mishmash of plastic tables and chairs in its big open-air courtyard. It's smaller than the more popular Cobal de Humaitá (*see p121*), and somewhat lacks its ambience, but is nevertheless a pleasant place to down a cold beer on a warm night, especially if there's been a big Flamengo match that day. Among the most popular places are Pizza Park (2512 1423) and Bar Boemia (2511 3122) at the entrance, which is open all day and serves a good range of meals and cachaças.

Copa Café
Avenida Atlântica 3056, Copacabana (2235 2947). Bus 136, 154, 523. **Open** 7pm-2am Tue-Sun. **Credit** AmEx, MC, V. **Map** p249 H15 ㉘
A 'chic burger-joint' may seem like a contradiction, but Copa Café is just that. The lounge downstairs is comfortable and smart, and filled with an arty, modish crowd sipping great caipirinhas. Upstairs, the dining area is downright romantic. Soft lighting, well-spaced tables and discreet and attentive waiting staff offer a welcome respite from the many mediocre tourist-oriented outdoor places along Avenida Atlântica. The menu is varied, but burgers are a house speciality, with beef, lamb, salmon and tuna options.

Devassa
Avenida General San Martin 1241, Leblon (2259 8271). Bus 132, 157, 433, 512. **Open** 5pm-last customer Mon-Fri; 2pm-5am Sat, Sun. **Credit** AmEx, DC, MC. **Map** p248 A17 ㉙
For a city so obsessed with beer, it's surprising that there aren't more micro-breweries, but Devassa is doing its best to fill the gap, opening new branches at a rapid rate since 2002. The original is a straightforward bar in the heart of Leblon, which always has room to squeeze in a couple more at the end of the long wooden tables. The beer's a welcome change from lager too.
Other locations: throughout the city.

Espelunca Chic
Avenida Ataulfo de Paiva 900B, Leblon (2512 9767/ www.conversafiadabotequim.com.br). Bus 125, 404, 591. **Open** noon-last customer daily. **Credit** MC, V. **Map** p248 B17 ㉚
Formely called Conversa Fiada, and along the same lines as the Belmonte, this is a clean-cut, trendy and modern bar. The interior is decorated with wooden shelves and stark white walls trimmed with black. The clientele are mostly groups of young singles and couples. Waiters circle about offering tapas style skewers of meat, pies and other savoury snacks; it's easy to fill up without ever picking up the menu.
Other locations: Rua Maria Quitéria 46, Ipanema (2247 8609); Rua Jardim Botânico 129, Jardim Botânico (2286 2111); Armando Lombardi 800, Barra (2496 3222).

Eat, Drink, Shop

Garota de Ipanema

Rua Vinicius de Morais 49A, Ipanema (2523 3787/ www.garotaipanema.com.br). Bus 132, 177, 433, 2017. **Open** 11am-3am daily. **Credit** AmEx, DC, MC, V. **Map** p249 F17 ❸❶

Lyrics man Vincius de Morais got the street named after him, musician Tom Jobim got the airport – it was inevitable that the bar where the magic was reportedly struck up should get the name of the famous bossa nova song. With its efficient service and sterile decor, it's hardly the sort of place to inspire songwriters nowadays, but they do serve up some musical history with your caipirinha and bar snacks. **Other locations**: throughout the city.

Jobi

Avenida Ataulfo de Paiva 1166, Leblon (2274 0547). Bus 132, 157, 433, 512. **Open** 11am-4am daily. **Credit** AmEx, DC. **Map** p248 A17 ❸❷

The Jobi is another one of those unremarkable bars that are nevertheless beloved by Cariocas. Small and welcoming, it's perhaps Rio's quintessential boteco. The beer is good and palate-stingingly cold, the snacks on the enormous menu are tasty and the three regular waiters are as cheerful as the two Portuguese owners are lugubrious. The Jobi has oodles of charm, though, as proved by the long queues outside each weekend evening. Stick around for a whole evening and watch time run backwards – older couples and relatively sober groups early on give way to younger crowds and hardened drinkers.

Lord Jim Pub

Rua Paul Redfern 63, Ipanema (2259 3047/www. lordjimpub.com.br). Bus 132, 177, 433, 2017. **Open** 6pm-2.30am Mon-Thur; 6pm-4.30am Fri; 1pm-4.30am Sat, Sun. **Credit** AmEx, DC, MC, V. **Map** p248 D17 ❸❸

Dark, dingy and reeking of smoke, the Lord Jim is a throwback to British pubs of yesteryear – which is no doubt part of the appeal for Cariocas. The attraction for visitors is the varied menu of sport on the pub's two plasma screens and eight TVs. Likeable landlord Doug has turned the Lord Jim into the place in Rio to catch British football, rugby and cricket, especially at weekends when it's packed even on the sunniest afternoons. Pub quizzes, special promotions, live rock'n'roll music including hotly contested 'battle of the bands' nights and regular happy hours, add to the fun during the week. Warning: partly because it's constantly full of gringos, the Lord Jim also attracts members of the world's oldest profession – and they aren't there for the quizzes or the cricket.

Manoel e Juaquim

Rua Barão da Torre 162, Ipanema (2522 1863/ www.manoelejuaquim.com.br). Bus 132, 177, 433, 2017. **Open** 5pm-last customer Tue-Sun. **Credit** DC, MC, V. **Map** p249 F16 ❸❹

A good-times Portuguese beer garden and restaurant chain with its hard-living cartoon mascots, the main draw for all ages is overstated portions of Portuguese food at understated prices. Finger-foods like shrimp pasties, cod-balls, shrimp with fried garlic and sausage sold by the metre give way to copious mains. Pizza is also on offer. It's not just food, though – the house has two versions of its own brand of cachaça made in Minas Gerais. **Other locations**: Avenida Atlântica 3806, Copacabana (2523 1128); Praça João Pessoa 7, Centro (2232 3775); Rua Siqueira Campos 12, Copacabana (2549 3550) Rua Almirante Tamandaré 77, Flamengo (2556 7385).

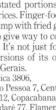

Home from home: a bit of sporting action at the **Lord Jim Pub**.

Natural e Sabor Juice Bar

Rua Visconde de Pirajá 611D, Ipanema (2239 4148).
Bus 132, 177, 433, 2017. **Open** 7am-11pm Mon-Sat.
Credit MC, V. **Map** p248 D17 ⑤
Rio is loaded with juice stands like Natural e Sabor,
but this place rates a mention for a few reasons.
First, they get the *açaí* right, mixed with guaraná
to your request, more if you want it sweeter, less if
you like the bite of the *açaí*. You can add granola
or protein supplements too, which should make you
feel healthier if you also go for the egg burger with
bacon. While savouring your icy *açaí*, check out the
location. Rua Visconde de Pirajá is a lively street,
full of drugstores, shops, newsstands, banks, clubs,
bars, restaurants and hotels. And here, where it
crosses with Avenida Henrique Dumont and where
Leblon turns into Ipanema, you'll find a highly controversial postmodern intersection designed by the
architects Paulo Case and Luiz Acioli. Natural e
Sabor is a perfect place in which to fuel up before
a walking tour of Ipanema.
Other locations: Praia de Botafogo 324A,
Botafogo (2552 5595)

Pizza Guanabara

Avenida Ataulfo de Paiva 1228, Leblon (2294 0797/
www.pizzariaguanabara.com.br). Bus 132, 157, 433,
512. **Open** 10am-8am daily. **Credit** AmEx, DC, MC, V.
Map p248 A17 ⑥
The most important thing to understand about
the Pizza Guanabara is that the pizzas are the
least important thing about it. They are generally
doughy and overrated, although the slices of *mara-
garita, mussarela, portuguesa* and *calabresa* are
good enough if you're really hungry. Rather, Pizza
Guanabara's attractions are its location and clientele. Of three bar/restaurants on a crossroads that
made this Leblon's hottest spot in the 1980s, it's the
only one to survive and thus holds a special place
in Cariocas' hearts. (Eating pizza at the counter
made *O Globo*'s list of 'Fifty things that real
Cariocas do'.) Today, it's hugely popular with the
attractive twenty- and thirtysomething crowd, especially during the wee small hours, when they flock
there looking to snack, chat and flirt, with a particular emphasis on the latter.

Talho Capixaba

Rua Ataulfo de Paiva 1022, Leblon (2512 8760/
www.talhocapixaba.com.br). Bus 132, 157, 433,
512. **Open** 7am-10pm Mon-Sat; 8am-9pm Sun.
Credit AmEx, DC, MC, V. **Map** p248 B17 ⑦
The Talho Capixaba is a café, butcher and delicatessen rolled into one, and its sandwiches are regularly voted the best in town by the *Veja Rio*
entertainment and listings magazine. The focaccia,
croissants and apricot tarts should not be overlooked. It also has wines and imported goods like
mustards, jams and chocolates as well as a fine
array of antipasti. Now serving breakfasts, it's the
delicatessen of choice for Leblon's old-money
crowd and made even more attractive thanks to the
cheery army of garçons.

The Lake

Bar da Graça

Rua Pacheco Leão 780, Horto (2249 5484).
Bus 409. **Open** noon-last customer Tue-Sun.
Credit AmEx, V. **Map** p248 B13 ⑧
Only a couple years old, da Graça has added a
splash of colour to the hillside neighbourhood above
the Botanical gardens. The papered walls, low
lights, lively decoration and friendly service set the
tone. A popular evening hangout with the numerous young artists and professionals who live in the
area, it's a good bet for a cachaça or two in boisterous yet pleasant company.

Bar Lagoa

Avenida Epitácio Pessoa 1674, Lagoa (2523 1135/
2287 1112/www.barlagoa.com.br). Bus 123, 128,
433. **Open** 6pm-2am Mon; noon-2.30am Tue-Sun.
Credit AmEx, DC, MC, V. **Map** p249 F16 ⑨
Bar Lagoa's signature food is German, a tradition
dating back to when the place was founded as Bar
Berlim in 1934. (The name was changed during
World War II.) But don't expect German formality
or efficiency here. The waiters, with their white coats
and white hair, are more likely to be snappish than
snappy: stay late and you might find one sipping a
chope and reading the newspaper while his tables
go thirsty. But that's part of Bar Lagoa's plentiful
charm. Check out the mirrors in the doors, the soft
pink Italian marble and the little internal balcony
where the orchestra used to play. Better still, sit on
the patio and gaze at the lake while sipping a cold
draft beer and picking on an appetizer of white or
red sausage. Bar Lagoa fills up most nights, with
patio tables especially in demand. If you're lucky
enough to land a table close to the street, apply bug
repellent to any bare legs.

Braseiro da Gávea

Praca Santos Dumont 116, Gávea (2239 7494/
www.braseirodagavea.com.br). Bus 158, 179, 572.
Open 11.30am-1am Mon-Thur, Sun; 11.30am-3am
Fri, Sat. **Credit** AmEx, MC, V. **Map** p248 A15 ⑩
There's no rational reason why the Braseiro da
Gávea is one of the best bars in Rio. It just is. The
decor is plain, the food is heavy and you have to get
there before 8pm to have a prayer of getting a seat.
But Rio's trendsetters crowd the pavement outside
and make the square hip. The food is deliciously filling as well as fatty, and it's marvellously informal
atmosphere has helped earn it the reputation as the
best place in town for flirting. *Photo p130.*

Café du Lage

Rua Jardim Botânico 414, Jardim Botânico (2538
1091). Bus 158, 409, 512. **Open** 9am-10.30pm
Mon-Thur; 9am-5pm Fri-Sun. **No credit cards.**
Map p248 D13 ⑪
Attached to the School of Visual Arts in Parque
Lage, Café du Lage is an amazing setting for a
leisurely weekend brunch – or a coffee and cake at
any other time. There's gentle live music from the

Palaphita Kitch.
See p130.

Rio's trendsetters flock to **Braseiro da Gávea**. *See p128.*

café's own flute, violin and cello trio and tasty own-made cakes and ice-creams – it's also where Snoop Dogg and Pharrell took their dates for a cup of tea and a dance in their *Beautiful* video.

Hipódromo

Praca Santos Dumont 106-108, Gávea (2274 9720). Bus 158, 179, 572. **Open** 9am-1am Mon-Thur; 9am-3am Tue-Sun. **Credit** AmEx, DC, MC, V.
Map p248 A15 ⓒ
The Hipódromo has been usurped as the number one bar in Baixo Gávea by the Braseiro across the road (*see p128*), but it's still a great place for a night out, as the regular crowds attest, and there isn't a lot of difference between the two. The clientele is the same, the menus are similar, the decor equally nondescript and the vibe in both places is young, hip and informal. The Hipódromo, however, is bigger, not quite as noisy and has air-conditioning.

Palaphita Kitch

Avenida Epitácio Pessoa s/n, Quiosque 20, Parque do Cantagalo, Lagoa (2227 0837/www.palaphita kitch.com.br). Bus 123, 128, 433. **Open** 6pm-1am Mon-Thur, Sun; 6pm-3am Fri, Sat. **No credit cards.**
Map p249 F16 ⓒ
Stuck among the identikit kiosks and restaurants overlooking the Lagoa, Palaphita Kitch is an oasis of strangeness in the area's rather pedestrian nightlife. There are no plastic chairs, no beer-sponsored parasols and no plain white tablecloths here. Instead, the open-air bar is scattered with spacious sofas and benches, small stools and massive coffee tables, all made from Amazonian wood (and all for sale). The food is disappointing and the cocktails are overpriced but the setting, overlooking the Lagoa with views of Christ the Redeemer and the Pedra da Gávea, more than makes up for it. The portakabin bathrooms lit with ultraviolet light take the prize in weirdness. *Photo p129.*

Zona Oeste

Barril 8000

Avenida Sernambetiba 8000, Barra (2433 1730/ www.barril8000.com.br). Bus 710A. **Open** 11am-4am Mon, Thur-Sat; 11am-midnight Tue, Wed, Sun. **Credit** AmEx, DC, MC, V.
There are two branches of Barril 8000, both in Barra. They are large and lively, attracting a young and very lively clientele. There's a varied programme of live music throughout the week, that attracts some weighty names in samba (from around 10pm).
Other locations: Downtown Shopping 105-107 Avenida das Américas 500, Barra (3153 7740).

Café Severino

Rio Design Barra, Avenida das Américas 7777, Barra (2438 7644/www.livrariaargumento.com.br) Bus 382, 1133, 1135. **Open** 10am-10pm Mon-Thur; 10am-midnight Fri, Sat, noon-11pm Sun. **Credit** AmEx, CD, MC, V.
A welcome oasis from the hustle and bustle of shopping, Café Severino, inside the Argumento bookshop, is a very civilised place to stop for the all-important *cafezinho*, or to enjoy a fresh, wholesome sandwich at lunchtime. The toasted cheese is out of this world – as are the freshly made cakes. For something more Brazilian, try the *broa de milho* (an anis-flavoured brioche). There is a very pleasant terrace outside, although due to the lack of shade it can be very hot in summer.
Other locations: Argumento, Rua Dias Ferreira 417, Leblon (2259 9398).

Shops & Services

Know your *sunga* from your *sunkini* and dress down for a hot day out.

By now you've learned lesson number one about Rio; it's the archetypal city of contrasts. In terms of shops and services this means you'll find a thriving service industry for all income levels. You can saunter into **Shopping Leblon** and cruise high-end Ipanema streets like Rua Garcia D'Avila. Or join the flow on one of the Centro's pedestrian streets, formerly known for their bargains but now attracting top designers. Do keep in mind that some of Rio's best shopping does not always give onto the street, so don't be put off small shops in commercial buildings – they're often the real finds.

Rio's fashion forte is clearly casual beach and swimwear; you'll find an endless array of options at any price range. If you want to take advantage of Rio's unbeatable selection of bikinis, but just aren't ready to bear almost-all, ask for a *sunkini*, which has a hotpant or boy-short style on the bottom. This comes from the term *sunga*, which is the more generous speedo-style cut the men wear. Other key beach accessories include a *canga* or beach wrap (taking a towel to the beach is a sure sign of a tourist) and a *saida de praia*, a long sleeved beach cover-up made of a cool, thin cotton, both of which can also readily be bought from the ever-present beach vendors.

Most street shops throughout the city open from 10am to 6pm or 7pm, Monday to Friday, but close around 2pm on Saturdays and all day on Sundays. Shopping malls offer a safe, air-conditioned and controlled environment as well as food, entertainment and, of course, shops. They generally open until 10pm, Monday to Saturday, and from 3pm to 9pm on Sundays and public holidays.

General

Department Stores

Lojas Americanas
Rua do Passeio 42 & 56, Centro (2524 0284/ www.americanas.com). Metro Cinelândia/406, 433, 464 bus. **Open** 7am 10pm Mon-Fri; 7am-8pm Sat; 9am-3pm Sun. **Credit** AmEx, MC, V. **Map** p245 I3.
A complete but no-frills department store for one-stop shopping for the whole family, with products including clothes, toiletries, CDs, electronics and homeware. The smaller Americanas Express have the same departments but less selection and no big ticket items like refrigerators.
Other locations: throughout the city.

Uptown shopping at the **Shopping da Gávea**. *See p132.*

Malls

In addition to the major malls, or *shoppings*, listed below, Rio, and especially the Zona Sul, has many smaller *galerias* – a species of arcade that may have anywhere from five to 85 shops and services.

Barra Shopping

Avenida das Américas 4666, Barra da Tuijuca (3089-1050/ www.barrashopping.com.br). Bus 179, 225, 523. **Open** *Shops* 10am-10pm Mon-Sat; 3-9pm Sun. *Restaurants* 10am-11pm daily.

One of the largest malls in South America, a visit to Barra Shopping is an event in itself. Besides all the major retail stores, you'll find the biggest indoor amusement park in Brazil, a bowling alley and the New York City Centre with cinemas and restaurants.

Casa Shopping

Avenida Ayrton Senna 2150, Barra da Tijuca (2108 8080/www.casashopping.com). Bus 225, 708. **Open** noon-10pm Mon; 10am-10pm Tue-Sat; 3-9pm Sun.

A modern open-air shopping centre with more than 100 high-end stores geared entirely to design and decor. You'll find local talent in Tamanduá Bandeira's rustic furniture next door to the latest in Italian kitchen design. It's well worth a window-shop even if you're not planning to buy.

Rio Design Leblon

Avenida Ataulfo de Paiva 270, Leblon (2430 3024/ www.riodesignleblon.com.br). Bus 571, 583, 584. **Open** 10am-10pm Mon-Sat; 3-9pm Sun & public holidays. **Map** p248 C17.

Originally open exclusively to design stores, this mall has now incorporated a variety of other boutiques like Mara Mac and Osklen. Full of friendly neighbourhood services, they offer parcel delivery by bicycle to addresses in Leblon, and are the only mall to let you bring your dog along while you shop.

São Conrado Fashion Mall

Estrada da Gávea 899, São Conrado (2111 4444/ www.scfashionmall.com.br). Bus 176, 546. **Open** 10am-10pm Mon-Sat; 3-9pm Sun & public holidays. **Map** p253 E3.

The Fashion Mall attracts an elite crowd of shoppers to its sophisticated mix of national and international fashion and design stores like Clube Chocolate (*see p136*), Emporio Armani, Ermenegildo Zegna and Bang & Olufsen.

Shopping Cassino Atlântico

Avenida Atlântica 4240, Copacabana (2523 8709/ www.shoppingcassinoatlantico.com.br). Bus 474, 503, 2016. **Open** 9am-9pm Mon-Sat; 2-8pm Sun. **Map** p249 H17.

Next door to the Sofitel Hotel, 80% of the shops are antique dealers, art galleries or jewellers. The antique market held throughout the mall is a local favourite for finding treasures, and a great option between 10am and 7pm on a rainy Saturday.

Shopping Cidade Copacabana

Rua Siqueira Campos 143, Copacabana (2549 0650/ www.shoppingcidadecopacabana.com.br). Metro Siqueira Campos/464, 584, 2019 bus. **Open** *Mall* 24hrs. *Stores* vary. **Map** p249 H13.

A quirky rabbit's warren of a shopping centre with a Guggenheim-esque ramp in the centre, it's one of the city's first malls, dating back to the 1960s. Locals call it Shopping Siqueira Campos, and with over 80 antique and retro design shops as well as numerous unpredictable little stores and services, it can be a fascinating shopping experience. There's also a 24 hour supermarket, Sendas.

Shopping da Gávea

Rua Marques de São Vicente 52, Gávea (2294 1096/ www.shoppingdagavea.com.br). Bus 504, 583, 2014. **Open** 10am-10pm Mon-Fri. *Shops* 3-9pm Mon-Fri. *Restaurants* noon-10pm Mon-Fri. **Map** p248 A15.

An upmarket shopping mall with over 200 shops and services as well as several performance spaces and art galleries. Especially big on jewellery designers such as Antonio Bernardo and Lisht. *Photo p131.*

Shopping Leblon

Avenida Afrânio de Melo Franco 290, Leblon (3138 8000/www.shoppingleblon.com.br). Bus 474, 504, 2016. **Open** *Shops* 10am-10pm Mon-Sat; 3-9pm Sun. *Restaurants* 10am-11pm Mon-Sat; noon-10pm Sun. **Map** p248 C16.

A brand spanking new shopping mall in upscale Leblon with lounge areas for the weary shopper complete with poofs and rugs, really ample corridors, ultra modern washrooms, a panoramic glass elevator and state of the art cinemas. Any shop worthy of its name is represented, including the biggest Livraria da Travessa in the city. There's a free tourist bus to and from hotels along the beach.

Shopping Rio Sul

Rua Lauro Müller 116, Botafogo (3527 7000/ www.riosul.com.br). Metro Botafogo/474, 505, 583 bus. **Open** 10am-10pm Mon-Sat. *Shops* 3-9pm Mon-Sat. *Restaurants & cinema* noon-10pm. **Map** p247 I12.

Conveniently located in Botafogo, just through the tunnel from Copacabana, Rio Sul is one of the biggest malls in the city with over 400 stores from most of the major Brazilian brands. It was recently expanded and renovated to let natural light in. There's a free tourist bus to and from hotels in the Zona Sul as well as from Cardeal Arcoverde metro.

Vertical Shopping

Rua Sete de Setembro 48, Centro (2224 0697/ www.verticalshopping.com.br). Metro Carioca/ 119, 128, 177 bus. **Open** 9am-8pm Mon-Fri. **Map** p245 I2.

A quiet refuge from the busy streets of Centro, Vertical Shopping has 45 styling stores, spread out on its nine floors. Check out stylish shoes at Via Mia and Sollas and the retro beach style of Totem Praia's beachwear. It closes a bit later than other shops in the centre, although it's not open on weekends.

The best Shops

For funky accessories
Mônica Carvalho's (see p151) gorgeous seed necklaces, Antonio Bernardo's jewels (see p142) and Gilson Martin's (see p143) modern vinyl bags and purses.

For shopping with a conscience
AmazonLife sells natural latex bags (see p143), Parceria Carioca (see p143) and Ação Comunitária do Brasil (see p142) objects from low-income communities.

For an afternoon's browsing
Tracks has racks of Brazilian groove (see p151), Livraria Argumento (see right) has coffee-table books galore, and Lidador (see p145) the best selection of caçhaca.

For Brazilian designer clothes
Novamente (see p138), Contemporânea (see p136) and Dona Coisa (see p136) stock the hottest designers.

For cool retro-style clothes
Favela Hype (see p136), Bruzundanga (see p136) and Totem Praia (see p138) all show a love of retro fabrics and designs.

For value for money
Fios e Artes (see p147) has great hair and beauty products, while Babilônia Feira Hype (see below) stocks work by new designers.

Markets

Babilônia Feira Hype
Itinerant venues (www.babiloniahype.com.br). **Open** 2-10pm Sat, Sun. **Admission** R$4; seniors & children free. **No credit cards.**
A biweekly fair held on weekends with clothing, accessories and homeware. Normally held in Gávea's Jockey Club or in Barra – check the website.

Feira Hippie de Ipanema
Praça General Osório, Ipanema (www.feirahippie. hpg.ig.com.br). Bus 132, 157, 512. **Open** 8am-6pm Sun. **No credit cards. Map** p249 F17.
Despite its name, very few hippies frequent this market, where you'll find arts and crafts, leather goods, children's toys and clothing galore.

Feira do Rio Antigo
Rua do Lavradio, Centro. Bus 176, 410, 433. **Open** 10am-6pm first Sat of month. **No credit cards. Map** p245 H3.
This lively antique and art fair also features music and dance performances throughout the day.

Specialist

Books & magazines

English language
All the bookshops listed offer something in the way of books in English, but for a decent selection of newspapers and magazines from around the world, head for the **Banca 33** news-stand (Rua Visconde de Pirajá, around number 371, Ipanema, 2523 2002).

General

Baratos da Ribeiro
Rua Barata Ribeiro 354, Copacabana (2549 3850/ www.baratosdaribeiro.com.br). Metro Siqueira Campos/464, 584 bus. **Open** 9am-8pm Mon-Fri; 11am-2pm Sat. **Credit** AmEx, MC, V. **Map** p250 H14.
Over 15,000 used books, including a good selection of English titles and 5,000 LPs including rock, tropicalismo, jazz, bossa nova and samba.

Livraria Argumento
Rua Dias Ferreira 417, Leblon (2239 5294/www. livrariaargumento.com.br). Bus 583, 2015, 2017. **Open** 9am-midnight Mon-Sat; 10pm-midnight Sun. **Credit** AmEx, MC, V. **Map** p248 B16.
During the military dictatorship, Argumento earned a following as one of the few sources of banned literature. Now it's a bookstore that sells more than just books with a café, music CDs and literary events.
Other locations: Barata Ribeiro 502, Copacabana (2255 3783); Rio Design Barra, Avenida das Américas 7777, Barra (2438 7644).

Livraria da Travessa
Travessa do Ouvidor 17, Centro (3231 8015/ www.livrariadatravessa.com.br). Metro Carioca/ 119, 128, 177 bus. **Open** 9am-8pm Mon-Fri. **Credit** AmEx, MC, V. **Map** p245 I2.
All its branches were made for book browsers and include a cosy café, but this romantic Centro shop wins on sheer charm. For English-language books, try the gigantic new Shopping Leblon location.
Other locations: Visconde de Pirajá 572, Ipanema (3205 9002); Shopping Leblon (3138 9600); Rio Branco 44, Centro (2519 9000).

Luzes da Cidade
Rua Voluntários da Pátria 35, Botafogo (2226 4108/www.luzesdacidade.com.br). Metro Botafogo/ 524, 583, 584 bus. **Open** 10am-10pm Mon-Fri; 4-10pm Sat, Sun. **Credit** MC, V. **Map** p247 H10.
A first class second-hand bookstore inside the Espaço Unibanco cinema. It also sells an impeccable range of mint condition vintage vinyl, CDs, DVDs and cool movie buff paraphernalia.
Other locations: Estação Ipanema, Visconde de Pirajá 605, Ipanema (2512 7693).

Eat, Drink, Shop

Market daze

The **Saara**, the biggest open-air shopping centre in Latin America, has been buying and selling since the 17th century, but now there's a newer wave of Oriental shops besides the traditional stalls set up by the original middle eastern and Jewish immigrants. The name, Portuguese for Sahara, dates only from the 1960s and is the acronym for the local business association, formed to save the area from being demolished to build a viaduct. Over 1,200 stores make up the complex, which can become so packed with people that designated meeting spots and holding on tight to the little one's hands are essential. Artists, fashion designers and creative types of all sorts can be found roaming the Saara's streets in search of great deals on the raw material they use in their work; and it's also a great source of cheap clothing and homeware.

The market is overflowing with almost anything you can think of. A selection of over 5,000 plant and flower extracts? Check. Watches, jewellery and accessories? Check. Games and wooden toys and sports equipment? You got it. Tasteful home decorations and lamps? That too. Fresh, dried and ready to eat food from around the country

and the world? Of course. Everything you might need to create a Carnival outfit? Where else would you look? There's also a whole lot more you wouldn't expect. Go digging and see what treasures you can find.

Nearby, the Centro de Comércio Popular da Uruguaiana, more popularly know as the **Camelódromo**, after the term *camelô* or street vendor, is the ultimate street market. Some 1,200 permanent stands operate side by side, selling everything from electronics to pirated CDs, DVDs and cheap knock-offs of brands such as Osklen and Billabong. The area between Avenida Presidente Vargas and Rua da Alfândega draws an alternative crowd who stop by to try on graffiti T-shirts or browse through vintage vinyl.

Saara Market
Between Rua dos Andrades, Rua Buenos Aires, Rua da Alfândega & Praça da República. Metro Uruguaiana/107, 125, 415 bus. **Open** 9am-6pm Mon-Fri; 9am-2pm Sat.

Camelódromo
Corner of Rua Uruguaiana & Avenida Presidente Vargas, Metro Uruguaiana/108, 125, 415 bus. **Open** 7am-8pm Mon-Sat.

Eat, Drink, Shop

Children

Fashion

Bebê Básico
Shopping da Gávea, Gávea (2294 6200/www.bebe basico.com.br). Bus 504, 583. **Open** 10am-10pm Mon-Sat; 3-9pm Sun. **Credit** MC, V. **Map** p248 A15.
Practical and comfortable basic cotton Babygros, sleepers, tops and bottoms for toddlers.
Other locations: Galeria Ipanema 2000 (2511 6858); Shopping Rio Design Barra (2431 3903).

Donna Chita
Rua Joana Angélica 192, Sala 103, Ipanema (2267 5127/www.donnachita.com.br). Bus 464, 572, 584. **Open** 9am-7pm Mon-Fri; 9am-2pm Sat. **Credit** AmEx, MC, V. **Map** p249 E16.
A real boutique for kids, with animal-print shoes, rock star T-shirts and fun labels like Santa Paciência and Margaridinhas. The Ipanema building is also home to several other small designer shops worth a visit.

Tag Kids
Rua Visconde de Pirajá 330, Loja 326, Ipanema (2523 5820/www.tagkids.com.br). Bus 464, 572, 584. **Open** 9am-7pm Mon-Fri; 9am-2pm Sat. **Credit** AmEx, MC, V. **Map** p249 E17.

Tag Kids stocks both regular line and outlet pieces from national and international children's labels. They carry Mini Humanos' onesies painted with gorgeous Amazon legends and Layana Thomaz's music idol T-shirts, as well as a line of Opa Looka bikinis.

Totem Kids
2nd floor, Shopping da Gávea, Gávea (2512 8772/ www.totempraia.com.br). Bus 504, 583, 2014. **Open** 10am-10pm Mon-Fri; 3-9pm Sun. **Credit** AmEx, MC, V. **Map** p248 A15.
The same psychedelic fabrics as the Totem Praia (*see p138*) adult clothing, but in mini versions, with a great line of kids swimwear.
Other locations: Galeria Ipanema 2000 (2540 9977).

Toys

Enfim Enfant
Shopping da Gávea, Gávea (2239 9298/www.bebe basico.com.br/enfim/enfim.htm). Bus 504, 583, 2014. **Open** 10am-10pm Mon-Sat. **Credit** AmEx, MC, V. **Map** p248 A15.
A really fabulous kids' toy store where it's all about old-fashioned creativity. Check out the beautifully crafted wooden human and animal characters made locally by Magoo, as well as the adorable memory games by Carioca designers Rei na Barriga.

Electronics & photography

General

Casa & Video

Praia de Botafogo 340, Botafogo (2508 3030/ www.casaevideo.com.br). Metro Botafogo/572, 583, 2018 bus. **Open** 9am-midnight Mon-Sat; 10am-midnight Sun. **Credit** AmEx, MC, V. **Map** p247 H10.

A kind of department store with just about everything but clothing, Casa & Video has a good selection of popular brands of electronics and appliances at competitive prices. Its late opening hours are a real bonus.

Specialist

For mobile phone rentals, there are a few services with delivery included. **Connect Com** (Avenida Nossa Senhora de Copacabana 195, 2275 8461, www.connectcomrj.com.br) offers a reliable service.

Amiel Câmeras & Acessórios

Rua Buenos Aires 93, Sala 103, Centro (2242 1722/ www.amiel.com.br). Metro Uruguaiana/107, 125, 179 bus. **Open** 8am-6pm Mon-Fri; 8am-1pm Sat. **Credit** MC, V. **Map** p245 I2.

Trust Amiel if your camera conks out on you – they buy, sell, trade and repair all brands of digital and still cameras as well as photographic equipment.

Qualidart

Travessa do Ouvidor 18, Centro (2224 8066). Metro Carioca/119, 128, 177 bus. **Open** 9am-7pm Mon-Fri. **Credit** AmEx, MC, V. **Map** p245 I2.

A full range of film and digital photography services and products, with computer kiosks available for editing individual or batch pictures before printing. **Other locations**: Rua Barata Ribeiro 450, Copacabana (2236 5837); Rua Visconde de Pirajá 142, Ipanema (2287 4953).

Shopping Edifício Central

Avenida Rio Branco 156, Centro. Metro Carioca/ 119, 128, 177 bus. **Open** varies. **Credit** varies. **Map** p245 I2.

Left your mobile phone charger in Salvador or spilled a caipirinha on your laptop? Your one-stop mall for anything electronics-related, Edifício Central is a three-floor maze of stores and kiosks where you can find sales or service representatives from all the major electronics brands as well as their generic counterparts.

Fashion

Designer

Atelier Real

Rua Real Grandeza 182, Casa 4B, Botafogo (2537 4924). Metro Carioca/119, 128, 177 bus. **Open** 9am-8pm Mon-Fri; 10am-2pm Sat. **No credit cards. Map** p246 G11.

Started by a trio fresh out of design school and looking for visibility, Atelier Real's store in a quaint Botafogo *villa* has fresh and funky looks for adults from a variety of new designers, as well as fun options for kids by Mini Humanos and Bebê com Açúcar. A lot of imagination has gone into their great selection of accessories too, which includes shoes by SRA.

Favela Hype. *See p136.*

Ausländer

Galeria Ipanema Secreta, Rua Visconde de Pirajá 371, Sala 205, Ipanema, (2227 4147/www.auslander. com.br). Bus 464, 572, 584. **Open** 10am-7pm Mon-Fri; 11am-3pm Sat. **Credit** MC, V. **Map** p249 E17.
Ausländer is all about hip T-shirts. Comfortable, modern cuts graced with photos of Audrey Hepburn or multilingual slogans, heavily sought after by the clubbing crowd.
Other locations: Fashion Mall (3875 8922).

Bruzundanga

Avenida Nossa Senhora de Copacabana 664, Loja 25, Copacabana (2549 6534). Metro Siqueira Campos/464, 572, 584 bus. **Open** 9am-7pm Mon-Fri; 9am-2pm Sat. **Credit** AmEx, MC, V. **Map** p250 H14.
A small shop big into 1970s style. Great patterned and striped long and short sleeved button-down shirts for men, funky baby Ts for the ladies, and pop culture buttons for all.

Clube Chocolate

2nd Floor, São Conrado Fashion Mall, São Conrado (3322 4155/www.clubechocolate.com). Bus 176, 546. **Open** 10am-10pm Mon-Wed; 10pm-midnight Thur-Sat; noon-10pm Sun. **Credit** AmEx, MC, V. **Map** p253 E3.
A 900sq m paradise revered by Carioca fashionistas, which carries international labels with hefty price tags, Clube Chocolate is contemporary luxury meets Brazilian sensuality. Its been a great platform for Brazilian designers like Daniela Martins, Zigfreda and Raia de Goeye. It also carries jewellery, flowers, music and homeware and hosts a highly rated restaurant (*see p117*).

Colcci

3rd Floor, Shopping Rio Sul, Botafogo (2244 0121/ www.colcci.com.br). Bus 474, 505, 583. **Open** 10am-10pm Mon-Sat; 3-10pm Sun. **Credit** AmEx, MC, V. **Map** p247 I12.
Designer Lila Colzani's label of men's and women's romantic street fashion is an international hit, thanks in part to the divine Giselle Bündchen's presence on the catwalk and in print campaigns.
Other locations: Barra Shopping (2431 9003); Shopping Rio Design Barra (3225 4767).

Contemporâneo

2nd floor, Rua Visconde de Pirajá 437, Ipanema (2287 6204/www.contemporaneobrasil.com.br). Bus 464, 572, 584. **Open** 10am-8pm Mon-Sat. **Credit** AmEx, MC. **Map** p249 E17.
Contemporâneo hand selects the best in fashion coming out of Brazil today, including Ronaldo Fraga and Nina Becker's lines, as well as stylish jewellery, and accessories. The store also has a smattering of cool home decor objects.

Dona Coisa

Rua Lopes Quintas 153, Jardim Botânico (2249 2336). Bus 409, 572, 583. **Open** 11am-8pm Mon-Fri; 11am-6pm Sat. **Credit** AmEx, MC, V. **Map** p248 C14.

A great selection of established and up and coming Brazilian designers, such as Glória Coelho and Juliana Jabour. A separate room is dedicated to elegant evening gowns. The swank Café Sudbrack on the second floor is another reason to visit.

Dversa

Rua Visconde de Pirajá 611B, Ipanema (2274 4732/ www.dversa.com.br). Bus 464, 572, 584. **Open** 9am-8pm Mon-Fri; 9am-4pm Sat. **Credit** AmEx, MC, V. **Map** p248 D17.
The practical fashionista will love Dversa's reversible and multi use looks: a cotton dress/skirt that can be tied and folded into 35 different looks, pants that unzip into shorts and a knapsack, or a jacket which doubles as a handbag. They also have a regular line with some retro urban dresses for those that prefer a more straightforward option, and also carry a few other small labels.
Other locations: 2nd Floor, Largo do Machado 29, Catete (2285 8117).

Espaço Lundgren

Avenida Viera Sotto 234, Ipanema (2523 2522/ www.espacolundgren.com.br). Bus 175, 503, 2018. **Open** 10am-8pm Mon-Fri; 10am-6pm Sat. **Credit** AmEx, MC, V. **Map** p249 F17.
A big 1920s beach chalet overlooking Ipanema beach is home to the creations of the higher echelon of Brazilian and international designers. Each designer's looks are displayed in a different area with attentive service, immense dressing rooms and an in-house restaurant.

Farm

Vertical Shopping, Centro (3852 2570/www.farm rio.com.br). Metro Carioca/119, 128, 177 bus. **Open** 9am-8pm daily. **Credit** AmEx, MC, V. **Map** p245 I2.
Some ten years ago Marcello Bastos and Kátia Barros set up a stand at the Babilônia Feira Hype, hawking hip and feminine beachwear. Success came quickly and with nine stores in Rio, several elsewhere in Brazil and one in Paris, Farm keeps creating colourful clothing inspired by the real Girls from Ipanema.
Other locations: throughout the city.

Favela Hype

Galeria River, Arpoador (3201 0406/www.favela hype.com). Bus 413, 426, 2018. **Open** 10am-7pm Mon-Sat. **Credit** AmEx, MC, V. **Map** p249 H17.
Kananda Soares' darling little boutique sells cool young labels for guys and gals like Ave Maria romantic looks and Kanvas shoes for men as well as her own Favela Hype label of alternative fashion and accessories. The inspiration for her collections comes from her love of everything kitsch and retro, from vintage films to caçhaça culture, and the results are sensual and edgy. *Photo p135.*

Forum

Rua Barão da Torre 422, Ipanema (2421 7415/ www.forum.com.br). Bus 464, 572, 584. **Open** 10am-10pm Mon-Fri; 10am-6pm Sat. **Credit** AmEx, MC, V. **Map** p249 E16.

Eu Amo Vintage. *See p141.*

Cool urban looks for both men and women with great jeans, a super sexy line of lingerie, prescription eyewear and sunglasses. The Forum by Tufi Duek label has more elegant fancy dress items as well as a line of perfumes.
Other locations: throughout the city.

Hering

3rd Floor, Shopping Rio Sul, Botafogo (2541 0481/ www.hering.com.br). Metro Botafogo/474, 505, 583 bus. **Open** 10am-10pm Mon-Sat; 3-9pm Sun. **Credit** AmEx, MC, V. **Map** p247 I12.
Practically a Brazilian institution, Hering makes a wide range of good quality, basic cotton clothing for the whole family at popular prices.
Other locations: Rua Uruguaiana 78, Centro (2222 1745).

Isabela Capeto

Rua Dias Ferreira 45-B, Leblon (2540 5232/ www.isabelacapeto.com.br). Bus 583, 2015, 2017. **Open** 10am-8pm Mon-Fri; 10am-6pm Sat. **Credit** AmEx, MC, V. **Map** p238 A17.
Romantic pieces are lovingly crafted like works of art at Isabel Capeto's. Her style is unmistakably her own, with a real love of fabric trims, old lace and sequins. No wonder she's sought after by some of the finest stores in Japan, England and France.

Maria Bonita

Rua Vinicius de Moraes 149, Ipanema (2287 9768/ www.mariabonita.com.br). Bus 464, 572, 584. **Open** 10am-8pm Mon-Fri; 10am-2pm Sat. **Credit** AmEx, MC, V. **Map** p249 F16.
Sophisticated contemporary looks for ladies with a bit of edge, Maria Bonita is known for impeccable tailoring, avant-garde cuts and clothes than hang just the right way. She also has an outlet for her sportier late twentysomething gear in Rio Sul.
Other locations: Barra Shopping, Barra (3326 1004); São Conrado Fashion Mall, São Conrado (3324 5465).

Novamente

5th Floor, Sete de Setembro 43, Centro (3852 8031/ www.lojanovamente.com.br). Metro Carioca/119, 128, 177 bus. **Open** 10am-9pm Mon-Fri; 10am-4pm Sat. **Credit** AmEx, MC, V. **Map** p245 I2.
This is a rare and a great find: a boutique that carries hot Brazilian labels like Fause Haten and Huis Clos, that isn't in the Zona Sul. Step off the elevator into fifth floor Novamente, conveniently located off Rua Quitanda in Centro, and you walk straight into a showroom with so many unique pieces you'll have a tough time deciding which one to splash out on.
Other locations: Rio Design Barra, (2487 5237).

Osklen

Rua Maria Quitéria 85, Ipanema (2227 2911/ www.osklen.com). Bus 464, 572, 584. **Open** 9am-8pm Mon-Fri; 9am-4pm Sat. **Credit** AmEx, MC, V. **Map** p249 E17.
A little bit laid-back California surfwear, a little bit Euro chic, Osklen is total Brazilian soul. Created by surfer, snowboarder, sport medic and avid traveller

Oskar Metsavaht, the label has seriously original and cool clothing for men and women. The feel is modern black and white with splashes of colours, sexy dresses, stylish bathing suits and chic leather and canvas shoes. Best worn with a golden tan.
Other locations: throughout the city.

Sandpiper

Rua Sete de Setembro 54, Centro (2222 0484/ www.sandpiper.com.br). Metro Carioca/119, 128, 177 bus. **Open** 9am-8pm Mon-Fri. **Credit** AmEx, MC, V. **Map** p245 I2.
Casual beachwear for men and women: cotton tanks and halter tops, surfing trunks and T-shirts, faded low-rise denims and lots and lots of floral prints, in typical surfing style.
Other locations: throughout the city.

Silvie Chic & Sweet

Rua da Quitanda 30, Sala 618, Centro (2221 7640). Metro Carioca/119, 128, 177 bus. **Open** 9am-6pm Mon-Fri. **No credit cards**. **Map** p245 I2.
Designer Silvia de Bossens creates curve-accenting jersey dresses that wrap and drape the body gorgeously, as well as classic-cut trench coats and oversized bags. As the shop doubles as her atelier, Silvia is always on hand to fit you into something feminine, with a touch of 1950s style.

Totem Praia

3rd Floor, Vertical Shopping, Centro (3852-3593/ www.totempraia.com). Metro Carioca/119, 128, 177 bus. **Open** 9am-8pm daily. **Credit** AmEx, MC, V. **Map** p245 I2.
Luckily for us, Fred D'Orey, Brazilian Surf champ in 1987, wasn't content with success just in the water. Back on land, he created an awesome line of clothing for men, women and even children in soft, natural fibres and with patterns that crossbreed the flower power of the 1960s with tribal Africa.
Other locations: throughout the city.

Via Flores

Rua Garcia d'Avila 66, Ipanema (2249 7145/ www.vifloresmultimarcas.com.br). Bus 464, 572, 584. **Open** 10am-8pm Mon-Fri; 10am-4pm Sat. **Credit** AmEx, MC, V. **Map** p248 D17.
A beautifully appointed store with a clean design on an upscale shopping street, Via Flores is a favourite among Zona Sul socialites who flock to buy new pieces by Alexandre Herchcovitch and Coven, or from Jo de Mer's simply divine swimwear line.
Other locations: Rua General Venâncio Flores 305, Leblon (2249 7909).

Zigfreda

Sala 201, Avenida Ataulfo de Paiva 1022, Leblon (2294 9821/www.zigfreda.com.br). Bus 571, 572, 583. **Open** 9am-6pm Mon-Fri. **No credit cards**. **Map** p248 B17.
Kátia Wille and husband Hans Blankenburgh's creations are modern and elegant with original, colourful patterns. She loves using silks and embroidery, and has recently introduced Babyzig, a fun line of clothes for children.

General

Casa Alberto Gentlemen

Rua Visconde de Pirajá 282, Ipanema (2522 6925/ www.albertogentlemen.com.br). Bus 464, 572, 584. **Open** 9.30am-7pm Mon-Fri; 9.30am-2pm Sat. **Credit** AmEx, MC, V. **Map** p249 F17.

An old school shop offering the finest in men's suits, shirts and accessories, with top-rate service.
Other locations: Shopping Rio Sul (2542 0536); São Conrado Fashion Mall (2422 3642); Avenida Nilo Peçanha 11, Centro (2219 8500).

Complexo B

Galeria River, Arpoador (2521 7126). Bus 413, 426, 2018. **Open** 10am-7pm daily. **Credit** AmEx, MC, V. **Map** p249 H17.

Funky clothes for men with a hint of attitude and no qualms with a flower print or two. It stocks a range of trousers, shirts, belts and shoes in bold patterns and colour combinations.
Other locations: Quartier Ipanema (2227 2312).

Draco

Rua Francisco Otaviano 55, Arpoador (2227 7393). Bus 413, 426, 2018. **Open** 10am-8pm Mon-Fri; 11-6pm Sun. **Credit** AmEx, MC, V. **Map** p249 H17.

Low-rise jeans, cool button-downs and laid-back menswear can be found at Draco, just next door to the Galeria River. *Photos p140.*

Nine

3rd Floor, Rio Design Leblon, Leblon (2239 1704/ www.nine9.com.br). Bus 571, 583, 584. **Open** 10am-10pm Mon-Sat; 3-9pm Sun. **Credit** AmEx, MC, V. **Map** p248 C17.

Nine brings together the best in designer maternity wear, with staff trained to attend to expecting clients. Every year, the owner invites a designer to add a new piece – recently designer Carlos Tufvesson created an exclusive line of maternity jeans for Nine. Check out its bikinis by Rygy, which flatter growing bellies.

Reserva

Galeria Quartier, Ipanema (2247 5980/www. reservaunanet.com.br). Bus 464, 572, 584. **Open** 9am-8pm Mon-Fri; 9am-6pm Sat; 11am-5pm Sun. **Credit** AmEx, MC, V. **Map** p249 E17.

Rony Meisler and Fernando Sigal, two authentic boys from Ipanema, created a line of original and edgy beach and streetwear for the modern man, and baptized it with the name of their favourite Rio beach, Reserva. Linen pants, patterned jackets and funky sungas abound in their sleek, loft-like shop.

Tear Gas

2nd Floor, Galeria 444, Ipanema (2267 6598/ www.teargas.com.br). Bus 464, 572, 584. **Open** 9am-7pm Mon-Fri; 10am-3.30pm Sat. **Credit** AmEx, V. **Map** p248 D17.

Designer Marcelo Labrude calls his range 'streetchic' and produces each exclusive line in small quantities. Look for haute couture jeans with really original cuts and designs. *Photo p146.*

Swimwear

Good one-stop swimwear shopping can be had on the fourth floor of Shopping Rio Sul or at the Galeria Forum de Ipanema, which both have numerous great chain boutiques. For something off the beaten track, check out Marine Levesque's **Quasi Nu** super stylish label for men and women (2255 1579, www. quasinu.com), by appointment only at her Copacabana studio. She uses high-tech, fresh touch and second skin fabrics that are exceptionally silky and comfortable; her geometrical and original cuts come in vivid colours and extra large bust sizes.

Blue Man

4th Floor, Shopping Rio Sul, Botafogo (2541 6712/ www.blueman.com.br). Metro Botafogo/474, 505, 583 bus. **Open** 10am-10pm Mon-Sat; 3-9pm Sun. **Credit** AmEx, MC, V. **Map** p247 I12.

Sexy swimwear in original prints and styles (including several inspired by the Brazilian flag). There's also an excellent selection of sungas for men.
Other locations: throughout the city

Bum Bum

5th Floor, Shopping Vertical, Centro (2509 0224/ www.bumbum.com.br). Metro Carioca/119, 128, 177 bus. **Open** 9-8pm Mon-Fri. **Credit** AmEx, MC, V. **Map** p245 I2.

Not only does Bum Bum hold the claim of opening the first bikini store in the world back in 1979, it also created some of the world's favourite bikini styles, including the *fio dental*, or dental floss. It's one of the few places that stocks larger sizes, so if the itsy bitsy teeny weenies are putting you off buying a bikini in Rio (an absolute must), look no further. They also stock a great selection of beach cover-ups.
Other locations: throughout the city.

Lenny

Forum de Ipanema, Ipanema (2523 3796/www. lenny.com.br). Bus 464, 572, 584. **Open** 10am-8pm Mon-Fri; 10am-3pm Sat. **Credit** AmEx, MC, V. **Map** p249 E17.

Lenny Niemeyer's sophisticated and glamorous ladies swimwear generally offers more body coverage than other swimwear lines, and can now be found on the racks at Bloomingales and Harrods. For real finds, check out the Lenny outlet store in Leblon (Carlos Goes 234, 2511 2739).
Other locations: Rua Garcia D'Avila 149, Ipanema (2227 5537); Shopping da Gávea (2259 3251); São Conrado Fashion Mall (3323 0315).

Salinas

4th Floor, Shopping Rio Sul, Botafogo (2275 0793/ www.salinas-rio.com.br). Metro Botafogo/474, 505, 583 bus. **Open** 10am-10pm Mon-Sat; 3-9pm Sun. **Credit** AmEx, MC, V. **Map** p247 I12.

Gorgeous selection of colourful and stylish swimwear for men and women as well as straw beach bags, flip-flops, cover-ups and wraps.
Other locations: throughout the city

Eat, Drink, Shop

Used & vintage

A Coqueluche do Momento

Rua Alice 217, Laranjeiras (2556 0634/www. acoquelechedomomento.com.br). Bus 153, 569, 584. **Open** 10am-7pm Mon-Wed; 10am-midnight Thur-Sat. **Credit** V. **Map** p246 G8.
Step right back in time in Victor Naves' shop – a house decked out in restored furniture ranging from the 1950s to the 1980s. Out the back, there's a laid-back garden bistro and a smaller house, which is where you'll find all the cool vintage clothes and accessories to go along.

Anexo Vintage

Rear parking lot, Shopping da Gávea, Gávea (2529 8253). Bus 504, 583, 2014. **Open** 10am-7pm Mon-Sat. **No credit cards. Map** p248 A15.
Owners Carla Pádua and Lila Studart have tapped in to the gently worn closets of Brazil's upper crust, and that means Manolo Blahniks, a Moschino jacket or a fab dress by a Brazilian designer you've never heard of, all for a steal. The shop is in a little house in the ground floor parking lot behind the Shopping da Gávea – go out the door at the back left of the mall, past the smoking area, and you'll find it.

De Salto Alto

Store 44, Rua Siqueira Campos 143, Copacabana (2236 2589/www.brechodesaltoalto.com). Metro Siqueira Campos, 464, 584, 2019 bus. **Open** 10am-7pm Tue-Sat. **No credit cards. Map** p249 H13.
Pop art, art deco lampshades, anything leopard print, 1950s glassware and loads and loads of vinyl… welcome to De Salto Alto. Not only will you find second-hand wares and enough animal prints to decorate a jungle, but also the store's own line of vintage-style dresses, shirts and men's and women's bathing suits.

Desculpa, eu ou chique

Rua Alice 75, Laranjeiras (2225 6059). Bus 153, 584, 569. **Open** 10.30am-7pm Mon Tue; 10.30am-midnight Wed-Sat. **No credit cards. Map** p246 G8.
This Laranjeiras store is pure heaven for the regular clientele, many of whom work in creative media and make weekly visits to see owner Sávio's new acquisitions. Complete coloured glassware sets, vintage orange juicers and other items for the home are on the first floor, while clothing and accessories share the second floor with a bar that hosts weekly theatrical shows.

Eu Amo Vintage

Itinerant vintage clothing stand (2208 9578). **Open** varies. **Credit** AmEx.
The girls who run Eu Amo Vintage pre-select fabulous vintage dresses and retro sunglasses, then set up shop at different markets on the weekends. Pieces for sale or rent might include a 1950s swimsuit or a collection of hats from the 1930s. You can find them at the Feira de Antigüidades da Gávea on Sundays, as well as at the monthly Feira de Rio Antigo. On other days you'll have to call. Visits to their Tijuca

stockroom are by appointment only. And yes, the shop does take American Express. *Photo p137.*

Carnival & costumes

The **Saara** (*see p134* **Market daze**) is ground zero for Carnival accoutrements and costumes and is worth visiting even if you've missed the festivities themselves. **Caçula** is the stand-out chain here and is **Tecidos e Carnaval** (Rua Buenos Aires 255-265, 3861 0928) where you'll find over 48,000 Carnival-related items as well as a colourful range of Havaianas. Its other branches have lots of other creative supplies and ideas, including: **Caçula Aviamentos** (Rua Senhor dos Passos 275, 2224 5945) for jewellery making and funky party and Christmas decorations; **Caçula Desenho e Pintura** (Rua da Alfândega 318, 2219 3820), which is chockful of paints, paintbrushes and everything else you might need to get messy and/or be creative; and **Caçula Papeleria e Informática** (Rua da Alfândega 325, 2509 3014), a one-stop school and office supply store.

Cleaning & repairs

Laundry Express

Rua Teixeira de Melo 31, Ipanema (2513 1558). Bus 464, 572, 584. **Open** 8am-8pm Mon-Sat. **Credit** V. **Map** p249 F17.
Laundry Express has over 18 years of experience in the heart of Ipanema, washing, ironing and dry-cleaning the dirty laundry of locals and tourists alike. They also pick up and deliver.

Oficina da Costura

2nd Floor kiosk, Galeria Ipanema 2000, (2512 1111). Bus 464, 572, 584. **Open** 8.30am-6pm Mon-Fri; 8.30-5pm Sat. **Credit** AmEx, MC, V. **Map** p248 D17.
Owner Jola Wajcman commands a crack squadron of seamstresses ready to take up a hem or perform any alteration needed, even on leather and often while you wait.

Sellkit

Shopping Rio Sul, Botafogo (2543 4709). Metro Botafogo, 474, 505, 583 bus. **Open** 10am-10pm Mon-Sat; 3-9pm Sun. **Credit** AmEx, MC, V. **Map** p247 I12.
In addition to performing lightning-quick alterations and repairs, Sellkit also sells the full line of sewing accessories, including lots of types of buttons, zippers, needles and thread.
Other locations: 2nd Floor, Rua Rodrigo Silva 18, Centro (2240 9332), Rua Vinicius de Moraes 100B, Ipanema (2523 6571).

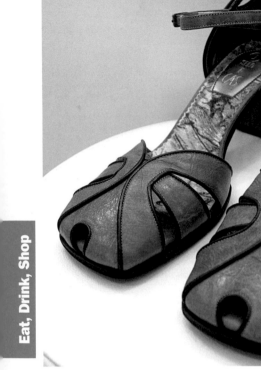

Kick up your heels at **Cas**. *See p144.*

Hats

Ação Comunitária do Brasil

*Rua da Candelária 4, Centro (2253 6443/www.
acaocomunitaria.com.br). Metro Uruguaiana/125,
404, 474 bus.* **Open** 10am-6pm Mon-Fri. **Credit**
AmEx, MC, V. **Map** p245 I1.

Stylish shoppers with a social conscience should
visit Ação Comunitária – a kind of small business
incubator for marginalised communities. Its Centro
store sells beautiful and unique hats as well as bags,
jewellery, clothing and home accents, some of which
are the results of partnerships and initiatives like
ModaFusion (www.modafusion.org).

Denis Linhares

*Shopping Cidade Copacabana, Loja 101, Copacabana
(2235 8132/www.denislinhares.com). Metro Siqueira
Campos/464, 584, 2019 bus.* **Open** 1-7pm Mon-Fri;
11am-3pm Sat. **No credit cards. Map** p249 H13.

Designer Denis Linhares hand-makes hats and hair
accessories, such as garlands, for all occasions, using
traditional wooden moulds, silk thread and the finest
of fabrics. You'll find one of a kind caps that the club
kids love alongside old-fashioned wide brimmed
hats, perfect for that summer wedding. If you have
the time, Denis can even style a hat especially for you,
like he does for the TV and theatre circuit.

Jewellery

Antonio Bernardo

*Rua Garcia D'Avila 121, Ipanema (2512 7204/
www.antoniobernardo.com.br). Bus 464, 572, 584.*
Open 10am-8pm Mon-Fri; 10am-4pm Sat. **Credit**
AmEx, MC, V. **Map** p248 D16.

One of Brazil's hottest jewellery designers and master goldsmiths, Antonio Bernardo's contemporary
designs play with movement, shape and texture.
Look for looping earrings, puzzle rings and gold
tipped leather cord necklaces.

Other locations: Forum de Ipanema (2523 3192);
Shopping da Gávea (2274 7796); São Conrado
Fashion Mall (3322 3113).

Atelier Schiper

2nd floor, Shopping da Gávea, Gávea (3874 3943/
www.atelierschiper.com.br). Bus 504, 583, 2014.
Open 10am-10pm Mon-Sat. **Credit** AmEx, MC, V.
Map p248 A15.
Sisters Alessandra and Aline Schiper have followed
in their jewel-making grandfather's footsteps and for
the past ten years have been creating contemporary
pieces using white and yellow gold and silver, with
a flourish of diamonds, pearls and gemstones.

Guerreiro

Galeria Forum de Ipanema (2521 8656). Bus 464,
572, 584. **Open** 10am-8pm Mon-Fri; 10am-3pm Sat.
Credit AmEx, MC, V. **Map** p249 E17.
Nothing at Guerreiro is understated: necklaces are
chunky and long, rings are laden with giant stones, earrings dangle with style. One of his trademark pieces is
a line of bracelets combining silver and leather.
Other locations: São Conrado Fashion Mall
(2422 3006).

H Stern

Rua Visconde de Pirajá 490, Ipanema (2274 3447/
www.hstern.com.br). Bus 464, 572, 584. **Open**
10am-7pm Mon-Fri; 10am-2pm Sat. **Credit** AmEx,
MC, V. **Map** p248 D17.
H Stern has come a long way since his first store,
opened up in the port area in 1949; his stunning creations with the most exquisite jewels are now prized
the world over. He invented the concept of designer
jewellery, with collections by the likes of actress
Catherine Deneuve and artist Roberto Moriconi.
Always a forward thinker, he was offering guided
tours of the jewellery making process way back in
the 1950s, and today thousands take advantage of
this behind the scenes look every month.
Other locations: throughout the city.

Parceria Carioca

Rua Jardim Botânico 728, Loja 108, Jardim
Botânico (2259 1437/www.parceriacarioca.com br).
Bus 409, 572, 583. **Open** 10am-7pm Mon-Fri;
10am-2pm Sat. **Credit** AmEx, MC, V. **Map** p248 C13.
A hard store to leave empty-handed from, Parceria
Carioca sells objects of art, fashion and design that
combine the best of Brazilian handicrafts with contemporary design. Great wide-banded bead bracelets
feature alongside accessories with kitschy religious
motifs. Many of the pieces are made in community
projects based in low-income communities.
Other locations: Shopping da Gávea, Gávea (2511
8023); Forum de Ipanema, Ipanema (2267 3222).

Lingerie & underwear

Objet du Désir

Rua Visconde de Pirajá 550, Sala 1114, Ipanema
(3502 1114/www.objetdudesir.com.br). Bus 464,
572, 584. **Open** 10am-6pm Mon-Fri; by appointment
Sat. **Credit** MC, V. **Map** p248 D17.
Philippine Bigorie, Melissa Monteiro and Deborah
Ribeiro create luxurious lingerie for girlie-girls who

are all grown up. Their results are playful with just
the right touch of frou-frou, and use fine materials
like tulle, silk crepe, lace, and ribbon... lots of ribbon.

Tutti e Due

Rua Dias Ferreira 64, Sala 104, Leblon (2294 1202/
www.tuttiedue.com). Bus 583, 2015, 2017. **Open**
10.30am-7pm Mon-Fri; 10.30am-5pm Sat. **Credit** MC,
V. **Map** p248 A17.
A small shop with excellent service and an impecca
ble selection of women's lingerie labels, including
Forum. It also stocks a great line of sexy and comfy
lace bras that are perfect for under halter tops.

Verve

Rua Garcia D'Avila 149, Ipanema (3202 2680/
www.verve.com.br). Bus 464, 572, 584. **Open** 10am-
7pm Mon-Fri; 10am-3pm Sat. **Credit** AmEx, MC, V.
Map p248 D16.
Verve's line of lingerie includes sexy laces, practical
cottons – all very feminine and 100% Brazilian.
Other locations: Shopping Rio Design Leblon
(2274 3294); Shopping Rio Design Barra (2431 0016).

Luggage & bags

All of your travel baggage needs can be met on
the strip of Rua da Carioca near República do
Paraguai, where you'll find six luggage stores
in a row including **Mala Amada** (2262 0676)
and **Bagaggio** (2215 9696, www.bagaggio.com).

AmazonLife

2nd Floor, Rua Visconde de Pirajá 499, Ipanema
(2511 7686/www.amazonlife.com.br). Bus 464,
572, 584. **Open** 10am-8pm Mon-Fri; 10am-6pm
Sat. **Credit** AmEx, V. **Map** p248 D17
AmazonLife has worldwide exclusivity to develop
and commercialize Treetap®, a natural latex produced from tapping rubber trees in the Amazon rainforest. The result is gorgeous courier bags and
knapsacks in rich colours and contemporary cuts.

Clutch

Rua Aristides Espínola 121, Sala 202, Leblon (2274
4288). Bus 583, 2015. **Open** 10am-7pm Mon-Fri or
by appointment. **No credit cards. Map** p248 A17.
Limited-edition bags of all sizes by Maysa Borges,
made with luxurious fabrics like leather and
chamois. She shares her studio space with shoe
designer Robert Wright's extravagant stilettos.

Gilson Martins

Rua Visconde de Pirajá 462B, Ipanema (2227 6178/
www.gilsonmartins.com.br). Bus 464, 572, 584.
Open 10am-8pm Mon-Sat. **Credit** AmEx, MC, V.
Map p248 D17.
Visual artist Gilson's vinyl bags, briefcases and wal-
lets come in an unusual variety of shapes, such as a
fried egg or a soccer ball, and feature kitschy Brazilian
icons such as Sugar Loaf and the Christ statue.
Other locations: Shopping Rio Sul, Botafogo
(2543 4390); Rua Figueiredo Magalhães 304A,
Copacabana (3816 0552).

Eat, Drink, Shop

Buying the body beautiful

'Why buy a new car when you can have a new nose for the same price!' remarks one cosmetic surgery worker in Rio.

Rio is obsessed with the body beautiful and the county has now overtaken the United States as the number one place in the world to get a nip and tuck. A recent survey by Unilever revealed that more than half of Brazilians would consider having some sort of cosmetic surgery. According to statistics from the Brazilian Society of Plastic Surgery there are around 600,000 operations a year with two thirds of those being cosmetic. Liposuction is the favourite, closely followed by breast augmentation and face-lifts.

Unlike in some countries, plastic surgery is not a taboo subject in Brazil. People in Rio especially spend hours virtually naked on the beach and many think nothing of being able to enhance what they've got if they can afford it. Young Brazilians in their twenties may get a new set of breasts or nose for their birthday and often take great delight in showing off the good work they've had done.

Brazil has become part of the huge boom in medical tourism. For around a third to half of the cost of an op in Europe or the States you can scoot off to Brazil for your hols and come back looking perkier and tighter, like a new woman or man, literally! If you really want to go the whole hog and have a Brazilian *bunda* you can even get silicone injected into your buttocks. Calf-enhancement is also very popular, though it's hard to fathom people's desire to look like a shot-putter.

The country's excellent reputation for cosmetic surgery is largely due to the pioneering efforts of a surgeon named Ivo Pitanguy. Now in his 80s, he is something of a legend in the profession. An expert in both reconstructive and aesthetic plastic surgery, he set up a clinic in Rio in the 1960s and has numbered Sophia Loren and Ava Gardner among his high-profile clients.

Rei das Malas

Rua Senhor dos Passos 96, Centro (2242 2750/ www.reidasmalas.com.br). Metro Uruguaiana/107, 125, 179 bus. **Open** 9am-7pm Mon-Fri; 9am-2pm Sat. **Credit** AmEx, MC, V. **Map** p245 H2.
For over 40 years, the 'King of Suitcases' has been repairing zippers, changing wheels and cleaning all type of cases, even on the same day if needed.

Shoes

Bianca Silveira

Quartier Ipanema, Loja 109, Ipanema (2227 2280/ www.biancasilveira.com.br). Bus 464, 572, 584. **Open** 9am-9pm Mom-Fri; 10am-2pm Sat. **Credit** MC, V. **Map** p249 E17.
Bianca's Ipanema store breathes luxury and so do her leather creations. Her shoes and bags are made with only the finest materials right down to the clasps and then adorned with delicate fabric flowers or Swarovski crystals.

Cas

Rua Dias Ferreira 64, Loja 201, Leblon (2249 4700). Bus 583, 2015, 2017. **Open** 10am-8pm Mon-Fri; 10am-5pm Sat. **Credit** MC, V. **Map** p248 A17.
Although the Cas label from São Paulo also includes clothing, it's the shoes that really have it going on.

Quite different from the delicate and feminine models you'll find in all the other shop windows in Rio, Cas's handmade shoes in thick colourful leather and with chunky heels really make a statement. *Photo p142.*

Casa Moreira Calçados

Travessa do Ouvidor 8, Sala 101, Centro (2224 9419). Metro Carioca/119, 128, 177 bus. **Open** 9am-6pm Mon-Fri. **Credit** AmEx, MC, V. **Map** p245 I2.
Still creating them like they used to, Casa Moreira has been tailor-making and repairing men's dress shoes and riding boots since 1939 at the same address on pedestrian Travessa do Ouvidor.

Constança Basto

Rua Visconde de Pirajá 371, Sobreloja 206, Ipanema (2247 9932/www.constancabasto.com.br). Bus 464, 572, 584. **Open** 10am-7pm Mon-Fri; 10am-2pm Sat. **Credit** AmEx, MC, V. **Map** p249 E17.
Constança's sexy slingbacks and stilettos can now be found on the tootsies of Cameron Diaz and Nicole Kidman. For her more casual line of footwear, bags and leather accessories, head to her Peach by Constança Basto stores in the Fashion Mall or Rio Design Leblon.
Other locations: São Conrado Fashion Mall (2422 0355).

It's largely down to Ivo Pitanguy that plastic surgery in Brazil is not just a vestige for the rich and famous. It was his goal in life 'to give to anyone regardless of their race, beliefs or social class, harmony and peace with their own image'. It's a philosophy he carries with him today in his work out of Santa Casa public hospital in Rio, which he visits every Wednesday to share his techniques and knowledge with budding plastic surgeons. They come from across the globe and from eastern Europe in particular to learn how to nip and tuck under his watchful eye. As well as performing reconstructive surgery he also offers cosmetic operations, a rare thing in an often under-funded public hospital, since most surgery is done privately. For a fraction of the price of a private clinic, the poorer people of Brazil can get access to this luxury.

In fact, one of the most famous devotees of plastic surgery in Rio is funk singer Tati Quebra-Barraca, who was born and grew up in Cidade de Deus favela. She recently admitted having liposuction and two ribs removed to make her more svelte.

Melissa

Galeria Menescal, Copacabana (2549 0805/www. m-br.com). Metro Siqueira Campos/464, 572, 584 bus. **Open** 9am-7.30pm Mon-Fri; 9am-5pm Sat. **Credit** AmEx, MC, V. **Map** p250 H14.
A multibrand shoe store that also features Melissa's own line of plastic footwear, including velvety felt slip-ons and colourful *aranha* (spider) jelly slippers. Karim Rashid, the Campana brothers, Alexander Herchcovitch and Judy Blame have all contributed designs to Melissa's array of eclectic and irreverent styles.
Other locations: Quartier Ipanema (3813 9328); Rio Sul, third floor, Botafogo (2279 1838).

Sollas

2nd Floor, Vertical Shopping, Centro (3852 6991). Metro Carioca/119, 128, 177 bus. **Open** 9am-8pm Mon-Fri. **Credit** AmEx, MC, V. **Map** p245 I2.
Head to Sollas in the Vertical Shopping mall or around the city for leather flats, funky platforms and fabric slip-ons designed by owner Carla Gugglielmetti. She also stocks a selection from the Schultz and Melissa brands, a good variety of men's casual shoes and a fabulous range of handbags and other accessories.
Other locations: Henrique Dumont 68, Ipanema (2511 5239); Shopping da Gávea (2239 4598).

Food & drink

Bakeries

Brasserie Rosário

Rua do Rosário 34, Centro (2518 3033/www. brasserierosario.com.br). Bus 121, 178, 340. **Open** 11am-8pm Mon-Fri; 11am-6pm Sat. **Credit** AmEx, MC, V. **Map** p245 J2.
The Brasserie's baked goods are nothing less than heavenly and include rosemary baguette, rye loaf with walnuts, fig danishes and pain au chocolat.
Other locations: Candelária (2516 2109).

Drinks

Lidador

Rua da Assembléia 65, Centro (2533 4988/www. lidador.com.br). Metro Carioca/119, 128, 177 bus. **Credit** AmEx, MC, V. **Map** p245 I2.
Since 1924, Lidador has been stocking its shelves with a wide variety of wines, champagnes, brandies and liqueurs from across the world. The prices range from everyday to special occasion purchases.
Other locations: Rua Vinicius de Moraes 120, Ipanema (2247 3863); Rua Barata Ribeiro 505, Copacabana (2549 0091); Botafogo Praia Shopping (2237 9063).

Markets

Feiras livres, or farmers' markets, are a great place to sample exotic fruit or to try local delicacies such as tapioca made into delicious crêpes with cheese and coconut. They usually start setting up stalls at the crack of dawn and wind down in the early afternoon, when prices drop sharply. The shortlist: Monday's **Rua Henrique Dumont** in Ipanema; Tuesday's **Praça General Osório** in Ipanema; Wednesday's **Rua Maria Eugênia** in Humaitá; Thursday's **Rua Ronald de Carvalho** in Leblon and **Rua Conde Lage** in Glória; Friday's **Praça Nossa Senhora da Paz** in Ipanema and **Praça Santos Dumont** in Gávea; Saturday's **Rua Frei Leandro** in Jardim Botânico, whose sophisticated offerings attract chefs and gourmets, and the organic food market on **Rua do Russell**, Glória; and Sunday's **Rua Augusto Severo** in Glória, one of the biggest in the city, and **Praça Tenente Gil Guilherme** in Urca.

Specialist

Alda Maria Doces Portugueses

Rua Almirante Alexandrino 1116, Santa Teresa (2232 1320/www.aldadocesportugueses.com.br). Both tram lines/206, 214 bus. **Open** 2-8pm Tue-Sun. **Credit** MC, V. **Map** p244 G5.

Eat, Drink, Shop

'Street chic' for the boys and girls at **Tear Gas**. *See p139.*

Alda uses over 500 eggs a day to make traditional Portuguese sweets such as Dom Rodrigo and Bem Casado, using recipes passed down from her grandmother. Her small shop doubles as a museum with objects, cooking utensils and recipes that tell the story of confectionary.

Casas Pedro
Avenida Tomé de Souza 113, Centro (2224 9819) Metro Uruguaiana/107, 125, 415. **Open** 9am-6pm Mon-Fri; 9am-2pm Sat. **No credit cards.** **Map** p245 H2.
One of the highlights of the Saara market (*see p134* **Market daze**) Casas Pedro stocks over 50 types of bulk spices, dried fruits, confectionary supplies, cheeses and foods from the Arab world here and at four other Saara locations.

Envidia
Rua Dias Ferreira 106, Loja A, Leblon (2512 1313/www.envidia.com.br). Bus 583, 2015, 2017. **Open** 11.30am-8pm daily. **Credit** MC, V. **Map** p248 A17.
A truly decadent chocolate shop with more than 60 types of *bonbons* made from Belgium chocolate and exotic fillings like plum with ginger, all displayed to entice shoppers on ritzy Dias Ferreira street. Recovering chocaholics should steer clear.

Kopenhagen
Rua Visconde de Pirajá 197, Ipanema (2287 7389/ www.kopenhagen.com.br). Bus 464, 572, 584. **Open** 9am-8pm Mon-Sat. **Credit** AmEx, MC, V. **Map** p249 F17.

Founded by sweet-toothed Lithuanian immigrants Anna and David Kopenhagen who introduced Brazil to marzipan in 1928, Kopenhagen now has over 180 stores providing the country with a range of high quality chocolate fixes. A must try is their Nhá Benta, a kind of malomar in original, strawberry or passion fruit flavours.
Other locations: throughout the city.

Mundo Verde
Rua Uruguaiana 82B, Centro (2507 0627/www. mundoverde.com.br). Metro Carioca/119, 128, 177 bus. **Open** 9am-7.30pm Mon-Fri; 9.30am-1pm Sat. **Credit** AmEx, MC, V. **Map** p245 I2.
The largest chain of health-food stores in Latin America, Mundo Verde has an extensive supply of natural food, beauty and health products as well as all the esoteric supplies you need. There's also a deli counter where you can grab a sample.
Other locations: throughout the city.

Gifts & souvenirs

Brasil & Cia
Rua Maria Quiteria 27, Ipanema (2267 4603/ www.brasilecia.com.br). Bus 464, 572, 584. **Open** 10am-7pm Mon-Sat; 10am-4pm Sun. **Credit** AmEx, MC, V. **Map** p249 E17.
Delicately embroidered textiles and colourful ceramic pieces from talented artisans that beg to jump in to your carry-on. They will also package and ship purchases to you back home, if your eyes are bigger than your suitcase.

Nativa Flores

*Cobal de Humaitá, Rua Voluntários da Pátria
448, Botafogo (2537 4252/www.nativaflores.com.
br). Metro Carioca/119, 128, 177 bus.* **Open** 7am-
8pm Mon-Sat; 7am-2pm Sun. **Credit** MC, V.
Map p246 F11.

Delicate orchid plants, fresh cut heliconias and dried
bougainvilleas in a rainbow of hues. Stunning bou-
quets and baskets can be delivered, guaranteed to
brighten up anyone's day.

O Sol

*Rua Corcovado 213, Jardim Botânico (2294 5099/
www.artesanato-sol.com.br). Bus 409.* **Open** 9am-
6pm Mon-Fri; 9am-1pm Sat. **Credit** AmEx, MC, V.
Map p248 B13.

O Sol is a kind of permanent art fair run by a social
agency to promote skilled artists and craftspeople,
many of whom live in the interior of Brazil, by providing transport and by displaying products in an
enormous showroom. Rugs made of stiff sisal fibres,
furniture from tropical lianas and chess sets armed
with handcrafted folkloric characters all feature.

Pé de Boi

*Rua Ipiranga 55, Laranjeiras (2285 4395/
www.pedeboi.com.br). Bus 153, 569, 584.* **Open**
9am-7pm Mon-Fri; 9am-1pm Sat. **Credit** AmEx, V.
Map p247 H8.

Pé de Boi buys intricate woven basketwork, tapes-
tries, hammocks and other gorgeous wares straight
from artisans across the country, including a superb
selection of hand-painted pottery with vases, pots,
bowls and water jugs.
Other locations: Assembleia 10, Centro (2232 7038).

Health & beauty

Hairdressers & barbers

Crystal Hair

*Barão de Jaguaripe 243, Ipanema (2513 2000).
Bus 464, 572, 584.* **Open** 10am-9pm Tue-Sat.
Credit V. **Map** p249 F16.

With an impressive list of rich and famous clients,
Crystal's top stylists are practically celebrities themselves, commanding top dollar to treat your locks.

Fios e Artes

*Rua Constante Ramos 74A, Copacabana
(2235 3192). Metro Cantagalo/464, 572, 584
bus.* **Open** 10am-6pm Mon; 8am-8pm Tue-Sat.
Credit AmEx, MC, V. **Map** p249 H15.

A low-key salon, where the owner and stylist
Giselle commands a following for giving modern
cuts at reasonable rates.

Hush Hush

*Rua Teixeira de Melo 31, Ipanema (2523 7500).
Bus 464, 572, 584.* **Open** 1-9pm Tue-Sat.
No credit cards. Map p249 F17.

Romulo runs the show at this small hair salon just
steps from the beach, which regularly fills up with
an alternative crowd.

Werner Coiffeur

*Rua Voluntários da Pátria 468, Loja A, Botafogo
(2537 1177/www.wernercoiffeur.com.br). Metro
Carioca/119, 128, 177 bus.* **Open** 9am-9pm Mon-Fri;
9am-8pm Sat. **Credit** AmEx, MC, V. **Map** p246 F11.

A sensibly priced chain of salons to be found throughout the city, overseen by master stylist and entrepre-
neur Rudy Werner. A full range of beauty services
are available, including haircutting, styling and
colouring, plus manicures, pedicures and waxing.
Other locations: throughout the city.

Opticians

Chili Beans

*Shopping da Gávea, 2nd floor, Gávea (2512 9985/
www.chilibeans.com.br). Bus 504, 583, 2014.* **Open**
10am-10pm Mon-Sat; 3pm-9pm Sun. **Credit** AmEx,
MC, V. **Map** p148 A15.

With stores and kiosks throughout many of Rio's
malls, Chili Beans have a cool and classy selection
of moderately priced shades to suit any style.
Other locations: São Conrado Fashion Mall (3322
0458); Shopping da Gávea (2239 8666).

Fotoptica

*Rua Visconde de Pirajá 197, Ipanema (2267 1676/
www.fotoptica.com.br). Bus 464, 572, 584.* **Open**
9am-7pm Mon-Fri; 9am-2pm Sat. **Credit** AmEx,
MC, V. **Map** p249 F17.

One of Brazil's largest eyewear chains, Fotoptica has
been combining optical and photographic services
under one roof since 1920. On-the-spot eye exami-
nations are available, and it sells contact lenses as
well as its own exclusive line of frames.

Lunetterie

*Rua Visconde de Pirajá 550, Ipanema (2239 8444/
www.lunetterie.com.br). Bus 464, 572, 584.* **Open**
9am-7.30pm Mon-Fri; 9am-3pm Sat. **Credit** AmEx,
MC, V. **Map** p248 D17.

Lunetterie sells its own line of super chic sunglasses as well as designer imports from Prada,
Chanel, Gucci and Dior. For the wee ones, check
out the Lunetterie Enfant section at the Shopping
da Gávea branch.

Pharmacies

There's at least one pharmacy on nearly every
corner in Rio. Not many are open 24 hours,
but most are open everyday and many will
do home deliveries.

Drogasmil

*Rua Visconde de Pirajá 294, Ipanema (2472 3000/
www.drogasmil.com.br). Bus 464, 584.* **Open** 24hrs
daily. **Credit** AmEx, MC, V. **Map** p250 F18.

A large chain of drugstores, most of them open 24
hours a day, with a full range of prescription, non-pre-
scription and cosmetic items. Delivery is available to
any location in the city within 45 minutes by calling
the 24-hour centralised customer service line.
Other locations: throughout the city.

Eat, Drink, Shop

Daqui do Brasil.

Granado

Rua Primeiro de Março 16, Centro (3231 6746/ www.granado.com.br). Metro Carioca/119, 177 bus. **Open** 8am-6.30pm Mon-Fri. **Credit** AmEx, MC, V. **Map** p245 J2.

Established in 1870, Granado still sells the same famous antiseptic talcum powders and glycerine soaps at the same Centro location, in addition to filling individualised pharmaceutical prescriptions. Also now selling ranges for babies and pets.

Other locations: Rua Conde de Bonfim 300, Tijuca (3231 6749); Rua General Artigas 470, Leblon (3231 6759).

Shops

Originallis

2nd Floor, Shopping Rio Sul, Botafogo (2295 9277/ www.originallis.com.br). Metro Botafogo/474, 505, 583 bus. **Open** 10am-10pm Mon-Sat; 3-9pm Sun. **Credit** AmEx, MC, V. **Map** p247 I12.

Luxurious massage oils and whatever else you could want for aromatherapy made from pure essential oils. Look for the revitalising range of fruity *caipim limão* shampoo, conditioner and bath oil made from lemon grass.

Other locations: São Conrado Fashion Mall (3204 8693) Shopping da Gávea, (2529 6564).

Perfumaria Lurdes

Rua Voluntários da Pátria 230, Botafogo (2539 0278). Metro Botafogo/572, 583, 2018 bus. **Open** 8am-7pm Mon-Fri; 8am-2pm Sat. **Credit** AmEx, MC, V. **Map** p246 G11.

Row upon row of colourful cosmetics and hair styling products neatly arranged on the shelves: nail polish, shampoo, hair colour, barrettes... no wonder it's the favourite haunt of the women who work at the nearby Mara Mac headquarters.

Shampoo Cosméticos

Rua Gonçalvez Dias 29, Centro (2507 0172/ www.shampoocosmeticos.com.br). Metro Carioca/ 119, 128, 177 bus. **Open** 9am-7pm Mon-Fri; 9am-1pm Sat. **Credit** AmEx, MC, V. **Map** p245 I2.

If you run out of that face cream you just can't live without, head to Shampoo, where you'll find a complete range of skincare, hair and cosmetic products including major imported brands.

Other locations: Rua Visconde de Pirajá 581, Ipanema (2259 1699).

Spas & salons

Do yourself a favour: take advantage of glorious and inexpensive beauty services while in Rio. Cariocas have perfected the art of the manicure, but you may be surprised when the attendant seemingly applies polish 'outside the lines'. Don't fret: she'll then wrap a piece of cotton on the end of a wooden manicure stick and deftly remove any superfluous bits. The results are impeccably covered nails. And if that new bikini you bought means you'll need a Brazilian wax, what you ask for is '*virilha cavada, por favor*'.

Base Nail Bar

Praia de Botafogo 416, Botafogo (2552 9540). Metro Botafogo/572, 583, 2018 bus. **Open** 10am-7.30pm Mon-Sat. **Credit** AmEx, MC, V. **Map** p247 H10.

Base offers reasonably priced beauty treatments, specialising in manis and pedis. Walk-ins are most welcome and you rarely have to wait.

Pello Menos Instituto de Depilação

2nd Floor, Rua Gonçalves Dias 89, Centro (2531 8810/www.pellomenos.com.br). Metro Carioca/119, 128, 177 bus. **Open** 8am-7pm Mon-Fri. **Credit** MC, V. **Map** p245 I2.

A popular chain devoted entirely to waxing away those unwanted hairs. No appointment is necessary, prices are very reasonable and the attendants follow strict hygiene codes.
Other locations: throughout the city.

Uluwatu Day Spa

2nd Floor, Rua México 119, Centro (2544 0351/ www.uluwatudayspa.com.br). Metro Carioca/119, 128, 177 bus. **Open** 9am-7.30pm Mon-Fri. **Credit** AmEx, V. **Map** p245 I2.

The spa of choice for busy professionals who work in Centro, Uluwatu was designed after the day spas in Bali. They offers quick services for those on a tight schedule, as well as full package treatments that can last glorious hours.

House & home

Antiques

Rua Lavradio in Lapa is the epicentre for antiques, with neighbouring Rua do Senado and Rua Gomes Freire starting to get some of the overflow. Antique lovers should make a point of visiting the **Feira do Rio Antigo**, the market held in Praça XV and both the Shopping Cassino Atlântico and the Shopping Cidade Copacabana malls. The popular music club **Rio Scenarium** (*see p179*), which also doubles as a prop house, is practically a museum in itself.

Armazén 161 Antigüidades

Rua do Lavradio 161, Lapa (2242 3342). Bus 176, 410, 433. **Open** 9am-6pm Mon Fri; 9am-2pm Sat. **No credit cards. Map** p245 H3.

An awesome collection of over 800 lamps and light fixtures of all kinds, painstakingly restored. A superb collection of colourful and playful designs.

Graphos Brasil

Stores 1 & 2, Shopping Cidade Copacabana, Copacabana (2256 3268). Metro Siqueira Campos/ 464, 584, 2019 bus. **Open** 10am-7pm Mon-Fri; 10am-2pm Sat. **No credit cards. Map** p249 H13.

Graphos Brasil's large showroom specialises in modern Brazilian furniture and object design from the 1940s to 1970s. For something a little older, its sister store Graphos Tradição (2255 8283) is on the same floor and has a fine array of furniture and objects from the 1920s and 1930s.

Hully Gully

Shopping Cidade Copacabana, stores 102 & 139, Copacabana (2236 6564). Metro Siqueira Campos/ 464, 584, 2019 bus. **Open** 11am-6.30pm Mon-Fri; 11am-4pm Sat. **No credit cards. Map** p250 H14.

Owner Nadia Bastos has filled her vintage store in Copacabana's mecca of such things with everything fun and kitsch she could find from the 1930s to 1970s, but her real forte is the 1950s. Among her curios you'll find standing ashtrays and apple-shaped coolers. Serious treasure hunters should make appointments to visit her warehouse.

Mercado Moderno

Rua do Lavradio 130, Centro (2508 6083/www. mercadomodernobrasil.com.br). Bus 206, 214, 398. **Open** 9am-6pm Mon-Fri, 9am-3pm Sat. **Credit** AmEx, MC, V. **Map** p245 I3.

In a beautifully restored building in Lapa, Mercado Moderno sells the coolest of cool Brazilian furniture from the 1950s to the 1980s, with pieces from revered names like Joaquim Tenreiro, Zalszupin, Sergio Rodrigues and Zanine. Along the same stretch of Rua Lavradio, several shops cover similar terrain: Mobix (2224 0244) at no.128, Movelaria Belmonte (2507 0873) at no.34 and Mobília (2232 3451) at no.172.

General

Daqui do Brasil

Avenida Ataulfo de Paiva 1174, Leblon (2529 8576/ www.daquidobrasil.com). Bus 571, 572, 584. **Open** 10am-8pm Mon-Fri; 10am-4pm Sat. **Credit** AmEx, MC, V. **Map** p248 A17.

A fabulous shop dedicated to young Brazilian designers where you'll find clever creations like Mari Lara's stencil wall stickers and Cris Oliveira's necklaces, brooches and belts made from felt. The newer Daqui Indumentaria (2529 8594) next door is a springboard for new fashion designers including OEstudio's unique fashion creations.

Dentro Design

Shopping da Gávea, Gávea (2239 4340/www. dentro.com.br). Bus 504, 583. **Open** 10am-10pm Mon-Sat; 3-9pm Sun. **Credit** MC, V. **Map** p248 A15.

Dentro showcases contemporary decorative objects, furniture and sculpture. Most of the pieces have a limited production run, so you can pick up a unique work of art like Elvira Schwartz's functional blown-glass creations at an accessible price.

Fernando Jaeger

Rua Corcovado 252, Jardim Botânico (2274 6026/ www.fernandojaeger.com.br). Bus 409. **Open** 10am-7pm Mon-Fri; 10am-2pm Sat. **No credit cards.** **Map** p248 B13.

Fernando Jaeger's furniture combines form and function, and a Scandinavian sense of simplicity with gorgeous Brazilian woods and traditional woodworking techniques. Everything sold here has a bit of a retro feel. Rugs come in untraditional colour combinations and sofas are upholstered with really cool fabrics.

Novo Desenho

Museu de Arte Moderna, Avenida Infante Dom Henrique 85, Glória (2524 2290). Metro Glória/ 404, 484, 583 bus. **Open** noon-6pm Tue-Fri; noon-7pm Sat, Sun & public holidays. **Credit** AmEx, MC, V. **Map** p245 J4.

Set in a refurbished restaurant at the Museum of Modern Art, this showroom for Brazilian contem-porary design has an outstanding selection of home and kitchen accessories, decorative objects and fur-niture along with cool gadgets and ingenious toys.

La Vereda

Rua Almirante Alexandrino 428, Santa Teresa (2507 0317). Both tram lines/206, 214 bus. **Open** 10am-8pm Mon-Sat; 10.30am-8pm Sun. **Credit** AmEx, MC, V. **Map** p245 H5.

Right next to the Santa Teresa hub of Largo dos Guimarães, La Vereda sells a prime selection of popular art from around Brazil, including creations by Rio artists. Owner Mavi also has a second space, just up the road at Rua Pascoal Carlos Magno 121, with larger-scale items like gorgeous wooden tables as well as Santa Teresa-based designer Wanderley Figueiredo's beautifully crafted wooden lamps. It's officially open on weekends from 2pm to 8pm, but if you're interested and there's a staff member free at other times, they're usually happy to take you over for a look.

Modern Sound.

Mônica uses seeds, branches, flowers, pods and other glorious 'leftovers' of Brazilian nature to make her unique organic art. Some of her pieces are purely decorative, framed into boxes or as a wall panel, but she also has a line of gorgeous accessories and home decor items. Her shop also sells her husband Klaus Schneider's amazing contemporary wooden sculptures and mobiles. *Photo p152.*

Music & entertainment

Modern Sound
Rua Barata Ribeiro 502, Copacabana (2548 5005/ www.modernsound.com.br). Metro Siqueira Campos/ 464, 572, 584 bus. **Open** 9am-9pm Mon-Fri; 9am-8pm Sat. **Credit** AmEx, MC, V. **Map** p250 H15.
A one-stop store with a huge array of CDs, DVDs and books on music from all over the world, although Brazil is its obvious forte. There are also jazz concerts in the in-house venue, Allegro Bistrô Musical (*see p125 and p181*). Famed Carioca writer Ruy Castro once said, 'As for me, one thing's for sure: when I die, I don't want to go to heaven. I want to go to Modern Sound.'

Tracks
Praça Santos Dumont 140, Gávea (2274 7182). Bus 504, 583, 2014. **Open** 10am-10pm Mon-Fri; 10am-9pm Sat. **Credit** MC, V. **Map** p248 B15.
Best to head into Tracks with time on your hands as you'll lose yourself in MPB, Brazilian jazz, soul and rock. Head up to the second floor loft and you can take most CDs or vinyl for a test spin before purchase. The staff are real music know-it-alls who can introduce you to new sounds and recommend hot shows to catch while in town.

Musical instruments
Whether you're looking to buy an *agogô, cuica, pandeiro* or *cavaquinho*, replace a guitar string, buy sheet music, or just be surrounded by stellar musical history, head to Rua da Carioca in Centro. Some five music shops offer an impressive array of national and imported instruments, along with advice and repairs. The best of the crop are **A Guitarra de Prata** (Rua da Carioca 37, 2262-9659), which has been around for almost 120 years, **Casa Oliveira de Música** (Rua da Carioca 70, 2252 5636) and **Musical Carioca** (Rua da Carioca 89, 2524 6029, www.musicalcarioca.com.br).

Sports & fitness
The first place for sports and fitness gear is **Galeria River** (Rua Francisco Otaviano 6, Arpoador). Not only is it the place to find all the clothing and equipment you need for surfing, skateboarding, rollerblading and adventure sports, but the store staff are excellent sources of info on events and services.

Specialist

Elementos da Terra
Rua Constante Ramos 61, Copacabana (2257 0017/ www.elementosdaterra.com.br). Bus 154, 434, 503. **Open** 9am-7pm Mon-Fri; 10am-4pm Sat. **Credit** AmEx, MC, V. **Map** p249 H15.
A chic home decor shop stocking pieces that have been handcrafted with incredible talent. Colourful woven place mats and embroidered napkins, hand-painted ceramic plates and an incredible selection of wooden furniture is stocked, with many items coming from the Oficina de Agosto, a cooperative of artisans in the state of Minas Gerais.

Mônica Carvalho
Rua Maestro Francisco Braga 442, Sala 101, Copacabana (2547 9989/www.monicacarvalho. com.br). Metro Siqueira Campos/154, 433, 434 bus. **Open** 10am-6pm Mon-Fri. **No credit cards** **Map** p249 H14.

Eat, Drink, Shop

Monica Carvalho. *See p151.*

Montcamp

2nd Floor, Rua Teixeira de Melo 21, Ipanema (2287 1143/www.montcamp.com.br). Bus 464, 572, 584. **Open** 10am-8pm Mon-Fri; 10am-3pm Sat. **Credit** AmEx, MC, V. **Map** p249 F17.
Montcamp carries all the major brands of adventure sport equipment and also has a service for cleaning and fixing knapsacks, tents and other outdoor gear.
Other locations: 2nd Floor, Avenida Rio Branco 50, Centro (2516 2525); Shopping Millenium, Barra (2438 0664).

Sport Society

Rua Visconde de Pirajá 419, Loja A, Ipanema (2267 8509/www.sportsociety.com.br). Bus 464, 572, 584. **Open** 9am-8pm Mon-Fri; 9am-6pm Sat. **Credit** AmEx, MC, V. **Map** p249 E17.
With all the latest styles from major international brands of trainers, Sport Society specialises in serious footwear for runners.
Other locations: malls throughout the city.

Track & Field

3rd Floor, Shopping Rio Sul, Botafogo (2295 5996/ www.tf.com.br). Metro Botafogo/474, 505, 583 bus. **Open** 10am-10pm Mon-Sat; 3-9pm Sun. **Credit** AmEx, MC, V. **Map** p247 I12.
Stylish athletic and streetwear in comfortable fabrics as well as great swimwear by Cia Marítima.
Other locations: throughout the city.

Tickets

Though there are some ticket agencies in the city, including **Ticketronic** (2542 4010, www.ticketronics.net) and **Ticketmaster** (0300 789 6846, www.ticketmaster.com.br), using them is yet to catch on either with Rio's general public or with tourists. Tickets for sports and music events are generally handled by the venues directly, and most of the really big events (such as international music acts on the beach) are free. For tickets for football matches, *see p204*, or check adverts for details of other events.

There are many resellers, but tickets for Carnival are sold by the **Liga Independente das Escolas de Samba de Rio de Janeiro** (LIESA) (Avenida Rio Branco 4/17, Centro, 3213 5151, http://liesa.globo.com).

Travellers' needs

For tour operators, including travel agencies that offer both city tours and itineraries for travel in Brazil and abroad, *see p53*. For renting mobile phones and fixing computers, *see p135*. A list of shipping agents is included on p225. For suitcase repairers and new luggage shops, *see p143*.

Arts & Entertainment

Features

Festivals & Events

Carnival's only one week of the party.

In case you hadn't heard, Rio likes to party, and has assembled a bewildering array of holidays and reasons for celebration. The city hall likes to inaugaurate new 'annual' festivals each year, some of which survive, but the biggest are connected with church festivals: Easter, Corpus Christi, All Souls' Day and Christmas. A comprehensive collection of events can be found in Riotur's *Rio Guide*, a bi-monthly publication, or on its website (www.riotur.com.br). For a list of public holidays, *see p233*.

January-March

Carnival
Dates 4-6 Feb 2008; 23-25 Feb 2009; 15-17 Feb 2010.
The Monday, Tuesday and Wednesday morning of Carnival are national holidays. *See pp25-29*.

Foundation of Rio de Janeiro
St Sebastian, Barra da Tijuca. **Date** 1 Mar.
The city of Rio de Janeiro was founded by Estácio de Sá on 1 Mar 1565; the date is celebrated by a mass.

It's All True
Various venues (www.itsalltrue.com.br). **Date** Mar.
An important international documentary festival held around the country since 1995.

It's smiles all round at **Carnival**.

April-June

Rio Boat Show
Marina da Glória, Avenida Infante Dom Henrique, Glória (www.rioboatshow.com.br). **Date** Apr or May.
Boat exhibitions and a regatta.

Day of the Indian
Museu do Índio, see p67. **Date** 19 Apr.
Marked with a week of exhibitions at Museu do Índio.

Tiradentes Day
Date 21 Apr.
A national holiday for Tiradentes (the 'teeth puller'), Joaquim José da Silva Xavier, executed for his part in the 1789 revolt against the Portuguese.

National Day of Choro
Various venues. **Date** 23 Apr.
Started in 2000 by the national government, the day is marked with live shows and jam sessions.

Saint George's Day
Igreja de São Jorge, Rua da Alfândega 382, Centro. **Date** 23 Apr.
A vigil to mark St George's day, a holiday in Rio.

International Leblon-Leme Race
Leblon (2292 7710/www.racersbrasil.com.br). **Date** early June.
An annual 8km (5 mile) beach race since 1979, which you can choose to either run or walk.

Rio das Ostras Jazz & Blues
Various venues in Rio das Ostras (www.riodasostras jazzeblues.com). **Date** early June.
Halfway to Buzios, Rio das Ostras hosts an annual festival where international names jam with local stars in three different waterside venues.

Dia dos Namorados
Date 12 June.
Love is in the air for the Brazilian equivalent of St Valentine's Day. Not the best time to visit a motel (*see p44* **Naughty and nice**) – the queues are horrendous.

Rio de Janeiro Marathon
Across the city (2223 2773/www.maratonadorio.com.br). **Date** late June.
Three routes through the city: the full marathon from Recreio along the coast to Flamengo, a half marathon and a 6km (4 mile) fun run.

Anima Mundi
Various venues (2541 7499/www.animamundi.com.br). **Date** late June, early July.
An exciting annual international animation festival.

July-September

Festa Literaria International de Parati
Various venues in Parati. **Date** early July.
Since 2003, the FLIP festival in Parati has become one of the world's leading literary festivals, with high profile visiting authors and an amazing setting.

Gay Pride Rio
(2238 8292/www.arco-iris.org.br). **Date** early July.
Out and about on the streets, the Pride Parade.

Portas Abertas
Various venues in Santa Teresa (www.arte deportasabertas.com.br). **Date** July.
A festival atmosphere is in the air when Santa Teresa artists open their studios to the public for a week.

Brazilian Grand Prix
Jockey Club, Praça Santos Dumont 31, Gávea (3534 9000). **Date** first Sun of Aug.
Not the Formula One race, which is in São Paulo, but the highlight of the horse racing calendar.

Independence Day
Date 7 Sept.
Anniversary of declaration of independence from Portugal signed by Dom Pedro in 1822.

Book Bienalle
Riocentro, Riocentro Avenida Salvador Allende 6555, Barra (3431 4000/www.bienaldolivro.com.br). **Date** mid Sept every other year.
The Bienal do Livro (next held in 2009) and early May's International Book Fair (also held at Riocentro every other year) are getting bigger each outing.

October-December

Festival do Rio
Various venues (www.festivaldorio.com.br). **Date** Oct.
Rio's high-profile annual international film festival.

Festival do Teatro
Various venues (www.riocenacontemporanea.com.br). **Date** early Oct.
Rio's most challenging theatre festival, with quality avant-garde and modern groups.

Nossa Senhora de Aperecida
Date 12 Oct.
Our Lady of Aperecida is the patron saint of Brazil and gets a national holiday, which also marks Children's Day, with events for kids.

International Short Film Festival
Various venues (www.curtacinema.com.br). **Date** Oct.
A sharp burst of short films from around the world.

Biennial Festival of Brazilian Contemporary Music
Sala Cecilia Meireles, Largo da Lapa 47, Centro (2224 4291/www.funarte.gov.br). **Date** late Oct.

Loud and proud: **Gay Pride Rio**.

A highbrow and challenging contemporary music festival; held in 2007 and then every other year.

Month of Rio Culture
Throughout the city. **Date** Nov.
Rio's month of culture, with special issues of magazines and a heightened cultural programme.

Panorama da Dança Contemporanea
Various venues (www.panoramafestival.com). **Date** early Nov.
Since 1992, Rio's annual cutting-edge contemporary dance festival, currently directed by Lia Rodrigues.

Republic Day
Date 15 Nov.
The anniversary of the day in 1889 when Dom Pedro left power. A national holiday.

Black Consciousness Day
Date 20 Nov.
The birthday of Zumbi, leader of Quilombo dos Palmares, a sanctuary for escaped slaves. A holiday in Rio de Janeiro marked by free concerts and events.

Hutúz Festival
Armazém 5, Avenida Rodrigues Alves, Centro (www.hutuz.com.br). **Date** late Nov.
Hip hop festival celebrating the great and the new.

National Samba Day
Central Station. **Date** 2 Dec; train leaves 8pm.
A tribute to the 1920s *sambistas* who used to jam on the journey to Oswaldo Cruz. Enjoyable chaos.

Revéillon
Date 31 Dec.
Dress in white and pick your choice of New Year's Eve party. A half-day holiday.

Arts & Entertainment

Children

Big excitement for little people.

With its reputation as a party city, Rio does not usually spring to mind as a traditional family destination. In reality it can be an excellent choice – there is plenty of normal life going on away from the clubbing and no shortage of options for keeping the kids entertained. One thing is for sure: Brazilians love children and will bend over backwards to make them feel welcome. Families will have a different experience to most tourists – but will perhaps get a better feel for the real Rio and the true warmth of its people.

Most Carioca children live on an entirely different routine to those from Western countries. Schools are split into morning and afternoon shifts, so half of them get a leisurely start to the day and consequently a very flexible bedtime, even during the week. The majority of restaurants welcome families with open arms and it is common to see even small children dining at 10pm or 11pm. For the smartest of restaurants and any serious night time exploring, however, it is essential to arrange a babysitter. Most venues in Lapa, for example, have a minimum age requirement of 18 years and are, in any case, no fun for kids.

But there is no need to skip the traditional Brazilian *churrascaria* (barbecue). These generally offer a half-price option for older children and don't charge for younger ones. Look out for **Porcão** in Ipanema (*see p102*) and **Barra Brasa** in Leblon and Barra (*see p106*); these branches all have monitored play areas. Parents of even the fussiest eater will relax soon after they discover the joy of eating in *por kilo* restaurants. You only pay for the weight of the food that you put on your plate and the options available range from simple to sophisticated so everyone is happy.

Outdoor activities

The city offers endless activities for youngsters and the main daytime tourist attractions are all fun for them to explore. Corcovado, Sugar Loaf and the Maracanã are all surefire hits.

Just like everyone else, kids have their favourite spots on the beach. The beach in Leblon is considered to be the most family friendly and between Postos 11 and 12 you'll find the ever popular **Baixo Bebê** (www.baixo bebeleblon.com.br), a free play area for smaller

kids. The nearby kiosk has nappy changing facilities and will even warm baby bottles for you. There is a similar but smaller area in Copacabana near Posto 4. In Barra, the Barraca do Pepe has a children's play area. Further afield the beaches of Prainha and Grumari attract families as well as surfers.

Older children can try body-boarding or surfing. The **Bean Surf School** (in front of the Arpoador Inn Hotel, Arpoador, www. beansurfschool.com.br) gives lessons. For a quieter option the sandcastle artists along the front give lessons in the tricks behind their elaborate creations.

Away from the beach there are other big open-air spaces such as **Quinta da Boa Vista**, the large park that surrounds the zoo, **Jardim Zoológico** (*see p96*). At weekends this fills with families and there are many attractions to amuse kids. Another great option is the area around Lagoa, with plenty to do and space to run around in. Here it is possible to rent bikes, skates and pedal boats. Other green places to burn off energy are the Jardim Botânico, which has a recently renovated play area, and Parque Lage (for both, *see p85*).

For fun excursions for all the family, take the boat to Ilha Fiscal (*see p62*) and visit the jewel-like castle that sits on it; explore the Floresta da Tijuca (*see p90* **The urban jungle**), or head out to sea on a boat trip. For those who like walking, kid-friendly hikes that don't require a guide are Morro dos Cabritos (*see p82*) and up to the Morro da Urca along the Pista Cláudio Coutinho (*see p64*). For something off the beaten track there are several tour companies that specialise in hikes for children and families. Recommended companies include **Moleque Mateiro** (8752 1171, www.molequemateiro.com.br), **Trilharte** (2225 2426, www.trilharte.com.br) and **Trilhas do Rio** (2425 8441, www.trilhasdorio.com.br).

Many small public playgrounds are scattered throughout the city and are often squeezed into any available space. The equipment is usually old and simple but well maintained, but beware that playground surfaces aren't always soft. Ever popular is Praça Nossa Senhora da Paz in Ipanema (Rua Visconde de Pirajá and Rua Joana Angélica), which has play equipment, ducks to feed, space to run around and trampolines and bungee swings.

Arts & Entertainment

Kids and Carnival

No need to feel guilty about leaving the tykes with the babysitter while you enjoy the biggest spectacle on the planet; these kid-friendly alternatives will keep 'em happy.

Blocos

These parades are held during the daytime but don't expect them to be any calmer for it. They range from the over-the-top Ipanema and Copacabana extravaganzas to a gentle neighbourhood stomp in Botafogo or Jardim Botânico. There's usually quite a crowd and it can get too boisterous for kids. Better to keep an eye out for *blocos* organised especially for younger children in the weeks preceding Carnival. They'll have a chance to don their favourite dressing-up gear, make mountains of noise and parade behind a scaled down samba band. A good example is the one that's held around General Osório in Ipanema. Contact Riotur (2542 8080, www.riotur.com.br) for dates and times.

Avenida Presidente Vargas

If you want to see the colourful costumes and floats of Carnival without going to the parade itself, take the children for a walk along Avenida Presidente Vargas outside the Sambódromo on the parade nights. This is where the schools line up before they parade.

Junior Samba Parade

This is the kid's Carnival – a parade by the children of the samba schools. Least touristy of all the Carnival events, it's colourful and fun to watch. The event lasts several hours, is free and is held in the Sambodromo on the Friday evening of the main Samba parade weekend. Contact Riotur (*see above*) for times.

Kids' costume parties

The kids get their own Carnival balls too and they can be elaborate affairs with music, dancing, food and a costume competition. Check with Riotur (*see above*) for times.

Splurge at Caçula

Visit Caçula (Rua Buenos Aires 261, 3861 9028), or any number of shops in Saara (*see p134* **Market daze**), to see what has to be the world's largest stockpile of sequins, feathers, beads and ribbons. Give them just a few small notes and let them shop alongside the Carnival costume-makers. Most of the stuff is available in R$2 packets, so they won't break the bank. When you get home again they will be occupied all afternoon making masks and headdresses. Don't forget to pick up some glue.

Parade of Champions

This is held the Saturday following Carnival in the Sambódromo. Even though this event does not have the competitive element of the main Carnival parades, the participants can let their hair down and you will still see the winning schools. The main advantage is that tickets are cheaper than the main parades so it doesn't hurt so much to leave early. As the schools finish parading, the participants often discard bits of their costume or throw them into the crowd.

Cidade do Samba

It's 'Carnival All Year Round' at the Cidade do Samba. It's fascinating to watch the floats being created and children get to learn about the different musical instruments that make up the Bateria of the Samba parade and are given the chance to get their hands on them and practice. After donning Carnival hats they will have a quick samba lesson and off they go in a spontaneous parade. Who knows when the next Carnival king or queen will be discovered? *See also p63.*

Sonho e Fantasia

Looking for kids' costumes that won't get relegated to the bottom of the dressing-up box? Then pay a visit to Sonho e Fantasia's 'dreams and costumes' (Rua Visconde de Pirajá, 2267 2011, www.sonhofantasia.com.br). This small Ipanema boutique has managed to mix together pyjamas with fancy dress to produce clothing that gives a whole new meaning to the word nightgown. Your princess is going to adore you – and for those with boys, pirates and superheroes are well represented too.

Arts & Entertainment

Good, clean fun on Rio's beautiful beaches.

Fazendinha Estação Natureza

*Estrada dos Bandeirantes 26645, Vargem Grande
(2428 3288/2428 3290/*www.estacaonatureza.
com.br*). Bus 382, 703, 749.* **Open** 10am-5pm Sat,
Sun. **Admission** R$22. **No credit cards.**
This little farm and petting zoo is a fun place to
spend a day away from Rio. Kids get to plant seeds,
feed the animals, ride chariots, try a bucking bron-
co machine and explore the forest.

Floresta Aventura

*Largo da Barra Velha, Barrinha, between São
Conrado & Largo da Barra on the old road to Joá
(2556 9462/www.florestaventura.com). Bus 557,
1133, 2113.* **Open** by reservation only 9am-4pm
daily. **Admission** R$35. **No credit cards.**
Older monkeys can swing through the trees at this
adventure park. The two different obstacle courses
mounted in the tree tops take about an hour each to
complete. Children must be six years or older and at
least 1m 30cms (four feet) tall to take part. Call ahead
to make a reservation.

Playgym Natureza

*Sociedade Hípica Brasileira, Rua Jardim Botânico
421, Jardim Botânico (2537 9541). Bus 415, 461.*
Open 9am-noon, 2-5pm Tue-Fri; 9am-1pm Sat, Sun.
Admission R$40 for a half-day session; free adults.
No credit cards. Map p248 D13.
For the really young set this outdoor discovery area
is divine. There's a clay pit to squelch in, dressing
up clothes, an art area, lots of water, musical instruments, animals and lots more. The kids will get dirty
and wet so dress them appropriately. Some staff
speak English and children aged four years and
older can stay without their parents present.

Rio Water Planet

*Estrada dos Bandeirantes 24000, Vargem Grande,
(2428 9000/www.riowaterplanet.com.br). Bus 703,
707.* **Open** 10am-5pm summer weekends & holidays.
Admission varies. **No credit cards.**

This is a great place to cool off with plenty of extreme
water rides and slides, as well as some calmer pools,
rivers to float down and three areas designated for
smaller children. Always call in advance to check
that this park is open.

Indoor activities

Rainy days in Rio require a little extra
planning. But here are some excellent options
for entertaining the whole family, including
the **Fundação Planetário** (Planetarium; *see
p86*), museums and the **Cidade do Samba**
(*see p63*). Particularly kid-friendly museums
are the **Museu Nacional** (*see p96*), the
Museu Histórico Nacional (*see p63*), the
H Stern gem museum (*see p143*) and the
Museu Casa do Pontal (*see p92*). Much
of the indoor entertainment for kids is found
in shopping malls where you'll find organised
activities that range from ice-skating to
bowling to mini-golf. (For information on
shopping malls, *see p132*).

There is a very full children's theatre
programme in Rio with shows commonly
held on Saturdays and Sundays at around 5pm.
These are, of course, in Portuguese but as the
subject matter is usually fairly predictable
and the production standards are high, it can
be an amusing way to spend an afternoon.

The cinema is another option, but be aware
that most children's films are dubbed into
Portuguese as soon as they are released.

To find one-off events and activities, check
Veja magazine and *O Globo* and *Jornal do
Brasil* newspapers. They all have listing
sections with activities and shows especially
for children. Look for 'Programção Infantil'
or 'Programação Crianças'.

Film

Had enough of golden sands? Then hit the silver screens.

Although silent films and 'part-talkies' were released throughout the 1920s, most mark the beginning of Brazilian film with Mário Peixoto's 1931 production *Limite*. A Belgian poet living in Brazil, Peixoto's classic – a sort of dreamy, Victorian ménage à trois in a boat – is a pillar in Brazilian film. Many critics and film buffs, however, prefer the psychological audacity and modernity of Humberto Mauro's *Ganga Bruta* (1934). Mauro's masterpiece deals with a man who kills his newlywed on their wedding night and then finds a sort of scandalous redemption. It was roundly rejected by traditional critics and short-sighted viewers. And despite the fact that Mauro helped launch the careers of actresses Carmen Miranda and Carmen Santos, and made the most groundbreaking film of his time, he and his work laboured in obscurity for nearly 20 years before being rediscovered in the 1960s by a new generation that would go on to create Brazilian cinema's most important movement, *cinema novo*.

Between the 1930s and the beginning of *cinema novo*, few films stand out more than *Orfeu Negro* (*Black Orpheus*, 1959). A French, Italian and Brazilian production, the film cleaned up at the awards ceremonies, winning the Palme d'Or in Cannes, a Golden Globe and an Academy Award for Best Foreign Language Film. Directed by Frenchman Marcel Camus

(no relation to Albert), *Orfeu Negro* is as much a celebration of Rio's dramatic beauty and rich culture as it is a powerful film. Filmed in a slum before drug trafficking and endemic violence plagued the favelas, sweeping panoramic views combine with intimate footage of full tilt, sweat-soaked carnival to frame an adaptation of a play by beloved scribe Vinicius de Moraes. Capping off the film's impact is one of the most influential soundtracks of all time featuring legends Antônio Carlos Jobim and Luis Bonfá introducing the world to a slick new jazz-infused style of samba that would later be called bossa nova.

CINEMA NOVO

The 1960s saw the arrival of the colossus Glauber Rocha and *cinema novo*; this was the golden age of Brazilian cinema The main precursor of the movement was *Rio, 40 Graus* (*Rio, 40 Degrees*, 1955), a neo-realist snapshot by director Nelson Pereira dos Santos of five young slum-dwellers up to no good on a hot Sunday in Rio. Rallying behind the mantra 'a camera in the hand is an idea in the head' a new wave of directors led by Rocha rebelled against hollow *chanchadas* – slapstick comedies replete with gaudy costumes and over-the-top musical numbers – that had previously dominated the industry. Setting many of his films in the barren, poverty-stricken north of Brazil, Rocha attacked Brazil's social problems with a jittery

Arts & Entertainment

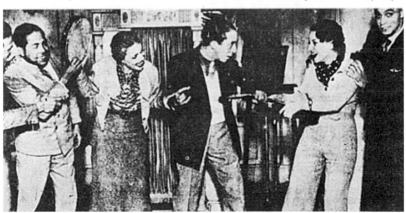

Star quality – **Carmen Miranda** (second from right) and friends.

camera and disregard for narrative that allowed him powerful images and juxtapositions. Rocha's 1964 masterpiece *Deus e o Diabo na Terra do Sol* (Black God, White Devil) – a poetic epic rooted in the mysticism of his native Bahia – is widely considered to be the best Brazilian film of all time.

THE CONTEMPORARY SCENE

By the 1980s, *cinema novo* had blown off its steam, the dictatorship was on its way out and national cinema was slipping into a period of creative decline that would last until the new millennium hailed a surge of investment and interest in making good films. But in spite of this, filmmaking today in Brazil is often overshadowed by beaches, flowers, beer, poverty and violence – it's often stunted by its own chaos before it's able to portray it.

However, the number of productions is on the rise. At the 2006 Latin American Film Festival in Cuba, Brazil presented more new films than any other Latin American country (24), and also came away with more gongs. And when the stars line up and one good film captures the intensity and depth of the nation, the product is invariably captivating and almost certainly profoundly disturbing. The last Brazilian movie to capture viewers' collective attention was the slickly made, gangster-cool *Cidade de Deus*

(*City of God*, 2002), directed by Katia Lund and Fernando Meirelles. By now an icon, the film, like *Orfeu Negro*, brought a budget and a solid artistic vision to the favela, creating a visually stunning film that meshes a crude portrait of the hyper-violent world of drug trafficking with the success story of a young photographer who overcomes his situation. Filmgoers again proved themselves madly attracted to all things gangster and the film was a hit locally and abroad. In an effort to paint a raw, real portrait of Rio, the directors plucked nearly all the actors from the slums.

Still, a certain sheen remains on *City of God*, falling far short of the raw grit of its main precursor, Hector Babenco's *Pixote* (1980). A disturbing epic about the exploitation of poor youth in São Paolo's slums, *Pixote* – like *City of God* 20 years later – used the neo-realist style and slum-dwellers for actors, riding a gut-wrenching performance by Fernando Ramos da Silva. Da Silva famously fell victim to the violence he portrayed, murdered in São Paulo at the age of 19. After *Pixote*, the Argentinian-born Brazilian national Babenco abandoned Brazil, working in the United States to making acclaimed movies like *Kiss of the Spiderwoman* and *Ironweed*, returning to Brazil in 2003 to make *Carandiru*, a film about a catastrophic prison riot in 1992 that left 111 prisoners dead.

Greek tragedy meets Carnival chaos: *cinema novo* and bossa nova in **Orfeu Negro**. *See p159.*

Cachaça and popcorn

The downtown area around the Cinelândia subway station was once packed with cinemas, most of which have since been demolished or turned into evangelical churches. The **Cine Odeon** complex (*see p163*) has survived, however, and, despite the fact it has only one screen, goes a long way to help the area live up to its billing as cinema fantasy land.

Inaugurated in 1926, the building behind the difficult to define and not altogether harmonious façade was slated to form part of a 'tropical Broadway' planned by its creator, the Spanish businessman Francisco Serrador.

Thankfully, the tropical Broadway concept didn't fly, and the cinema has been able to develop its own personality. Unveiled after extensive refurbishment in 2000 at the opening of Rio's annual film festival, the new and improved Cine Odeon has top-shelf infrastructure, great programming, diverse events relating to all things celluloid, including one of the hippest party nights in town.

The refurbished theatre itself has over 600 luxurious seats from which you can appreciate the great sound and picture. The neoclassical ceilings were restored as were charming art nouveau touches that can be seen in both of its cafés, one next to the entrance in the ground floor and the other on the first floor.

Usually on the first Wednesday of every month (sometimes it's the second; check the website at www.cstacaovirtual.com.br) is **Cachaça Cinema Clube**, an event that uses a brilliant formula to unite young people's passion for film and booze. A R$10 fee gets you into a screening – usually quality shorts or good local films – and when the film is over a cachaça tasting booth waits outside. After plowing through a number of R$1 samplers of cachaça, partygoers head upstairs for yet more booze and DJs spinning hits well into the night.

Another novelty night at Cine Odeon is the movie marathon. Residents of Rio aren't reputed as night owls, often burning off their energy during daylight hours at the beach, but Cine Odeon gives paler Cariocas a night out on the first Friday of every month. Films are shown from 11pm to 6am with a DJ and dancing during the breaks between screenings.

Remaining Wednesdays are **Cinema Clube** nights, without the cachaça for the purists who don't need the lure of drink and dance to go out and see a film. Quality films are shown and experts like the editors of the *Contracampo* magazine are on hand to lead post-function discussions.

Cine Odeon hosts all kinds of other cultural events too, from Carnival parties to World Cup games to film premières.

Cidade de Deus (City of God).

Another modern giant is Walter Salles. Salles directed the acclaimed *Central do Brasil* (*Central Station*, 1998), a gritty drama set in Rio's central train station, and appeared to be poised to carry the torch as Brazil's next big director into the new century. After making the tepidly received *Abril Depedaçado* (Behind the Sun) in 2001, Salles too sought greener pastures, making the hit *The Motorcycle Diaries* and a remake of the Japanese horror film *Dark Water*.

Cinemas

As in most places, the mall multiplexes have the bulk of Rio's silver screens, but low-key, two-screen cinema's are also common, have good screens and sound and charge about the same. In the south of the city, most of the cinemas are in the Botafogo and Catete areas, but there are also a few screens in Leblon, Ipanema and Copacabana. Retrospectives and themed screenings are usually promoted under the rubric of '*cineclube*' and show anything and everything. Cinelândia's Cine Odeon (*see p161* **Cachaça and popcorn**) is the key venue for these evenings, but cultural centres like Caixa Cultural or Centro Cultural Banco do Brasil are also used, as well as more esoteric places like bars and the French consulate. Places like Museu da Cidade in Catete and Espaço Paço in Praça XV show quality recent releases for R$4 to $5.

INFO, TIMINGS AND TICKETS
A high percentage of English-language films are shown with Portuguese subtitles, but it doesn't hurt to ask ahead to be sure they aren't dubbed. Reliable newspapers will indicate that films are dubbed by putting 'dub' after the title in the listings. Foreign and Brazilian films at festivals and sometimes at *cineclube* nights are shown with English subtitles.

Listings can be found in newspapers; those in *O Globo* tend to be the most complete. *O Globo* also comes with short reviews and recommendations and Friday's cultural supplement, 'Rio Show', is comprehensive and informative. Online, check out www. estacaovirtual.com.br for information on films and film-related events at the Estaçao cinemas throughout the city. Portuguese speakers will also want to check out the online magazine forum *Contracampo* (www.contracampo.com.br). Most types of official international student cards pay big dividends, gaining up to 50 per cent off in almost all cinemas. Matinées, before 2pm in some places and before 5pm in others, and films after 9pm are generally a bit cheaper.

The centre

Cine Santa Teresa
Rua Pascoal Carlos Magnos 136, Santa Teresa (2507 6841/www.cinesanta.com). Either tramline/ 206, 214 bus. **Open** from 2pm daily. **Tickets** R$12; R$6 Wed. **No credit cards**. **Map** p245 H5.
The owner presents films with a few words and a raffle for food or beers at local establishments, giving the small, 60-person cinema a homely feel.

Centro Cultural Banco do Brasil
Rua Primeiro do Março 66, Centro (3808 2007, www.bb.com.br). Metro Uruguaiana/125, 404 bus. **Open** from noon Tue-Sun. **Tickets** R$6. **Credit** AmEx, MC, V. **Map** p245 I1.

With a strong programme showing everything from animation festivals to new Brazilian cinema, CCBB has the most dynamic line-up in the city, plus, on weekends, a free kid's film at 2pm.

Odeon BR
Praça Floriano 7, Cinelândia (2240 1093/www. estacaovirtual.com.br). Metro Cinelândia/107, 136, 157 bus. **Open** from 2pm Mon-Sat. **Tickets** R$10. **No credit cards. Map** p245 I4.
Although Cine Odeon has only one screen, it's a firm favourite among Rio's legions of film buffs and hosts the legendary Cachaça Cinema Clube (*see p161* Cachaça and popcorn).

South of the centre

Cinemark Botafogo
Praia de Botafogo 400 (2237 9484/www.cinemark. com.br). Metro Botafogo/119, 154, 434 bus. **Open** from noon daily. **Tickets** R$15-17 Thur-Tue (matinees Mon, Tues & Thur $R13); R$11 Wed. **No credit cards. Map** p247 H10.
In Botafogo Praia Shopping, there are six screens that mostly show Hollywood blockbusters.

Estação Ipanema
Rua Visconde de Pirajá 605, Ipanema (2279 4603/ www.estacaovirtual.com.br). **Tickets** R$17; R$10 Mon-Thur before 2pm & after 9pm. **No credit cards. Map** p248 D18.
This decent complex comprises three smallish, fully equipped cinemas and shows new releases.

Estação Laura Alvim
Avenida Vieira Souto 176, Ipanema (2267 4307, www.estacaovirtual.com.br). Bus 177, 382, 503. **Tickets** R$15 Mon-Thur; R$10 Mon-Thur before 2pm & after 9pm; R$17 Fri-Sun. **No credit cards. Map** p249 F17.

The newest of Estação's cinemas, it has three good screens and shows a variety of new releases.

Espaço Unibanco de Cinema
Rua Voluntários da Pátria 35, Botafogo (2226 1986/www.estacaovirtual.com.br). Metro Botafogo/136, 179, 503 bus. **Open** from noon daily. **Tickets** R$14 Mon-Thur; R$16 Fri-Sun; R$10 before 2pm & after 9pm. **No credit cards. Map** p247 H10.
Three screens show European arthouse film, new Brazilian releases and quality international films. A shop next door sells DVDs, books and paraphernalia.

Roxy
Avenida Nossa Senhora de Copacabana 945A (2461 2461/www.severianoribeiro.com.br). Bus 132, 473, 521. **Open** from noon daily. **Tickets** R$12.40 Mon, Tue, Thur before 5pm & all day Wed; R$13.40 Mon, Tue, Thur after 5pm; R$15.40 Fri-Sun. **No credit cards. Map** p249 H15.
A fixture on a busy Copacabana corner since as far back as 1938, Roxy underwent a comprehensive renovation in the 1990s that replaced one big theatre with three smaller, more modern screens with good sound quality, that show mostly first-run film releases from the United States. Fortunately, the priceless art deco entrance and stairway survived the makeover intact.

UCI New York City Center
Avenida das Américas 5000, Barra (2461 1818/ www.ucicinemas.com.br). Bus 234, 523, 707. **Open** from noon daily. **Tickets** R$18; R$15 Wed; R$12 Mon,Tue, Thur before 5pm; R$16 Fri-Sun before 5pm. **Credit** AmEx, DC, MC, V.
This huge and popular multiplex has 18 state-of-the-art screens and shows mainstream films. Check on the website or at the box office before you go, since films are often dubbed here.

Galleries

Rio begins to develop its own style.

Rio's visual arts scene has long lived in the shadow of São Paulo's Bienal de Arte and the now annual contemporary art fair SP-Arte, but a new generation of artists and gallery owners is starting to put the city back on the artistic map.

Over the past several years, a fresh crop of contemporary galleries has emerged, catering to a more dynamic market, inhabiting less traditional venues and offering a greater range. Watch too for the rapidly expanding **Arquivo Geral** showcase, timed to take advantage of the art world's trek to São Paulo for the Bienal.

The greatest concentration of commercial galleries can be found in Ipanema, Gávea and the Cassino Atlântica shopping mall in Copacabana, which houses 20 galleries of one type or another. Many of the city's commercial galleries are located in shopping centres or smaller arcades, also known as *galerias* (for addresses, *see p132*), but don't be put off. Some pleasant exceptions are **Galeria de Arte Ipanema**, **HAP Galeria** and **Mercedes**

Viegas Arte Contemporânea. These last two don't even have a sign on the door.

To find out what's happening at galleries, museums and cultural centres, check out the free bimonthly *Mapa das Artes* (www.mapadasartes.com.br). It offers the most comprehensive information, but only in Portuguese. Look out too for annual festivals like Santa Teresa's **Arte de Portas** (www.artedeportasabertas.com.br) and Jardim Botânico's **Circuito de Artes** (www.circuitodasartes.com.br), during which artists open their studio doors for public visits. Unless otherwise mentioned, admission for all galleries and museums is free.

Galleries

A Gentil Carioca

2nd & 3rd floor, Rua Gonçalves Ledo 17, Centro (2222 1651/www.agentilcarioca.com.br). Metro Presidente Vargas or Uruguaiana/107, 125 bus. **Open** noon-7pm Tue-Fri; noon-5pm Sat. **Map** p245 H2.
Opened by now internationally hot Ernesto Neto, Márcio Botner and Laura Lima, A Gentil Carioca is breathing new life into both its neighbourhood and Rio's art scene through provocative exhibitions, artistic exchange and educational projects.

Arte 21

Shopping Cassino Atlântico, Units 122 & 123, Copacabana (2227 7280/www.arte21galeria.com.br). Bus 474, 503, 2016. **Open** 10am-7pm Mon-Fri; noon-6pm Sat. **Map** p249 H17.
A well-designed and appealing basement space. Exhibitions are sassy, provocative and include contemporary paintings, sculpture and new media.

Arte em Dobro

Rua Dias Ferreira 417/205, Leblon (2259 1952/ www.arteemdobro.com.br). Bus 583, 2015, 2017. **Open** 10am-6pm Mon-Fri. **Map** p248 B16.
Follow the lane to the right of the Argumento bookstore and walk upstairs to this charming second floor gallery and its fine collection of paintings, sculptures and installations, including works by Fernando Velloso, Felipe Barboso and Cabelo.

Box 4

Rua Teixera de Melo 53, Ipanema (2247 8809/ www.galeriabox4.com). Bus 464, 572, 584. **Open** 10am-7pm Mon-Fri; noon-4pm Sat. **Map** p249 F17.
Just across the hall of the main floor shopping arcade from her mother Silvia Cintra's space, Juliana Cintra is making a name both for herself and her gallery – one

This way in to **A Gentil Carioca**.

Off the wall

Street art may have got a late start in Brazil, but both the São Paulo and Rio movements have had a prominent influence on graffiti styles across the globe. Rio's physical and social geography – high walls to keep violence out or to contain a hilly terrain – mean paintable surfaces abound. Prime graffiti spotting areas are Jardim Botânico – the long Jockey Club wall is a favourite – as well as Santa Teresa and Lapa. Key players include Flesh Beck Crew, the all-female TPM Crew (whose witty name is Portuguese for PMS), Acme, Smaêl, Santa Crew, Núia, Nação Crew, TM1 and Marcelo Eco. Graffiti use is also booming in Brazilian advertising and design, which means *grafiteiros* are no longer being sought by the cops but instead by top art directors and interior designers.

Haus Arte Contemporânea (*see p166*) represents various graffiti artists including Acme, Toz, Plá and Smael, while **Severo 172** (*see p167*) houses a graffiti gallery and hip hop music venue in a converted garage. For graffiti supplies head to **Junkz** in Copacabana (Rua Francisco Sá, 95, 2525 6774, www.junkz.com.br) or **Ink Graffiti Shop** in Barra (Shopping Città America, 2494 9117) with an Ipanema branch opening soon. And watch out for the **Hutúz Festival** (*see p155*) in November, dedicated to hip hop cultural expression that includes graffiti interventions and workshops.

of the best places to see works by the new generation of contemporary artists. Names to watch include Maria Klabin, Rodrigo Matheus and Pedro Motta.

Galeria Anna Maria Niemeyer

Shopping da Gávea, Unit 205, Gávea (2239 9144/ www.annamarianiemeyer.com.br). Bus 504, 583, 2014. **Open** 10am-10pm Mon-Sat. **Map** p248 A15.
One of the most established names in town *and* daughter of architect Oscar Niemeyer, Anna Maria represents a long roster of the country's top contemporary artists. Her main gallery in Shopping da Gávea hosts temporary exhibits, while the much more amenable second space on Praça Santos Dumont shows works from her permanent collection. **Other locations**: Praça Santos Dumont 140/A, Gávea (2540 8155).

Galeria de Arte Ipanema

Rua Anibal de Mendonça 27, Ipanema (2512 8832/ www.galeria-ipanema.com). Bus 464, 584. **Open** 10am-7pm Mon-Fri; 10am-2pm Sat. **Map** p249 D17.
Just steps from the beach, Galeria de Arte Ipanema is a quaint white house working mostly with big-name Brazilian modern artists like Di Cavalcanti, Volpi, Portinari and Iberê Camargo, since 1965.

Sound on paper: multimedia at Multiplicidade, part of the **Espaço Cultural Oi Futuro**.

Galeria Paulo Fernandes

Rua Visconde de Itaboraí 6, Centro (2233 1537).
Bus 404, 474, 2014. **Open** noon-6pm Tue-Sat.
Map p245 J1.
A fixture on the art scene for well over two decades, Paulo's gallery on a pedestrian street corner behind the Centro Cultural Banco do Brasil includes a main space, and a window display next door open for 24-hour viewing. A few large-scale sculptures by artists such as José Resende are exhibited on a rotating basis in the square in front of the gallery.

Galeria Tempo

Rua Visconde de Pirajá 414, Room 305, Ipanema
(2227 2221/www.galeriatempo.com.br). Bus 464,
572, 584. **Open** noon-7pm Mon-Fri; by appointment
only Sat. **Map** p249 E17.
Opened in 2006, Galeria Tempo works exclusively with photography and video art. This small gallery in an office space above an Ipanema shopping mall hosts temporary exhibits and represents both Brazilian and international artists.

HAP Galeria

Rua Abreu Fialho 11, Jardim Botânico (3874
2830/www.hapgaleria.com.br). Bus 409, 572,
583. **Open** 10am-7pm Mon-Fri. **Map** p248 B13.
Heloísa Amaral Peixoto took a historic house and turned it into a gallery with two ample floors. The renovations earned a design award and gave her a great space for showing large-scale sculptures and installations. HAP represents and exhibits top-notch artists including Beatriz Milhares, but there's no name on the door – buzz the intercom to be let in.

Haus Arte Contemporânea

Shopping Cassino Atlântico, Unit 213, Arpoador
(2227 6895/www.hausarte.com.br). Bus 474, 503,
2016. **Open** 10am-9pm Mon-Sat. **Map** p249 H17.
One of the first spaces to bring local graffiti artists such as Smael and Pia off the streets and into a gallery, Haus represents *grafiteiros*, abstract painters and a photographer or two – all with a very urban vibe. The space is small for the number of large, colourful canvases it wants to exhibit, a problem that has been remedied by spilling out over into the corridor outside the second-floor gallery.

Laura Marsiaj Arte Contemporânea

Rua Teixeira de Melo 31C, Ipanema (2513 2074/
www.lauramarsiaj.com.br). Bus 464, 572, 584.
Open 10am-7pm Tue-Fri; 3-8pm Sat. **Map** p249 F17.
At the forefront of the contemporary art scene, Laura's inviting streetfront space is on one of Ipanema's hippest streets. There is a main gallery with rotating solo exhibits and a smaller annex next door, aptly named Anexo, which shows bold installations and site specific works.

Lurixs Arte Contemporânea

Rua Paulo Barreto 77, Botafogo (2541 4935/
www.lurixs.com). Metrô Botafogo/524, 583, 584
bus. **Open** 10am-7pm Mon-Fri; by appointment Sat.
Map p247 H11.

A highly respected art collector for many years, Ricardo Rego opened his own gallery in 2003. The works displayed are from nine established Brazilian artists, including José Bechara and Geraldo de Barros. A second exhibit space across the street can be visited upon request.

Mercedes Viegas Arte Contemporânea

Rua Jõao Borges 86, Gávea (2294 4305/www. mercedesviegas.com.br). Bus 504, 583, 2014. **Open** 2-7pm Mon-Fri; 4-8pm Sat. **Map** p253 F1.
Mercedes' space is a tranquil delight, set on a quiet residential street in upscale Gávea. The exhibitions often extend into the tropical garden, with sculptures set against the vine-covered walls or installations hanging from the trees. The gallery represents several well-known Brazilian sculptors like Ana Holck, Angelo Venoso and Ivens Machado.

Severo 172

Avenida Augusta Severo 172, Glória (no phone or website). Metro Glória/178, 571, 572 bus. **Open** 2-10pm Sat, Sun. **Map** p245 I4.
Brainchild of local businesswoman Lilly Barbato, whose garage this is, Severo 172 displays the work of some of the city's most talented *grafiteiros*. The 'gallery' is open only on weekends; during the week, it doubles as a hip hop venue.

Silvia Cintra Galeria de Arte

Rua Teixeira de Melo 53, Ipanema (2521 0426/ www.silviacintra.com.br). Bus 464, 572, 584. **Open** 10am-7pm Mon-Fri; noon-4pm Sat. **Map** p249 F17.
A veteran of the art scene, Silvia Cintra represents some of the country's best artists such as Miguel Rio Branco, Daniel Senise and Amilcar de Castro. She is also a fierce promoter of new talents.

Museums, foundations & cultural centres

Besides those listed below, the city has a wide variety of great exhibition spaces listed elsewhere: the refined Fundação Eva Klabin (*see p81*); the charming Museu Casa do Pontal (*see p92*); the gravity defying Museu de Arte Contemporâneo de Nitéroi (*see p98*); the modernist Museu de Arte Moderna do Rio de Janeiro (*see p68*); the folkloric Museu de Folclore Edison Carneiro (*see p68*) and the Museu Internacional de Arte Naif do Brasil (Rua Cosme Velho 561, Cosme Velho (2205 8612, www.museunaif.com.br) – it's actually currently closed due to lack of funding, though may be open for groups if booked in advance.

Centro Cultural Hélio de Oiticica

Rua Luís de Camões 68, Centro (2242 1012). Metro Carioca/119, 128, 177. **Open** 11am-7pm Tue-Fri; 11am-5pm Sat, Sun & public holidays. **Map** p245 J5.

This three-floored cultural centre is named after one of the city's greatest artists. It shows both national and international exhibits, plus many of Oiticica's works. Frustratingly, city funding has dwindled to a trickle and this promising space is often empty.

Espaço Cultural Oi Futuro

Rua Dois de Dezembro 63, Flamengo (3131 3060/ www.oifuturo.org.br). Metro Largo do Machado/434, 571 bus. **Open** 11am-8pm Tue-Sat. **Map** p247 I7.
This telephone-sponsored multidisciplinary centre has several exhibition spaces on its eight floors showing local and international contemporary art with a strong emphasis on photography, technology and multimedia. It's also home to the bold Multiplicade series (www.multiplicidade.com) and its innovative multimedia performance events.

Espaço Tumbao de Malevo

Rua Pascoal Carlos Magno 121, Santa Teresa (2242 9434/www.tumbaodemalevo.com). **Open** 4-10pm Wed-Sun. **Map** p245 H5.
Tumbao de Malevo is a breezy indoor-outdoor venue for productions from the rest of Latin America; Brazilians tend to know little about their continental neighbours. Up a set of stairs in an old colonial house, it hosts art exhibits, clown performances and an open mic night. There's always great Latin American music playing and drinks at the bar.

Instituto Moreira Salles

Rua Marquês de São Vicente 476, Gávea (3284 7400/www.ims.com.br). Bus 504, 583, 2014. **Open** 1-8pm Tue-Sun. **Map** p253 F3.
This cool white modern cultural centre was built for the Moreira Salles family (son Walter is one of Brazil's top film directors). The stunning house and gardens have six discrete spaces showing top quality exhibits. There is also an intense cultural programme that includes great music events. A visit here is highly recommended; check the website for details.

Museu da Chácara do Céu

Rua Murtinho Nobre 93, Santa Teresa (2507 1932/ www.museuscastromaya.com.br). Tram both lines/206, 214 bus. **Open** noon-5pm Wed-Mon. **Admission** R$2; free Wed. **Map** p245 H4.
This museum houses an excellent collection of modern art, furnishings and decorative objects from Brazil, Europe and Asia, though it hit headlines for an audacious robbery in 2006, when thieves made off with a Picasso, a Dali, a Matisse and a Monet in broad daylight. There's also a lovely garden with views of both Sugar Loaf and Corcovado.

Museu Nacional de Belas Artes

Avenida Rio Branco 199, Centro (2240 0068/ www.mnba.gov.br). Metro Cinelândia/409, 434, 571 bus. **Open** 10am-6pm Tue-Fri; 2-6pm Sat, Sun. **Admission** R$4; free Sun. **Map** p245 I3.
The imposing building on Avenida Rio Branco houses some fine examples of Brazilian and foreign art: more than 16,000 paintings, sculpture, drawings and etchings and a great collection of popular art,

Arts & Entertainment

Gay & Lesbian

Everything you've heard is true. And that's only the half of it...

Regarded as one of the world's key gay destinations, Rio is not in fact overtly queer in terms of bars, clubs and other entertainment. The reality is that gay culture is in some ways quite mainstream. Although society here is definitely (and defiantly) macho, Cariocas for the most part do not bat an eyelid when it comes to homosexuality. True, there are many fun gay places in which to have a good time, but what Rio does not have is a pumping, party-fuelled gay scene along the lines of Miami South Beach or Ibiza.

So what you will find is a 'gay beach' where young straight Cariocas and their families happily co-exist with super buff 'barbies' (the local name for muscle marys) and gay cafés that are not exclusively gay. Most of the places we've listed in this chapter are gay friendly rather than gay exclusive, and, except for the gay baths, lesbians are welcome and encouraged at most gay clubs and parties.

Foreign visitors need to take care in Rio. Prostitution is not uncommon. There are regular stories of 'gringos' being duped. The prevalence of street crime means you should avoid walking between clubs and bars late at night or in the early morning, particularly if you are looking the worse for wear. Just take common sense precautions, such as taking a taxi or going out as part of a group.

You will often hear or read the abbreviation GLS (Gays, Lesbians and Sympathisers), which means that anyone with an open mind is welcome. Rio has a far more integrated scene than many other major gay capitals, and it won't disappoint.

Resources

Arco-Iris
Rua Doutor Otávio Kelly, 15A Tijuca (2238 8292/2208 2799/www.arco-iris.org.br).
Rio de Janeiro's leading gay rights organisation works to improve local quality of life for homosexuals.

Rio Gay Guide
www.riogayguide.com.
Informative website about gay life in Rio.

Rio Gay Life
www.riogaylife.com.
A well laid out website for the gay traveller. Check out its calendar for upcoming events.

Where to stay

Gay and lesbian guests are openly welcome at most hotels in Rio. There are very few exclusively gay-owned and operated hotels or bed and breakfasts in Rio. Your best option is to choose a gay friendly area like Ipanema, Copacabana or Leblon for your stay. Gay-friendly hotels include **Ipanema Plaza** (*see p45*), **Leme Othon Palace**, **Olinda Othon Classic** and **Sol Ipanema** (*see p43*).

Bars & clubs

A Casa da Lua
Rua Barao da Torre 240A, Ipanema (3813 3972/www.idealparty.com.br). Bus 175, 432, 457.
Open 12.30pm-2am Tue-Sat; 4pm-12.30am Sun.
Credit MC, V. **Map** p249 I16.
A small neighbourhood bar for lesbians with house and techno music played. No cover charge.

Bofetada
Rua Farme de Amoedo 87A, Ipanema (2227 1675). Bus 175, 432, 457. **Open** from 6pm daily.
Credit AmEx, MC, V. **Map** p249 F17.
This no-frills bar on the city's gayest street is a sure bet. Boys with buff bodies returning from the beach stop off for a few beers. This bar attracts a big crowd, especially in summer and during Carnival, when it spills out on to the street.

Le Boy
Rua Raul Pompéia 102, Copacabana (2513 4993/www.leboy.com.br). Bus 127, 457, 574. **Open** from 11pm Tue-Sun. **Credit** AmEx, MC, V. **Map** p249 H17.
Rio's biggest and most openly gay nightclub, Le Boy is an institution on the local scene. With capacity for 1,000 hardcore hedonists, the venue is a guaranteed crowd puller, especially on Sunday nights. Cariocas of all ages strut their stuff to uplifting house and high camp disco along with hunky go-go dancers and tourists. On most nights there are drag shows too. Dark and cruisey in parts. For extra entertainment there's easy access to the Le Boy Fitness and Sauna suite.

Cabaré Casanova
Avenida Mem de Sá 25, Lapa (2221 6555).
Bus 434, 464, 572. **Open** from 10pm Fri-Sun.
No credit cards. Map p245 I4.
The superb drag shows at Cabaré Casanova are the real reason to visit this Rio classic. They also have go-go boys on Sunday nights.

Cine Ideal

*Rua da Carioca 64, Centro (2221 1984/www.
cineideal.com.br). Metro Carioca/119, 128, 177
bus.* **Open** 11pm-6am Sat, Sun. **No credit cards.**
Map p245 I2.

Set in an old cinema, this club draws a pumped-up
crowd. Hit the roof terrace to escape the techno.

Copa Bar

*Rua Aires Saldanha 13A, Copacabana (2256
7412/www.thecopa.com.br). Bus 128, 473, 571.*
Open from 9pm Thur-Sat. **Credit** AmEx, V.
Map p249 H15.

This is a small 1960s-inspired venue but with a
smart crowd. Light snacks are served from 9pm, but
the crowd doesn't usually start arriving until around
11pm, when you will most likely have to queue to get
in. Modern pop tunes normally provide the soundtrack.

La Cueva

*Rua Miguel Lemos, 51, Subsolo Copacabana. Bus
464, 473 (2267 1364/www.boatelacueva.com).*
Open 10pm-4am Mon; 10pm-6amTue-Sun.
Credit MC. **Map** p249 G15.

Designed to look like a cave, this bar/club is for the
mature gay man. There are lots of small booths.

Dama de Ferro

*Rua Vinicius de Moraes 288, Ipanema (2247 2330/
www.damadeferro.com.br). Bus 132, 177, 433.*
Open from 10pm Wed-Sun. **Credit** AmEx, MC, V.
Map p249 F16.

There are no shortage of bars on **Rua Farme de Amoedo** – a hub for Rio's gay community.

An interesting combination of lounge and club set over two floors with dancing upstairs. Different DJs play each night. Eclectic mix of patrons from gym bunnies to fashion victims.

Fosfobox Bar/Club

Rua Siqueira Campos 143, 22A, Copacabana (2548 7498/www.fosfobox.com.br). Metro Siqueira Campos/ 464, 584, 2019 bus. **Open** from 11pm Thur-Sat. **Credit** MC, V. **Map** p249 H14.
Known simply as Fosfo, this is a trendy club playing alternative music, from rock to new wave. Attracts a local crowd.

Galeria Café

Rua Teixeira de Melo 31, Ipanema (2523 8250/ www.galeriacafe.com.br). Bus 132, 177, 433. **Open** from 4pm Wed-Sat. **Credit** AmEx, MC, V. **Map** p249 F17.
This dark venue works better as a bar late in the evening. Unusual art installations line the walls and there's a small dancefloor. The resident DJs play a mixture of house and techno, enjoyed by a good-looking crowd that is mainly drawn from Rio's smart and fast professional set. Be sure to sample one (or preferably several) of the bar's speciality cocktail, the tangerine caipirinhas. On Sundays, the bar turns into Galeria Bazar, an alternative clothing shop that's open from noon to 8pm.

La Girl

Rua Raul Pompéia 102, Galeria, Copacabana (2247 8342/www.lagirl.com.br). Bus 127, 457, 574. **Open** from 10pm Mon, Wed-Sun. **Credit** V. **Map** p249 H17.
This is easily the biggest lesbian club in Rio, brought to you (no surprise here) by the same owners as Le Boy. The interior is crisp and modern with plenty of mirrored surfaces.

Redondo Lounge

Avenida Bartolomeu Mitre 450, Leblon (2540 9076). Bus 432, 435. **Open** from 10pm Sun. **Credit** AmEx, V. **Map** p248 B16.
Held here every Sunday evening, 'Girls and Guys Let's Have Fun On Sundays' is a super smart event. Sophisticated and party-hungry Cariocas come out to play in this cool venue.

Star's Club (Buraco da Lacraia)

Rua André Cavalcânte 58, Centro (2242 0446/ www.buracodalacraia.com). Bus 410, 464, 572. **Open** 11pm-5am Fri, Sat. **Credit** AmEx, MC. **Map** p245 H4.
Slightly off the tourist radar but well worth a visit. This part of the Centro is not a known tourist hangout, but as long as you take a taxi you'll be safe. You'll find great music, pool tables, a dark room and waiters who wear nothing but a bow tie and apron to cover their modesty.

X-Demente

Marina da Glória, Avenida Infante Don Henrique, Glória (no phone/www.xdemente.com). **Open** varies. **Map** p245 K5.

If you like your parties big then visit X-Demente, one of the best circuit party producers in Rio. Usually held twice a month (check the website for details), these 2,500-strong parties are for those who like it large, sweaty and pumping. Muscle boys, trannies, straights, gays and lesbians grind away to local and international DJs playing mainly house and techno. The laser shows are spectacular.

Restaurants

Rio caters to diners with all kinds of tastes but particularly those who like meat more than veg. The restaurants and cafés listed below are not exclusively gay but very gay friendly.

00

Avenida Padre Leonel Franca 240, Gávea, inside Planetário da Gávea. (2540 8041/www.00site. com.br). Bus 432, 435. **Open** *Club* from 8pm Thur-Sun. *Restaurant* 8pm-1am Tue-Sun. **Credit** AmEx, MC, V. **Map** p248 A16.
One of the smartest venues in Rio, 00 attracts a gay and gay-friendly crowd on Thursdays and especially Sundays. It's popular with the fashion crowd. Both the club and the restaurant are inside, while the bar, with its amazing outdoor terrace, is packed when the weather holds. Lounge on the day beds underneath the palms or head inside to check out the club's pumping dance music. The menu inside is Asian-Brazilian fusion. Interesting and fun. *See also p189.*

Café New Natural

Rua Barão da Torre 173, Ipanema (2287 0301). Bus 132, 177, 433. **Open** 7am-11pm. **Credit** AmEx, MC, V. **Map** p249 F17.
A Bohemian café/restaurant with a few tables and chairs outside on the street. Very busy at lunchtime with a huge buffet selection. This is a *por kilo* restaurant and you are charged by the weight of food on your plate. Just around the corner from Bofetada Bar/Café (*see p168*), this place is popular with gay locals and also offers great vegetarian options.

Pecado

Rua Barão da Torre 152, Ipanema (2522 5198/ www.pecadosite.com.br). Bus 132, 177, 433. **Open** 7pm-midnight Tue-Thur; 7pm-2am Fri; noon-2am Sat; noon-midnight Sun. **Credit** AmEx, MC, V. **Map** p249 F17.
Bolivian chef Checho Gonzales' menu is very Latin with a modern interpretation. He uses many typical South American ingredients, including tropical fruit, in some of his sauces. Brazilian staples like *moqueca* (fish stew) are given a new twist. Unfussy decor and a gay-friendly crowd.

Rainbow Kiosk

Avenida Atlântica, in front of Copacabana Palace Hotel (no phone). **Map** p250 I14.
This is a kiosk set right on the beach. A great place to have a cocktail and a pizza at the end of the day and watch the antics of the transvestites. Impromptu shows are performed regularly.

I, Yi, Yi, Yi, Yi, I like you very much...

Carmen Miranda seductively sang these words in the 1941 Hollywood film *That Night in Rio*. The cinema-going world had never experienced anything like this performer, the Brazilian Bombshell as she soon became known. Carmen made the world sit up and notice her.

'Look at me and tell me if I don't have Brazil in every curve of my body,' Carmen famously once said.

The Brazilian icon, who died over 50 years ago, still casts her spell over Rio and her influence is found everywhere. With her lavish costumes, flamboyant jewellery and infectious smile, Carmen Miranda has been immortalised, copied, mimicked and loved by the gay community worldwide.

Carmen took samba to an international audience with great style, amplifying it with colour, gusto and her own personal touch. Take away the show-stopping costumes and Carmen is remembered locally as a great singer. She helped popularise a new modern Brazilian sound in 1930s Brazil.

Born in Portugal, Carmen moved to Brazil when she was only one year old. For the major part of her life Rio became her home before she conquered Hollywood.

The singer considered herself a local and she gave Carioca women (and subsequently drag artists) a new role model. Strong, proud and sexy, Carmen was not afraid of achieving or performing. After recording her first song in Rio in 1929, the samba 'Não vá Simbora', she went on to have a successful career before being lured by Broadway, in 1939, and subsequently Hollywood.

There is a whole museum in Rio dedicated to Carmen (*see below*). It houses some of her costumes, jewellery, photographs of her career and other memorabilia. Each year the the museum celebrates the birthday of Carmen Miranda on 9 February with special exhibitions and a film festival.

Her influence on local culture can even be seen on the gay section of the beach at Ipanema. One of the male beach sellers, wearing nothing but a bathing suit and an elaborate hat made of tin foil and plastic fruit, walks along the beach selling fresh fruit salad. Elsewhere in Rio drag queens pay homage to her in nightly shows and her iconic style is copied during Carnival and gay pride. The higher the fruit, the closer to God.

Carmen proudly wore Brazil on her sleeve and despite, or perhaps because of, her outrageous persona, she is still widely admired and adored.

Museu Carmen Miranda

Avenida Rui Barbosa 560, Flamengo (2299 5586). **Open** 11am-5pm Tue-Fri; 2-5pm Sat, Sun. **Admission** free.

Arts & Entertainment

Leave the book at home – Rio's beaches are an integral part of the social scene.

Gyms & saunas

Body Tech Gym
Rua Gomes Carneiro 90, Ipanema (2287 8531/
www.bodytech.com.br). Bus 132, 177, 433. **Open**
6am-11pm Mon-Fri; 9am-11pm Sat, 5-10pm Sat; 9am-2pm
Sun. **Credit** V. **Map** p249 G17.
Within walking distance of the gay section on
Ipanema beach, this gym attracts a large gay clientele. The buff boys of Rio pump iron here before
going to the beach, or before venturing out to a bar
or club in the evening. Hi-tech facilities include a
swimming pool and all the latest in cardio torture
machines. This large and stylish chain also has
two other branches in Ipanema, plus one in
Copacabana and one in Leblon (where all the local
television stars work out).

Club 117
Rua Candido Mendes 117, Glória (2252 0160/
www.club117.com.br). Bus 434, 571, 572.
Open 3pm-1am Tue-Sun. **Credit** AmEx, MC, V.
Map p245 I5.
One of the oldest, largest and most respected
saunas in Rio. Set over three floors the sauna has
steam rooms, a video lounge and two bars. The
main bar feels like a nightclub, with its resident DJ
and shows performed every night – from strippers
to go-go boys, each night is different. This sauna
is extremely busy at the end of the working day,
with a large array of escorts.

Nova Leblon
Rua Barão da Torre 522, Ipanema (2247 9169/
www.termasleblon.com.br). Bus 132, 177, 433.
Open noon-6am daily. **Credit** AmEx, MC, V.
Map p248 D16.
This sauna does not attract escorts like some of the
others in Rio. It has private cabins, both wet and dry
steam rooms, a dark room and masseurs. The beach
crowd come here to get down and dirty at the end of
the 'working' day.

Projeto SB Club
Rua 19 de Fevereiro 162, Botafogo (2244 4263/
www.projetosb.com.br). Bus 435, 572, 584. **Open**
3pm-midnight daily. **Credit** MC, V. **Map** p247 I11.
This sauna is extremely smart and wins major
points for cleanliness. There are massage rooms,
a cybercafé and bar, hydro massage, lounge, cinema and private rooms. This sauna sets a new standard for quality and modernity on the Rio scene,
with its many added-value touches, including toiletries and headsets.

Beaches

Cariocas take body presentation to a new level.
Living by the sea and with some of the best
beaches in the world on their doorstep, the
locals spend a lot of time on the sands. Looking
good is a *sine qua non*. Cariocas are not fans
of beach towels – instead they take a *kanga*

(sarong) to the beach. Tourists are easily
spotted if they are using a beach towel.
  Another Carioca idiosyncracy is that they
hardly ever lie down to sunbathe – instead
they prefer to stand. This allows them to survey
the crowd (and the competition), chat to friends
and show their best physical attibutes in their
full, three-dimensional glory. So don't be shy.
If you've got it, flaunt it. If you haven't got it,
flaunt it anyway.
  A crucial, almost obligatory, beach
accoutrement is the square piece of lycra known
as the *sunga*. Both straight and gay locals wear
this piece of swimwear almost as a uniform.

Copacabana beach
Avenida Atlântica
The area between the Copacabana Palace Hotel and
Rua Fenando Mendes is the gay and transvestite
section. You will encounter more hustlers on this section of the beach, so take care. To avoid any hassle
just say no. Gay saunas are a safer option.

Grumari & Abrico beaches
Avenida Estado da Guanabara.
About a 30-minute drive west of Rio you'll find the
nudist beach, Abrico, set in the nature reserve of
Grumari. Most people on the left section of the beach
are male, although it's not easy to find. Head out
west past Barra de Tijuca, follow the coastline till
you come to Macumba beach and then Prainha (little beach). At the top of the road near some large
rocks is the first path. Follow that down to the beach.
No public transport goes here, so you will need a car.

Ipanema beach
Avenida Vieira Souto.
Rio's most openly gay side of life is on this beach,
between Posto 9 and Posto 8, the section in front of
Rua Farme de Amoedo, is the most popular gay
and lesbian stretch of sand in Rio for both tourists
and locals. Just look out for the rainbow flags. It's a
great place to collect flyers promoting different club
nights and special events.

Gay Carnival

Rio throws one of the biggest parties in the
world: Carnival. Besides the famous parade of
the Samba schools, Rio's gay community joins
in the festivities, throwing their own parties
all over town during Carnival. The brashest
and most opulent is the Gala Gay held on the
Tuesday night of Carnival at Scala. People
come and stare at the outrageous transvestites.
Other clubs and bars also host their own Carnival
events. Check websites in advance for special
events and tickets.

Scala Gay Carnival
Avenida Afrânio de Melo Franco 296, Leblon
(2239 4448/www.scalario.com.br). **Map** p248 C16.

Arts & Entertainment

Music

Whatever you came for, you leave with the music.

Samba & choro

CHORO

The Brazilian classical composer, Heitor Villa-Lobos, once described choro as 'the true incarnation of the Brazilian soul'. Its roots go back to the start of the 19th century when the Portuguese royal family imported instruments like the clarinet and the piano to Brazil. It developed into a popular music form towards the end of the 19th century on the outskirts of Rio de Janeiro where civil servants who lived in the city's poor outskirts came together for jam sessions based around a flute and a guitar.

More commonly referred to these days as 'chorinho', choro is perhaps the only form of popular Brazilian music to be heavily influenced by Europe. Early choro composers, like the flautist Joaquim Calado, mixed polka and the waltz with African rhythms. The result was a massively intricate sound that required rapid fingerwork and a complete control over the instrument.

Choro is unique in bridging the gap between classical music (known rather pompously n Brazil as 'erudite music') and popular music, particularly samba. Classically trained musicians like the pianist Chiquinha Gonzaga and Ernesto Nazareth were key to the evolution of choro during the 1910s and 1920s, when the core of the choro repertoire was composed, never to be superseded. Among the best-known tracks are 'Odeon' and 'Apanhei-te Cavaquinho', both composed in 1914 by Ernesto Nazareth, and 'Noites Cariocas', a standard in most samba and choro gigs around Rio.

During the 1950s and '60s, a time when most Cariocas were more interested in bossa nova, the choro scene in Rio focused around the home of Jacob do Bandolim, a superb *bandolim* (mandolin) player who often crossed over into samba and made three LPs with the singer Elizeth Cardoso mixing *samba-canção* and choro.

Choro experienced a revival in the 1980s and is in the midst of another revival at the moment. Foremost among the groups playing in Rio today are **Trio Madeira Brasil** and **Regional Carioca**, while Hamilton de Holanda, a Brasilia-born *bandolim* player, and Yamandu Costa (*see p176* **Living legends and rising stars**), are perhaps the best known solo artists. Mauricio Carrilho, a musician who has been at the heart of choro for several decades, recently set up an independent label called **Acari Records** (www.acari.com.br) to promote further the genre, and in 2000 the **National Day of Choro** was created by the Brazilian government – marked each year on 23 April with live shows and jam sessions.

SAMBA

Despite being firmly rooted in African rhythms imported by slaves, samba is a genuinely Brazilian beat, which emerged from the spontaneous get-togethers in the outskirts and favelas of Rio de Janeiro. It's now recognised throughout the world – but it's a Rio thing. These days other regional genres, like forró and *brega*, sell more records and fill more clubs across the country, but samba remains at the centre of cultural life in Rio de Janeiro.

Samba was born at the beginning of the 20th century with a song recorded in 1917 called 'Pelo Telefone'. The track remains one of the definitive samba songs, and set the tone for much of the early music that offered up *crônicas* (stories) of Brazilian workers and musicians.

Samba's big breakthrough came in the 1930s when, under the Getúlio Vargas dictatorship, the country's radio network was massively expanded as a means of disseminating government propaganda. Virtually overnight households across the country had access to the latest sambas coming out of the studios in Rio de Janeiro. Also at this time – now known as the golden era of samba – the first samba schools began to appear (*see pp25-29*), forming the centrepiece of Rio's Carnival.

Despite samba's growing name, many of the composers – mostly impoverished men from the city's shantytowns – remained unknown in these first decades. The situation began to change in 1965, when **Elizeth Cardoso**, one of Brazil's most treasured female voices, released one of the era's defining records, *Elizeth Sobe o Morro* (*Elizeth Goes up the Favela*). The record brought together Cardoso, the queen of Rio's casinos and radio waves, and the voices from Rio's hilltop favelas, among them Cartola, Nelson Cavaquinho, Candeia and Jair do Cavaquinho, and included tracks like 'Vou Partir', 'A Flor e o Espinho' and 'Luz Negra' – all now samba standards.

Elizeth's involvement propelled the invisible *sambistas* – who had previously scratched a

Trapiche Gamboa. *See p179.*

Living legends and rising stars

The Old Guard

NELSON SARGENTO is one of the key members of the Mangueira Samba school, who in the 1950s composed alongside the king of samba, Cartola. Despite being well into his 80s, he can still be seen singing in Rio's nightclubs and dancehalls.

WILSON MOREIRA was born and raised in northern Rio and is today one of the most loved members of Rio's *Vehla Guarda* – the old guard. Alongside his partner Nei Lopes he has composed hits like 'Lady Liberty', championing black rights and social equality.

WILSON DAS NEVES is a drummer and to this day is part of Brazilian composer Chico Buarque's band. As a session musician he has played across the world. These days, he can be seen frequently on the stages of Lapa, either solo or with the excellent Orquestra Imperial Carnival group.

TIA SURICA, or Auntie Surica, has been a key member of the Portela samba school for nearly four decades but only recently finished recording her first solo record and still hosts legendary samba parties at her home. She can be seen performing alongside rising stars like Batuque na Cozinha.

MONARCO, more formally known as Hildmar Diniz, is the king of the Portela Samba school's Old Guard. Born in 1933, his long career continues with recently composed sambas for the Brazilian singer Marisa Monte – and he can still be seen most weeks singing in Rio.

WALTER ALFAITE (Walter the Tailor) is a self-taught singer, composing since he was a teenager but he was officially discovered in the 1970s by samba star Paulinha da Viola. Over his 50 year career he has recorded over 200 sambas and two solo records.

DONA IVONE LARA (Yvonne Lara da Costa) is the undisputed Queen of Samba. Born in Rio in 1921, she studied the *cavaquinho* as a child and in 1965 joined the Império Serrano composer's group.

ELTON MEDEIROS worked with Ze Keti in the 1940s and later became a member of the samba group A Voz do Morro (The Voice of the Favela). He has worked alongside many of Rio's most celebrated samba composers, including Guilherme de Brito and Cartola.

The New School

DIOGO NOGUEIRA is the son of samba king João Nogueira. His deep voice and dashing good looks have made him a constant crowd puller in the last couple of years. In 2007, he composed the samba theme for one of Rio's biggest samba schools, the Portela.

NICOLAS KRASSIK, a French jazz violinist, moved to Rio in 2000 and has never looked back. Playing a mixture of samba, forró and choro, he has recorded two albums, *Na Lapa* and *Caçuá*, and has slotted right into the scene, playing alongside some of Brazil's most famous musicians. For more information and audio clips, see www.nicolaskrassik.com.

HENRY LENTINO is the Jimi Hendrix of samba and choro. From the south of Brazil, he moved to Rio in 2000 where he has wowed audiences with his unconventional, rock-like style of playing the *bandolim* (mandolin). He is currently working on his first solo album, *Batucada Urbana*, and second album with his group Tira Poeira. For more, see www.henrylentino.com.br.

YAMANDU COSTA, originally from Brazil's south, is one of the most established musicians of this emerging scene, renowned across Brazil for his mind-bogglingly rapid style of guitar and his mixture of Brazilian, Argentinian, Paraguayan and classical rhythms. These days, Yamandu spends half of his life on the road, touring Brazil and the world, but if you're lucky you just might catch him propping up a late-night jam session in Lapa. For more, see www.yamandu.com.br.

THAIS VILLELA is one of many 'divas of Lapa' the talented female singers in the samba heartland. She began her career at the legendary Comuna do Semente jam sessions, and these days can be seen playing regularly in Lapa's best clubs. For more information, on her debut album and perfrmances see www.thaisvillela.com.

living selling tracks and cleaning cars – from the favelas into the mainstream. Zicartola, a restaurant in central Rio where the sounds and flavours of the favelas were played to the 'official Rio', suddenly became gossip-column material, and musicians from all possible backgrounds suddenly acquired a common bond.

In the 1970s and '80s, a new generation of sambistas began to spring up – musicians and singers like Joao Nogueira, Clara Nunes, Paulinho da Viola and Martinho da Vila, who borrowed heavily from roots samba but simultaneously modernised it, bringing in new instruments and upping the tempo. Joao Nogueira created the **Clube do Samba**, a hugely popular samba knees-up that continues to this day in different clubs in Lapa – it was recently revived by Joao's wife, Angela Nogueira, after he died in 2000.

Another key *sambista* during this era was **Bezerra da Silva**, who became the unofficial spokesman for Rio's favelas, with tracks that laid bare the harsh realities of everyday slum life. He recorded 28 albums before his death in 2005, 11 of which went gold, three platinum and one double platinum. Many Brazilian rappers now describe him as the 'Godfather of Gangsta Rap', partly because of his role in developing *partido alto*, a freestyle form of samba singing.

Pagode – a tacky, romantic and watered down version of samba – is the order of the day in most parts of Brazil, with bands like Revelação selling by far the most number of records. But purists needn't despair. *Samba de raiz* (roots samba) and choro, in many ways an instrumental cousin of samba, can be found in hundreds of bars and clubs across Rio and Niterói. As they say in Rio: *Tudo dá samba* ('everything ends up in samba').

For up-to-date and comprehensive information on artists and events, check www.samba-choro.com.br (in Portuguese).

Bar da Ladeira

Rua Evaristo da Veiga 149, Lapa (2224 9828/ http://matrizonline.oi.com.br/bardaladeira). Metro Cinelândia/107, 157 bus. **Open** from 6pm Wed-Sat. **Admission** R$7-$10. **Credit** MC, V. **Map** p245 I3.
Following the trend for early 20th-century mansions in Lapa being converted into watering holes, Bar da Ladeira is a good venue for great samba and choro.

Bip Bip

Rua Almirante Gonçalves 50, Copacabana (2267 9696). Bus 154, 433, 523. **Open** 6.30pm-1am daily. **Admission** free. **No credit cards. Map** 249 H16.
A miniscule samba bar with a huge reputation for legendary jam sessions. It gets so packed that the customers inevitably spill onto the pavement outside and so good that they often continue at the kiosk across the road on Copacabana beach after closing hours.

Café Cultural Sacrilégio

Avenida Mem de Sá 81, Lapa (2222 7345/ www.sacrilegio.com.br). Bus 434, 464, 572. **Open** from 2pm Wed-Fri; from 8.30pm Sat. **Admission** R$16. **Credit** AmEx, DC, MC, V. **Map** p245 H4.
Another rock of the samba revival in Lapa, Sacrilégio is a charming old townhouse converted into a bar and show venue with live music most nights harking back to the golden days of samba.

Carioca da Gema

Avenida Mem de Sá 79, Lapa (2221 0043/www. barcariocadagema.com.br). Bus 434, 464, 572. **Open** from 6pm daily. **Admission** R$15-$25. **No credit cards. Map** p245 H4.
One of Lapa's most famous and highly rated, although increasingly expensive, samba joints in the heart of Lapa. It also features regular performances from choro groups like Regional Carioca.

Clube dos Democráticos

2nd Floor, Rua do Riachuelo 91, Lapa (2252 4611/www.clubedosdemocraticos.com.br). Bus 410, 464. **Open** from 11.30pm Wed-Sat; 8pm-midnight Sun. **Admission** R$8-$24. **No credit cards. Map** p244 G4.
Founded in 1867, Democráticos is one of Rio de Janeiro's oldest Carnival clubs. This huge second-floor dancehall has a slightly dodgy sound system but it does host some of the hottest samba and forró shows in the city. Look out for the excellent Semente da Musica Brasileira project (www. sementedamusicabrasileira.kit.net) each Friday, when the pick of samba's oldest and youngest musicians take over. *Photo p178.*

Clube Renascença

Rua Barão de Sao Francisco 54, Andaraí (2572 2322). Bus 217, 226, 433. **Open** 3-9pm Mon; 4-10pm Sat. **Admission** R$6 men; R$4 Mon; R$5 Sat women. **No credit cards.**
It's a bit of a journey to get to if you're staying in the southern zone, but this place is well worth the schlep. The Samba do Trabalhador (Workers' Samba), which takes place on Mondays, is a linchpin of Rio's samba scene – a raucous, hedonistic daytime party attended by some of the scene's biggest hitters.

Comuna do Semente

Rua Joaquim Silva 138, Lapa (2509 3591). Bus 409, 571, 572. **Open** from 10pm. **Admission** R$10 **No credit cards. Map** p245 I4.
A tiny but extraordinary club, directly under the Arcos da Lapa. The Comuna is one of the favourite hangouts for young Brazilian musicians. Its weekly programme includes choro, a *roda de samba* and residencies from some of the scene's new stars.

Estrela da Lapa

Avenida Mem de Sá 69, Lapa (2507 6686/ www.estreladalapa.com.br). Bus 434, 464, 572. **Open** from 9pm Tue-Sat. **Admission** R$10-$50. **Credit** MC, V. **Map** p245 H4.

Clube dos Democráticos. *See p177.*

Any venue opened by novelist and musician Chico Buarque cannot possibly be bad and the 'Star of Lapa' does not disappoint. Shows include bossa nova, jazz and MPB bands.

Estudantina

Praça Tiradentes 79. (2232 1149). Metro Carioca/ 107, 125, 178 bus. **Open** from 10pm Wed-Sat. **Admission** R$15. **Credit** V. **Map** p245 H2.

Estudantina is a *gafieira*, or traditional dance hall, where couples spin and glide on the parquet floor as a live orchestra belts out the best in Latin ballroom, from samba to salsa. It's a lot of fun. The place has recently started to put on forró nights directed by a wicked accordion player called Chico Chagas.

Mangue Seco Cachaçaria

Rua do Lavradio 23, Lapa (3852 1947/www. manguesecocachacaria.com.br). Bus 107, 154, 158. **Open** from 11am Mon-Sat. **Admission** free-R$12. **Credit** AmEx, DC, MC, V. **Map** p245 H3.

This is the sister club of the Rio Scenarium (*see below*) across the street. Mangue Seco is a two-storey mansion that hosts great choro and samba groups, and boasts a selection of potent *cachaças*.

Rio Scenarium

Rua do Lavradio 20, Lapa (3147 9001/www.rio scenarium.com.br). Bus 107, 154, 158. **Open** from 6.30pm Tue-Thur; from 7.30pm Fri, Sat. **Admission** R$15-$25. **Credit** DC, MC, V. **Map** p245 H3.

A stunning antique shop and nightclub, recently voted as the world's eighth best bar by the UK's *Guardian* newspaper for its superb music, including choro, forró and samba, and great atmosphere. The entrance fee has shot up in recent years as the club has become popular with Rio's high society but it's still the place to really enjoy the Lapa thing.

Teatro Rival

Rua Álvaro Alvim 33, Centro (2240 4469/www. rivalbr.com.br). Metro Cinelândia/125, 170 bus. **Open** varies. **Admission** R$10-$25. **No credit cards**. **Map** p245 I3.

A big basement auditorium right next to the Cinelândia metro station with a collection of great street bars on the tiny cobbled street out front. The Rival is not exclusively dedicated to samba and choro, but it does stage shows by big names in samba most weeks and also plays host to musicians from across Brazil.

Trapiche Gamboa

Rua Sacadura Cabral 155, Gamboa (2516 0868) Bus 123, 170, 177. **Open** from 6.30pm Tue-Thur; from 8.30pm Fri, Sat. **Admission** R$10-$16. **Credit** AmEx, DC, MC, V. **Map** p245 H1.

In a gorgeous old building in the city's port zone, an area currently being revitalised by the town hall, Trapiche is one of the favourite venues among Rio's samba and choro musicians. It draws a friendly crowd from all over the city to dance. All the way up the stairs at the back is a tiny and unexpected beer garden. Highly recommended. *Photo p175.*

Forró

Very big right now, forró hails from the great north-east of Brazil and is spreading all over the country and the world. Its dance style has been modernised for the big stage and it's often performed for large, dancing crowds by a fully choreographed band. In Rio, its public tends to be lower and middle class, including many immigrants from the north-east, and the music and fashion can sometimes be very tacky, but it's well worth overlooking that for the sheer amusement and the great dancing.

Asa Branca (*see below*) has become the main focus for forró in the centre of town. A more culturally interesting experience can be had at the **Feira São Cristóvão** (*see p95*) – a mammoth, enclosed (thus practically crime-free) fair that stays open from Friday evening all the way through till Sunday evening non-stop. Big forró bands play on a huge main stage until 6am, and smaller stages are packed with forró, *repentista* music and other styles.

Asa Branca

Avenida Mem de Sá 17, Lapa (2224 9358). Bus 434, 464, 572. **Open** from 10pm Wed-Sun. **Admission** R$10. **Credit** AmEx, DC, MC, V. **Map** p245 I4.

A forró club in the heart of Lapa, which until recently had a slightly sleazy reputation. The club, however, was recently revamped and has since been hosting some riotous forró nights. They're not a whole lot more sophisticated, but much, much more fun.

MPB

Like much of Brazil's cuisine, its religious practices and even its fashion, Musica Popular Brasileira (MPB) is a syncretised blend of ingredients and influences from all corners of the earth; a pot-au-feu of urban music simmering in Brazil since the late 1960s and intensifying its complex, smoky flavours ever since.

In its early days – and to some extent today – MPB was a movement of musical culture and a bastion of leftist politics. Its performers criticised the country's military regime, social injustice, police corruption and culture of violence. In solidarity with the country's vast underclass, MPB was built on a foundation of traditional Brazilian styles, often with syncopated, African-influenced rhythms played on local percussion instruments. Its main melodic instruments were voice and Brazilian guitar.

To show its erudition and world awareness, however, MPB tapped into ideas from world pop and rock of the time, including Jimi Hendrix and the Beatles, and added psychedelic riffs, rare time signatures, raunchy electric

Next generation: Caetano's son (left), Domenico and Kassin are **Moreno Veloso + 2**.

guitar, rock drums or even full string and horn sections. MPB was said to be a 'cannibalistic' sound, unashamed to mix and match existing styles. Present day MPB has borrowed from electronica, hip hop, dance-pop and the singer-songwriter tradition, but guitar and vocals still play the dominant role.

In the **Tropicalia** movement of the late 1960s, artists like Gilberto Gil, Caetano Veloso and Gal Costa, from Bahia's mecca of Afro-Brazilian culture, turned out highly unique pop-rock. Tropicalia lyrics alternated between innocent love ballads, to scathing political manifestoes like Veloso's famous anti-censorship chant-rant 'E prohibido prohibir' ('It's Forbidden to Forbid').

Such open defiance would eventually land Veloso and Gil in jail and later to exile in London. That only served to inject even more bravado and foreign influence into Brazilian music upon their return in 1972. Songwriter and composer Chico Buarque eluded the censor's red marker, writing more subtle protest songs. Tom Ze, whose surrealist lyrics (and lifestyle) were later a major influence on Talking Heads front man David Byrne, used (low-brow) subterfuge to dodge the censors. The cover of his 1973 LP *Todos Os Olhos* (*All*

the Eyes) appeared to feature an eye, but was in fact a soft-focus photo of an anus and a glass marble.

Today's MPB scene includes pioneers like choro-influenced Marisa Monte (*photo p182*), who recently brought out the brilliantly produced *Tribalistas* album, silky-voiced Rio pop phenomenon Adriana Calcanhotto, schmaltzy love-ballad king Djavan, aging maestro of favela samba-rock Jorge Benjor, Sao Paulo's grande dame of soft-rock Rita Lee, and Bahian dancing queen Daniela Mercury. New faces to look out for include Os Hermanos, Moreno Veloso (Caetano Veloso's son; *photo above*), Maria Rita (daughter of 1970s-era MPB great Elis Regina), Lenine, and soon-to-be superstar Seu Jorge.

Canecão

Avenida Vencesláu Brás 215, Botafogo (2543 1241/www.canecao.com.br). Bus 413, 512, 2019. **Open** *Box office* noon-9.20pm. *Shows* 7.30pm. **Admission** varies. **Credit** V. **Map** p247 I11. This show venue may not be known for its acoustics or food, but it's become a Rio institution and an enduring monument to MPB. For more than 30 years it has consistently attracted the biggest talents in Brazilian music and a fair few big-name visitors to a relatively small and intimate hall.

Circo Voador

*Rua dos Arcos, Lapa (2533 0354/www.circovoador.
com.br). Bus 434, 572.* **Open** varies. **Admission**
varies. **No credit cards. Map** p245 I3.
The 'Flying Circus' is an outdoor, covered amphitheatre in Lapa that reopened in 2004 after it had
been shut down for eight years. This rock and MPB
temple features both Brazilian and international acts
and plenty more besides.

Citibank Hall

*Shopping Via Parque, Avenida Ayrton Senna 3000,
Barra da Tijuca (0300 789 6846/www.citibankhall.
com.br). Bus 225, 2113.* **Open** varies. **Admission**
varies. **Credit** AmEx, DC, MC, V.
This 10,000-seat modern venue is one of the largest
show houses in Latin America, and its good acoustics
attract many of the biggest international bands, and
top Brazilian acts when they come to Rio.

Fundição Progresso

*Rua dos Arcos 24, Lapa (2220 5070/www.fundicao.
org). Metro Carioca or Cinelândia/410, 433, 438
bus.* **Open** varies. **No credit cards. Map** p245 I3.
Right next door to the Circo Voador (*see above*) and run
by the same owners, the Fundição Progresso is a hi-
tech space for shows, theatre and dance performances
and for staging anything else there's an audience for.

Vivo Rio

*Avenida Infante Dom Henrique 55, Aterro do
Flamengo (2272 2902/www.vivorio.com.br). Bus
121, 133, 404, 474.* **Open** *Box office* noon-9pm
Mon-Sat; noon-8pm Sun. *Shows* varies. **Credit** MC,
V. **Map** p245 J4.
The newly erected Vivo Rio hall, built on to the side
of the Museum of Modern Art, is one of the largest
show venues in the city and has a privileged location in Flamengo, across from the Sugar Loaf and
overlooking the shimmering Guanabara Bay. It's a
tech-savvy, well-designed theatre that has already
played host to big international names.

Bossa nova & jazz

Bossa nova is the music of Rio's most famous
mestres, musical demi-gods like pianist/
composer Tom Jobim and guitarist Joao
Gilberto, whose sounds took the world jazz
scene by storm in the 1960s. The mix of
European instruments like the guitar and piano,
with the city's established samba rhythms, plus
a rich street and beach life where jam sessions
are common, has helped Rio produce legendary
grooves. Bossa nova, literally 'new rhythm',
emerged as a group of young musicians sought
to trailblaze a new Brazilian sound, drawing
on samba, choro, jazz and other genres.

By the late 1950s, much of American jazz had
evolved – or devolved – into highly virtuosic
bebop with very little pop or 'crossover' appeal.
Everybody knew that Charlie Parker and John
Coltrane were ultra hip, but few listeners could

figure out their music. But down in the
southern hemisphere, jazz seemed to swirl
in the opposite direction, and Rio's new,
mellifluous tone lacked the jagged edge of
American jazz of the era.

Bossa nova had some good reasons to be
upbeat. The 1950s and '60s were a golden age
for the city's creative elite, in music, film and
architecture. Carioca musicians, mostly from
a light-skinned elite, set out to create a sound
that would capture the light-hearted nature
of Rio's posh Zona Sul, the sun and surf, the
body-beautiful and the lush aesthetic of the
city's surroundings.

Bossa nova's pleasures and fancies seemed
simple, even if some of its musical constructions
were, in fact, quite complex; with sappy lyrics,
catchy melodies, slow rhythms and sweet
harmonies, bossa nova tunes were crafted to
immediately gratify most listeners, and not
just the musicians themselves. Perhaps that's
why 'Girl from Ipanema' is one of the most
recorded songs in history.

Bossa's prime years may be over, and many
of its most famous pioneers, like the hard-living
Vinicius and Tom, are already gone. Others,
including guitarists Joao Gilberto, Carlos Lyra
and Roberto Menescal, and pianist Sergio
Mendes, live on and can sometimes be caught
performing in Rio. And a new generation of
Bossa-influenced artists has emerged, led by
singers like Rosa Passos, Paula Morelembaum
and Bebel Gilberto, Joao's Gilberto's daughter,
who's promoting the sound around the world.

Allegro Bistrô Musical

*Modern Sound, Rua Barata Ribeiro 502D,
Copacabana (2548 5005/www.modernsound.
com.br). Metro Siqueira Campos/154, 433, 523
bus.* **Open** *Café* 9am-9pm Mon-Fri; 9am-8pm Sat.
Shows 4pm, 7pm, days vary. **Credit** AmEx, DC,
MC, V. **Map** p249 H14.
The large, handsome, air-conditioned Modern Sound
megastore (*see p151*) was created by a jazz-lover
almost 40 years ago and is still the centre of Rio's
musical set today. *See also p125.*

Bar do Tom

*Rua Adalberto Ferreira 32, Leblon (2274 4022).
Bus 410, 523, 2019.* **Open** from 10pm Thur-Sat;
from 8pm Sun. **Admission** R\$30-R\$50. **Credit**
AmEx, DC, MC, V. **Map** p248 B16.
A small temple to bossa nova and Brazilian jazz
with consistently good performances, and music,
often bringing in some of the biggest names in
Brazilian jazz, old and new.

Centro Cultural Parque das Ruinas

*Rua Murtinho Nobre 169, Santa Teresa (2252 1039/
2252 0112). Either tramline/206, 214 bus.* **Open**
Centre 8am-8pm Tue-Sun. *Shows* 7.30pm Thur.
Admission free. **No credit cards. Map** p245 H4.

Choro-influenced **Marisa Monte** – a pioneer of contemporary MPB. *See p180.*

This handsome, neocolonial mansion and cultural centre set above Rio's downtown area features live jazz shows from 7.30pm to 9.30pm on Thursdays showcasing Santa Teresa's homegrown talent.

Maze Inn

Rua Tavares Bastos 414/66, Catete (2558 5547/ www.jazzrio.info). Metro Largo do Machado/ Catete then taxi. **Open** 10pm-4am, first Fri of mth. **Admission** $15. **No credit cards.** **Map** p245 H6.

Better known as the 'Casa de Bob' after its eccentric English owner, who's bagged one of the best views in Rio from his terrace, and now opened it up to visitors to these monthly jazz nights. The jazz inevitably takes second place to the view and the wierdness of it all, but it's good music just the same.

Piano Bar Ouvidor

Rua do Ouvidor 43, Centro (2221 7743). Bus 123, 132, 177. **Open** from 7pm Tue, Wed. **Admission** free. **No credit cards.** **Map** p245 J2.

Bossa-heavy shows on Tuesday and Wednesday evenings for the late happy-hour crowd in this cosy, central location.

Songbook Café

Rua Conde Bernadotte 26/111, Leblon (2249 9772). Bus 410, 523, 2019. **Open** *Café* from 10am. *Shows* varies. **Admission** from R$7. **Credit** AmEx, DC, MC, V. **Map** p248 B16.

This small café located inside a shopping gallery offers the occasional jazz or samba show (call in advance or look at show listings at www.oglobo.com.br) with jazz pianists and big names such as legendary guitarist/singer Joao Bosco.

Toca do Vinicius

Rua Vinicius de Moraes 129C, Ipanema (2247 5227/ www.tocadovinicius.com.br). Bus 132, 177, 433, 2017. **Open** 9am-10pm Mon-Sat; 11am-6pm Sun. **Credit** AmEx, DC, MC, V. **Map** p249 F17.

A record store, bookshop and sometimes a small performance venue whose theme is all things bossa nova. The shop has a good selection of hard to find jazz CDs, books and sheet music, and very helpful, tourist-friendly staff. It also offers an exellent selection of the best samba and choro music, as well as souvenirs.

Vinicius

Rua Vinicius de Moraes 39, Ipanema (2287 1497/ www.viniciusbar.com.br). Bus 132, 177, 433, 2017. **Open** *Restaurant* 9am-2am daily. *Shows* varies. **Admission** R$25-$38. **Credit** AmEx, DC, MC, V. **Map** p249 F17.

This modest-sized upstairs bar and restaurant draws a lot of tourists, but the shows are quite authentic bossa nova, often featuring such famous artists as the singer Maria Creuza. The service can be uneven, but the music is the saving grace.

Rock

Never let it be said that Rio doesn't know how to rock. Just ask a surviving Ramone or, of course, a Rolling Stone. The latter played their largest ever show in Rio in 2006, to crowds of more than 500,000. Like many of Rio's biggest shows, it was free of charge and held on Copacabana beach. **Rock in Rio** is the continent's most famous festival (though it now seems to have decamped to Lisbon). Deep in Rio's rock history too are seedy nightclub performances by Janis Joplin and the heyday of 'O Rei' (The King), crooner Roberto Carlos, Brazil's long-haired answer to Elvis.
Rio remains a major tour stop for international rock bands. It's also a key destination on the *rock nacional* circuit. Popular in Rio are Brazil's surf-rock and reggae-rock acts, like Skank and O Rappa; and 1980s-era 'stadium-rock' bands like Barão Vermelho and Paralamas do Sucesso from Rio, Titãs from Sao Paulo and Legiao Urbana from Brasilia are still held in high esteem. Check listings for visiting bands who generally play in venues listed elsewhere in this chapter. To listen to rock in clubs try **Casa da Matriz** (*see p185*) and **Emporio** (*see p188*); live rock bands play at the **Lord Jim Pub** (*see p127*) from Sunday to Thursday.

For big events, don't miss Rio's free beach shows, common on weekends and public holidays on Ipanema, Copacabana and Flamengo beaches. The stages go up days in advance with banners announcing the artists. **Oi Noites Cariocas** offers live shows from the crème de la crème of Brazil's rock/pop/MPB scene to an exclusive crowd of beautiful people atop the Morro da Urca on summer weekends (http://oinoitescariocas.oi.com.br).

Hip hop

Hip hop touched down in shantytowns of Rio de Janeiro in the late 1980s, and since then the movement has steadily grown. Traditionally the Brazilian hip hop scene has been associated with São Paulo and groups like the Racionais MCs or Facção Central, but in the last ten years grafitti, breakdancing, rapping and DJing have all gained in popularity in Rio.
The neighbourhoods of Lapa and Madueira have become the main focus of the Carioca hip hop scene, hosting weekly showcases of the city's rappers and DJs. Events are also frequently held in favelas across the city and even in the upper-class Zona Sul, which seems increasingly interested in the 'sound of the favelas'. Many of Rio de Janeiro's rappers describe their work as *hip hop consciente* – a socially engaged form of music – and devote large amounts of time to social projects in their communities. Others are evangelical Christians who perform 'gospel' hip hop preaching the 'word up' of the Lord. Some of the most exciting rappers to look out for in Rio are MC Funk, Dom Negrone, Papo Reto, Marechal and the group A Resistência.

Finding shows and parties requires an ear to the ground as most of them move around like they're illegal. Clues as to where to start looking, and further information on shows, releases and downloads, can be found (in Portuguese) at www.realhiphop.com.br.

Madureira

Viaduto Negrão de Lima, Madureira (3355 7471). Train Madureira/254, 284 bus. **Open** from 10pm Sat. **Admission** *Men* R$10. *Women* R$6.
No credit cards.
Spending the night under a flyover in north Rio probably isn't what most people come to the Marvellous City for, but the Saturday night hip hop parties underneath the Viaduto Negrão de Lima, billed as 'ground zero for black culture in Rio', are not to be missed. This *baile charme* – the type of *baile* people used to go to before funk – is legendary among fans of soul and hip hop in Rio and draws crowds of around 2,000 each week.

Classical music

Rio has a small but respectable classical music scene, including two well-trained symphony orchestras, regular chamber music recitals and occasional opera and ballet performances. Of special interest are classical guitarists, such as Brazilian guitar great Turibio Santos and newcomer, virtuoso Yamandu Costa (*see p176* **Living legends and rising stars**).
There's only a handful of performance spaces, though, and most of them are shared with dance and opera. The **Sala Cecilia Meireles** (Largo da Lapa 57, Lapa, 2224 4291, box office 1-6pm) is one of Rio's best concert venues. Originally built in the late 1880s, it has great acoustics and a central, downtown location. It hosts recitals and some of the best classical performances in the city. The **Theatro Muncipal** (*see p193*) has a full repertoire in suitably elevated surroundings, and the **Centro Cultural Banco do Brasil** (*see p63*) can also be relied upon for quality performances; it currently has a series of free classical music concerts on Tuesdays at lunchtime. Recent offerings have included an international harp festival, vocal choir recitals and a European chamber music festival.
There's good, up-to-date information on all things classical in Rio and the rest of the country at www.vivamusica.com.br.

Arts & Entertainment

Nightlife

How to unwind after a hard day at the beach.

As you'd expect from the city that puts on Carnival, in addition to a world-class live music scene Rio offers a decent selection of places to shake your *bunda* if you want to leave the samba bands behind for a night. Most clubbers choose to be part of one of two categories: the 'beautiful people' and the casual and colourful beach/skate/ surf and student crowd. The former like to splash cash (generally mum's and dad's cash) and snack on sushi, while the latter seek out interesting spots in off-beat areas to listen to DJs and/or live music. Both can be immense fun, and it definitely pays to get out of the main tourist spots for good clubs and nights.

What's on depends on the particular night, so it's worth checking out individual club websites or asking a Carioca with their ear to the ground. Another good place to check what's going on is www.riothisweek.com, which lists club nights day by day and also the daily 'Segundo Caderno' listings section of *O Globo* newspaper, although this tends to be a more 'arty' than 'street'. *O Globo* also runs a good pull-out called 'Rio Show' on Fridays.

Note: most clubs in Rio don't get going until midnight. Those in the popular areas such as Ipanema, Copacabana and Lapa can be reached easily by bus but those in the more residential areas are often in backstreets and it may be much easier and safer to take a taxi. Most of the time, entrance charges will be cheaper for women than men – usually half the price or less.

Festivals & events

Outside regular clubs there are some good one-off nights in Rio. Although it may not be as cutting edge as São Paulo, Rio does pull-in big name DJs. Among those the city has played host to are Fatboy Slim, who even turned up on Brazilian Big Brother, and Deep Dish, who played to thousands at the **Jockey Club** (Praça Santos Dumont, Gávea, 2512 9988), which often holds big parties. On a smaller scale, but with a much cooler crowd, are the electronic parties that can be found by visiting www.moo.com.br. Another good place to check for events is **Circo Voador** (Rua dos Arcos, Lapa, 2533 0354, www.circovoador.com.br). As well as being a huge centre for street culture during the day, offering courses in anything from parkour to breakdancing, there are some excellent nights held there, particularly hip hop

nights. Decent throwdowns include the Eu Amo Hip Hop (I love hip hop) and Eu Amo Baile Funk festivals, which are annual events and showcase the best in home-grown Brazilian talent. The Circo Voador website (*see above*) has details and you can also check their blog at www.euamohiphop.blogspot.com. A lot of DJs will also play at the many summer festivals, which are in great locations (often the beach), and very often free.

Venues

The Centre

For many, Lapa is the first taste of nightlife in Rio and remains one of the best places for a long and exciting night out. As well as having fantastic live music venues, the majority of the clubs have something to suit all tastes. Friday nights tend to be the best for experiencing the street life here – grab a cheap caipirinha from the many bar stalls, wander along Avenida Mem de Sá and just soak up the atmosphere. You can pretty much choose anything from reggae and hip hop to *baile funk* or rock. Or if you want, you can do them all, sometimes in the same place. Admission prices range from between R$10 and $15 at the weekend and sometimes include a free drink.

Casarão Cultural dos Arcos

Avenida Mem de Sá 23, Lapa (2266 1014/2509 5166/http://matrizonline.oi.com.br/casaraocultural). Bus 434, 464. **Open** 11pm-5am Fri, Sat. **Admission** R$12-$16. **Credit** MC, V. **Map** p245 I4.

Casarão Cultural used to be a cinema in Lapa but now specialises in all things rock. Think classics like The Doors to more up-to-date stuff, often featuring the hottest new British guitar bands (Arctic Monkeys, and so on). With a bit of house music too, its best to check the website to see what's happening but it remembers the kids wanna rock!

Club Six

Rua das Marrecas 38, Centro (2510 3230/www.club six.com.br). Metro Cinelândia/434, 464 bus. **Open** from 10.30pm Fri, Sat. **Admission** R$10-$40. **Credit** AmEx, MC, V. **Map** p245 I3.

For the best in US and Brazilian hip hop and funk, and a big club experience in Lapa, Club Six is the place. It's an impressive industrial-looking building over three floors with five bars. There's also rooms of house music, decent local MC battles and even live acts.

Arts & Entertainment

An alternative crowd getting happy on the dancefloor at **Pista 3**. *See p186.*

Dito e Feito

Rua do Mercado 21, Centro (2509 1407/2222 4016/www.ditoefeito.com.br). Metro Uraguaiana/ 415, 474 bus. **Open** from 6pm Mon-Sat. **Admission** R\$15 women; R\$30 men. **Credit** AmEx, DC, MC, V. **Map** p245 J2.

During the day Dito e Feito functions as a reasonably good restaurant but come nightfall it turns into a crazy drinking den with cheap booze for the ladies – and plenty of other treats too. On 'Ladies nights' men aren't allowed to enter before 8pm, by which time the ladies have had enough free drinks for anything to happen.

Febarj

Avenida Mem de Sá 373, Lapa (no phone). Bus 434, 464. **Open** from 9pm Fri, Sat. **Admission** R\$2-\$4. **No credit cards. Map** p245 H3.

Febarj (Federação dos Blocos Afro do Rio de Janeiro) gets busy to hip hop classics every weekend with a relaxed laid-back vibe. There's always a good crowd hanging outside and it's super cheap.

Teatro Odisséia

Avenida Mem de Sá 66, Lapa (2266 1014/ http://matrizonline.oi.com.br/teatroodisseia). Bus 434, 464. **Open** from 9pm Thur-Sat. **Admission** R\$15-\$24. **Credit** AmEx, MC, V. **Map** p245 I4.

Just a little way away from the main drag of Mem de Sá, this interesting building, an old theatre, has a good mix of eclectic music and alternative events, from samba to rock. One of Rio's best places to hear music from the rest of Brazil, and occasionally the rest of the world. Another arm of the same innovative group that runs Casa da Matriz.

The Bay

There's a great selection of different clubs in these neighbourhoods, often convertions of the huge old mansion houses that dominate the area. They attract a decent, down-to-earth local crowd and are well worth leaving the tourist 'comfort' zone for.

Casa da Matriz

Rua Henrique de Novaes 107, Botafogo (2266 1014/ http://matrizonline.oi.com.br). Bus 154, 434, 435. **Open** from 11pm Wed-Mon. **Admission** R\$10-\$25. **Credit** AmEx, MC, V. **Map** p246 G11.

Club nights at Casa da Matriz have a loyal following among hipsters who prefer the Ramones and drum 'n' bass to samba. Two good-sized dancefloors packed with Vans and Chuck Taylors attract some of the city's best DJs, and the place

00. See p189.

fills with locals. Upstairs is electronic music and downstairs DJs spin themed sets. The downstairs is one of the few places in town you'll hear sounds from the likes of the Arcade Fire and Joy Division. There's also a lounge area to rest weary feet and assorted arcade games spread about, including Space Invaders. *Photo p188*.

Pista 3
Rua São João Batista 14, Botofogo (2266 1014/ www.pista3.com.br). Bus 154, 434, 435. **Open** from 11.30pm daily. **Admission** R$10-$16. **Credit** AmEx, MC, V. **Map** p246 G11.
Another venture of the Casa de Matriz owners and located just down the road, this club goes for a more urban sound. DJs mix up old-school funk classics with hip hop, R&B and a slice of electro making for a soulful session. *Photo p185*.

The Hills

There are a lot of parties going on in Santa Teresa, but not many organised regular events... yet. Keep an ear to the ground for one-off parties, though, especially in Aprazível and early evening happenings in the **Espaço de Convivência Tumbao de Malevo** (*see p167*).

Aprazível
Rua Aprazível 62, Santa Teresa (2508 9174/2507 7334/www.aprazivel.com.br). Tram Dois Irmãos/ 206 bus. **Open** noon-1am Thur-Sat; 1-7.30pm Sun. **Credit** AmEx, DC, MC, V. **Map** p245 H5.
Aprazível is actually a restaurant in Santa Teresa but throws some excellent one-off parties, particularly the 'High Noon' series on summer Sunday afternoons.

It's in a wonderful location in a leafy area of this very Bohemian part of Rio. Check the website for details or ask a Carioca in the know.

Casa Rosa
Rua Alice 550, Laranjeiras (3309 9417/www.casarosa. com.br). Bus 583, 584. **Open** from 11.30pm Fri, Sat; from 5pm Sun. **Admission** R$8-$15. **Credit** MC, V. **Map** p246 G8.
The huge pink house, set on a hill in Laranjeiras, is a cultural centre throughout the week and a first-rate music venue at weekends. There are three rooms set around an open-air courtyard with different music in each. Sundays are hugely popular here with a *roda de samba* and food plus a smattering of *funk carioca*. It all makes for a good vibe – perfect after a day at the beach.

The Beaches

For many this is the first point of contact with Rio and there's a decent mix of venues in the area. Most in Ipanema and Leblon cater towards the affluent residents of this neighbourhood but there are some cheaper options. With some unfortunate exceptions, Copacabana offers more of a relaxed clubbing experience that's also easier on the pocket. Generally, there's a crowd of friendly locals as well as tourists.

Baronneti
Rua Barão da Torre 354, Ipanema (2247 9100/ www.baronneti.com.br). Bus 132, 435, 584. **Open** from 10pm Wed-Sun. **Admission** R$30-$40 women; R$90-$100 men. **Credit** AmEx, MC, V. **Map** p249 E16.

What the funk?

'Prepare o popozão!' ('Get your booty ready!') For many young people in Rio the raw sound of funk (pronounced 'funky') outweighs traditional samba in the popularity stakes. Thousands can be found gyrating and bouncing their backsides to its infectious beat at weekend funk parties, mostly in one of the city's 700 favelas.

Funk, or *funk Carioca* to give it its full name (the term *baile funk*, as it's known elsewhere, means 'funk dance'), is indigenous to Rio and far removed from traditional US funk. In fact, its roots are in Miami bass. In the late 1980s, Brazilian DJs got hold of tracks from Miami by artists like Stevie B, played with the synth-electro sounds, added their own lyrics and Brazilian percussion and funk was cultivated through the 1980s and early 1990s. The first official hit by MC Batata was released in 1989 and funk exploded.

Since its conception, funk has had a colourful and interesting history and one that continues to evolve. Although the musicians came from the poorer areas, funk wasn't always in the favelas and parties used to be held in big social clubs or samba schools. The widely publicised and often misrepresented phenomenon of Baile de Corredor in the mid 1990s (where the crowd would line up on two sides of the room to take part in orchestrated fighting) put many

venue owners off holding the parties. It was then the parties moved into the favelas.

Some funk lyrics do focus on life in the favelas and problems in society, but the rest make hip hop seem politically correct. The most recent style is the overtly sexual *putaria* (literally 'whorehouse', roughly translated as 'totally smutty') practiced by both male and female MCs. Other favela *bailes* revolve around *proibidão*, a gritty, aggressive and expletive-strewn homage to gun battles, AK-47s and drug factions.

Now much of Rio reverberates to funk every weekend, with huge dances going on in many of the favelas and often clearly audible in neighbouring districts. The parties mostly feature a DJ and a line up of funk MCs. Good names to look out for include DJ Sany Pitbull, who mixes up electro and funk, MCs Junior and Leonardo and MC Gringo (who's actually German). Violence is rare at a funk party but nevertheless it is not a good idea to go wandering into a favela alone at night without a guide. If you don't have one, **Be a Local** (9643 0366/www.bealocal.com) runs a good Sunday night trip to one of the best locations, Castelo. Otherwise you can hear funk at various venues around Rio. Call **Circo Voador** (2533 0354), which runs regular 'Eu Amo Baile Funk' nights. Plus it's worth looking at www.riofesta.com.br ('*festas*') for funk nights in various clubs.

Arts & Entertainment

Casa da Matriz.
See p185.

This club has a reputation for being one of the most expensive and stylish joints in Rio, where the 'beautiful people' gather – leave the havaianas at home for this one. Two floors play the latest hip hop and house to a young and sophisticated crowd. Saturdays are rammed. If it all gets too much there's an excellent sushi bar upstairs.

Bombar

Avenida General San Martin 1011, Leblon (2249 2161/www.bombar.com.br). Bus 132, 157, 433, 512. **Open** from 10pm Tue-Sat. **Admission** free-R$40. **Credit** MC, V. **Map** p248 B17.
A club that advertises itself as a place for 'beer drinkers and hell raisers', which pretty much sums it up. An energetic, mixed crowd enjoys a lively party atmosphere to hip hop, funk and house. Hot

and sweaty in all respects, its Tuesday nights of free booze before midnight are legendary.

Bunker

Rua Raul Pompéia 94, Copacabana (3813 0300) Bus 128, 523. **Open** from 10pm Wed-Mon. **Admission** R$10-$25. **No credit cards. Map** p249 H17.
Appropriately named, if you're a hip hop head then this is a place to check out. Resident DJs play a selection of the latest hip hop and classics as well as a good slice of *baile funk* to a friendly local crowd. Check out the MC battles, usually on Thursdays.

Empório

Rua Maria Quitéria 37, Ipanema (3813 2526). Bus 132, 464, 584. **Open** from 8pm daily. **Admission** free-R$30. **No credit cards. Map** p248 E17.

If it's all getting a bit too sophisticated, there's always Empório for 'rocking out' and downing a few JDs. Largely due to the fact that it's open later than anywhere else in the area, it attracts a relaxed, mixed and colourful crowd including a good number of gringos looking for a bar that could, at a stretch, remind them of home. If there's still a crowd left when things get really late, they often head down to the 24-hour kiosk at the end of the street on Ipanema beach. Local bar-workers and waiters head here to let loose when they've finished their shift.

Fosfobox

Rua Siqueira Campos 143/22A, Copacabana (2548 7498/www.fosfobox.com.br). Metro Siqueira Campos/128, 132 bus. **Open** from 11pm Thur-Sat. **Admission** R$10-$15. **Credit** MC, V. **Map** p250 H14.
One of the few underground clubs in this 'touristy' area of Rio, Fosfobox hosts a good range of Brazilian DJs offering the minimal techno of São Paolo's Anderson Noise to the raw funk of DJ Sany Pitbull. It also has very gay nights and full on rock, so it's a good idea to check the programme first.

Galeria Café

Rua Teixeira de Melo 31, Ipanema (2523 8250/ www.galeriacafe.com.br). Bus 175, 177, 557. **Open** *Café* from 4pm Wed-Sat. *Bar* from 10.30pm Wed-Sat. **Admission** R$15 $20. **Credit** AmEx, MC, V. **Map** p249 F17.
Galeria Café adroitly combines an art gallery, a bazaar and a club for a largely gay, thirtysomething clientele. With plenty more class than LeBoy and LeGirl, there's drum 'n' bossa on the musical menu as well as the more straightforwardly gay 'house, hitz and glitz' night.

Mariuzinn

Avenida Nossa Senhora de Copacabana 435, Copacabana (2545 7672/www mariuzinn.com.br). Metro Cardeal Arcoverde/128, 132, 523 bus. **Open** 11pm-6am Thur-Sat. **Credit** DC, MC, V. **Map** p250 H14.
An old-school legendary Copacabana hang-out, with decor to match, which plays a mixture of disco classics, hip hop and funk along with more traditional Brazilian musical styles such as *forro* and *pagode*. It's quite a favourite with the student crowd so arrive early to avoid the queues.
Other locations Avenida Rio Branco 277, Centro (2533 8787).

Melt

Rua Rita Ludolf 47A, Leblon (2512 1662/2249 9309). Bus 132, 157, 433, 512. **Open** from 8pm daily. **Admission** R$30-$50. **Credit** AmEx, MC, V. **Map** p248 A17.
Pronounced 'melch' by locals, this lounge bar-cum-club caters to a mixed crowd, offering a clubbing experience that's more down-to-earth than the likes of Baronneti, but still very smart and trendy. It also has the advantage of being close to lots of other good places, so you can move on at any time if you want to. DJs spin US hip hop and house.

Redondo Lounge

Avenida Bartolomeu Mitre 450, Leblon (2540 9076) Bus 432, 435. **Open** from 8pm Wed-Sat. **Admission** R$15-$35. **Credit** AmEx, DC, MC, V. **Map** p248 B16.
This laid-back lounge bar caters to a pre-clubbing set bound for Baronneti with a similar dress code. There are plenty of places to sit and a decent DJ playing dance and R&B. Arrive earlier for this one, around 9pm for a fresh fruit caipirinha and light food, to mix with the young and affluent set until 11ish.

The Lake

There's some great nightlife on the 'other' side of the Lagoa for the affluent local residents, with a shot in the arm from the hedonistic students of PUC university; but the majority of the scene is centered around the bars and live music venues that cluster around and close to the lake. The area makes up for it, though, with one of the city's best clubs, **00** (*see below*).

00

Avenida Padre Leonel Franca 240, Gávea (2540 8042/www.00site.com.br). Bus 432, 435. **Open** from 10pm Wed-Sun. **Admission** R$20-$50. **Credit** AmEx, MC, V. **Map** p248 A16.
Zero Zero offers one of the best clubbing experiences in Rio. In behind an outdoor bar and a restaurant (*see p170*) is a small dancefloor with a cutting-edge and varied music selection. Breakbeat and electronica to R&B and dub get played out in beautiful surroundings to a friendly and stylish crowd. You can even chill under leafy palms and snack on sashimi from the sushi bar. Thursday nights here are the pick for discerning clubbers. A good vibe. *Photo p186.*

Zona Oeste

For good or ill, Barra and its environs is known as the 'Miami of Rio' and its clubbing scene requires a similar approach; that is to say, most people cruise around the area by car. There's a few clubs that come and go according to what's fashionable at the time – but starting at Nuth (*see below*), a well-established venue, is an excellent way in to find what's going on. It's also in a good location near to several bars and restaurants.

Nuth

Avenida Armando Lombarda 999, Barra da Tijuca (3153 8595/www.nuth.com.br). Bus 175, 225, 523. **Open** from 9pm Mon-Sat; from 8pm Sun. **Admission** R$10-$70. **Credit** AmEx, MC, V. **Map** p253 A3.
Pronounced 'nooch', this is the most established, and most popular club in Barra for the well heeled of the area and visitors from Zona Sul. Nuth's take on the high life is an upbeat mix of poppy R&B and hip hop in very pleasant surroundings with a beautiful, but very friendly, crowd.

Performing Arts

Plays, dirty dancing – and soap.

Theatre

Brazilian theatre has been alive as long as the country, with 19th-century literary cornerstones Machado de Assis and José de Alencar leading the charge, writing plays dealing with issues relating to the country's fledgling nationality.

Nelson Rodrigues (1912-1980) is one of the most recognisable names in Brazilian theatre, renowned for enabling the national scene to overcome the prevailing *chanchadas* (cheap musical comedy films) with the 1940s hit *Vestido de Noiva* (Wedding Dress). Always a problem for the establishment, Rodrigues' plays dug into the dark side of Brazil's upper class, often suffering censorship or being banned. Recent translations have raised his stock in the English-speaking world, but he remains largely unknown outside academic circles, where he's revered and often mentioned along with Eugene O'Neil, Tennessee Williams and David Mamet.

Crossovers are common in Rio's theatre scene. Poet and musician Vinicius de Moraes wrote *Orfeu de Conceição* – later to be adapted into the hit film *Orfeo Negro* – and several other plays. Musician and novelist Chico Buarque also wrote several works for the stage, including the noteworthy *Ópera do Malandro*. Film director Walter Lima Jr recently switched over to theatre, directing several critically acclaimed works in recent years.

Brazil's most important theatre export is Gerald Thomas, an avant-garde director heavily influenced by the theatre of the absurd and German expressionism, who has also done operas with the likes of Phillip Glass. Another Brazilian director highly respected in international circles is Augusto Boal. Seen as an enemy of the state for his plays steeped in Marxism, Boal was arrested, tortured and exiled to Argentina in 1971. He went on to create the revolutionary Theatre of the Oppressed, an unconventional approach looking to turn classical theatre on its head that's now practised in over 70 countries and has been highly influential in modern theatre. Boal moved back to Brazil when the dictatorship lifted and opened **O Centro de Teatro do Oprimido** in Lapa.

The most challenging of Rio's festivals is the **Festival do Teatro** (www.riocena contemporanea.com.br; *see p155*). Run since 2001, the festival is held at the beginning of October and attracts quality avant-garde and modern theatre from around Brazil and good European organisations.

As with much of Rio's cultural life at the moment, Lapa is where things really happen. **Cia dos Atores** (*see p193*), one of the most active troupes in Rio, is based there. The popular group **Tá Na Rua** (www.tanarua. com.br) has been a fixture of Lapa's theatres and streets since they were formed in an effort to free up Rio's theatre scene from the oppression of the dictatorship in 1980. This fertile ground also gave rise to Eduardo Tolentino's **Grupo TAPA**, now one of Brazil's foremost groups and working out of São Paulo.

Started in 1986 as a social programme to promote interest in theatre in the slum Vidigal (between Leblon and São Conrado), **Nós do Morro** has become an established company with its own theatre. The school feeds soap operas and movies, and provided many of the actors for *City of God*. For those willing to dig, there are endless smaller groups who do plays of varying quality and audacity.

GENERAL INFORMATION

There are several theatres funded by the national government in Rio. State-run theatres have cheaper tickets (normally between R$10-$20) than privately owned theatres, and tend to put on commercial plays, musicals, or revivals of classics, although some do put on smaller, local productions.

Privately owned theatres are more expensive (R$30-$70) and are more likely to showcase local talent. Tickets for big shows can be bought via **TicketMaster** (0300 789 6846, www.ticketmaster.com.br) or **Ticketronics** (www.ticketronics.net). The most complete on-line listings can be found at www.teatro paratodos.com.br, which breaks down shows according to neighbourhood and price. **Teatro Para Todos** also has a stand in the Cinelândia plaza that sells tickets (10am-6pm Mon-Fri, 10am-2pm Sat, cash only). In Zona Sul, tickets can be bought at the music store **Modern Sound** (*see p151*). '*Postos de venda*' on the Teatro Para Todos website lists other ticket stands, some of which move. The best print media listings come in *O Globo*, especially the Friday cultural supplement 'Rio Show'.

Theatro Municipal. *See p193*.

Arts & Entertainment

Super trupers

Intrépida Trupe was born out of a strange kind of alchemy. A cultural mission to Mexico for the 1986 World Cup found members of Brazil's prestigious National Circus School thrown together with theatre actors and dancers for performances. The result was something different, something like choreographed circus performance but with a distinctive dramatic edge. It was a combination that placed the troupe on the cutting-edge of the performing arts scene and vaulted them swiftly onto the international circuit.

Fuelled by the artistic freedom afforded by the lifting of the military dictatorships in South America, Intrépida mirrored other theatre movements, like Argentina's successful De La Guarda. The group has always been prodigiously dynamic, maintaining its roots of street performance while continually developing new stage productions using more and more advanced equipment, special effects and techniques.

After the highly successful *Metegol* in 2006, Intrépida closed out the year with a 20th anniversary show, a retrospective montage that took audiences through two decades of performances. Broken into three parts by video clips labelled 1986, 1996 and 2006, the whirlwind show jumped from early hip hop dance numbers to Chaplin-style Vaudevillian antics to languorous, amber-tinted trapeze acts, showing the richness and depth of Intrépida's productions.

Intrépida Trupe has sent members on to Cirque du Soleil – the holy grail for circus performers – but some Brazilians will make the bold statement that Intrépida is better than the hallowed Canadian troupe. On a level of talent, no other group can compete with Cirque du Soleil, but what Brazilians are referring to is not necessarily the physical prowess or the cleaness of the numbers – neither of which Intrépida lacks – but the spirit; something distinctly Brazilian, difficult to describe but easy to recognise. In short, Intrépida Trupe overflows with all the exuberance, spontaneity, diversity and grit that characterises the country.

Just as it's blended circus, theatre and dance, Intrépida Trupe has inevitably incorporated Brazil's blend of Portuguese, African and native cultures. In this spirit of diversity, Intrépida's influences embrace and jump freely back and forth over regional, racial and class divisions. While a polished performance in a theatre can cost punters up to R$30, most of Intrépida's performances can be staged in the streets or on the beach and the troupe is known to ply its trade just about anywhere. Local fame has also made it a perennial Carnival favourite, where it often performs with samba schools.

Classes given by members of the troupe are open to the public at **Fundição Progresso** (Rua dos Arcos 24, Lapa, 2220 5070, www.fundicao.org).

State-run theatres

Teatro Carlos Gomes

Praça Tiradentes, Centro (2232 8701/2224 3602/www.teatrocarlosgomes.com.br). Metro Carioca/107, 154, 158 bus. **Box office** 2-6pm Tue-Sat. **Performances** 7pm Thur, Fri; 8pm Sat; 6pm Sun. **Tickets** R$10-$20. **No credit cards. Map** p245 H3.

Once the heart and soul of Rio's theatre scene, Praça Tiradentes has since largely been taken over by prostitution and poverty. Teatro Carlos Gomes has survived thanks to subsidies from the city government, and puts on musicals about the history of Brazil, popular international plays and concerts.

Teatro João Caetano

Praça Tiradentes, Centro (2221 1223) Metro Carioca/107, 154 bus. **Box office** 2-7pm Tue-Sun. **Performances** 7pm Thur, Fri; 8pm Sat; 6pm Sun. **Tickets** R$10-$20. **No credit cards. Map** p245 H2.

The large João Caetano hasn't fared so well of late, but while the facilities may be lacking, the rustic, crumbling setting does manage to evoke the survivalist spirit of the theatre, originally built on the site in 1813. The theatre puts on comedies, musicals, revivals of classics and occasional concerts.

Teatro Maria Clara Machado

Rua Padre Leonel França 240, Gávea (2274 7722). Bus 157, 179, 410, 432. **Box office** 4-9pm Tue-Sun. **Perfomances** 9pm Thur-Sat; 8pm Sun. **Tickets** R$10-$20. **No credit cards. Map** p248 A16.

Teatro Maria Clara Machado is considered to be the most progressive theatre run by the city government. Strictly dedicated to staging independent theatre up until 1994, the theatre still hosts challenging new monologues and dramas beside some good-quality mainstream plays.

Teatro Nelson Rodrigues

Avenida República do Chile 230, Centro (2262 5483). Metro Carioca/107, 154, 158 bus. **Box office** 3-8pm Tue-Sun. **Performances** 7.30pm or 8pm Thur-Sun. **Tickets** R$10-$25. **No credit cards. Map** p245 I3.

A piece of modernist architecture geometrically blocked between the Petrobras building and the Cathedral and fronted with a koi pond and babbling fountains, Teatro Nelson Rodrigues has a strangely spectacular stage. Its large stage brings in bigger productions as well dance and circus acts like the Intrépida Trupe (*see p192* **Super trupers**).

Teatro Villa Lobos

Avenida Princesa Isabel 440, Leme (2275 6695/ 2543 5782). Bus 125, 472, 523, 2018. **Box office** 3-7pm Wed; 3-9pm Thur-Sun. **Performances** 9pm Thur-Sat; 8pm Sun. *Children's theatre* 5pm Thur Sun. **Tickets**?? **No credit cards. Map** p250 J13.

Set on the busy Avenida Princesa Isabel, Teatro Villa Lobos hides three different stages behind its narrow modernist façade. Mostly sticking to revivals of time-tested classics, it also boasts the city's most complete line-up of children's theatre. Dance performances are put on here.

Theatro Municipal

Praça Floriano, Centro (2299 1711/www.theatro municipal.rj.gov.br). Metro Cinelândia/176, 434, 571, 572 bus. **Open** *Tours* 8am-10pm daily. *Box office* 8am-9pm Tue-Sun. **Performances** vary. **Tickets** R$10-$150. **Credit** V. **Map** p245 J3.

The costliest theatre built outside of Europe, Theatro Municipal is a lofty, art nouveau affair capping the east end of Praça Floriano. Patterned after Paris's opera house, it's a sight to behold when lit up at night and the city's top spot to see opera, ballet and classical music. Although stage plays are put on less frequently, the theatre still attracts prestigious international groups and globetrotting local icons like Gerald Thomas. *Photo p191.*

Other theatres

Casa de Cultura Laura Alvim

Avenida Vieira Souto 176, Ipanema (2247 6946). Bus 177, 503, 2018. **Box office** 5-9.30pm Wed-Sun. **Performances** 9pm Wed, Thur, Sat; 8pm Sun. **Tickets** R$20-$50. **No credit cards. Map** p249 F17.

A three-storey house built in 1906 by scientist Alvaro Alvim, and named in honour of his daughter, Casa de Cultura Laura Alvim has a 250 seat theatre that puts on irreverent comedies by local groups in the heart of Zona Sul.

Espaço Cia dos Atores

Rua Manoel Carneiro 10, Lapa (2212 4176/ www.ciadosatores.com.br). Bus 409, 433, 464. **Map** p245 I4.

The home space of Lapa's busy Companhia dos Atores is currently undergoing renovations. The company comprises an energetic group of actors who also run many other projects in the city and abroad, from soap operas to teaching to organising theatre festivals. Check website for details of opening times and performances.

Espaço SESC

Rua Domingos Ferreira 160, Copacabana (2547 0156/www.sescrj.org.br). Bus 136, 154, 433, 523. **Box office** 3-7pm Thur-Sun. **Performances** from 9pm Thur-Sat; 7.30pm Sun. **Tickets** R$10-$30. **No credit cards. Map** p249 H15.

An energetic proving ground for young thespians, Espaço SESC works to promote creativity in the underground theatre scene. The Copacabana branch is also home to other cutting-edge performing arts events, like festivals showcasing local experimental music and modern dance.

Teatro Clara Nunes

3rd Floor, Shopping da Gávea, Marquês de São Vicente 52, Gávea (2274 7246). Bus 157, 170, 410. **Box office** 2-10pm Wed-Sun. **Performances** 11pm Fri, Sat; 10pm Sun. **Tickets** R$40-$65. **No credit cards. Map** p248 A15.

Arts & Entertainment

Part of the popular grouping of three theatres in Shopping da Gávea (*see below* Teatro dos Quatro), Teatro Clara Nunes puts on polished comedies geared at teenagers and adults. Occasional appearances by big-name talent pull in Zona Sul's jet set.

Teatro do Leblon
Rua Conde doBernadote 26, Leblon (2294 0347/ www.teatrodoleblon.com) Bus 464, 522, 2019. **Box office** 3-9pm Tue-Sun. **Performances** 7pm, 9pm, 11pm Tue-Sun. **Tickets** R$40-65. **Credit** MC, V. **Map** p248 B16.
The popular Teatro do Leblon started with one stage in 1994 and now has three, with a slick multipurpose cultural centre and bookstore next door too. The three theatres stage plays neatly divided into adult, alternative and children's theatre.

Teatro Maison de France
Avenida Presidente Antônio Carlos 58, Centro (2544 2533/www.teatromaisondefrance.com.br). **Metro** Cinelândia/107, 123, 132 bus. **Box office** 2-7pm Tue-Sun. **Performances** 9pm Fri, Sat; 7pm Sun. **Tickets** R$40-$60. **No credit cards.** **Map** p245 J3.
After undergoing a number of renovation projects, the downtown Teatro Maison de France now has some of the city's most modern facilities. It attracts polished, big-budget plays often starring well-known television personalities. The theatre also has a live music programme and screens some excellent arthouse films.

Teatro dos Quatro
2nd Floor, Shopping da Gávea, Marquês de São Vicente 52, Gávea (2274 9895). Bus 157, 170, 410. **Box office** 2-8pm Tue-Sun. **Performances** 8pm Thur-Sun. *Children's theatre* 5pm Sun. **Tickets** R$40-$65. **No credit cards.** **Map** p248 A15.
On the second floor of Gávea's frenetic and fashionable shopping mall, dos Quatro has similar programming to its upstairs neighbour Teatro Clara Nunes (*see above*), but leans more towards plays for adults. Sunday afternoons are reserved for excellent kids' circus shows.

Teatro Ziembinski
Rua Heitor Beltrão, Tijuca (2254 5399). Bus 415, 426, 438. **Box office** 3-9.30pm Fri-Sun. **Performances** 8pm Fri-Sun. *Children's theatre* 5pm Fri-Sun. **Tickets** R$20-$60. **No credit cards.**
One few theatres in the north of the city, afternoon slots are reserved for children's shows, but later on you're more likely to catch a monologue or a small production delving into the angst of existence.

A busy schedule at **Teatro do Leblon.**

Dance

Rio is synonymous with samba, but it's not the only dance in town. Cariocas like to move their bodies, and contemporary dance, ballet and even breakdancing have all cut out their own piece of rug in the city. Of the city's secondary genres, contemporary dance is the runner-up to samba, with several companies who have achieved international recognition, and a couple of notable festivals. Although not exactly a dance troupe, Intrépida Trupe (*see p192* **Super trupers**) draws heavily from contemporary dance and former members have produced their own successful dance troupes, the most visible being Deborah Colker. Her challenging choreography and creative mixture of floor and aerial techniques have made her Companhia Deborah Colker a hit in Rio and abroad. Another Intrépida offshoot is Dani Lima, whose group also uses floor and aerial techniques along with video to put together cutting-edge performances. The most successful Brazilian contemporary dance troupe internationally is **Grupo Corpo**, founded in Belo Horizonte in 1975. When not globe-trotting on far-flung world tours, Grupo Corpo performs in Brazil's top theatres, usually showing at Theatro Municipal when in Rio.

For the top ballet in Rio, take a trip to the Theatro Municipal to check out the 100-member **Ballet do Theatro Municipal**. Despite the numbers of established troupes and renewed interest from the public and private sectors in dance, most of the groups working in Rio have only been around for about ten years and new groups find it difficult to get start-up money. **DeAnima Ballet Contemperâneo** is an exception. Managing to get healthy chunks of money from both the city government and businesses, it's now one of the rising companies in Rio's dance scene. Founded in 2001, DeAnima puts on acclaimed shows and has a strong social programme, providing courses in ballet, hip hop and theatre for underprivileged youths.

Of the many dances stemming from Brazil's African roots, capoeira is the most prevalent. Technically a martial art, the 'dance' – something of a cross between kick-boxing and ballet – was developed by slaves in the 16th century and simulates fighting with slow fluid kicks, leg sweeps and swings that nearly graze the partner but make no contact. Accompanied by a line-up of percussion including *berimbau* and tambourine, capoeira is practiced in living rooms and on beaches.

A type of salon samba, forró is the second-most practised dance in Rio, taught at schools and cultural centres around the city and performed at clubs like **Asa Branca** (*see p179*) and at the **Feira de São Cristóvão** (*see p95*).

Less frenetic than samba, forró is popular among foreigners who want to learn some Brazilian dance steps but are intimidated by samba's ferocious pace.

Venues

Brazil's most prestigious venue for dance is the Theatro Municipal (*see p193*). The theatre dedicated nearly solely to dance performances is **Teatro Cacilda Becker** (Rua do Catete 338, Catete, 2265 9933). Although it normally hosts concerts, **Canecão** (*see p180*) also holds quality dance performances. Multi-purpose spaces like **Centro Cultural Banco do Brasil** (*see p63*), **Espaço Cultural Oi Futuro**, **Teatro Maison de France** (*see p194*) and **Teatro Nelson Rodrigues** (*see p193*) are all good places to see dance.

A nightly show at **Plataforma** (Rua Adalberto Ferreira 32, Leblon, 2274 4022, www.platforma.com) showcases different forms of Brazilian dance. It does have a tendency to veer into the kitsch at times, but has also earned a reputation among foreigners for its prodigious displays of capoeira and extravagant line-up of Carnival costumes.

Telenovelas

Besides being the ultimate thermometer of popular culture in the country, and being wildly popular and very entertaining, *telenovelas* (soap operas) are very often the bread and butter day jobs, or sometimes the dreamy career goals, for Rio's theatre professionals. Channel surfing during the soap hours (for details, *see p229*) can offer up just about anything: narcotics police busting in on a wedding to take away the groo... no – gasp! – to take away the bride! Nuns cloistered with a television being swept away by the lascivious euphoria of Carnival... The acting is so demonstrative that language is no barrier to following the plot.

The soaps follow the ups and downs that are the rollercoaster of political and social life in Brazil, while simultaneously dictating trends in clothes and pop music. Most of all, they give people something to talk about. Popular soaps can paralyse Rio, leaving streets empty and quiet as Cariocas are glued to their sets. The popular myth about the legendary *Roque Santeiro,* by seminal soap scribe Dias Gomes, says the show achieved 100 per cent ratings. Whether you believe that or not, the show did give its name to Angola's – and some say Africa's – largest street market. Brazilian soaps, mostly from Rio, are currently shown in over 85 countries.

Arts & Entertainment

Sport & Fitness

Can't sit still for more than a minute? You've come to the right place...

Participation sports

Rio de Janeiro is an energetic city. Copacabana, Ipanema and Leblon are some of the most densely packed neighbourhoods in the world. Kinetic energy that builds up during the day is released in bursts of activity. Cariocas easily spend more time being active than other Brazilians, making their city a sporting heaven. As long as it's not raining, Rio de Janeiro is a city in perpetual motion.

During the early morning hours beach-side *calçadões* (pavements) and bike paths from Flamengo to Leblon are full of locals jogging, biking, or speed-walking, often chatting at pace. Surfers and bodyboarders abound in the water, especially from May to November, when the waves are consistent.

Further down the coast, just before the famous Praia da Pipa beach in Barra da Tijuca, kite surfers check their gear before ripping through the waves just off the shore where the underwater shelf extends further out than at other beaches. The shallow water area is an ideal testing ground for beginners.

In the evening hours, after the sun's heat has dissipated, activity doubles. Walk along the beach in Ipanema, from Aporador rock to lifeguard Posto 10 an hour before sunset and

you'll see dozens of people practicing capoeira (www.nestorcapoeira.net) and playing volleyball, *futevollei* and football in the sand.

In the summer months, local gyms sponsor open-air free weight stands and work out sessions close to lifeguard Posto 9. At intervals along most of Rio's beaches, you'll find sit-up and push-up posts, as well as pull-up and chest-dip bars. The beach bordering Botafogo bay has permanent goal posts, and the beaches in Ipanema, Leblon and Copacabana are lined with volleyball nets.

Running on the sand is also very popular, especially on rainy days when there's more space and firmer sand. Otherwise, rain stops all but indoor activity in Rio, but it doesn't stop Cariocas from exercising; swimming, jiu-jitsu (*see p200* **Get a grip**), *futesala*, racquetball and basketball are all viable wet weather alternatives.

When the rain stops, the forest comes alive. In the crisp morning air after a night shower, rock climbers and outdoor enthusiasts head to the city's nature centres. Rio is home to the world's largest national park inside a metropolitan centre. Tijuca park (*see p198*) has hundreds of kilometres of hiking trails to explore. Rock climbing on Urca hill, Sugar Loaf and Pedra da Gávea is common.

The **Lagoa bike and running track**. *See p201.*

Arts & Entertainment

From the top of the rocks, hang-gliders float gently down to the forest below, joined by paragliders, who choose parachutes over the hang-glider's fixed wing. Skydivers drop from the clouds. Once the chute opens, the float down affords the best view of Rio de Janeiro. Watching them land on São Conrado beach is encouragement enough to join them.

It's all there to do. The challenge is not in finding but in choosing the sport you want to practice, experiment or learn.

Beach football

Copacabana beach, between Postos 4 and 5, is wide enough to fit at least two mini football fields side by side. The length of the stretch between the lifeguard posts is filled with beach footballers on most weekends and sunny days during the summer. Just indicate you're interested in playing and you should get a game. The same goes for the beach football courts in Ipanema. Smaller courts just before Posto 9 are usually used for *escolhinha* (kids' day school) – to take on the big boys, head for the larger court just past Posto 8, to find the games played just before the canal that separates Ipanema and Leblon, or the far end of Leblon beach. Held all over the city, games are usually in the evening, and most can accommodate an extra player or two.

Cycling

There are a number of spots along the walkway in Copacabana to rent a bike, especially between lifeguard Postos 3 and 5 – but the dubious quality of these bikes may leave you with a flat tire or worse. More reliable are Bike & Lazer and Special Bike. Be careful, though, when bicycling around Rio, stick to cycle lanes or beach roads – other roads are extremely dangerous.

Bike & Lazer
Rua Visconde de Pirajá 135B, Ipanema (2521 2686/ www.bikeelazer.com.br). Bus 132, 157, 512. **Open** 9am-7.30pm Mon-Fri; 9am-2pm Sat. **Rates** R$15/hr; R$60/day. **Credit** AmEx, MC. V. **Map** p249 F17. **Other locations**: Rua das Laranjeiras 58A, Laranjeiras (2285 7491).

Special Bike
Teixeira de Melo 53J, Ipanema (2513 3951/ www.specialbikebotafogo.com.br). Bus 132, 433, 512. **Open** 9.30am-7pm Mon-Fri; 9am-2.30pm Sat. **Rates** R$15/hr; R$45/day. **Credit** V. **Map** p249 F17.

Frescobol

One of the most popular beach sports combines fun in the sun with two wooden racquets and a solid core rubber ball. The racquets are about

Beach football.

Arts & Entertainment

twice the size of ping-pong bats and the ball is like a tennis ball but slightly smaller and more solid. Two players stand about five metres apart and knock the ball back and forth – simple as that. Frescobol sets can be purchased in Ipanema at Lojas Americanas (*see p131*) or around the city. Cariocas play the sport wherever they find space on the sand, usually in front of the ocean.

Golf

Rio has only recently become a golfing destination. There are two private golf courses in the city worth a swing, and most holes have beautiful views of the mountains, beaches or both. The private **Gávea Golf & Country Club** (Estrada da Gávea 800, 3323 6050, www.gaveagolf.com.br) in São Conrado has 18 holes and is a par 68, 6,000-yard course. Holes ten to 14 are along the seaside, while the home stretch is tucked against the Pedra da Gávea. The **Itanhangá Golf Club** (Estrada Barra da Tijuca 2005, 2494 250, www.itanhanga.com.br) has a full 18-hole golf course with an additional nine holes of what's been dubbed 'target golf', for its narrow fairways and tiny greens. Both courses are private and non-member players must be invited as member guests, but some of Rio's luxury hotels have an agreement with Gávea Golf Club. For a cheap, cheerful and more or less accessible public course, head for **Banana Golf** (*see below*) out in Recreio, where you can hire clubs to hack twice around their nine-hole course. For more on golf in Rio, and for courses elsewhere in the state, see www.fgerj.com.br (in Portuguese) or the Brasil Bureau of Golf Tourism site (www.brasilgolfe.com.br).

Banana Golf

Rua Serviente 4/9, Vargem Grande (3411 6110/ www.bananagolf.com.br). Bus 1133. **Open** 2.30-10pm Wed-Fri; 8am-10pm Sat; 8am-9pm Sun. **Rates** R$60-$80 for 2 rounds. **Credit** AmEx, MC, V.

Gyms

Most gyms in the southern zone require visitors to pay for a minimum amount of time, usually a week or more, before allowing them to work out there. Fortunately most hotels also have decent gyms, and there are many other ways to break a sweat in Rio. **Body Tech**, one of the group's largest gyms in the Zona Sul, has various sites across Leblon and Ipanema and offers guest passes and spa services.

Body Tech

Visconde de Pirajá 356b/202, Ipanema (2523 3838/ www.bodytech.com.br). Bus 132, 433, 512. **Open** 6am-10pm Mon-Fri; 8am-8pm Sat. **Rates** vary; R$60 day pass. **No credit cards**. **Map** p240 G18.

Hang-gliding

Imagine running down a ramp that drops off into nothing... and soaring into the air over rainforest hundreds of metres below. Rio's hang-gliders and parasailers make this experience safe and packed with adrenaline for anyone brave enough to take a tandem flight. Taking off from Gávea rock, one of the city's highest points, and soaring over São Conrado, the views of Barra da Tijuca to the east, Leblon and Ipanema to the west and the Lagoa to the north are spectacular. Turn up on the Praia do Pepino between 9am and 6pm daily to make arrangements directly with the instructors there or check with **Rio Super Fly** (3322 2286, www.riosuperfly.com.br), Konrad Heilmann with **Rio Hang Gliding** (9843 9006, www.riohang gliding.com) or **Just Fly** (9985 7540, www.just fly.com.br). The ramps are at Pedra Bonita, seven kilometres (four miles) from Pepino Beach. Take the Estrada das Canoas from São Conrado. Current information and a list of licensed instructors can be obtained from the **Hang-gliding & Parasail Association** (3322 4176, www.avlrj.com.br).

Hiking

Rio's Tijuca national park is the largest national park within city limits in Latin America – and probably in the world. Dozens of trails snake underneath a canopy of rich Atlantic rainforest, one of the last places in the world where it still flourishes. For tour operators, *see pp90-91* **The urban jungle**.

Kite surfing

This is a relatively new sport in Rio, but like any other sport, Cariocas practice it with passion and persistence. Most kite surfers can be found along the beaches in Barra da Tijuca, west of Barra's Praia da Pipa, where there's maximum wind exposure. Unless you're an experienced kite surfer with your own equipment, you should take a day or two with a local professional to learn some techniques and to hire equipment. Marcelo Cunha (mobile 8859 2112, www.kitepointrio.com.br) gives kite surfing lessons in Barra. For R$200 he'll give you a three-hour class to get you started. He also offers equipment for rent.

To really get going, consider a course of lessons along the coast in Cabo Frio, where there's less crowd and more wind. See www.jerrykitesurf.com for details.

For windsurfing, try **Rio Wind** (Avenida Prefeito Dulcídio Cardoso 400, Barra, 2438 2723, www.riowind.com.br).

Hang-gliding from the Pedra Bonita.

Besides beaches, football and a beautiful landscape, Rio de Janeiro has also become home to what many have accepted as the most comprehensive style of martial arts in the world. Brazilian jiu-jitsu is a style adapted from the Japanese grappling martial art that dates back to the Samurai. Unarmed warriors used jiu-jitsu to attack the throat and arms, the only vulnerable areas on an opponent otherwise protected by bamboo armour. Since then, the martial art has developed into a number of distinct styles, each with its own disarming set of chokes, locks, sweeps, take downs and defence.

The patriarch family of Brazilian jiu-jitsu, known as the Gracies, adapted what two brothers learned from a Japanese judo master over years of training and practice. One of these brothers, Helio Gracie, became known internationally as the founder of Brazilian jiu-jitsu after spending much of his fighting career challenging world boxing, wrestling and judo champions from the United States and Japan.

Jiu-jitsu gained its current renown when Helio's son, Royce Gracie, won the first and second Ultimate Fighting Championships in the United States. He won again in the fourth championship, forcing all multi-martial

art practitioners to seriously consider jiu-jitsu as a fundamental practice for any professional fighter today.

As jiu-jitsu's popularity has grown around the world, the practice moved from the preserve of professional fighters to men, women and children interested in a complete knowledge of self-defense. Many travel to Rio de Janeiro, Brazil's jiu-jitsu centre, specifically to train with the world's best, but anyone can sit in on a class or sign up for a week's instruction.

Most academies are located in Copacabana or in Barra da Tijuca. Big teams include Brasa and De la Riva (www.delarivajiujitsu.com.br) but Gracie Barra and the Brazilian Top Team (*see p203*) are the most visitor friendly and also offer classes for beginners all year. Most can rustle up a clean kimono too, just in case a curious traveller walks through the door.

Jiu-jitsu is certainly not for everyone. But arm bars and chokes should not prevent you from learning more about this fascinating martial art. Some who give it a try do so once. Most come back for more and fall in love with the sport, which in turn often changes their lives. Returning home from Brazil, you're likely to find a jiu-jitsu studio nearby to continue your quest for the black belt.

For information on schools, *see p203*.

Rafting

Whitewater rafting is one of the few sports that requires travel outside of Rio. Fortunately, there are companies that will pick you up early in the morning and drop you back in time for dinner. In the mountains between Rio de Janeiro and the city of Belo Horizonte is Tres Rios, a small town about 100 kilometres (60 miles) from Rio that boasts some of the region's best, though certainly not its only, stretches of whitewater. Rafting trips make for a good break from the city and are an adrenaline fuelled day. There are a number of companies that offer rafting packages, but few are reliable. Check first with **Tuareg Rafting** (2463 1095, www. tuaregrafting.com.br) for day-long rafting expeditions before using the service suggested by your hotel or hostel.

Rock climbing

From gentle upwards rambles to full-on ascents, just about every rock face in Rio is climbable – there are over 50 routes up the Sugar Loaf alone, and even more companies that will take you. Alexandre from **Aribira** (2235 3716, www. aribira.com.br) runs a range of expeditions in Rio and beyond, taking groups to the tops of mountains. He specialises in working with beginners but is happy to spend the day with experts too. For longer, expedition-length climbs, try **Climb in Rio** (Rua Alice 1512A, Laranjeiras, 2557 6093, www.climbinrio.com). The boys with Climb in Rio tend to be a little more hardcore and work well with clients with experience of the technological intricacies of multi-pitch and expedition climbing.

Running

The bike and jogging paths lining the beaches of Copacabana, Ipanema and Leblon are perhaps the best places for running and jogging in the Zona Sul, where even the most exercise-averse will see the attraction. They are also lined with stands selling coconut water for refreshment. The small, two-lane pathway clogs with human traffic in the morning between 9am and 10am and in the evenings for an hour before sunset. If you can avoid these times, do so.

Around the Lagoa is another bike and jogging path. It's popular with runners because of stretch and workout stations placed at intervals around the loop. The path is considerably wider, so any time of day is fine. A run around the Lagoa is one of the best options for combining a tour of one of the most beautiful areas in Rio with a good workout (see p84 **Rambling in Rio**).

Skydiving

Apart from dropping into a three-metre wave, skydiving is probably the most extreme sport you can do inside Rio's city limits. Tandem jumps strap you together with a master jump instructor, who on the count of three will throw the both of you out of the side of a plane, 4,000 metres (13,000 feet) above sea level. You will fall for 40 seconds before opening the parachute. For first-time jumpers, it will probably be the most memorable minute of your life, and experienced skydivers won't need further encouragement. Get in touch with **Barra Jumping** (3151 3602, www.barrajumping. com.br) or **Rio Turismo Radical** (9224 6963, www.rioturismoradical.com.br) for more information.

Surfing

Rio has long been known as a surfers' city, but as there's a changing sand bar and no reef breaks, it's hard to nail down exact spots along the beach front. Generally speaking, the break in front of Posto 10 in Ipanema and Posto 11 in Leblon is constant. In Copacabana, there's a constant break a few hundred metres past Posto 5, towards Posto 4. The breaks at Arpoador rock and at the very end of Leblon fire with good swell, as does the break in Recreio. Prainha is perhaps the best local surf spot, but it's accessible only by car, taxi or the **Surf Bus** (see p91). This excellent service can be booked from many hotels and surf stores, leaves four times a day and can pick you up from any prearranged spot in Botafogo, Copacabana, Ipanema or along the coast. For further information on swells, competitions and breaks www.waves.com.br (in Portuguese) has it all; and for good prices on used and new boards and all the equipment you'll need, **Galeria River** (Rua Francisco Otaviano 67, Arpoador) is the place to go.

For beginners, or those wanting to improve their technique, there are a number of surf schools loosely based on Barra beach. Most of them move around, looking for the best surf, but Evandro Guimarães of **Barriga Assada** (2442 1908, mobile 9424 3336, Avenida Lúcio Costa, between Postos 3 and 4, in front of the Windsor Hotel) does at least have a thatched *barraca* on the beach – and is a good teacher.

Swimming

Most pools in Rio de Janeiro are connected with hotels, private sports clubs or gyms (see p198), but the best option by far is the ocean. From Ipanema to Leblon is probably the best stretch

Arts & Entertainment

for swimming, especially between the months of December and March when there tends to be less off-shore storm activity or rainfall in the city. After as little as a half-day of rain, the ocean can turn discoloured, especially around the outflow of the canal that separates Ipanema and Leblon. People in the water is a good sign, generally speaking, but always remember that the Guanabara Bay is more polluted than the ocean, so check which side of the Sugar Loaf mountain you are on. Always be very careful with heavy surf as waves can generate strong long shore and rip currents.

Tennis

Tennis in Rio is mostly a sport played in the type of private club that requires a lot of money to join. There are some free public courts around the Lagoa if you bring your own racquet and are prepared to wait your turn, and there are also free courts on the Aterro do Flamengo, with amazing views of the Sugar Loaf mountain, but they might be shared with football-playing kids from the neighbouring favelas. More regular courts that can be booked involve a journey out west to the **Rio Sport Center** (*see below*) in Barra.

Rio Sport Center

Avenida Ayrton Senna 2541, Barra da Tijuca (3325 6644/www.riosportcenter.com.br). Bus 175, 750. **Open** 6am-10.30pm Mon-Thur; 6am-10pm Fri; 8am-8pm Sat; 9am-1pm Sun. **Rates** (day pass) R$28 Mon-Fri; R$17 Sat, Sun. **No credit cards**.

Wakeboarding

There are few places in the world where you can wakeboard or waterski literally in the middle of the city. Rio's Lagoa is an amazing spot to spend a day or two learning how to wakeboard, or where the more experienced can rent the equipment and boat time for an afternoon zipping around on the water. For the really advanced, there are also a series of freestyle rails and ramps for performing tricks and getting big air. Marquinhos Figueiredo at the **Rio Wake Center** (Lagoa Rodrigo de Freitas, in front of Rua Garcia D'Avila, 2239 6976, www.riowakecenter.com.br) can give instruction and more information.

Yoga

There are a number of private, yoga-only centres located around Rio. Minimum payment is generally for a month, though arrangements can be made to pay in weekly instalments. Generally the first couple of classes in each place are free, so shop around. Centres include **Academia Hermógenes de Yoga** for Hatha Yoga (Rua Uruguaiana 118, 2224 9189, www.profhermogenes.com.br), **Sivananda Center** (Rua das Palmeiras 13, Botafogo 2266 4896, www.yogasivananda.com.br) and **Nirvana** (Jóquei Clube, Praça Santos Dumont 31, Gávea, 2187 0100, www.enirvana.com.br). Nirvana covers all the range of yoga styles, and has two native Brits, Matthew and Nick, among their ashtanga teachers.

Hitting Rio's waves: the city offers a number of good surf spots. *See p201.*

Cultural sports

Capoeira

About as rootsy as you can get, capoeira was developed as a form of self-defence by African slaves in the Brazilian plantations from as early as the 16th century. Prohibitions on fighting made them disguise the operation as a traditional dance, complete with musicians around them in a *roda* (circle). While it's much more common in Bahia, Rio is home to enough capoeiristas for there to be a vibrant community. Near Arpoador rock on Fridays just before sunset, you can catch a traditional *roda de capoeira*. On the corner of Prudente de Moraes and Farme de Almoedoa in Ipanema, you can also often catch street capoeira performers. There are plenty of teachers if you want to try it yourself, but they tend to be unreliable. Call **Mestre Espiga Capoeira** (3435 2703, mobile 7821 9217, www. capoeirarj.com) for information, or better still, ask at the *roda de capoeira* near Arpoador.

Jiu-jitsu

If you're interested in training for a day, a week, or more, you should consider checking out Gracie Barra or the Brazilian Top Team in Rio. Another alternative would be to go through a tour company. Rio Sports Tour is probably the best option as it has close contacts with jiu-jitsu gyms that are more focussed on martial arts than marketing. *See also p200* **Get a grip.**

Brazilian Top Team
Athletic Association of the Bank of Brazil, Avenida Dorges de Medeiros 829, Lagoa (2274 4722/www. braziliantopteam.com). Bus 128, 157, 434. **Rates** R$35 registration; R$135/mth training; first class free. **No credit cards. Map** p248 C16.

Gracie Barra
ByFit Academy, Avenida Comandante Júlio de Moura 300, Barra da Tijuca (2493 1188/www.graciebarra. com.br). Bus 175, 225, 234. **Rates** vary; first class free. **No credit cards.**

Rio Sports Tour
Avenida Rio Branco 100/18 (2507 7709/www.rio sportstour.com). Bus 123, 127, 177. **Rates** vary; call for info. **Credit** call for info. **Map** p245 I2.

Spectator sports

Football

Rio's **Maracanã** stadium (*see p94*) is one of the world's great stadiums, and being a part of its crowds and colourful displays can be as much fun as the game itself. The stadium thunders when the Brazilian national team invites other nations to test their mettle. Recently refurbished for the 2007 PanAmerican Games, the Maracanã is where Flamengo, Fluminense, Vasco da Gama, and Botafogo, Rio's four major football clubs, play most of their games. The Campeonato Carioca during February and early March guarantees a lively crowd.

...ets are offered by many hotels and tour ...ators, or can be bought in advance from ...club houses of the team playing – Botafogo, ...lamengo and Fluminense, but not Vasco de Gama, have an agreement between them to sell tickets to each others' matches. Check the club websites for fixtures and other sales points.

As the stadium never sells out, tickets can also be found just before the game on the walkway between the Maracanã metro stop and the stadium, though touts will add their own surcharge. Prices depend on the game and where you sit, but on average expect to pay R$30 for the 'neutral' white seats (where tourists and families generally sit), R$25 for slightly rowdier green seats, R$20 for the full-on bottom section of the stands (blue) or R$100 for the relative tranquility of an *especial* seat. Expect to pay around R$20 for a normal season game and double that for championship time. Afternoon matches start at 4pm, evening matches at 7pm. Bear in mind that the green stands, with their grandstand view of the Corcovado, may be better in the afternoons as spectators in the white stands are forced to stare into the sun to watch the game.

The famous **Fla-Flu** (Flamengo-Fluminense) derby is usually the most rowdy match, closely followed by matches between Rio teams and São Paulo teams. The Brazilian Football Federation site has details of news and game schedules (http://cbfnews.uol.com.br).

For big games, most Cariocas either head to the Maracanã or stay home, resulting in a limited number of places to belly up and watch the game from a bar with beer in hand. **Shenannigans** (Rua Visconde de Piraja 112, Ipanema, 2267 5860), with its large screen for televised games, is probably the best place around and it's got Guinness on tap. The **Lord Jim Pub** (*see p127*) is another option, but without the large screens or cover charge.

For more on football in Rio, *see pp30-34*.

Botafogo
Avenida Vencesláu Brás 72, Botafogo (2543 7272/ www.botafogonocoracao.com.br). Bus 123, 125, 132, 175. **Ticket office** 11am-5pm daily. **No credit cards. Map** p247 J11.

Flamengo
Avenida Borges de Medeiros 997, Lagoa (2159 0100/www.flamengo.com.br). Bus 128, 157, 434. **Ticket office** 11am-5pm daily. **No credit cards. Map** p248 C16.

Fluminense
Rua Moura Brasil, Laranjeiras (2553 7240/www. fluminense.com.br). Bus 126, 435, 456. **Ticket office** 11am-5pm daily. **No credit cards. Map** p247 H8.

Vasco de Gama
Rua General Almério de Moura 131, São Cristóvão (2176 7373/www.crvascodagama.com) Bus 433, 472, 473. **Ticket office** 10am-5pm Mon-Fri. **No credit cards.**

Horse racing

The **Jockey Club** (*see below*) located near the Lagoa is the only venue for live horse racing in Rio. Situated close to the water and tucked between the mountains of Tijuca National Park and the beaches of Ipanema and Lelbon, it's a beautiful spot for a racetrack. Opened in 1926 by the jockey club of Brazil, this course and the adjoining grandstands, restaurants and bars are as splendid as ever. There are four races each week, held on Fridays at 4.30pm, Saturdays and Sundays at 2pm and Mondays at 6.30pm. All races are open to the public. The big date in the calendar is the Brazilian Grand Prix, held every year on the first Sunday of August.

Jockey Club
Praça Santos Dumont 31, Gávea (3534 9000/ www.jcb.com.br). Bus 158, 172, 179, 409. **Open** 6-11pm Mon; 4-10pm Fri; 1.30-10pm Sat, Sun. **Admission** free. **No credit cards. Map** p248 B15.

Jockey Club.

Arts & Entertainment

Trips Out of Town

Features

Parati

Pirates, book festivals and beaches: the buried treasures of Parati.

There's a tendency to groan when you hear about a town whose sole purpose is tourism, and an urge to turn to the pages where the 'real' places and 'real' people are. This time, though, don't – Parati (also sometimes known as Paraty) has a bittersweet history of piracy, slaves, gold and sugar, plus a superb location just 240 kilometres (150 miles) south of Rio down the beautiful BR101 coastal highway, making it the perfect weekend getaway. Add to that a hefty programme of festivals and cultural events, a growing reputation as a mecca for culinary enthusiasts and an explosive nightlife, and you'll realise why Parati has gone from ghost town in 1966, when its entire city centre was declared a World Heritage site by UNESCO, to one of the most popular and vibrant destinations on Brazil's east coast.

One of the town's most pleasant aspects is its lack of road traffic. No vehicles are permitted in the centre, a farsighted civic strategy that helps to maintain the town's tranquil, romantic ambience. The town was originally laid out in a 'T' shape facing northward in order to create a coastal bulwark against raiding pirates and, if you believe the rumours, as a symbolic representation of Masonic precepts.

Parati's sudden transformation into a tourist destination is deeply bound up with its turbulent history. Within 200 years of its foundation in 1600, the town had become the second most important port in Brazil, exporting huge amounts of gold and importing shiploads of slaves to work in the mines. When piracy grew to unbearable proportions and an alternative gold trail was created straight from the Minas Gerais to Rio de Janeiro, Parati set its population of slaves to producing sugar. Cachaça or *pinga* (sugar cane liquor) became for a time synonymous with Parati, and you can now visit the old distilleries and buy their cachaça for an historic caipirinha.

The extent to which Parati's economy depended on slavery is revealed dramatically by the mass exodus in 1888, when slavery was finally abolished – 16,000 inhabitants became 600 in a matter of weeks. The abandoned town remained preserved, a relic from the past, until it was rediscovered in 1954 and declared a national historic monument 12 years later. Now Parati is once again exploding into life, trading this time not in gold, sugar or slaves,

but in tourism. The abandoned houses of the town's 19th-century residents have been imaginatively transformed into shops, bars, restaurants, museums and cultural centres, and in summer the lumpy, stone-filled streets are heaving with local and foreign visitors. The port from which countless gold was shipped out to Europe is now filled with schooners and small converted fishing boats offering day trips round the bay. The beaches from which pirates launched their nefarious expeditions are scattered with small bars and kiosks, where you can lounge and watch the sun go down with a caipirinha or fresh *coco gelado*.

You're bound to coincide with one or other of Parati's festivals and cultural events, because the town always seems to be celebrating something. Carnival week at the end of February is famous for its **Bloco da Lama**, in which hundreds of people splatter themselves in mud from the nearby Jabaquara beach and parade through the streets imitating cavemen. For something a little more refined, don't miss the **Festa Literaria Internacional de Parati** (FLIP) in August. Well-known and respected authors, poets and journalists come from all over Brazil and the world to take part in four days of readings, workshops, shows and other celebrations of literary culture. Almost all FLIP events have simultaneous Portuguese-English translation, and are open to all – see www.flip.org.br or call 24 3371 7082 for more details. Food, dance and music celebrations are liberally scattered throughout the calendar, and the programme varies every year – a full list can be found from the tourist information website: www.paraty.com.br.

TOURIST INFORMATION

The official tourist information office can be found on Avenida Roberto Silveiro (24 3371 6553, www.paraty.com.br) at the entrance to the historic centre. Another useful website is www.eco-paraty.com.

There are numerous tour agencies scattered in and around the centre. The biggest of these is **Paraty Tours** (Rua Roberto Silveiro 11, next to tourist information, 24 3371 2651, www.paratytours.com.br), but other agencies offer variations with bike hire and trips in kayaks and jeeps. In general, however, most of what Parati has to offer is easily managed without the need for expensive tours and guides.

Beaches

The best things to do in Parati are actually away from the sand, but that doesn't mean there aren't beaches aplenty in and around the town. The best are in Trindade, a 35-minute bus ride from Parati. In previous years, Trindade was used by pirates to attack ships carrying gold to Rio, but it's unlikely you'll find any buried treasure now. What you will find is a lovely old fishing village, several beautiful beaches (including the popular surf spot Cepilho and the nudist beach Praia dos Pelados), and a fantastic natural pool created by huge volcanic stones enclosing part of the sea. The latter is the perfect place for sunning yourself on a rock like a mermaid – ask one of the men on the Praia do Meio to take you to the 'Piscina do Cauxadaço' on his speedboat (around R$5 each way), or follow the trail at the far end of the beach if you feel up to a steep and slippery hike.

Prais dos Ranchos is another attractive beach with plenty of bars. The best of these is **Rock & Beach** where you can listen to retro tunes and sample the perfect caiprinhas mixed by the owner, Eduardo. You can also charter speedboats from here that will take you to some one of the translucent natural lagoons just off the coast – perfect for scuba divers.

Boat trips

A fine alternative to the beach is a five-hour schooner trip round the bay, stopping at four different islands for swimming, with lunch served on board. One of the most popular trips, organised by Paraty Tours, costs around R$20, plus an optional R$15 for a full lunch. For a bit more privacy and freedom simply head down to the harbour, where you'll find a host of converted fishing boats and their friendly owners, all willing to take you out for as long as you like, whenever and wherever suits. You can usually hire a good boat and skipper for around $50 for three hours. Highly recommended is Fabiano (81 322 543), who will take you round the isolated coves and beaches of Ilha Rasa, Ilha Comprida, Praia de Lula and Praia Vermelha. Some tour companies organise overnight boat trips, with all meals included from around R$60 per person.

The **Port**.

Trips Out of Town

Waterfalls & gold trails

If you've ever fantasised about bathing in a small, intimate natural pool, surrounded by trees and fed by a small waterfall, you can live out your dream for the price of a bus ride to **Tobogá** (R$2.60, direction Penha). Take your swimming things and follow the path behind the hut to the pool. There are no facilities and a lot of insects, so do take plenty of water and insect repellent, although if you haven't unwound enough already you can relax afterwards with a beer at the bar in Tobogá while waiting for the bus home.

A visit to the waterfall of Tobogá can be combined well with a tour of the **Caminho do Ouro**, the old trail along which thousands of slaves carried the gold which made Parati famous and Portugal rich. The first part of the trail, from Tobogá itself, can only be visited with a guide, and it's well worth the R$15 fee to have the history and nature explained as you trek the few kilometres through the trees. Portuguese language tours leave at 11.30am every day and can be booked through most tour agencies; English-speakers may have to hire a private guide so do ask in advance.

You can, if you like, hike up a good section of the trail by yourself, either by continuing on up after the guided tour ends or by getting off the bus two kilometres after Tobogá. A well-signposted path leads up through the forest and ends in a small site (entrance R$10, where you'll find a simple restaurant and pousada, some lovely waterfalls and natural pools, the ruins of an old toll house and the finest view over Parati from anywhere around. A map can be bought in advance from **Paraty Adventure** (Avenida Roberto Silveria 40, 24 3371 6135, www.paratyadventure.com).

Where to eat

Parati's reputation for fresh fish and home-style cooking (try the Bahian style *moqueca de peixe*, fish stew or whatever happens to be the dish of the day) has become increasingly established in the last few years, and there are now around 150 restaurants in and around the centre. The **Refugio** restaurant (Praça da Bandeira, 24 3371 2447) is cosy and finely decorated, and although fairly pricey has a good reputation for innovative fish and seafood dishes. Another good place for fish is the **Sabor do Mar** (Rua Domingos Conçalves de Abreu, 24 3371 1872) – you can choose your own fish in the market and sit back while they prepare it for you. For some unpretentious, excellent value Brazilian meat and fish you can't beat **Netto** (Rua da Lapa 402, 24 3371 0049) and if you're yearning

for granny's homely cooking head for the **Restaurante Panela de Ferro** (Rua Domingos Conçalves de Abreu, 24 3371 0049). Cheaper pay-by-weight restaurants and snack bars can be found between the *rodaviária* and the entrance to the historic centre. Otherwise, simply take the local advice – the busiest restaurant is usually the best.

For a special occasion, **Restaurante da Matriz** (Aurea Mello, Praça da Matriz N6, 24 3371 2820, www.paraty.com.br/matriz; *photo p210*), in a 17th-century stone house, rustles up some of the finest seafood in Parati. Typical dishes include a delicious *casquinhas de sire* (stuffed crab). The owner – a descendant of a famous cachaça-producing family – offers samplings of her families best home-brews. For cheaper but perfectly recommendable fare, both **Restaurante Paraty** (Rua de lapa s/n, 24 3371 2282) and **Corte Maltesse** (Rua da Comercio 130, 24 3371 2758) are family-run restaurants that mix hearty food with a bustling atmosphere. For a convivial drink, head no further than tiny **Bar Verdinho** (in front of the Praça Cachafaris), which has occasional live music and a busy barman who serves up ice-cold beers (R$3) and *petiscos* (bar snacks) until the wee hours.

Foodies should visit during the annual **Folia Gastronômica** in mid November, a festival of gourmet cookery in which top chefs are contracted from all over Brazil to prepare sumptuous feasts in the 35 or so restaurants that actively take part. They also organise a series of demonstrations, workshops and courses in cookery and barmanship open to all, especially if you book in advanc; see www.foliagastronomica.com.br for details.

Nightlife

The Brazilians are never ones to sit in silence, and some of the best places to eat in town have some of the best live music. Beware hefty cover charges at the **Café Paraty** (Rua do Comércio 253, 24 3371 1464), **Paraty 33** (Rua da Lapa 357, 24 3371 7311) and **Margarida Café** (Praça do Chafariz, 24 3371 2441), but the nightly live bossa nova, MPB and jamming sessions are well worth the price.

More informal, but often just as lively, music can often be found in the **Praça da Matriz**, which is heaving at the weekend with strollers tackling huge ice-creams and lounging in bars in the light of the Igreja Matriz. Here locals regularly practice capoeira and several of the bars have free live music on an irregular basis.

If you're after some night-time entertainment that's a bit less deafening, book a ticket for the tiny **Teatro Espaço** (Rua Dona Geralda 327, 24 3371 1575, www.paraty.com.br/teatro),

Cachaça isn't the only tipple available at Parati's classic liquor stores.

which puts on its famous puppet shows (*teatro de bonecos*) every Wednesday and Sunday at 9pm (R$40, book in advance). The troupe has played around the world, to the appreciation of reviewers from the *New York Times*, *Le Monde* and many more. You have to suspend belief slightly and avoid looking at the black-clothed puppeteers manipulating the lit-up puppets, but the effect is surprisingly realistic – particularly in the rather disturbing final act of their 'best of' show *Em Concerto*, which portrays a semi-naked puppet-girl masturbating herself to ecstasy. Nightlife in Parati is many and varied.

Where to stay

There are literally hundreds of hotels and *pousadas* in and around Parati, although most are booked up during weekends in summer. Most of the cheaper options (around R$50 for a double room) can be found between the Rodoviária and the entrance to the historic centre – many are excellent value but do check that lights and fans work, and whether hot water is available, before agreeing.

For a bit more peace, a friendly family atmosphere and the best view in Parati, head for the **Pousada Morro do Forte** just over the bridge from the main town (Rua Orlando Carpinelli 21, 24 3371 1211, www.pousada morrodoforte.com).

If you want all the mod cons of a city hotel – TV, minibar, bar, games room, swimming pool, sauna, room service – and don't mind paying for the privilege, the central **Pousada Porto Imperial** should fit the bill (Rua 10, Francisco Antonio, 24 3371 2323, www.pousada portoimperial.com.br). A good, cheaper option is **Pousada dos Contos** (Rua Marechall Deodoro 1, 24 3371 7505, www.pousada doscontos.com.br, double R$95-$R120), which has eight rooms, king-size beds, a good tropical breakfast buffet and friendly, multilingual staff.

Out of the centre, **Pousada das Canoas** (Avenida Roberto da Silveira 61, 24 3371 1133, www.redehoteis.com.br) has over 50 apartments kitted out for couples and groups, with separate swimming pools for children and adults. Doubles start at R$180.

Getting there

Parati is 241 kilometres (150 miles) south-west of Rio along the BR101. There are regular buses to and from Rio's Rodaviária with the Costa Verde company, which also stop at the pretty fishing village of Angra dos Reis (*see p214*). The journey takes four hours, costs R$44 each way, and seats should be booked well in advance at weekends and for holidays.

Restaurante da Matriz. *See p208.*

Búzios

Summer buzzing.

Just 191 kilometres (118 miles) north-east of Rio de Janeiro, Armação de Búzios, known simply as Búzios, offers a perfect bolthole from Rio's urban stress. Styled as a resort for the ultra chic, it sits at the peak of a beach-studded peninsula that pokes out into the transparent waters of the Atlantic. As prime tourist brochure material it attracts not just Rio's moneyed set but planeloads of visitors from São Paulo, Buenos Aires and further afield.

The area was originally discovered and populated by indigenous tribes, and then by Jesuit missionaries who took its natural beauty as incontrovertible proof of the existence of God. Later it become a refuge for pirates, the scene of great sea battles and a hotspot for slave trafficking before settling down as a quiet fishing village. All its history paled into insignificance beside the events of 1964 when Búzios really made its way onto the map – Brigitte Bardot retreated here for the summer with Bob Zaguri, her Brazilian boyfriend, and invited the world's press to take some photos.

In those days, Búzios was just another picturesque seaside village, with a scattering of fishing huts and a population of 300. There was no running water or electricity, and the only pousada telephone was to be found in the Pousada do Sol (where BB used to stay). Even meat was scarce. Amália de la Maria, a fellow Búzios pioneer and owner of Casas Brancas (see p213) tells the story of how a dog was 'lynched' the day it stole a piece of meat from a kitchen table.

Today, Búzios has a lot more to offer than just a beautiful setting. The heart of the village lies along the two main drags, the shoreline Rua das Pedras and Rua Turibe de Farias, where cafés, restaurants, travel agencies and internet centres jostle for the public's attention. Here too are small boutiques, stocked with the sort of high street fashion and classy ornaments that chic Cariocas and visiting tourists demand. On a sunny day, the cobbled streets are quiet and peaceful, but come nightfall, they're invaded and transformed by sun-kissed fun seekers returning from the beaches.

Still, certain aspects of Búzios' roots and former tranquility remain intact: fishing boats still chug out to sea, returning at sunset with their hulls laden (though the demands of the local restaurants have become more

sophisticated in the intervening years). And the locals still congregate for a chat each evening in the Praça Santos Dumont, before the evening turns to night and the parties get started.

Búzios's natural beauty is everywhere. With over two dozen beaches dotted around the rugged coastline, all within 20 minutes of the main centre, there's a beach for everyone (see below The best). Its less heralded reasons of success can be attributed to the simplicity and natural friendliness of the locals, and the government's ability to resist the pressure to construct large hotel complexes.

Only time will tell if this policy continues. But for now, with an average of 300 days of sunshine per year and an exceptionally high level of security, the future looks bright.

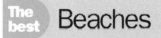

Beaches

For snorkelling
Praia João Fernandes, **Praia Azeda** and **Praia Azedinha** have transparent waters with coral reefs.

For families
Praia Ferradura (*p213*) is top choice for placid waters, soft sands and beach huts.

For topless sunbathing
Whip it off at **Praia Azedinha** or **Praia Azeda**.

For windsurfing and kitesurfing
Strong winds and choppy waters at **Praia Manguinhos** and **Praia dos Ossos** guarantee tight sails and lots of air.

For reading a book
Praia João Fernandinho is a small, peaceful beach sheltered from the wind.

For surfing
Praia Geribá, **Praia Tucuns** and **Praia Brava** (*p216*) are long sandy beaches and meeting points for surfers.

For a sunset caipirinha
Raise a toast as the sun slip over the edge at **Praia dos Ossos** or **Praia da Ferradura** (*p213*).

Trips Out of Town

The lovely view from **Pousada Casas Brancas**.

Where to eat & drink

Búzios prides itself on its seafood, with plenty of fish restaurants dotted around the port as well as many types of Asian cuisine. Restaurants on the main drag are two a penny, with some excellent pay-by-kilo restaurants among the usual cheap pizza and beer traps.

Boom

Rua Manoel Turibe de Farias 110 (22 2623 6245/www.boombuzios.com.br). **Main courses** R$39/kilo. **Open** noon-11pm daily. **Credit** AmEx, DC, MC, V.

Designed by local darling, Helio Pelegrino, Boom is an airy and comfortable upmarket pay-by-kilo restaurant that serves up some of the best barbecued meat and fish in the resort. The condiments are also pretty special; try the creamy pomegranate dressing, the giant capers or the chilli sauce.

Café Atlântico

Morro do Humaitá 10, Búzios (22 2623 1458/ www.casasbrancas.com.br). **Main courses** R$40-$90. **Open** 8am-10pm daily. **Credit** AmEx, V.

La crème de la crème. Sitting over the local port, Pousada Casas Brancas' brilliant restaurant does more than offer the resort's best views – the food (Mediterranean/Brazilian), multilingual service and sex appeal are second to none. Kick start the night with a fruity caipirinha before heading into a menu that includes racks of lamb, *magret de canard* and the pick of the fisherman's nets. A meal here is an event in itself.

Chez Michou

José Bento Ribeiro Dantas 90 (22 2623 2169/www. chezmichou.com.br). **Main courses** R$8-$20. **Open** noon-5am Tue-Sun. **Credit** AmEx, DC, MC, V.

The hub of the pre-clubbing scene and a Búzios classic, Chez Michou has something for everyone: fantastic chocolate crêpes, live football, cocktails, ice-cold beers and plenty of tacky music. But it's most recommendable for its relaxed atmosphere that allows locals and tourists to chat and dance freely with each other.

Sawasdee

José Bento Ribeiro Dantas 422, Orla Bardot (22 2623 4644/www.sawasdee.com.br). **Main courses** R$35-$70. **Open** 6pm-1am Thur-Tue. **Credit** AmEx, DC, MC, V.

Facing the docile waters of the port of Búzios, Marcos Sodré's Sawasdee adds spice and herbs and no end of creativity to the local catches and beef herded in from the state of Rio. Try the delicious chicken or prawn kebabs in Satay sauce or the *nam katee pla* – a cherne (grouper) cooked in a coconut and ginger sauce. Round off proceedings with banana flambada doused in Cointreau with tangerine and chocolate sauce and vanilla ice-cream. A classy restaurant better suited to intimate evenings for couples than for a large group of friends.

Where to stay

With over 300 pousadas to chose from, Búzios has plenty of options (though you'll still need to reserve well in advance during the high-season). They vary from the chic and modern to the isolated and off-beat, with the average price in low season being around R$160 per night, and in high R$300. Most are run by their owners.

Glenzhaus Lodge

Rua dos Coqueiros 27 (22 2623 2823/www. glenzhaus.com.br). **Rates** R$250-$600. **Rooms** 10. **Credit** AmEx, DC, MC, V.

One of the continent's best lodges, Cris Glenz put together his dream lodge with ideas gathered over 30 years of travelling around the world. Apart from all the standard amenities to be expected in a place of this calibre, Glenzhaus affords sea views and a secluded pool area surrounded by thick vegetation.

Pedra da Laguna

Rua 6, Quadra F, Praia da Ferradura (22 2623 1965/www.pedradalaguna.com.br). **Rates** R$250-$300. **Rooms** 25. **Credit** AmEx, DC, MC, V.

At a safe distance from the buzz and bustle of the centre, and yet tantalisingly close to Praia da Ferradura, this charming lodge is a real find. The lodge boasts a spa, outdoor bar, a tennis court and a large pool to cool off in.

Pousada Casas Brancas

Alto do Humaitá 10 (22 2623 1458/www. casasbrancas.com.br). **Rates** R$400-$750. **Rooms** 32. **Credit** AmEx, V.

Every article written about Búzios purrs over the award-winning Casas Brancas – and with good reason too. The property is beautifully designed with whitewashed walls and rooms adorned with beautiful mosaic-tiled floors and traditional carvings, setting the backdrop for a stay of unrivalled comfort and class. The best rooms gravitate around the heart of the pousada, where the pool and terrace area offer spectacular views across the Praia da Armação. Every year owner Amália de la Maria embarks on some new development – this year, it's a tapas bar.

Pousada Vila do Mar

Travessa dos Pescadores 88 (22 2623 1466/www. viladomar.com). **Rates** R$140-$220. **Rooms** 18. **Credit** AmEx, DC, MC, V.

Ideally located – at the edge of the main village and a few yards from the seaside promenade – Vila do Mar has a restaurant, small pool and the added boon of the Gran Cine Bardot, a cinema attached to the main entrance. Rooms vary in size and quality but all are clean and aptly equipped with televisions, minibars and large comfortable beds.

Getting there

Short of hiring a private jet, by far the most convenient way to reach Búzios is by road, the trip taking about three and a half hours (depending on traffic). Most hotels and pousadas offer transfer services between Rio de Janeiro and Búzios. A round-trip, in an air-conditioned car, costs around R$130 per person, while a van costs R$70. Buses leave frequently from the Rodoviára Novo Rio bus station terminal (Avenida Francisco Bicalho 1, Santo Cristo, 3213 1800, www.novorio.com.br). Viação 1001 (21 2516 1001) offers one-way tickets for R$18-$25.

Praia da Armação.

Trips Out of Town

Angra & Ilha Grande

More beaches, fewer people.

Angra dos Reis

Spurred on by the beauty of Guanabara Bay, a group of Portuguese explorers pushed on down the Brazilian coast dropping anchor on 6 January 1502 in a sheltered creek that was to be christened Angra dos Reis (King's Creek). Once a foothold was established, Angra dos Reis became a thriving port, where agricultural goods and gold were shipped off to Europe and slaves brought in to work the coffee plantations. These days, its history has more to do with rock stars, models and Brazilian celebrities who use Angra as a stepping stone to the 365 islands and 2000 pristine white beaches that surround her littoral. The beauty of the surrounding flora and fauna cannot be overstated.

But this small fishing town – with its crumbling forts, convents, churches and monuments – is still worth a visit. It's also the perfect spot to jump on a boat to head to one of the islands, or to charter your own (with or without skipper) through Angra Charter Boats, (24 9979 0886, www.angracharterboats.com).

For the active, Angra is 15 minutes away from the rapids of the Mambucaba River. The breathtaking 90-minute descent takes you through crystal-clear waters and rainforests.

Angra's highlight is the New Year Sea Procession. It's a real one-of-a-kind event, with thousands of colourfully decorated boats and some unrivalled maritime partying.

Where to eat

Seafood is top of the bill in Angra, led by restaurants such as **Ananás** (Unit 101, Shopping Pirata's Mall, Estrada Municipal 200, 24 3367 6285 main courses R$18-$50), and at bar **Sambura** (Rua Maria Jose Lucas Peixoto 286, Parque das Palmeiras, 24 3377 2730 www.angranews.com.br/sambura).

Where to stay

Angra dos Reis is synonymous with luxurious resorts. Most of the brochures offer the same – pools, sandy beaches, white smiles and an all-inclusive package-deal – but only one boasts an 18-hole golf course. At 12 kilometres (7 miles) from the centre, **Hotel do Frade and Golf Resort** (Praia do Frade, BR 101 KM 513, Angra dos Reis, 24 3369 9500, R$1400-$1800 double all inclusive, www.hoteldofrade.com.br) is particularly popular with Brazilians. The golf course cuts a picturesque line through the

Pousada Sankay. *See p216.*

Trips Out of Town

rivers and lakes around the deep hillside forest. Attracting a more cosmopolitan crowd, the **Hotel Pestana** (Estrada Vereador Benedito Adelino 3700, Retiro, Angra dos Reis, 24 3364 2005, www.pestana.com, call for prices) – set between the forest and the beach – has 27 rooms, oriental spas and the most spectacular views of the Bahia. In a similar vein, **Blue Tree** Resorts (Estrada Vereador Benedito Adelino 8413, Fazenda Tanguá, Angra dos Reis, 24 3379 2800, www.bluetree.com.br, R$660 to $850 doubles all included) has large kidney-shaped pools, 319 large rooms, impeccable service and a pristine white beach.

Ilha Grande

Ringed by secluded beaches hemmed in by fringes of palms and crystal-clear waters, Ilha Grande is an island paradise just a half-day trip out of Rio de Janeiro. Beyond all the natural beauty, the island comes laden with lore from a history that spans five centuries – from nearly-nude Tupi Indians to camera-toting gringos with plenty of smuggling, slave trading and penal colonies in between.

In the 16th century, the island's attractive bays and inlets quickly became favourites among smugglers and, after the Spanish and Portuguese struck gold, pirates and raiders frequented the islands, intercepting ships coming from Peru and the ports of nearby Angra dos Reis and Parati. Before becoming part of Brazil, Ilha Grande changed hands between the Dutch, Spanish and Portuguese – even the Argentines made a half-hearted three-boat attack in 1827 that was easily turned back. Around the mid 1880s, ships started to jettison lepers and passengers stricken by cholera, leading to the construction of a quarantine hospital in Abraão, to date the island's hub. A large prison and aqueduct were built close to Abraão – the ruins of both can be visited by taking a short stroll east of town. In the 1930s, the fishing industry started in earnest, giving rise to around ten solid drying and canning industries that lasted into the 1970s before being squashed by the big fisheries. After suffering an economic collapse and partial exodus, the island looked to its natural beauty and the tourist industry to help it stay afloat.

Now, most of Abraão's 3000 inhabitants live on the booming tourist industry. The high season – mid December to the end of February – sees boatloads of tourists arrive at the town's docks each morning and evening, and there are new inns, hostels and tour companies popping up at a fast rate, causing debate about how to juggle tourism and preserve natural treasures.

There are two piers in Abraão, the eastern-most is used for transport to and from the mainland, and the pier to the west is used for tour boats around the islands. Between the piers and extending either side, a line of restaurants and gifts shops follow the arc of the bay. Two streets with more of the same head back toward the hills behind the city. Devoid of cars, save for a couple police cars, ambulances and an all-purpose garbage truck, it's a pleasure to stroll the cobbled or sand streets.

Travel agencies abound in the town centre, offering schooner trips, snorkelling, scuba diving, kayaking, fishing, sailing and surfing. If you can, join with fellow visitors – groups of at least ten have a chance of negotiating better prices for boat tours; don't be afraid to ask around as prices do vary. Much of the island is protected by state parks and reserves that harbour numerous bird species, monkeys, snakes and rich flora. For those fond of walking in the woods, trails circumnavigate the island, scaling steep headlands before dropping down to secluded beaches. The open ocean Lopes-Mendez Beach – one of the hundreds of 'most beautiful beaches in Brazil' – can be reached by a three- to four-hour walk, but there's also an option to take a cheap boat ride from Abraão that cuts the walk to about 40 minutes. Strong hikers can look into scaling the 959-metre (3146-foot) peak of Pico do Papagaio for stunning 360-degree views and a chance to see the wildlife. Much of the open ocean coastline is a biological reserve closed to tourists, but almost all the boat companies go to beaches close to the reserve. Las Palmas, the beach north of Abraão, has a small community and three good places to eat – one even takes credit cards – for those who want to have lunch away from it all.

Where to eat & drink

For good seafood, just past the church and plaza on Abraão's main street is the popular **Adega do Cosario Negro** (Rua Professora Alice Kuri 06, 34 3361 5002, main courses R$20-$60). Also recommended for seafood and great steaks is **Lua e Mar** (Veja 95, 34 3361 5761, main courses R$30-$80). To get to Lua e Mar, walk west of town until the boardwalk ends and continue along the beach until you see the blue awnings and candlelit tables on the beach.

On moonlit nights, nothing beats a boat trip to dine in the unlikely culinary outpost of the secluded Saco do Ceu bay. Of the three restaurants in the bay, Reis e Mago and Coqueiro Verde are generally thought to be superior. Ask about dinner prices with the tour company when you arrange your boat trip. Nightlife is sparse in Abraão, but the restaurants around the plaza usually have a

Trips Out of Town

It's easy to get away from it all in Ilha Grande, with a boat trip around the islands.

few people looking to drink and chat, and local dances are sometimes spontaneously arranged.

Where to stay

Prices listed are for the high season and drop during low season. Over New Year and Carnival most places are considerably more expensive.

Lodgings have sprouted up all around Abraão, but as often happens with accelerated growth, some are far better than others. The most unique place in town is the **Pousada Aquario** (Praia da Julia, 24 3361 5405, www.aquariohostel.com, R$90 double, R$35 dorm room), ideally situated on the rocky headland west of town. Less than a ten-minute walk from the piers, Aquario features a stunning location, easy beach access, clean rooms, ceiling fans, boat trips, barbecues and a good crowd. Another decent option west of town is the beachfront **Pousada Porto Girasol** (Rua da Praia 65, 24 3361 9527 or 2437 1056, R$180 double with beach view, R$130 facing forest).

For a more exclusive stay outside of Abraão, there are a number of 'mini-resorts' dotted around the island, usually accessible only by boat. Still within the Bay of Abraão is the charming, nine-room **Sagu** (Praia Brava, 3361-5660, www.saguresort.com, R$320 double) and the **Asalem** (Praia da Crena, 24 3361 5602, www.asalem.com.br, R$260 double), where the fully equipped rooms have huge doors that open on to the garden. Further to the west is the 12

room **Pousada Sankay** (Enseada do Bananal, 24 3365 1090, www.pousadasankay.com.br, R$400-$490 double), a resort with a Japanese flavour. Arrive directly from Angra on the resort's own boat service, which also runs a daily tour of the surrounding coves and beaches. Unlike the rolling waves of Lopez Mendez beach, the waters in the northern coves are tranquil and silent.

Getting there

By road

Costa Verde (2573-1484) buses leave from the Rodoviária Novo Rio terminal every hour or half hour from 4am to 10.30pm. The two and half hour trip costs around R$30. From the bus station in Angra, take a taxi to the terminal where the boats leave. The ferry leaves for Abraão at 3.30pm on weekdays (when it costs R$5) and 1.30pm on weekends (R$18). Schooners that cost around R$15 also come and go early in the day and in the late afternoon from Angra to Abraão. The other option is to take a bus from Rodoviária to Mangaratiba, but check boat times to avoid getting stranded. Mini-resorts offer their own travel arrangements. Travel agencies and hotels will give details of private car operators that drive to Angra, for around R$300.

By sea

There are no regular direct services but boats can be chartered for the trip. Ask at Dehouche (2512 3895, www.dehouche.com).

Upstate Rio

Over the hills – and not so far away.

Petrópolis

While travelling the Estrada Real to Ouro Preto in 1822, Pedro I fell in love with the cooler air and the stunning mountain scenery of the Petrópolis region. His son, Pedro II, turned the settlement into a fascinating imperial city. In 1843, he declared that during the summer months, he would run his government from the newly named Petrópolis. Construction of the Imperial Palace, now home of the **Museu Imperial** (*see below*), began in 1845 and the building was finished in 1862.

In 1884, building work started on the cathedral, **Catedral São Pedro de Alcântara** (*see below*), although it was 1925 before the building was finally inaugurated. Additions and alterations to the structure continued up until the 1960s. The cathedral houses the Imperial Mausoleum, which became the final resting place for several members of the royal family.

Also in 1884, the amazing **Palácio de Cristal** (*see below*) was constructed for Princess Isabel. Built in France, it arrived here in prefabricated form. It houses a greenhouse and fountains, and every Saturday, *Som e Cristal* (Sound and Crystal) concerts are held there, featuring both local and nationally recognised artists. Other attractions include the **Casa do Barão de Mauá** (Praça da Confluência 3, Centro), the home of one of Brazil's first entrepreneurs; **Casa de Santos Dumont** (Rua do Encanto 22), named for the father of Brazilian aviation (who also gets a footnote in history as being the inventor of the wristwatch); and **Museu Casa do Colono** (Rua Cristóvão Colombo 1034, Castelânea), a German colonial house.

In spite of its royal history, the town has a very central European feel, brought by the German immigrants who chose to settle in territory more familiar to them than the tropical coast. There are many other buildings of historical significance in the town. It makes an easy day trip from Rio.

Catedral São Pedro de Alcântara

Rua São Pedro de Alcântara 60, Centro (24 2242 4300). **Open** 8am-noon Mon, 8am-noon, 2-6pm Tue-Sun. **Admission** free.

Museu Imperial

Rua da Imperatriz 220, Centro (24 2237 8000/ www.museuimperial.gov.br). **Open** 11am-6pm Tue-Sun. **Admission** R$8 adults; R$4 concessions.

The museum houses a huge and varied historical archive of documents and photos and a busy programme of visual art exhibitions. Son et Lumière shows take place each evening at 8pm from Thursday to Saturday, costing R$30.

Palácio de Cristal
Rua Alfredo Pachá, Petropolis (24 2247-3721).
Open 9am-6.30pm Tue-Sun. **Admission** free.
Each Saturday at 6pm, local and national artists put on a musical performance called Som e Cristal.

Where to eat

There are a variety of restaurants in the town centre, including the bistro at the Museu Imperial, *por kilos* and *churrascarias*. For something special, **Locanda della Mimosa** (Alameda das Mimosas 30, Vale Florido, Petrópolis, 24 2233 5404) offers a regularly updated Italian-inspired menu, put together by chef Danio Braga, who's the inspiration behind **Boa Lembrança** (Good Memories) scheme: participating restaurants offer diners a hand painted ceramic plate if they order the establishment's signature dish.

Where to stay

The **Pousada Monte Imperial** (Rua José de Alencar 27, Petrópolis, 24 2237 1664, www.pousadamonteimperial.com.br, R$215 double including taxes) is a chalet-style pousada just a short but steep walk from the historic centre. This pousada has a sister hotel in an old house in the town centre, the **Pousada Monte Imperial Koeller** (Avenida Koeller 99, Petrópolis, 24 2237 1664, www.pousadamonte imperial.com.br, R$145 double).

Itaipava

A little way beyond Petrópolis is the small town of Itaipava. This is worth a trip solely to visit the pottery, **Cerâmica Luiz Salvador** (Estrada União e Indústria 10588, Itaipava, 24 2222 2712, www.ceramicaluizsalvador.com.br). There is a huge variety of tableware, household goods and ornaments, all made and hand-painted on site. There are several good restaurants, especially pizza places, along the street where the factory is located.

Teresópolis

The main reason to visit Teresópolis is the dramatic scenery and the mountain climate, which offer superb opportunities for hiking and other outdoor activities. Though it used to be a favoured retreat of Empress Teresa Cristina, the town itself does not have much to lure the visitor these days.

The premier attraction is the Parque Nacional da Serra dos Orgãos, with its spectacular rock formations, such as the 1,692-metre (5,500-foot) Dedo de Deus (Finger of God) and 2,263-metre (7,500-foot) Pedra do Sino (Bell Rock). One of the most popular treks is the 40-kilometre (25-mile) hike between Teresópolis and Petrópolis, which takes three days. The National Park office (Avenida Rotariana s/n, 2642 1070, www.ibama. gov.br/parnaso, 8am to 5pm Tuesday to Sunday) offers advice on the trip. Alternatively, it can be arranged through Brazil Ecotravel, in Rio (Rua Visconde de Pirajá, Ipanema, 2512 8882, www.brazil-ecotravel.com).

Where to eat

Teresópolis is full of European-style restaurants; try the **Cremerie Geneve** (Estrada Teresópolis-Friburgo km 16, 21 3643 6391), with more cheese at **Casa do Fondue** (Avenida Feliciano Sodré 221, Centro, 21 2742 0480). For Brazilian fare (and sushi), there's **Churrascaria Novilho de Ouro** (Avenida Delfim Moreira 720, 21 2641 6384).

Where to stay

There are a few hotels in the town centre – one recommended choice is the **Hotel Várzea Palace** (Rua Prefeito Sebastião Teixeira 41, 21 2742 0878), but most popular are the resort hotels outside the town, which offer all kinds of leisure opportunities. The **Hotel St Moritz** (Estrada Teresópolis, Friburgo Km 36, 21 2641 1115 or 21 2239 4445 for reservations) offers lots of outdoor activities.

Nova Friburgo

Nova Friburgo is another popular destination for overheated Cariocas. The original Swiss immigrants from the Friburg canton must have felt right at home in the alpine scenery and their influence is evident in the architecture. There are woods, waterfalls and a forestry reserve open to walkers, plus plenty of hotels and restaurants in town. From the Praça Teleférica in the centre of town, a cable car runs to the top of the **Morro da Cruz** at 1,800 metres (6,000 feet).

Nova Friburgo is now best known for its lingerie industry, which started when a local bra factory closed and the workers decided to start their own businesses. Many Rio residents visit the town regularly, just to restock their underwear drawers with cut-price goodies.

Coffee Valley

The Brazilian coffee boom of the 19th century outstripped the country's previous economic

Fazenda Ponte Alta.
See p220.

Trips Out of Town

cycles, which were centred on *pau-brasil* wood, followed by sugar and then gold and precious stones. Coffee quickly became the country's main export. The initial expansion of production – which turned coffee from a local product into a desirable international commodity – started just outside Rio, in the **Vale do Paraíba**.

This boom transformed the lives of individuals and the city of Rio. During the height of coffee's success, slavery was finally abolished in Brazil. In order to keep the plantations running, large numbers of immigrants were encouraged to come to Brazil. Many Portuguese, Spanish, Italian and German families flocked to Brazil to escape turmoil and urbanisation in their native lands, to work the land of the new world.

A new moneyed class emerged – the coffee barons. In their wake followed the first great Brazilian entrepreneurs. Barão de Mauá was one of the most successful. He quickly saw that capital liberated from the slave trade could be put to productive use through industrial investment. One of Mauá's many achievements was bringing gas lighting and a proper water supply to Rio.

São Paulo later became the centre of coffee production, but the legacy of Rio's success lies in the magnificent coffee *fazendas* scattered across the state – old plantation houses set in rolling countryside and surrounded by lush farm land. Many can be found clustered around the towns of Barra do Pirai, Vassouras, Valença and Rio das Flores.

Once unknown and overlooked by outsiders, many have now been restored to their former splendour. Others have become havens of tranquility for weekends away, offering all sorts of leisure and sporting activities. Some are still in the same family, others are still working farms. One – Taquara (*see below*) – still produces coffee. An organisation, Preservale (www. preservale.com.br), was formed in 1994 to protect, develop and promote this important slice of Brazil's heritage and encourage tourism.

For the visitor, there are plenty of fazendas to choose from. Most lie to the north and west of the city of Rio, and many are only a one- to two-hour car ride away. A few are listed below and many others can be found at the Preservale website, which provides lots of details about individual estates. For a day trip, consider using a tour operator such as Indiana Jungle Tours (*see p90* **The urban jungle**).

Fazenda Arvoredo

Along the Pirai to Barra do Pirai road (RJ-145), off Rodovia Presidente Dutra (24 2447 2001/www.hotel arvoredo.com.br). **Open** daily for visits, weekend packages. **Admission** (includes lunch & high tea) R$60. *High tea only* R$25. *Overnight stay* R$480 double for Fri-Sun package, including all meals (children R$120 each). **No credit cards.**

This is the place to take the family. There's lots of outdoor entertainment, including a swimming pool, a lake with a water slide and a treetop adventure area. Visitors can watch cows being milked (and have a go too) and go for horse rides. There are also guided excursions, such as raft building and nature walks, but it's possible to trek through the beautiful surrounding country unaccompanied. A highlight is *Chá Imperial* (Imperial High Tea) at 6pm on Saturdays, complete with the 'baron'. Food is good and plentiful, while the accommodation is clean and comfortable. The fazenda is around 120kms from Rio.

Fazenda Ponte Alta

18 km along the Pirai to Barra do Pirai road, off Rodovia Presidente Dutra (24 2443 5005/www.ponte alta.com.br). **Open** daily (telephone in advance). **Admission** R$10. *Traditional lunch buffet* R$39. *Overnight stay* R$297 double. **Credit** MC, V.

The fazenda is beautiful, its setting picturesque and its integrity well preserved. The *senzala* (old slave quarters), slave hospital and *engenho* (mill) are more-or-less intact. There's a small slave museum and some interesting antique furniture, ornaments and books. Guided tours are offered in several languages, along with a play presenting the history of the coffee era. The buffet lunch is delicious, in the elegant surroundings of the main building. Guest rooms are pleasant and of a good size and there's a small swimming pool. The fazenda is around 120kms from Rio. *Photo p219.*

Fazenda da Taquara

Off RJ-145, shortly after Barra do Pirai, heading towards Valença (24 2443 1221/24 2444 7900) **Open** daily, by appointment. **Admission** R$20, includes tour. **No credit cards.**

Taquara is a small but attractive house, chock full of treasures, original furniture and memorabilia from the coffee era – the house has been in the same family for six generations. It's distinguished by the fact that it still produces coffee (along with farming pigs). A traditional country lunch is available, if booked in advance.

Getting there

The only way to travel inland is by car or bus – Petrópolis is 60 kilometres (40 miles) from Rio and easily reachable by bus from the Rodoviára Novo Rio (Avenida Francisco Bicalho 1, Santo Cristo, 3213 1800, www.novorio.com.br); buses leave every 15 minutes from 7am to 10pm and cost around R$10. Teresópolis is around 100 kilometres (60 miles) from Rio and can be reached by bus directly from Rio or via Petrópolis. Nova Friburgo is 130 kilometres (80 miles) from Rio, two and a half hours by bus from Rodoviária Novo Rio. The coffee fazendas are harder to reach without your own transport, though many tour operators will be keen to help get you there and the fazendas themselves can generally suggest easy routes.

Directory

Features

Directory

Getting Around

Arriving & leaving

By air

Rio de Janeiro is served by two airports. The **Aeroporto Internacional Antonio Carlos Jobim** (3398 4526, www.infraero.gov.br), located 20 kilometres (13 miles) north of the city centre on Ilha do Governador (a big land mass in the bay of Guanabara) is where international flights arrive and depart. It's better known as Galeão airport and most of the main airlines also fly here from São Paulo. Buses and taxis are the easiest ways to travel into Rio. Taxis can be prepaid at the airport and there are always regular cabs waiting outside (but make sure their meters are cleared before you start). An hourly airport shuttle bus stops at major hotels in the centre.

There's also the **Aeroporto Santos Dumont** (3814 7070), which is used for some domestic flights. It's located by the bay right in the city centre.

Aerolineas Argentinas International Airport Terminal 1 (3398 3737/3398 3720).
Air France/KLM International Airport Terminal 1 (3398 3490/ 0800 891 8640).
American Airlines International Airport Terminal 1 (0300 789 7778).
BA/Qantas International Airport Terminal 1 (4004 4440).
Continental International Airport Terminal 1 (3398 3023).
Gol International Airport Terminal 1 (3398 5136).
Iberia International Airport Terminal 1 (3398 3425).
TAM International Airport Terminal 2 (3398 2134).
TAP International Airport Terminal 2 (3398 2051).
United International Airport Terminal 2 (3398 2450).
Varig International Airport Terminal 1 (3398 2122).

By rail

Brazil has no national rail network but some commuter train lines do exist within Rio (*see below*).

By road

Rio is within easy driving distance of São Paulo to the south-west and Belo Horizonte to the north-east. The BR116 leads to Sao Paulo, while the BR040 goes to Belo Horizonte.

By sea

Rio is a stopover for many international cruises. The port is at **Praça Mauá** in Centro.

Public transport

Rio has no shortage of public transport since it's the main way of getting around the city for most Cariocas. Buses are most popular and there are hundreds of routes. Competing with the buses are 'vans', which are illegal but popular. There's also a clean, efficient and safe metro system.

Metrô

Rio has two metro lines. Linha 1 goes from Saens Peña station in Tijuca, through the centre and down to Cantagalo station in Copacabana. Linha 2 starts at Estácio station in Centro, and goes through the Zona Norte up to Pavuna. At certain stations there's an efficient integrated 'Metro Bus' service to connect other districts of Rio to the metro lines at no extra cost. These are blue and silver and easy to distinguish from regular buses. Those serving the Zona Sul run from Siqueira Campos station to Ipanema, Leblon and Gavea. The stop is outside the station on Rua Siqueira Campos.

The metro is open 5am to midnight from Monday to Saturday and 7am to 11pm on Sundays and public holidays.

Buses

You don't have to wait long for the bus in Rio – the streets are clogged with them and because there are so many they don't operate to specific timetables. Each bus route has a number, and this will be clearly marked on the front of the bus, along with the destination. On the side next to the door there's also a useful list of the main stops along the way. The fare is always marked on the front of the bus. Tickets usually cost R$2, though air-conditioned buses are slightly more expensive.

Rail

There are some commuter trains in Rio, called Supervia, operating out of the **Estação Dom Pedro II**, also known as Central do Brasil. They serve stations in the Zona Norte of the city and the outskirts but are notorious for crime.

Trams

There are two short tram lines still in existence linking the Santa Teresa district to the centre of the city. The trams, called *bondinhos*, leave from Rua Lélio Gama, about 200 metres from the Carioca metro station. There's one every 30 minutes between 7am and 8.30pm and both the lines cross the historic Arcos da Lapa and

Staying safe

Among other (better) things, Rio is famous for its violent crime. Fortunately for travellers, however, the majority of what you may read in the news occurs in the city's northern zone, far from the beaches, nightclubs and restaurants you'll frequent in the city's southern districts. Petty theft and mugging remain a possibility. Some areas should be avoided and, as in most large cities, travellers should exercise caution at all times.

Generally speaking, using city buses in Rio is not a major risk as long as you're circulating in the city's southern zone. If you have any reason to travel to the northern zone, consider taking a trusted cab driver or going with locals. Taxi drivers are for the most part trustworthy. Make sure they start the meter before you set off.

The smaller passenger vans and Volkswagen minibuses are not a good option. Their drivers are some of the most reckless, helping make Rio a traffic accident hotspot.

Neighbourhoods in Rio's southern zone are mostly safe. There are some spots, however, that you should consider avoiding during the evening.

The area that's known as the Aterro de Flamengo, its beaches and walkways, and the football courts along Rua do Flamengo should all be avoided.

The two blocks on either side of the tunnel that connects Copacabana with Ipanema at Rua Miguel Lemos on Avenida Barata Ribeiro, and the area known as the Corte Cantagalo, up Rua Miguel Lemos toward the mountain should be avoided after sunset.

A three block radius around the Copacabana nightclub Help is teeming with pickpockets and amateur muggers. The path around the lagoa should be avoided after 10pm, when most of the foot traffic dwindles to a trickle. In Ipanema, Praca General Osorio after dark is not dangerous but its proximity to a well-known favela, called Pavão, dictates caution. Praça Nosso Aúxiliador in Leblon should be avoided after dark. And Avenida Niemeyer, beyond the Sheraton hotel is not a good place to be at any time, unless you're passing by on a bus or in a cab.

Favelas, generally speaking, should be avoided at all times. They are small communities where outsiders are quickly recognised. All favelas in Rio's southern zone are controlled by organised crime groups whose members will not take kindly to random visits from unwanted gringo guests. Take an organised favela tour if you're interested, but don't arrange your own private viewing.

---

go to the Largo dos Guimarães in the centre of Santa Teresa. From there the lines split, one going to Largo das Neves, and the other, the Dois Irmãos line, to Largo França in Cosme Velho. The trams are a magnet for pickpockets; make sure all your valuables are concealed.

Vans

Along most major bus routes, you'll also find white vans operating. These have been set up by locals wanting to cash in on the demand for transport. The number of the bus routes they follow will be visible in the front window along with the destination and point of origin. They usually cost the same as ordinary buses but check when you get on board.

Water transport

There are plenty of ferries linking Rio de Janeiro to Niterói and the islands in Guanabara bay.

The Niterói ferries leave from the quays near Praça XV regularly from 6am until 12.10am. Overnight there's one ferry every hour. At weekends and during holidays there's one ferry every 30 minutes during the day. They take about 20 minutes and cost R$2.30 one way.

There are usually nine ferries a day to Paquetá island during the week and slightly fewer at the weekends. The price varies too – a single ticket costs R$4.20 Monday to Saturday and R$8,50 at weekends. The journey takes 70 minutes.

Ferries also go to the Ilha do Governador from Monday to Friday. There are ten trips a day, taking 55 minutes and costing R$3.00.

In addition to the ferries, there are also hydrofoils to Niteroi. They leave every 15 to 20 minutes and are slightly quicker with a journey taking 15 minutes. Before 5pm, the outbound ticket costs R$3, while the return costs R$5. After 5pm, the outbound ticket is R$5, and the return costs R$13.

There are also catamarans to Charitas island. They leave every 15 to 20 mins and a single ticket costs R$5.50 up to 4pm and R$6.50 after. The journey takes 15 minutes.

Taxis

Taxis in Rio are abundant, cheap and relatively safe. The most common ones are yellow (with a blue stripe down the side) and many belong to a cooperative operating out of a certain area. The name and number of the cooperative is painted on the side of each cab at the back and it's worth making a note of these in case of problems such as lost property. The meter starts at R$4.30 and there are two tariffs. Tariff 1 is used Monday to Saturday from 6am to 9pm. Overnight, on Sundays and bank holidays the meter will be set to Tariff 2, which is more expensive. If the driver tells you the meter is broken then get out and get another cab – there are enough cabs around.

There are also *taxis especiais* (special taxis), which are more expensive but safer. The fares to different parts of the city are fixed and paid in advance. The taxis can be booked either at the kiosks at the airport or over the phone. As well as the advantage of safety, *taxis especiais* also make it the driver's responsibility to make sure you leave nothing in the taxi – so if you were to leave something by mistake, you're sure to get it back at no extra cost. Below are some numbers for *taxis especiais*:

Cooptex 3272 2360
Cootramo 3976 9944
Transcoopass 2590 6891
Transcootur 2590 2300

Driving

Brazil has a terrible road safety record and drivers in Rio can be aggressive and dangerous. They hardly ever indicate, change lanes on a whim and will only step on the brake if they really have to. If you're still intent on driving around the city then there are plenty of car rental firms and all you need is to be over 25,

have a credit card and a driving licence. Although an international one is preferred, the majority of firms will happily accept foreign licences. The speed limit in cities is 80 kilometres per hour (50 miles per hour) and on highways it's 110 kilometres per hour (68 miles per hour). After 9pm, drivers won't stop at traffic lights unless there's traffic coming. This is because of a problem with car-jacking. The usual practice is to slow down approaching the junction, check the way is clear, and then carry on.

You can buy local road maps from any *livraria* (bookshop) but if you're hiring a car, the company should provide you with one.

Car hire

Away from the airports, the biggest concentration of car rental firms is on Avenida Princesa Isabel in Copacabana. There are so many within walking distance of each other that it's easy to shop around for the best price.

Europcar *Avenida Princesa Isabel 245/ABC, Copacabana (2275 0460/Call Centre 0800 703 3876).*
Hertz *Avenida Princesa Isabel 500, Copacabana (2275 7440); Aeroporto Internacional Antonio Carlos Jobim (3398 4421); Aeroporto Santos Dumont (2262 0612).*
Localiza Rent A Car *Aeroporto Internacional Antonio Carlos Jobim (3398 5445); Avenida Princesa Isabel 150, Copacabana (2275 3340); Aeroporto Santos Dumont (2220 5095).*
Unidas *Avenida Princesa Isabel 166/A, Copacabana (3685 1212); Aeroporto Internacional Antonio Carlos Jobim (3398 2286); Aeroporto Santos Dumont (2240 6715).*

Fuel stations

There are plenty of fuel stations in Rio but if you've hired a car make sure you know which type of fuel it uses. In Brazil, many cars run on alcohol or can take a mixture of both petrol and alcohol.

Parking

Like any major city, parking in Rio is tricky. Car parks aren't very common and are very expensive. Most Cariocas park on the streets but almost every stretch is claimed by *flanelinhas*, self-declared security staff who hover around while you park. The idea is that you give them a few *Reais* and in return they'll watch your car while you're away. R$2 should usually be enough. Normally you pay when you return though some may ask for it before. Some of these *flanelinhas* are officially employed by the *Prefeitura* (city council). They'll charge you in advance and should also give you a ticket for you to put on the dashboard.

Cycling

While cycling on Rio's roads involves dicing with death, the city mercifully has plenty of *ciclovias* (cycle paths) and the authorities are creating more all the time. They're an ideal way to get around and enjoy the city. The best paths are alongside the beaches starting in Leblon and ending in the Centro. There's also a *ciclovia* around the Lagoa and through Botafogo and Flamengo. There are plenty of places to rent bikes (*see p197*).

Walking

Most of Rio is fairly flat except for the favelas – and travellers are strongly advised not to venture into those unaccompanied. As a result it's perfectly possible to stroll around neighbourhoods such as Ipanema or Leblon during the day. It's always worth bearing in mind that tourists are a target for muggers anywhere in Rio at any time of day so don't be too conspicuous and keep valuables out of sight.

Resources A-Z

Age restrictions

The minimum legal age for driving, drinking, smoking and having sex in Brazil is 18.

Attitude & etiquette

Meeting people

Brazilians are known for their friendliness and openness. Compared to most of Europe and the US, they're very tactile. When greeting each other it's customary to kiss women on both cheeks. Men who know each other well will usually hug or give an arm wrestle-style handshake accompanied by a pat on the back. However, for people you don't know well, it's best to stick to a regular handshake.

In general few ordinary Brazilians speak English and will always appreciate any attempt made to speak Portuguese so a basic knowledge is useful.

When it comes to punctuality, Brazilians are notoriously unreliable, so be prepared to wait for them to turn up. Also be aware that plans often change at the last minute and social engagements can suddenly be cancelled. Culturally, it's a country where people live very much in the present and what may have seemed a good idea three days ago might later cease to be the case.

Due to the climate, Brazilians dress more casually than in Europe or the US but across the country there are regional variations. Cariocas are much less conservative than their nearest big-city neighbours in São Paulo and even when it comes to business will not necessarily wear a suit and tie. That said, they always dress neatly and are well turned out.

Although friendly, Brazilians are direct, even pushy, so be aware of this, particularly when it comes to any financial transactions. Being equally direct though polite in return will always earn respect.

Business

Doing business in Brazil is often about who you know so it helps to have personal contacts. Many clients and contractors are found through word of mouth recommendations. Most business professionals do speak basic English and are keen to use it.

Conventions & conferences

Rio has a heavy schedule of conventions and conferences and most top hotels have their own organisations (*see pp35-50*). In addition to these, there are also some dedicated convention centres.

Centro de Convenções Mario Henrique Simonsen *Avenida das Américas 3434 Bloco 8, Barra da Tijuca (3431 3509).*
Centro de Convenções Ribalta *Avenida das Américas 9650, Barra da Tijuca (2432 6015).*
Rio Convention & Visitors Bureau *Rua Visconde de Pirajá 547/610, Ipanema (2259 6165).* Map p248 D17.
Riocentro – GL Events Centro de Convenções *Avenida Salvador Allende 6555, Barra da Tijuca (2442 1300/2442 1330).*

Couriers & shippers

FedEx (*see below*) have a customer service centre and drop-off point for packages close to Galeão airport, and authorised shipping centres across the city. The Brazilian postal service (Correios; *see p230*) runs an international service (SEDEX) but there's a limit of 30 kilograms (66 pounds) and maximum size of 1.5 metres (five feet) as the sum total of the three dimensions. There are also many independent shippers.

Aguiar Comissaria de Despachos Ltda *Rua Acre 83/505, Centro (2233 8169).* Map p245 I1.
Andréia Gomes de Oliveira Rua Ruy *Porto 50B, Barra (2433 1056).*
Atrade Cargo Brasil Ltda *Avenida Vieira Souto 100/501, Ipanema (2522 1168).* Map p249 F17.
Este Asiático Comércio Navegação Ltda *Avenida Pref Dulcídio Cardoso 2800/801, Barra da Tijuca (3325 8215).*
FedEx Station *Rua Nair 135, Olaria (0800 703 3339).*
O Lisboa Despachos Internacionais Ltda *Avenida Venezuela, 27/310, Saúde (2516 8449).* Map p245 H1.
Saile Comissária de Despachos e Carga Aérea Ltda *Rua Eduardo Nadruz 490, Portuguesa (2462 1755).*

Office & computer hire

Alecsander Heiser *Avenida Passos 115, Centro (2253 1685).*
Alexandre Crispim Ferreira *Rua Visc de Inhaúma 58/204, Centro (2233 7927).*
Ana Márcia Mello Pereira *Rua Hilário Gouveia 66/504, Copacabana (2256 4022).*
Flexioffice Avenida Presidente *5th Floor, Avenida Presidente Wilson 231, Centro (2103 7600).*
Luciano Cezar Sturzeneker *Rua 2 Dezembro 78/G01, Flamengo (2557 9693).*
Novo Mundo Building *12th Floor, Avenida Presidente Wilson 164, Centro (2103 7600).*

Translators

Besides the public translators that your embassy can provide, these are recommended.

AS Campbell Tradutores Associados Ltda *Avenida Nilo Peçanha, 50 S 2605/06, Centro (2240 1315/2262 3383/2524 4624).*
Marília Rotler Oliveira Rebello *Rua Pacheco Leão, 1842/401, Jardim Botânico (2511 1509).*

Useful organisations

Amcham

5th Floor, Praça Pio X 15, Centro (3213 9200/www.amchamrio.com.br). **Map** p245 I1.
American Chamber of Commerce for Brazil.

Associação Comercial do Rio de Janeiro

11th Floor, Rua da Candelária 9, Centro (2291 1229). **Map** p245 I1.
Commercial Association of Rio de Janeiro.

Britcham

Avenida Graça Aranha 1/6, Centro (2262 5926). **Map** p245 J3.
UK Chamber of Commerce for British businesses in Brazil.

Centro de Informações das Nações Unidas

Avenida Marechal Floriano 196, Centro (2253 2211). **Map** p245 H2.
The UN Information Centre.

MRE Regional Office

Avenida Marechal Floriano 196, Centro (2263 1257/2263 5214). **Map** p245 H2.
The Ministry for Foreign Affairs is the government department that deals with foreign business.

Rio de Janeiro Stock Exchange

Bolsa de Valores do Rio de Janeiro, Praça XV de Novembro 20, Centro (2514 1069/www.bvrj.com.br). **Map** p245 J2.

Consumer

Consumers in Brazil are protected by the *Código de Defesa do Consumidor*, a law introduced in 1990. In event of trouble, the following organisations should be able to provide help and give advice.

PROCON

2nd Floor, Rua Buenos Aires 309, Centro (1512). **Map** p245 H2.
Programa Estadual de Orientação e Proteção ao Consumidor (State Programme to Guide and Protect the Consumer) is a state-run organisation that helps consumers make complaints, with a special phone number for inquiries.

Comissão de Defesa Municipal do Consumidor

0800 285 2121, 9am-5pm daily.

A freephone number run by the city council for consumer complaints and inquiries.

Defesa do Consumidor

0800 282 7060, 9am-5pm Mon-Fri.
Consumer defence hotline.

Customs

Travellers entering Brazil are allowed to bring in two litres of spirits and other goods bought at the duty-free shop, including cigarettes, worth up to US$500 dollars. In addition to this, visitors are allowed goods bought abroad worth up to US$500. Travellers returning to the UK are allowed to take one litre of spirits and one carton of cigarettes or 50 cigars. US citizens returning home are allowed one litre of spirits and goods worth up to $800.

Disabled

Acessibilidade Brasil *Rua Conde de Lages 44/502, Glória (2232 1848/3852 3559).* **Map** p245 I4.
Associação Brasileira Benficente de Reabilitação *Rua Jardim Botânico 660, Jardim Botânico (2294 6642/2294 9893).* **Map** p248 C13.

Drugs

Drug trafficking is widespread in Brazil. If you're caught trafficking, or in possession, the penalties are severe.

Electricity

Voltage across Brazil varies but in Rio de Janeiro it's 110V/60 cycles. Most sockets take both the US style flat two pins or European rounded two pins. Some hotels take 220 volts to cater for travellers.

Embassies & consulates

Australian Honorary Consulate *23rd Floor, Avenida Presidente Wilson 231, Centro (3824 4624).* **Open** 10am-7pm Mon-Fri. **Map** p245 J3.

British Consulate-General *Praia do Flamengo 284/2, Flamengo (2555 9600).* **Open** 8.30am-4.45pm Mon-Thur; 8.30am-4.30pm Fri. **Map** p247 J7.
Canadian Consulate-General *5th Floor, Avenida Atlântica 1130, Copacabana (2543 3004).* **Open** 8.30am-1pm Mon-Fri. **Map** p250 J13.
Irish Honorary Consulate *Rua 24 de Maio 347, Riachuelo (2501 8455).* **Open** 9am-1pm Mon-Fri.
New Zealand Embassy House *Brasília DF (61 3248 9900).* **Open** 8am-5pm Mon-Thur; 8am-1.30pm Fri.
US Consulate-General *Avenida Presidente Wilson 147, Centro (3823 2000).* **Open** 8am-4.45pm Mon-Fri. **Map** p245 J3.

Emergencies

The following are the emergency numbers used in Brazil; all are available 24 hours daily.

Ambulance *192*
Civil Defense *199*
Civil Police *197*
Federal Police *194*
Fire *193*
Military Police *190*

Gay & lesbian

Grupo Arco-Íris de Conscientização Homossexual

Rua Doutor Otávio Kelly 15/A, Tijuca (2552 5995). **Open** 1-7pm Mon-Thur; 1-11pm Fri.
Grupo Arco-Iris is a gay and lesbian community group with weekly meetings and support groups for people with HIV and AIDS.

Disque Defesa Homossexual

3399 1111
A helpline for victims of homophobic abuse or attacks.

Health

Brazil does offer foreign visitors emergency medical treatment for accidents and unforeseen illnesses in its public hospitals.

However, public hospitals in Brazil tend to be crowded and they are not obliged to offer treatment for existing illnesses, or once the patient's condition has become stable. All visitors are strongly advised to take out adequate health insurance before travelling to the country.

Rio is not a malaria-risk area, but there have been outbreaks of dengue fever, which is also carried by mosquitoes. While there is no vaccine against it, you can minimize risk by using insect repellent and wearing suitable clothing at night. You should have vaccinations against all major diseases including yellow fever.

Officially, tap water in Rio is supposed to be safe to drink but to avoid unnecessary risk, visitors are strongly advised only to drink water that's been filtered, or bottled water.

Should you need to seek medical advice, your embassy should have a list of doctors who can speak English

Disque-Saúde (0800 611997) is the Brazilian government's helpline for general health problems. It's open daily from 8am to 6pm but is more for practical orientation towards the right health services and for formal complaints.

Accident & emergency

Hospital Municipal Lourenço Jorge *Avenida Ayrton Senna 2000, Barra da Tijuca (3111 4600).*
Hospital Municipal Miguel Couto *Rua Mário Ribeiro 117, Gávea (3111 3600/3111 3610).* Map p2248 B16.
Hospital Municipal Paulino Werneck *Estrada da Cacuia 745, Ilha do Governador (3111 7700).*
Hospital Municipal Salgado Filho *Rua Arquias Cordeiro 370, Méier (3111 4100/3111 4177).*
Hospital Municipal Souza Aguiar *Praça da República 111, Centro (3111 2600/3111 2729).* Map p244 G3.

Complementary medicine

Rio's *prefeitura* (city council) offers complementary treatments, like acupuncture, massage therapy, homeopathy

Travel advice

For current information on travel to a specific country, including the latest news on health issues, safety and security, local laws and customs, contact your home country's government department of foreign affairs. Most have websites with useful advice for would-be travellers.

Australia
www.smartraveller.gov.au

Canada
www.voyage.gc.ca

New Zealand
www.safetravel.govt.nz

Republic of Ireland
http://foreignaffairs.gov.ie

United Kingdom
www.fco.gov.uk/travel

USA
http://travel.state.gov

and tai chi at some of its health centres around the city (called *'centros'* or *'postos de saude'*, *see below* **Contraception & abortion**). There are also two homeopathic pharmacies:

Farmacia Homeopatica Aymore *Rua 7 de Setembro 219, Centro (2221 0573).* Map p245 I2.
Medkatus *Avenida Ataulfo de Paiva 1079/219, Leblon (2540 8110).* Map p248 B17.

Contraception & abortion

Abortion in Brazil is illegal. Contraceptives like the pill and condoms are offered free of charge at all the *prefeitura*'s *centros de saude* such as the ones listed below. You can also get all types of contraceptives from pharmacies (*see below*).

Centro Municipal de Saúde João Barros Barreto *Rua Tonelero 262, Copacabana (2549 2769/2547 7122/2256 2202).* Map p249 H14.
Centro Municipal de Saúde Manoel José Ferreira *Rua Silveira Martins 161, Flamengo (2225 7505/3862 2019).* Map p245 I6.
Centro Municipal de Saúde Píndaro de Carvalho Rodrigues *Avenida Padre Leonel Franca, s/n°, Gávea (2511 2619/2274 2796/ 2274 6495).* Map p248 A16.
Posto de Saúde Fernando Antônio Braga Lopes *Rua Carlos Seidl 1388, Caju (2580 2024/3860 2613).*

Dentists

There's no shortage of dentists in Rio and the stiff competition means it's quite common to find dental flyers being given out on street corners. For emergency work, the Prefeitura's *postos de saude* deal with dental problems. The following private practices also offer 24 hour emergency call outs.

My Way Odontologia *Avenida Nossa Senhora de Copacabana 749/601, Copacabana (3208 1908/9699 7490).*
Simone Fabiano Alves *Rua Visconde de Pirajá 111/314, Ipanema (2521 2448).*

Hospitals

The main hospitals are listed above (*see above* **Accident & emergency**). Check with medical insurers for other doctors and hospitals.

Opticians

See p147.

Pharmacies

See p147.

STDs, HIV & AIDS

Treatment of HIV and AIDS in Brazil is highly sophisticated

Directory

and once again, the first port of call is one of the Prefeitura's *postos de saude*, listed above. The gay community group Arco-Íris has a support group for people with HIV and AIDS (*see p226* **Gay & lesbian**). Disque-Aids (2518 2221) also run a helpline for people with HIV and AIDS on weekdays from noon to 8pm.

Helplines

The following helplines should have someone on duty who can speak some basic English, though they are principally for Portuguese speakers.

Alcoólicos Anônimos 2233 4813/2235 3086
Coordenadoria de Prevenção ao Uso Indevido de Drogas (Drug helpline) 2588 9016
Disque-Mulher (Women's helpline) 2299 2121
Narcóticos Anônimos 2533 5015
Neuróticos Anônimos 2233 0220/ 2233 6053
Nepad – Atendimento a Dependentes de Drogas (Drug helpline) 2589 3269/2587 7163/2587 7148/2589 4309.

ID

In Brazil everyone is required by law to carry identification. As foreign visitors are advised not to carry important documents, a certified copy of the main page of the passport is acceptable. You can get photocopies certified at any *Oficio de Notas* (notary).

Insurance

All visitors to Brazil are strongly advised to take out comprehensive travel insurance (including medical insurance) before travelling.

Internet

There are dozens of internet cafes all over Rio. Most of them are in the main tourist districts like Copacabana and Ipanema. Prices vary from R$3 to $12 per hour of use. Most hotels also have internet access and some ordinary cafés and restaurants are beginning to offer free Wi-Fi connections.

Language

Written Portuguese can often be guessed at by English speakers and much more so by Spanish speakers, but it's strangely unphonetic when spoken and can take some getting used to. A little knowledge of Portuguese can go a long way.

Left luggage

Twenty-four hour left luggage is available in the airports and the Novo Rio bus station. At Galeão, the left luggage is at Terminal 1 on the second floor in the Green Area (3398 3141). The cost of leaving one item for 24 hours is between R$7 and $12. The same company has a left-luggage desk at Santos Dumont airport, open from 6am until midnight daily.

There are two left-luggage counters at Novo Rio bus station (2263 8581), one in departures and the other in arrivals. It costs R$8 to leave a normal sized suitcase for 24 hours.

Legal help

It's best to contact your consulate or embassy for any legal help (see above). The following are English-speaking solicitors with experience of dealing with foreign clients

Gustavo Villela Filho *11th & 12th Floors, Rua Rodrigo Silva 18, Centro (2220 8210)*. **Map** p245 I2.
Paulo Lins e Silva *9th Floor, Rua Visconde de Pirajá 351, Ipanema (2522 3030)*. **Map** p249 F17.
Pedro Jardim de Mattos *Rua Visconde de Pirajá 463/201, Ipanema (3204 3168)*. **Map** p249 F17.

Libraries

The largest library in Brazil is the Biblioteca Nacional (*see below*). Most of its archive is in Portuguese, but it does have many English books and periodicals.

Biblioteca Nacional *Avenida Rio Branco 219, Centro (3095 3879)*. **Open** 9am-7.30pm Mon-Fri; 9am-2.30pm Sat. **Map** p245 J3.

Lost property

If you lose anything on public transport then contact the bus or taxi company you were travelling with in the unlikely event that it's been handed in.

Media

Magazines

Epoca

A recent rival to the well-established *Veja*, it covers similar issues and has a very similar format.

Isto é

Another quality magazine focused more on politics and the economy.

Veja

A quality weekly magazine covering all issues, from current affairs and the economy to religion and health.

Newspapers

O Globo

This broadsheet is the staple read for most middle-class Cariocas. Although it's a Rio newspaper it offers informed national and international stories and comment. It also has an extensive classified listings, especially on Sundays.

O Dia

A tabloid alternative to *O Globo*, this newspaper is thinner on current affairs but has plenty of sensational crime stories and more celebrity news and gossip.

Extra

A stablemate of *O Globo*, *Extra* was launched to appeal to the masses and to compete with *O Dia*. Its news values are aimed at the working and lower middle classes.

Jornal do Brasil

Once a mighty and well-respected newspaper, the *Jornal* used to be the preferred choice of politicians and people of influence. It's still regarded as a quality read, though financial difficulties mean it's trying to reinvent itself.

Television

Bandeirantes

This is a serious channel with considered dramas and documentaries as well as political and religious programmes.

Globo

The powerhouse of Brazilian TV, this is the channel with the flamboyant *telenovelas* exported around the world. They're usually on between 6pm and 8pm, with one more after the evening news. It also usually secures the rights to major sporting events.

Record

The oldest TV channel in Brazil, Record is popular for its *telenovelas* and variety shows.

Rede TV

A pop culture channel with plenty of celebrity gossip programmes.

SBT

This is Brazil's second most popular channel after Globo. It has many chat shows and game shows with studio audiences.

TVE

This is an educational TV channel with different regional networks including one in Rio. It's run by the government's Ministry of Education and broadcasts documentaries.

Money

The Brazilian currency is the *real* (plural, *reais*) and hovers around two to the US dollar and four to the British pound.

Denominations of bank notes are 100 (light blue), 50 (brown), 20 (yellow), ten (red or blue/orange plastic), five (purple), two (dark blue) and one (green). There's also a one *real* coin.

A real is made up of 100 *centavos* and there are coin denominations of 50, 25, 10 and 5. Confusingly, there are two types of coin for each – and some look remarkably similar. One *centavo* coins also exist but are rarely used.

When paying small amounts of money (for example on the bus or to a street vendor) don't use high denomination notes. They won't be able to change them.

Banks & ATMs

There are banks on every corner in Brazil and you'll always find a foyer of ATMs inside. However, not all of them will accept foreign cards – look for the appropriate symbol on the machine. Most ATM foyers used to close after 10pm because of the risk of *seqüestros* where people are held up and forced to withdraw cash at gun-point. These days some foyers stay open 24 hours but it's not a good idea to withdraw cash after dark in Rio. There has also been a rise in card cloning, with security staff inside banks using CCTV to get pin numbers. Cover your hands when punching in the number and never leave the withdrawal receipt in the bank.

It's pretty much impossible for a foreigner to open a bank account in Brazil unless you're willing to invest a small fortune in the country. Even then bureaucracy means it's a lengthy and frustrating process. A common way to receive money in Brazil is through Western Union.

Bureaux de change & travellers' cheques

Travellers cheques are becoming increasingly difficult to use and are rarely accepted by businesses. You can change them in banks and some bureaux de change but the rates are much worse than for cash. Banks generally have worse exchange rates than bureaux, plus they charge commission for exchanging both foreign currency and travellers' cheques. It's better to compare prices in the many bureaux de change found in Copacabana, Ipanema or the Centro. **American Express** *Hotel Copacabana Palace, Avenida Atlântica 1702/01 (Customer call centre 0800 702 0777).*

Credit cards

Credit cards are accepted in the vast majority of places in Rio. The most popular are Visa (V), MasterCard (MC) and American Express (AmEx) although Diners Club (DC) is often accepted too.

Lost & stolen cards

American Express *0800 78 50 50*
Diners Card *4001 4444*
Mastercard & Visa *4001 4456*

Tax

Brazil doesn't have a uniform sales tax as such, but every manufacturer, distributor, retailer or provider of most types of merchandise is required to pay the state ICMS tax (*Imposto sobre Circulação de Mercadorias e prestação de Serviços*). However, since this tax is a hidden one and the percentage paid on different goods varies, it's difficult to establish how much it is.

Natural hazards

Recently, prolonged torrential rain during the summer has lead to landslides in the state of Rio de Janeiro. So far though this has not affected the city itself. The rain can cause disruption to transport though so take that into account when travelling during inclement weather. Rio is not affected by malaria, however there have been cases of dengue fever, a potentially life-threatening illness also carried by mosquitos. There's no vaccine against it but you can minimise the risk by using repellent and wearing appropriate clothing at night.

Opening hours

Banks

These are open from Monday to Friday, 10am until 4pm.

Directory

Bars

There are as many different opening hours as there are bars. Those serving food will usually open at lunchtime, others in the early evening. Closing time can be anywhere from 11pm up until when the last person leaves.

Business hours

Office hours are usually from 9am until 6pm, Monday to Friday.

Post offices

All branches are open from 9am to 5pm from Monday to Saturday. Some of the larger branches are also open on Saturdays from 9am to 1pm.

Shops

Generally shops open from 9am until 7pm on weekdays and 9am until 1pm on Saturdays – though many will stay open on Saturday afternoon. Shopping Centres are generally open from 10am until 10pm, Monday to Saturday and 3pm to 9pm on Sundays.

Police

There are three different types of police force in Rio; visitors wishing to report a crime should go to the *Delegacia Especial de Atendimento ao Turista* (Tourist Police). The office is open round the clock and staff speak reasonable English. The main office of the Policia Federal is where visitors need to go to extend visas. For emergency numbers, *see p226*.

Delegacia Especial de Atendimento ao Turista *Avenida Afrânio de Melo Franco 159, Leblon (3399 7170).* Map p248 C16.
Policia Federal *Avenida Venezuela 2, Centro 2203 4000/2203 4183).* **Open** 8am-4pm Mon-Fri. Map p245 H1.

Postal services

Brazil's postal service is called Correios and their post offices and boxes are easy to spot because of the clear branding (blue lettering on a yellow background).

Ordinary international airmail costs R$1.70 to send up to 20 grams anywhere in the world, but the service is irregular and mail can take up to one month to arrive. There's a priority service to most countries that costs between R$2 and R$2.50 for the first 20 grams and takes five to 11 working days. Then there's an express service (EMS) that costs R$60 to the US, R$64 to the UK and R$67 to Australia for up to 500 grams. EMS takes three to five working days to arrive.

For information on couriers and shipping, *see p225*. The main post office branches are listed below, all open 9am to 5pm Monday to Friday as well as any extra times noted.

Empresa Brasileira de Correios e Telégrafos

Rua Primeiro de Março 64, Centro (2219 5315); Avenida Presidente Vargas 3077, Centro (2273 5998/ 2273 5360/2503 8467); Praia de Botafogo 324, Botafogo (2503 8496/2226 1122); Avenida Nossa Senhora de Copacabana 540/A, Copacabana (2256 1439/2256 1448); Rua Prudente de Moraes 147, Ipanema (2521 1543/2521 1845); Rua Visconde de Pirajá 452/ss box 7, Ipanema (2267 6197); Avenida Ataulfo de Paiva 822, Leblon (2503 8388); Aeroporto Internacional do Rio de Janeiro, Avenida 20 de Janeiro s/n, Ilha do Governador (3367 6028).

Poste restante

Any mail sent to Rio de Janeiro with no further address would end up at the Central Post Office in Rua Primeiro de Março. But you can also send *postas restantes* to any other post office in Rio if you use the full address. The addressee can pick up the mail with ID.

Religion

There are as many different religions in Brazil as there are exotic fruit juices. So while it's the world's biggest Catholic country, it also has the world's largest Spiritualist community and there are plenty of other beliefs, including African ones brought by the slaves such as Candomblé and the hybrid Umbanda.

Anglican
Igreja de Cristo *Rua Real Grandeza 99, Botafogo (2226 7332).* **Services** 8am, 10.30am Sun; 9am Tue. Map p246 G11.
Capela de Nossa Senhora das Mercês *Rua Visconde de Caravelas 48, Botafogo (2266 8297).* **Services** 9.30am Sun. Map p246 G11.

Baptist
Igreja Batista Internacional *Rua Desembargador Alfredo Russel 146, Leblon (2239 8848).* **Services** 10.30am, 7pm Sun; 8am Tue; 7.30pm Wed. Map p248 B16.

Buddhist
Sociedade de Budismo Tibetano *Estrada dos Bandeirantes 25636, Recreio dos Bandeirantes (2428 6711/2428 1245).*

Candomblé
Ilê Asé D'Osalà *Rua Seridó Lote 20 Quadra 16, Nova Iguaçú (2556 9009/2557 2139).* **Services** 4pm Mon, Sat.

Jewish
Associação Religiosa Israelita *Rua General Severiano 170, Botafogo (2543 6320/2295 6599).* **Services** 6.30pm Fri, 9.30am Sat. Map p247 I11.

Methodist
Igreja Metodista do Jardim Botanico *Rua Jardim Botanico 648, Jardim Botanico (2294 9179).* **Services** 9am-7pm Sun; 8pm Tue, Thur; 3.30pm Wed; 8am Fri. Map p248 C13.

Muslim
Sociedade Beneficente Muçulmana *Avenida Gomes Freire 176/205, Centro (2224 1079).* **Services** 10am-noon, 1-5pm daily. Map p245 H3.

Orthodox (Greek)
Igreja Santo André *Rua Darque de Mattos 46, Bonsucesso (2590 3735).* **Services** 11am, 2nd & last Sundays of the month.

Orthodox (Russian)
Igreja Ortodoxa Russa Santa Zinaida *Rua Monte Alegre 210, Santa Teresa (2252 1471).* **Services** 10am Sun. **Map** p244 G5.

Roman Catholic
Catedral Metropolitano de São Sebastião *Avenida República do Chile 245, Centro (2240 2669).* **Services** 11am Mon-Fri, 10am Sat, Sun. **Map** p245 I3.

Spiritualism
União das Sociedades Espíritas do Estado do Rio de Janeiro *Rua dos Inválidos 182, Centro (2224 1244).* **Services** 2.30pm Mon, Tue; 7pm Thur. **Map** p245 H3.

Umbanda
Centro Espírita Caminheiros de Verdade *Rua Comendador João Carneiro de Almeida 133, Engenho de Dentro (2594 6336).* **Services** 6pm Mon, Thur, Sat; Kardecism 6pm Tue.

Safety & security

Thousands of tourists visit Rio every year and never encounter any problems. However, levels of mugging, often involving weapons, are high so it's wise to take precautions. Only carry around with you the money you need for any trip and avoid wearing jewellery or watches that look expensive. Keep other valuables such as phones or cameras out of sight and, rather than using a rucksack for carrying belongings, use a supermarket bag. Dress down and dress like the locals too so that you don't stand out as a tourist. Never attempt to resist muggers. More often than not they'll be carrying weapons and aren't afraid to use them.

See also p223 **Staying safe**.

Smoking

Brazil doesn't yet have the stringent anti-smoking laws in place across much of Europe and the US. Having said that, smoking is not as common as in neighbouring countries in South America. Many bars and restaurants choose to have a no smoking policy. Others

have ashtrays on the table. If in doubt, ask. Smoking is banned on all public transport.

Study

Hundreds of students from all around the world come to study in Rio, spending anything from a few months to a year. The trips are organised through their academic institutions back home that have links with universities here. There are many universities in Rio – mostly privately owned. Only the largest are listed here.

Universidade Candido Mendes *Edifício Candido Mendes, Rua da Assembléia 10 (Terreo), Centro (0800 282 5353/www.ucam.edu.br).* **Map** p245 J2.

Universidade Estácio de Sá *Rua do Bispo 83, Rio Comprido (3231 0000/www.estacio.br).* **Map** p252 D6.

Universidade Estadual do Rio de Janeiro *7th Floor, Bloco F, Rua São Francisco Xavier 524, Maracanã (2567 7209/2587 7385/2587 7435/ www.uerj.br).*

Universidade Federal do Rio de Janeiro *2nd Floor, Avenida Pedro Calmon 500, Cidade Universitária (2562 2010/www.ufrj.br).*

PUC Rio (Pontifícia Universidade Católica do Rio de Janeiro) *8th Floor, International Programs Central Coordination Office, Rua Marquês de São Vicente 225, Edifício Padre Leonel França, Gávea (3527 1578/ www.puc-rio.br).* **Map** p253 F2.

Language classes

For foreigners wanting to learn Portuguese, there are plenty of language schools to choose from, including these three:

Bridge Lingua Tec *Avenida Nilo Peçanha 151/201, Centro (2220 8659).* **Map** p245 I2.

Mais Brasil *Avenida Rio Branco 181/103, Centro (2533 0065/2532 1537).* **Map** p245 I2.

Plan Idiomas Direcionados *Avenida Presidente Wilson 164/101, Centro (2544 0440/2491 3116).* **Map** p245 J3.

Telephones

Since the privatisation of the telecommunications industry in Brazil, the system has become complicated. There are

several companies competing for the market and they each have a two-digit code, so that for long distance or international calls you choose which company you wish to use by including the code in the number.

CTBC	12
Brasil Telecom	14
Embratel	21
Intelig	23
GVT	25
Telemar/Oi	31
TIM	41

Dialling & codes

All telephone numbers in Brazil have eight digits. Each area also has a two-digit area code. The main ones are:

São Paulo	11
Rio de Janeiro	21
Belo Horizonte	31
Curitiba	41
Porto Alegre	51
Brasília	61
Salvador	71
Recife	81
Belém	91

To call long distance, you dial as follows: 0 + telecom company code + area code + eight-digit number.

So, to call Salvador from Rio using Telemar, you would dial: 0 31 71 followed by the eight digit number.

With international calls you also have to use the telecom company code; the sequence is: 00 + telecom company code + country code + area code + number.

So, to call a number in London, UK using Embratel, you would dial: 00 21 44 207 + number.

Mobile phones

Mobile phones in Brazil use 900Mhz and 1800Mhz wavelengths, as in Europe, and in some cases the 850Mhz wavelength used in the US. If you wish to use your own mobile in Brazil you'll have to check that it uses these bands (European dual band phones will get good coverage but US ones will not).

Directory

To use a Brazilian SIM card, make sure your phone is unlocked. Pay-as-you go SIM cards (called *chips*) are very cheap, costing around R$20, and most of the mobile phone companies offer them in their shops. Mobile phone companies often have counters in electronics shops and department stores too. To buy one, all you need are your passport details and an address. You can then add credit by buying top-up cards available in newsstands and phone shops. Mobile phones are also available for rent.

Operator services

There's no single operator service since each different telecom company seems to have its own.

To make local reverse charge (collect) calls without going via an operator, dial 90 90 + the number you wish to dial.

To make national or international reverse charge calls, dial 90 + telecom company number + area/country code + number.

Business directory enquiries
0800 703 2100
Calls via operator 101 (24 hours)
Directory enquiries 102 (24 hours)
Embratel operator services
0800 902 111
Intelig operator services 103 23
International directory enquiries 0800 703 2111
National rates 108 (24 hours)
Reverse-charge (collect) calls
0800 703 2121
Reverse-charge calls via operator 107 (24 hours)
Speaking clock 130.
Telemar operator services
103 31

Public phones

There are plenty of public phones in Brazil. They're the large, light-blue shells that can be found on pavements and are called *orelhões* – 'large ears'. You need a card (*cartão telefónico*) to use them. These can be bought at newspaper

stands or shops. The most expensive time to call is between 8am and 8pm weekdays. The cheapest is between 11pm and 6am or on Sundays.

Some international phone cards exist where you call a freephone (0800) number and then punch in a pin number from the back of the card. However, they're not nearly as cheap as the ones found in Europe or the US.

An alternative to public phones are phone centres. There are plenty of them, especially in Copacabana and Ipanema. However, check out the cost in several different ones first because prices can vary a great deal.

Time

Rio de Janeiro is three hours behind GMT, which then becomes four hours behind during the northern hemisphere summer. However, Rio has daylight saving during its own summer. Clocks go forward an hour at the end of November and go back again in late February. During these three months, Rio is just two hours behind GMT.

Tipping

Brazil doesn't have a big tipping culture. Restaurants and bars with table service will add a ten per cent service charge to the bill automatically so there's no need to add any more. It's also not customary to tip taxi drivers. At the most, you might round up the fare to the nearest *real*. Occasions when tips are given are for home deliveries (water, shopping), for porters in hotels and in the hairdressers.

Toilets

Unfortunately, the only public toilets used in Rio seem to be the pavements, especially

during Carnival. Nor do staff in bars and restaurants take kindly to people wandering in just to use their toilets. The best thing to do is to pick a bar that's too busy for them to notice or to buy something cheap. Shopping malls are also a good bet for clean, decent facilities.

Tourist information

The best source of tourist information is the department of the *Prefeitura* (local authority) dedicated to tourism, called Riotur. They have a detailed website in both Portuguese and English www.riode janeiro-turismo.com.br. They have a phone information line in English too called Alô Rio (0800 285 0555 or 2542 8080), open Monday to Friday from 9am to 6pm.

There are also tourist information kiosks in the following locations.

International Airport
Terminal 1 International Arrival Hall, Blue Area (3398 4077). **Open** 6am-11pm daily. *Terminal 1 Domestic Flights Arrival Hall, Green Area (3398 3034).* **Open** 7am-11pm daily. *Terminal 2 International Arrival Hall (3398 2245).* **Open** 6am-midnight daily. *Terminal 2 Domestic Flights Arrival Hall (3398 2246).* **Open** 6am-midnight daily.

Novo Rio Bus Station Arrival Hall
Avenida Francisco Bicalho 1, Santo Cristo (2263 4857). **Open** 7am-7pm daily. **Map** p244 D1.

RioTur Information Centre
Avenida Princesa Isabel 183, Copacabana (2541 7522/2542 8004/2542 8080). **Open** 9am-6pm Mon-Fri. **Map** p250 J13.

Secretaria Especial de Turismo
9th & 10th Floors, Praça Pio X 11, 9/10th Floor, Centro (2588 9146/7). **Map** p245 I1. Federal government tourism department.

Directory

TurisRio Information Centre

Rua México 125, Centro (0800 282 2007/2544 7992/www.turisrio. rj.gov.br). **Open** 9am-6pm Mon-Fri. **Map** p245 J3.
Rio de Janeiro state tourist office.

Visas & immigration

Foreign visitors from the United Kingdom, Ireland and New Zealand do not need a visa to enter Brazil, but do need a passport valid for at least six months prior to departure. United States, Canadian and Australian citizens do need a visa and will have to apply to the Brazilian embassy at their country of origin before travelling. Visitors are allowed an initial stay in Brazil of up to 90 days. This period can be extended for a further 90 days by applying to the Policia Federal. A fee is involved. If you over-stay, you'll be fined at the airport on the day of your departure. If you're visiting Brazil from a country affected by yellow fever it's compulsory to have a vaccination certificate, which you'll need to show when you arrive.

Weights & measures

Brazil is completely metric. Distances are measured in metres and kilometres, liquids in litres and weights in kilograms. Temperatures are only ever given in Celsius.

When to go

Climate

Rio is just within the tropics and has the temperatures and rainfall to match. The summer months are from December to March and winter from June to August, although it doesn't

really experience seasons in the way Europe and the US do. It's generally wetter during the summer than during winter, although there's always the chance of a huge downpour at any time of year.

Public holidays

New Year's Day 1 Jan.
Carnival Mon & Tue before Ash Wednesday (6 Feb 2008; 25 Feb 2009).
Good Friday Fri 21 Mar 2008; Fri 19 Apr 2009.
Easter Sunday Sun 23 Mar 2008; Sun 21 April 2009.
Tiradentes Day 12 Apr.
St George's Day (Rio de Janeiro city only) 23 Apr.
Labour Day 1 May.
Corpus Christi June (varies).
Independence Day 7 Sept.
Children's Day 12 Oct.
All Soul's Day 2 Nov.
Proclamation of the Republic Day 15 Nov.
Black Awareness Day 20 Nov.
Christmas Day 25 Dec.

Women

Although the Latin American macho male mentality exists in Brazil, it's not as intense as in neighbouring countries. Brazilian men like to flirt and are not subtle about it, but they're rarely aggressive and will usually take a brush-off in good humour. The

testosterone kicks in when they get behind the wheel.

There's a special division of the Policia Civil dedicated to women, called the *Divisão de Polícia de Atendimento à Mulher*. The office in Rio is at Rua Visconde do Rio Branco 12 (3399 3370, 2224 6643). Female officers are on hand to deal with victims of sexual abuse and domestic violence.

There's also an excellent helpline for women who are the victims of violence (*see p228* **Helplines**).

Working in Rio de Janeiro

Any foreigner wishing to work in Brazil must have a temporary work visa. To obtain this, the employer will have to apply to Brazil's Ministry of Labour and Employment (Esplanada dos Ministérios, Bloco F, Brasília, 3317 6000) to obtain authorisation. Foreigners looking to invest in Brazil will naturally find it easier to obtain a visa. However, you have to invest in excess of 50 thousand US dollars to be able to set up your own company here.

Weather report

Average daytime temperatures in Rio de Janeiro

Month	Average high	Average low
January	29°C (84°F)	23°C (69°F)
February	29°C (84°F)	23°C (67°F)
March	28°C (80°F)	22°C (63°F)
April	27°C (73°F)	21°C (57°F)
May	25°C (66°F)	19°C (51°F)
June	24°C (60°F)	18°C (46°F)
July	24°C (59°F)	17°C (45°F)
August	24°C (63°F)	18°C (48°F)
September	24°C (66°F)	18°C (50°F)
October	25°C (73°F)	19°C (55°F)
November	26°C (78°F)	20°C (56°F
December	28°C (83°F)	22°C (65°F)

Language & Vocabulary

Written Portuguese seems reassuringly familiar if you speak Spanish, with many recognisable words. The shock comes when you hear it spoken. The pronunciations given in this section are specifically for Portuguese as spoken in Rio. Brazilian accents vary widely but if you can understand Cariocas, you should have no problem with people from other regions.

Pronunciation

Once you know how each letter is pronounced, Portuguese is actually pretty much phonetic. Stress falls on the penultimate syllable in most words, on the last syllable for words ending in consonants (except for **s**, and in most cases **m**). Words with accents have the stress on the syllable with the accent.

Vowels

Many Portuguese vowel sounds are nasal and don't really have equivalents in English. Nasal vowels in written Portuguese are usually seen with a tilda (~) over the **o** or **a**.

ão is similar to the 'oun' in lounge but is much more nasal.
ãe is like the 'in' in mine, again more nasal.
õe is similar to the 'oin' in boing.

Some vowels are also nasalised when they're followed by **m** or **n** at the end of a syllable. An example of this everyone will hear here is in *sim* (yes).

a is close to the English *a* in cat
e is like the English *ey* in they
é or **ê** is like the English 'e' in bet
e unstressed at the end of a word is like the English 'ea' in tea
i is also pronounced like 'ea' in tea
o is usually like the English 'o' in local
ó, ô and occasionally stressed **o** is like the 'o' in hot
final **o** is like the 'oo' in foot
u is also pronounced like the 'oo' in 'foot'

Consonants

The letters **b**, **f**, **k**, **p**, **v** and **w** are pronounced as in English. So are **d**, **g** and **t**, except when they're followed by **i** or an unstressed **e**. In these cases they are softened: **d** becomes like the dg in *judge*; **t** becomes like the ch in *cheese*; **g** becomes like the **s** in *pleasure*. This sound is also the way to pronounce the Portuguese **j**.
c is hard like the c in *canal*, except when it has a cedilla (ç) or is followed by **e** or **i**, which soften the sound to like the c in *ceiling*.
h is always silent.
When **l** follows a vowel it becomes like an English **w**.
lh together make the sound like the lli in *million*.
m and **n** at the end of a word or syllable and immediately following a vowel will nasalise the vowel.
r at the beginning or end of a word, and **rr**, are pronounced like the Scottish ch in *loch*.
s is like the English **s** except when it's between two vowels when it's pronounced like an English **z**. In the middle of a word followed by a consonant it's pronounced either like the **s** in *pleasure* or like the English **sh** depending on the consonant.
x is usually pronounced like the English **sh**, but can sometimes be pronounced like the English **s** or **x**.

Basics

hello *oi*
good morning *bom dia*
good afternoon *boa tarde*
good evening/night *boa noite*
yes *sim*
no *não*
maybe *talvez/pode ser*
how are you? *como vai?*
Sir/Mr *Senhor*;
Madam/Mrs/Ms *Senhora*
please *por favor*
thanks *obrigado* (or *obrigada*)
sorry *desculpe/perdão*
excuse me *com licença*
I don't speak Portuguese *não falo português*; do you speak English? *você fala inglês?*
I don't understand *não entendo*
good *bom/boa*; well *bem*
bad/badly *mal/ruim*
small *pequeno*; big *grande*
a bit *um pouco*; a lot/very *muito*
with *com*; without *sem*
and *e*; also *também*
this *este/esta*; that *aquele/aquela*
because *porque*
what? *o quê?*; who? *quem?*; when? *quando?*; which? *qual?*; why? *por quê?*; how? *como?*; where? *onde?*; where to? *para onde?*

I am English *sou inglês/inglesa*; Irish *irlandês/irlandesa*; American *dos Estados Unidos*; Canadian *canadense*; Australian *australiano/a*; a New Zealander *neozelandês/neozelandesa*.
what time is it? *qué horas são?*
forbidden *proibido*
out of order *não funciona*
bank *banco*; post office *correios*

Emergencies

Help! *socorro!*
I'm sick *estou doente*
I need a doctor/hospital *preciso de um médico/um hospital*
there's a fire! *tem um incêndio!*

Getting around

airport *aeroporto*
station *estação*
ticket *passagem*
single *ida*; return *ida e volta*
bus/coach station *rodoviária*
entrance *entrada*; exit *saída*
left *esquerda*; right *direita*
straight on *direto/em frente*
street *rua*; avenue *avenida*;
motorway *estrada*
map *um mapa*
speed limit *limite de velocidade*
petrol *gasolina*

Shopping

how much? *quanto custa?*
expensive *caro*; cheap *barato* sale *liquidação*
is there... /are there... *tem... /têm...* I would like... *eu gostaria de...* can you give me a discount? *tem desconto?*
what size? *qual tamanho?*
can I try it on? *posso experimentar?*

Days, months & seasons

morning *manhã*; afternoon *tarde*
night *noite*; tomorrow *amanhã*; yesterday *ontem.*
Monday *segunda-feira (2ª)*;
Tuesday *terça-feira (3ª)*;
Wednesday *quarta-feira (4ª)*;
Thursday *quinta-feira (5ª)*;
Friday *sexta-feira (6ª)*;
Saturday *sábado*; Sunday *domingo*
January *janeiro*; February *fevereiro*; March *março*;
April *abril*; May *maio*; June *junho*;
July *julho*; August *agosto*;
September *setembro*; October *outubro*; November *novembro*;
December *dezembro*

Further Reference

Books

Non-fiction

Alex Bellos *Futebol: The Brazilian Way of Life* All about football and its influence on the culture. *See pp30-34.*
Sarah de Carvalho *The Street Children of Brazil* It takes a higher calling to give up everything and work amongst foreign street kids. A bold account of one such journey.
Ruy Castro *Rio de Janeiro* The biographer of Garrincha and Bossa Nova writes on his own city.
Barbara Danusia *Restaurantes do Rio 2007* The tried and trusted annual roundup of Rio's eateries, with an English translation included.
Marshall C Eakin *Brazil: The Once and Future Country* A clear account of the country's troubled present bookended between an enviable past and future.
Marc Ferrez *O Rio Antigo* Fascinating photos of all parts of the city taken by the photographer between 1865 and 1918.
Gilberto Freyre *The Masters and the Slaves: A Study in the Development of Brazilian Civilization.* A groundbreaking work on slavery written in the 1930s that helped to redefine the country.
Joseph A Page *The Brazilians* A readable and insightful introduction to the country and its people.
Fernando Tasso Fragoso Pires *Fazendas The Great Houses and Planatations of Brazil* A gorgeous coffeetable book about historic coffee fazendas in and around Rio.
Patrick Wilcken *Empire Adrift* The very entertaining story of the Portuguese Court in Rio 1808-1821.

Literature

Jorge Amado *Dona Flor and Her Two Husbands* Magic and comedy from Brazil's best author – made into a successful film in 1978.
Machado de Assis *Dom Casmurro* Published in 1899, this classic and tragic tale of love set in Rio de Janeiro is a realist masterpiece.
Chico Buarque *Budapeste* Brazil's answer to Ishiguro goes on a surreal tour through Rio and Hungary.
Paulo Coelho *The Alchemist* Rio's most famous literary export is known for his philosophy rather than his style. This is his biggest work.
Rubem Fonseca *The Lost Manuscript* A hardboiled tale of crime and Carnival.
Paulo Lins *Cidade de Deus* The original novel whose author was

himself born and bred in the City of God housing estate. In parts even more shocking than the film.
Clarice Lispector *The Hour of the Star* A short and disturbing masterpiece telling the adventures of a poor girl from the north east who comes to Rio in search of a new life.
Nelson Rodrigues *The Wedding Dress* Brazil's first modern play and a big success for Rio's most celebrated dramatist.

Film

Central do Brasil (*Central Station*) dir. *Walter Salles* (1998) Part travelogue, part neo-realist fable, the film works as well as the director refuses to play up the sentimentality.
Cidade de Deus (*City of God*) dir. *Fernando Meirelles* (2002) A global hit which also caused a rethink of security issues. Look too for City of Men, a telenovela produced by the same people and now out on DVD.
Flying down to Rio dir. *Thornton Freeland* (1933) Featuring both the first pairing of Fred and Ginger and the classic line: 'What have these South Americans got below the equator that we haven't?'
Madame Satã dir. *Karim Aïnouz* (2002) A film about the true-life trials of transvestite João Francisco (aka Madame Satã) in 1920s Lapa features a rich ambience and a great performance by Lazaro Romero.
Notícias de uma guerra particular (*News From a Private War*) dir. *Kátia Lund and João Moreira Salles* (1999) Sharp social analysis and a dynamic shooting and editing style in this exemplary documentary on the forces at play in the drug battles of Rio's favelas.
O Caminho das Nuvens (*The Middle of the World*) dir. *Vicente Amorim* (2003) A touching story starring Claudia Abreu, one of Brazil's best actors. Terrific.
O Primeiro Dia (*Midnight*) dir *Walter Salles and Daniela Thomas* (1998) Betrayal, sin, redemption and rebirth against the backdrop of the world's biggest New Year's Eve celebration. A sensual feast.
Orpheu Negro (*Black Orpheus*) dir. *Marcel Camus* (1959) Backstage Carnival footage, breathtaking views and a landmark soundtrack.
Rio Babilônia dir. *Neville de Almeida* (1982) Dismissed by some as pornography and lauded by others as a brutally insightful portrayal of the decadence of upper-class Cariocas, this film still makes waves.
Vinicius dir. *Miguel Faria Jr.* (2005) Documentary about the life and loves

of one of the founders of Bossa Nova, Vinicius de Moraes. Includes fine archive footage of Rio and interviews with most of his nine wives.

Music

Joao Gilberto *Getz Gilberto* (1964)
Baden Powell *Os Afro-Sambas* (1966)
Tom Jobim *Wave* (1967)
Elizeth Cardoso *Ao Vivo no Teatro João Caetano* (1968)
Cartola *Cartola* (1974)
Clara Nunes *Claridade* (1975)
Chico Buarque *Meus caros amigos* (1976)
Elis Regina *Falso Brilhante* (1976)
Gonzaguinha *Começaria tudo outra vez* (1976)
Jorge Ben Jor *Africa Brasil* (1976)
Milton Nascimento *Travessia* (1978)
Tim Maia *Descobridor dos sete mares* (1983)
Romero Lumambo e Raphael Rabello *Shades of Rio* (1992)
MV Bill *Traficando Informação* (1999)
Zeca Pagodinho *Deixa e vida me levar* (2002)
Yamandu Costa *Yamandu live* (2003)
Teresa Cristina *Sings Paulinho da Viola* (2002)
Ana Costa *Meu Carnaval* (2006)
Mart'nália *Menino do Rio* (2006)

On the web

www.brazilnuts.com.br hard news and inside stories from this guide's Consultant Editor.
www.samba-choro.com.br the full guide to samba and choro shows and venues (in Portuguese).
www.cariocaforever.com the informative online magazine of Rio's English-speaking community.
www.brazilbrazil.com persevere past the old school graphics for maps, photos, trivia and much more.
www.brazilmax.com useful tips and essays on Rio and the country.
www.riothisweek.com good photos and a few handy bilingual pointers to what's going on in Rio.
www.loronix.blogspot.com an incredible collection of downloadable out of print classic Brazilian music.
www.multiplicidade.com a new home for colourful Brazilian designs and multimedia events.
www.riodejaneiro-turismo.com.br/en listings and useful information from the city's tourist board.
www.radar55.com fashion tips for shops and trends (in Portuguese).

Directory

Index

Accommodation

Restaurants

Bars, cafés & botecos

Area name	**IPANEMA**
Place of Interest and/ or entertainment	■
Park	▨
Pedestrian road	▨
Ciclovia	– – – –
Estação de Metrô	Ⓜ
Hospital	✚
Church	✚
Tourist information	ⓘ

Maps

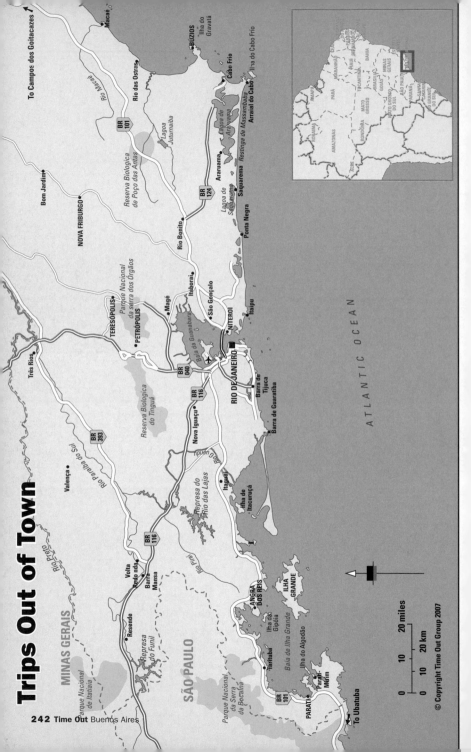

Trips Out of Town

© Copyright Time Out Group 2007

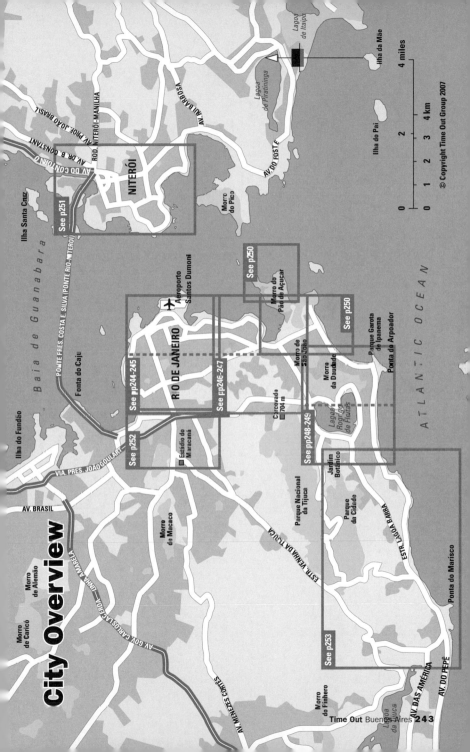

City Overview

Morro de Caricó

Morro de Alemão

Morro de Caricó

Ilha do Fundão

Baía de Guanabara

Ilha Santa Cruz

See p251

NITERÓI

Ilha da Mãe

Ilha do Pai

Lagoa de Itaipa

Lagoa de Piratininga

4 miles

© Copyright Time Out Group 2007

4 km

AV. DO FOSTE

AV. NI BARBOSA

ROD. NITERÓI-MANILHA

AV. DR. B. CONSTANT

AV. DO CONTORNO

RDD. NITERÓI-NITERÓI

AV. PROF. JOAO BRASIL

LINHA VERMELHA

PONTE PRES. COSTA E SILVA (PONTE RIO / NITERÓI)

Fonta do Caju

VIA. PRES. JOAO GOULART

AV. BRASIL

Morro do Pico

Aeroporto Santos Dumont

See p250

Morro do Pão de Açucar

See p250

RIO DE JANEIRO

See pp244-245

See p252

See pp246-247

Estádio do Maracanã

Morro de São João

Parque Garota de Ipanema

Ponta de Arpoador

Morro da Dauhade

Circovado 704 m

ATLANTIC OCEAN

Lagoa Rogr.gq de Flutas

See pp248-249

Parque Nacional da Tijuca

Jardim Botânico

Parque da Cidede

ESTR. VENHA DA TIJUCA

AV. GOV CARLOS LAL

LINHA AMARELA

AV. MENEZES CORTEL

Morro de Macaco

ESTR. LAGOA BARRA

Morro do Finhero

See p253

Ponta do Marisco

Lagoa da Juca

AV. DAS AMERICA

AV. DO PEPE

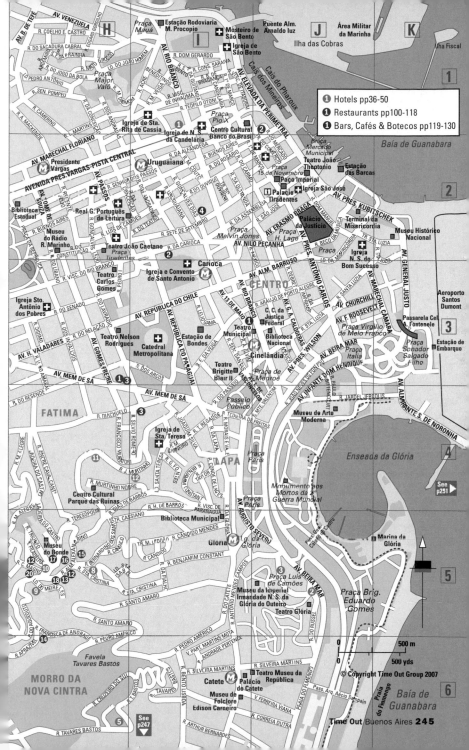

AV. VENEZUELA

Praça Mauá

Estação Rodoviaria M. Procopio

Puente Alm. Arnaldo luz

Área Militar da Marinha

Ilha Fiscal

Mosteiro de São Bento

Igreja de São Bento

J

Ilha das Cobras

K

1

❶ Hotels pp36-50
❶ Restaurants pp100-118
❶ Bars, Cafés & Botecos pp119-130

Baía de Guanabara

2

Igreja de Sta. Rita de Cassia

Centro Cultural Banco do Brasil

Praça Pio X

Praça Mercado Municipal

Teatro João Theophoto

Estação das Barcas

Igreja de N.S. da Candelária

Praça 15 de Novembro

Paço Imperial

Palácio Tiradentes

Igreja São João

Presidente Vargas

Uruguaiana

Biblioteca Estadual

Real G. Português de Leitura

Palácio da Justiça

Praça Melvin Jones

Praça H. Lage

Terminal da Misericordia

Museu Histórico Nacional

Museu do Rádio

Teatro João Caetano

Praça Tiradentes

Igreja N.S. do Bom Sucesso

Carioca

Igreja e Convento de Santo Antonio

CENTRO

Aeroporto Santos Dumont

3

Igreja Sto. Antônio dos Pobres

Teatro Carlos Gomes

C. C. da Justiça Federal

Praça Virgilio de Melo Franco

Teatro Municipal

Biblioteca Nacional

Praça Italia

Passarela Cel. Fontenele

Estação de Embarque

Teatro Nelson Rodrigues

Estação de Bondes

Catedral Metropolitana

Cinelândia

Praça Senador Salgado Filho

Teatro Brigitte Blair II

Praça de Monroe

Teatro Nelson Rodrigues

Passeio Público

FATIMA

Igreja de Sta. Teresa

Museu de Arte Moderna

LAPA

Praça Paris

Enseada da Glória

4

See p251

Centro Cultural Parque das Ruinas

Praça Paris

Monumento aos Mortos da 2ª Guerra Mundial

Biblioteca Municipal

Gloria

Museu do Bonde

Igreja da Glória

Marina da Glória

5

Praça Luis de Camões

Museu da Imperial Irmandade N.S. da Glória do Outeiro

Teatro Glória

Praça Brig. Eduardo Gomes

Favela Tavares Bastos

MORRO DA NOVA CINTRA

Teatro Museu da República

Catete

Palácio do Catete

Museu de Folclore Edison Carneiro

Museu da República

Baía de Guanabara

6

See p247

0   500 m
0   500 yds

© Copyright Time Out Group 2007

Praia do Flamengo

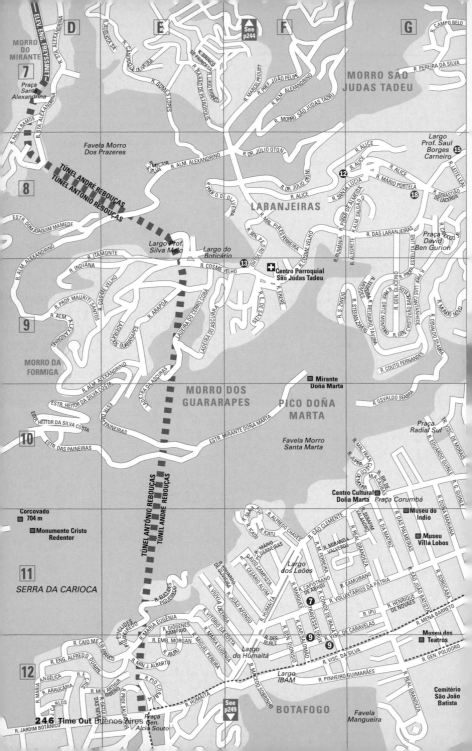

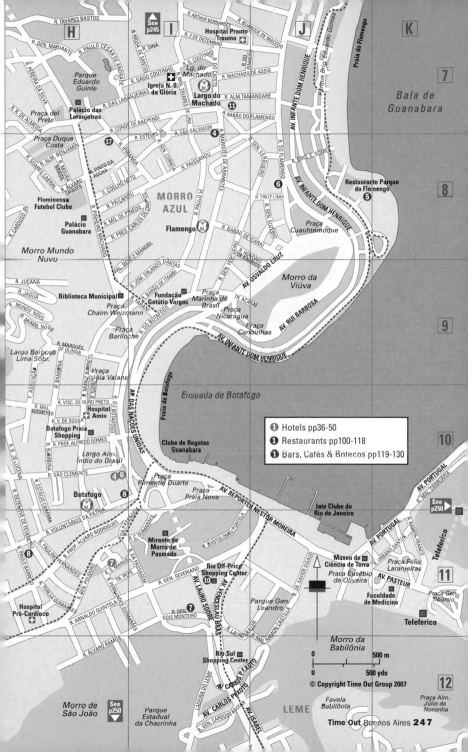

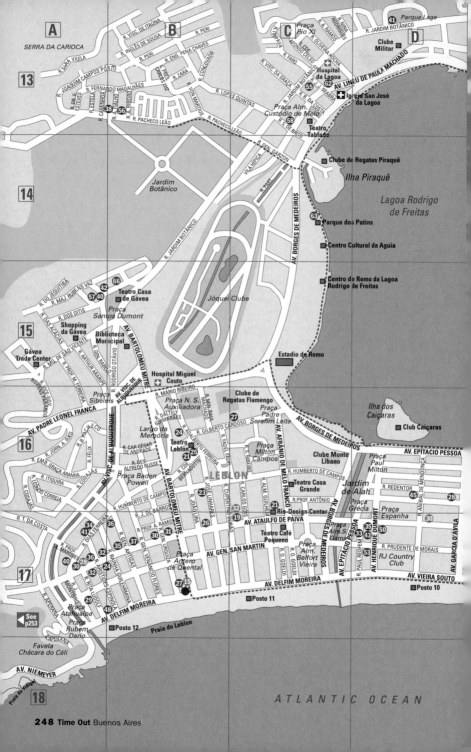

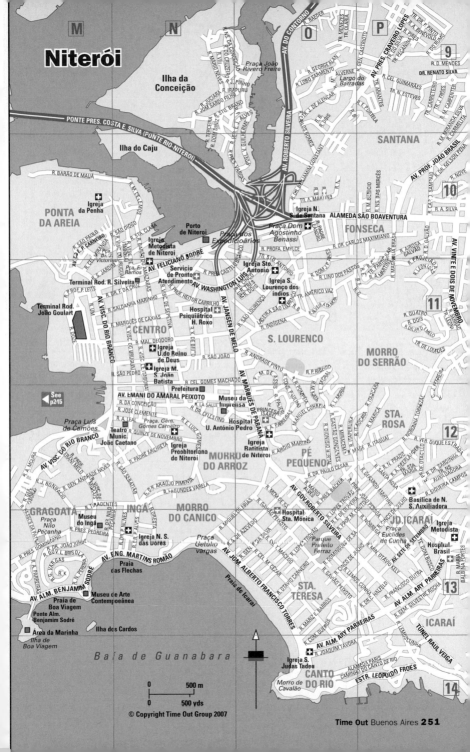

Niterói

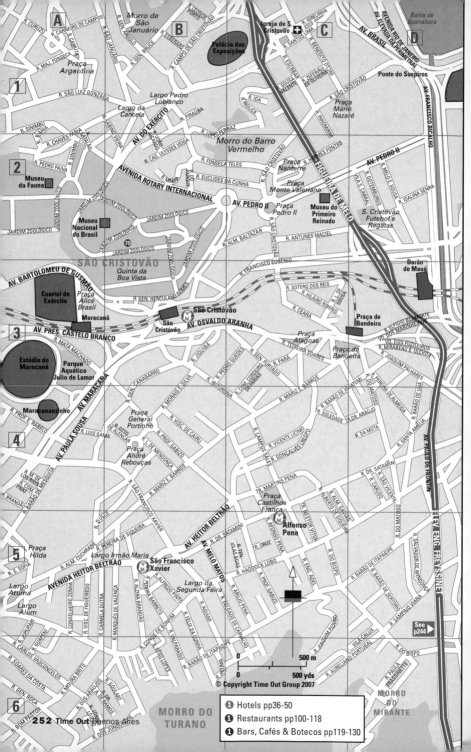

© Copyright Time Out Group 2007

❶ Hotels pp36-50
❶ Restaurants pp100-118
❶ Bars, Cafés & Botecos pp119-130

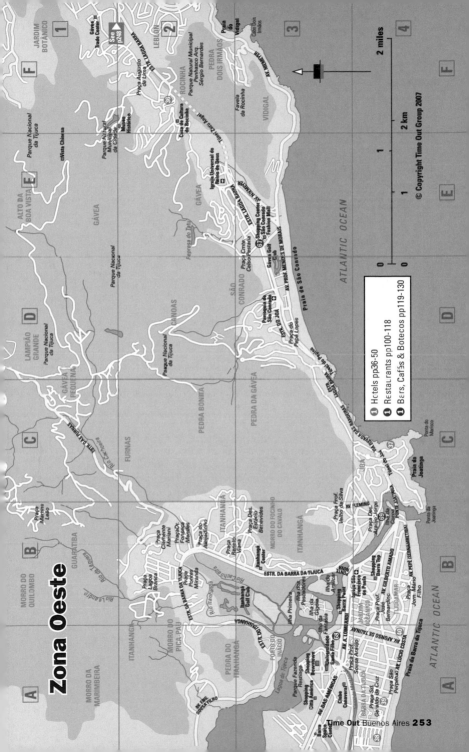

Zona Oeste

Hotels pp36-50
Restaurants pp100-118
Bars, Cafés & Botecos pp119-130

2 miles

2 km

© Copyright Time Out Group 2007

ATLANTIC OCEAN

Street Index